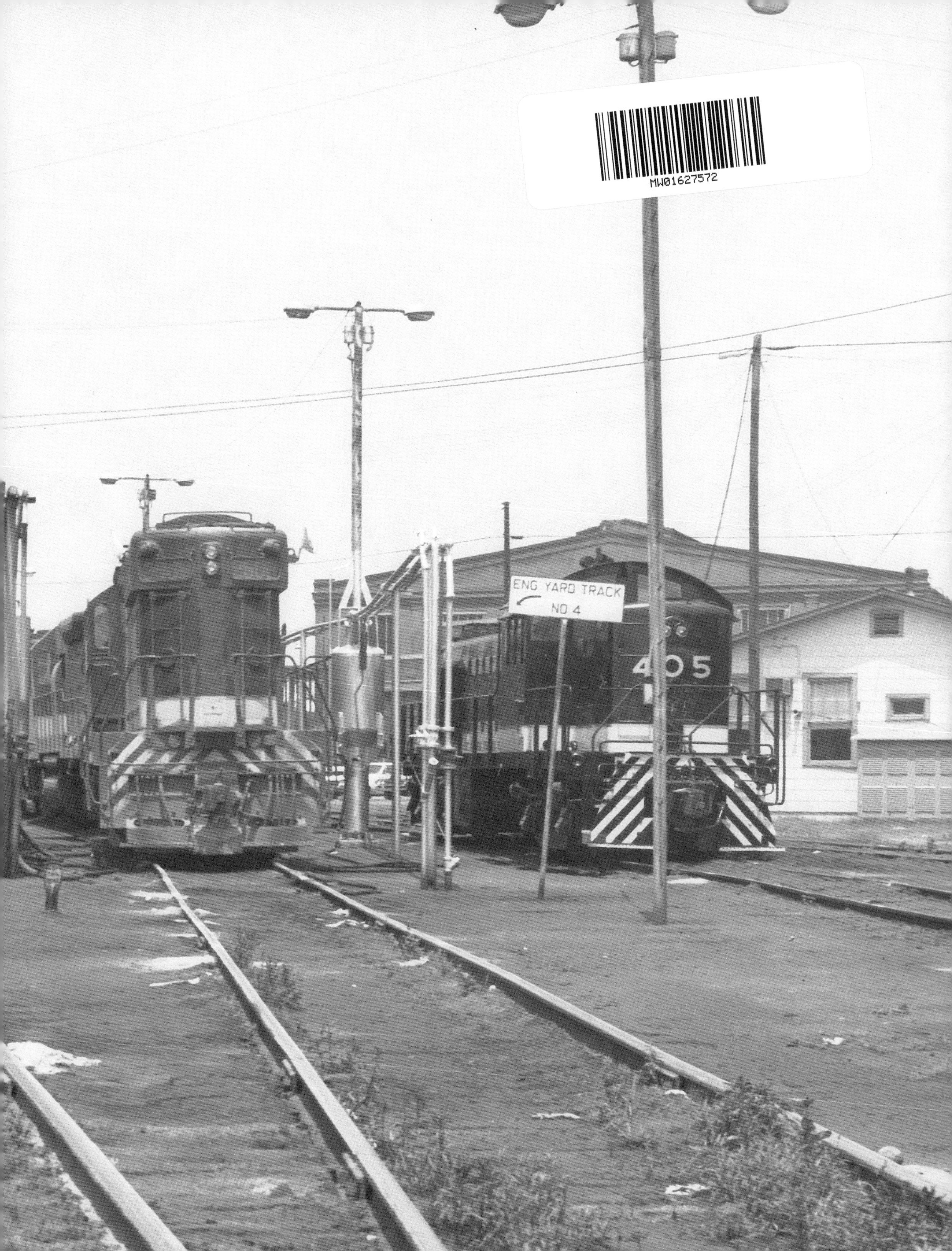
MW01627572
ENG YARD TRACK
NO 4
405

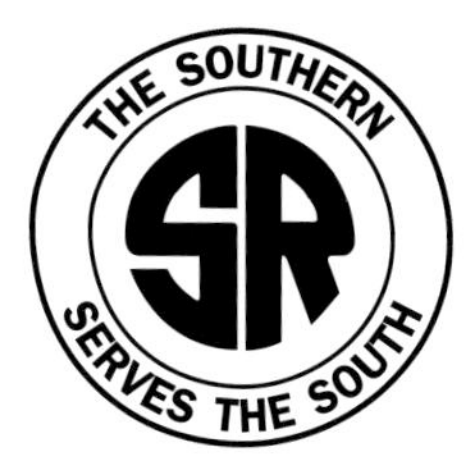

SOUTHERN RAILWAY
Diesel Locomotives and Trains
1950-1982 • Volume One

BY
CURT TILLOTSON, JR.

2003
TLC PUBLISHING INC.
1387 WINDING CREEK LANE
LYNCHBURG, VA 24503-3776

Endsheet Photo

Front: A variety of motive power awaiting the call to duty on the ready track at the Spencer, North Carolina shops.
Back: System map of the Southern Railway not long after the beginnings of dieselization.

Table of Contents

Editors Note

Usually book design is straightforward and will go through the process fairly quickly. That was not the case for this volume. Normally, the reason for difficulty is not enough quality material to work with. In this case, there are too many excellent images and it was difficult to leave any out, therefore, this is first of two volumes. Volume Two will have different photos, and coverage of some of the classes missing in this volume.

Kenneth L. Miller

Library of Congress Control Number 2002109706
ISBN 1-883089-82-4

Layout and Design by Kenneth L. Miller
Miller Design & Photography, Salem, Va.

Printed by
Walsworth Publishing Co. Marceline, Mo. 64658

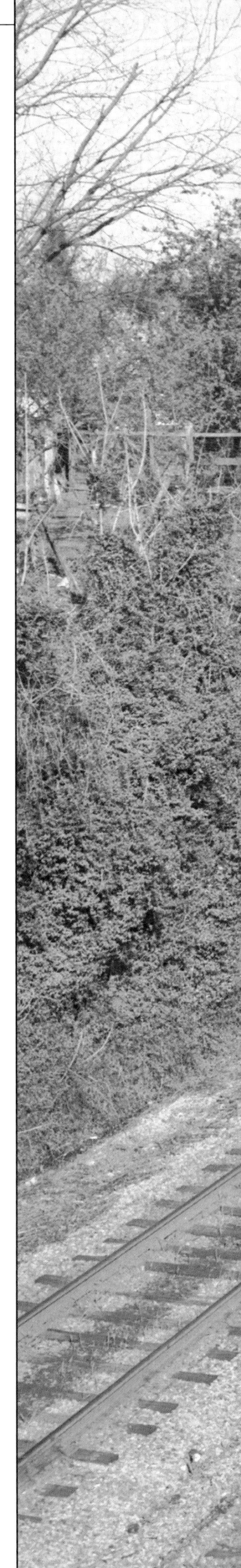

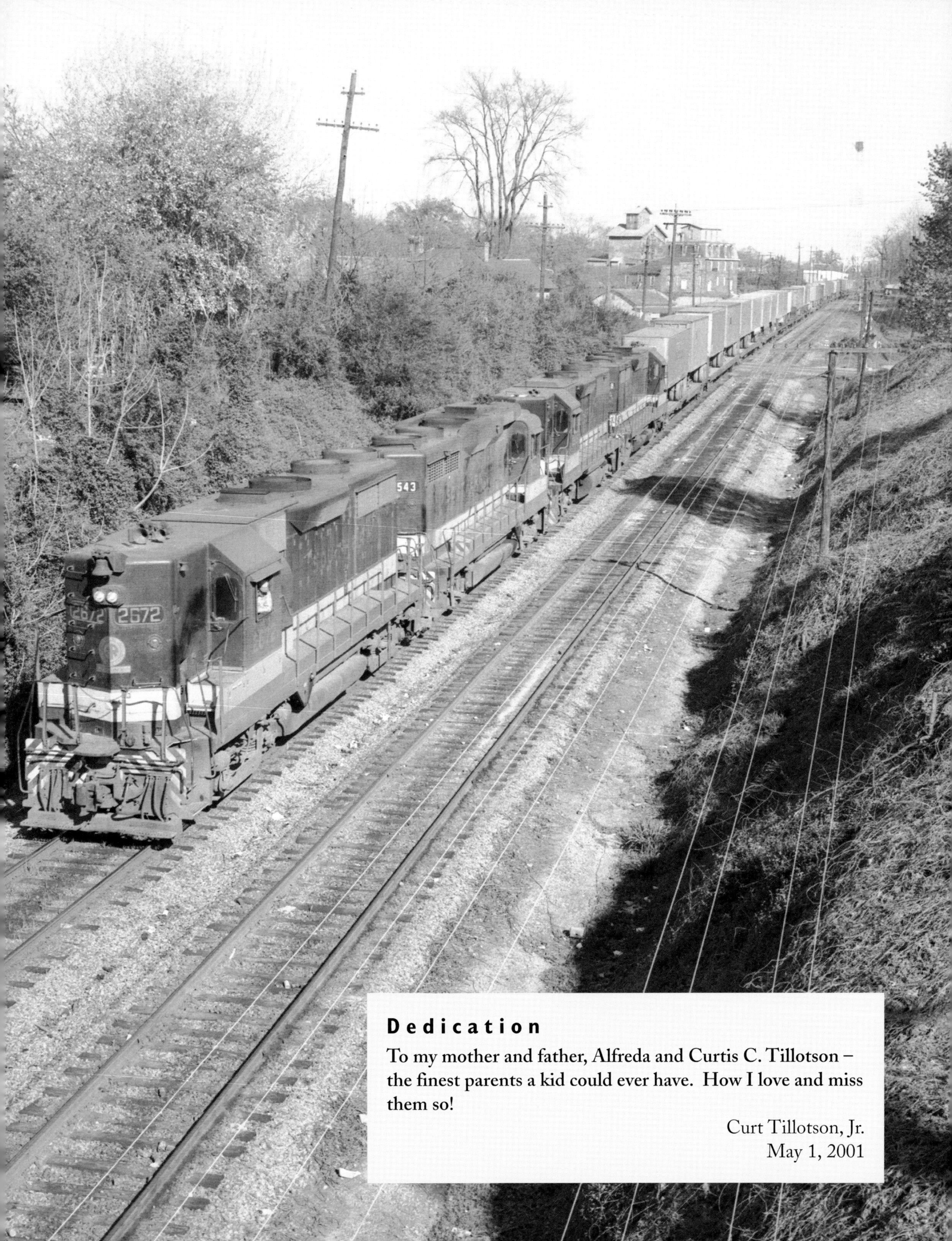

Dedication

To my mother and father, Alfreda and Curtis C. Tillotson – the finest parents a kid could ever have. How I love and miss them so!

Curt Tillotson, Jr.
May 1, 2001

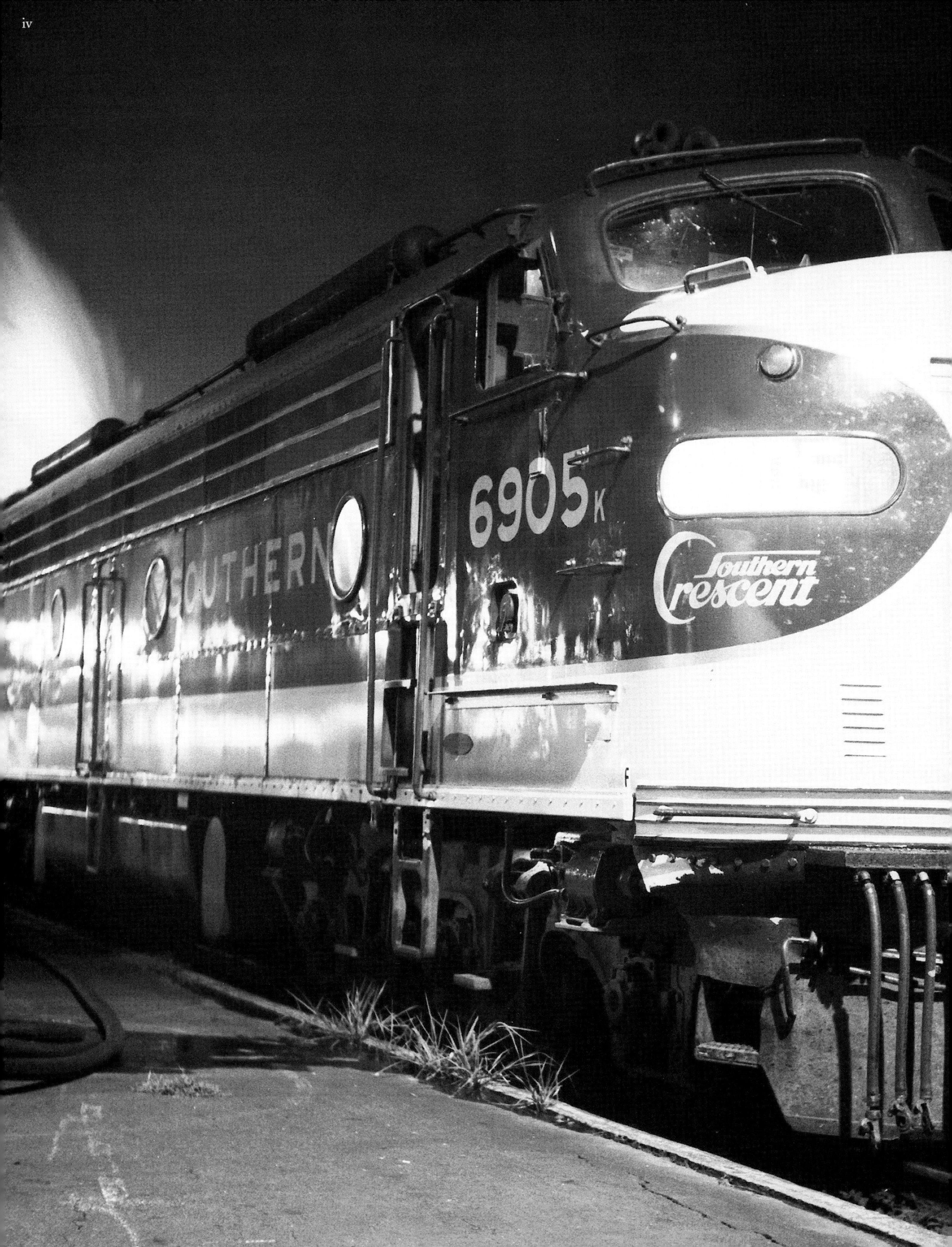
6905 K
SOUTHERN
Southern Crescent

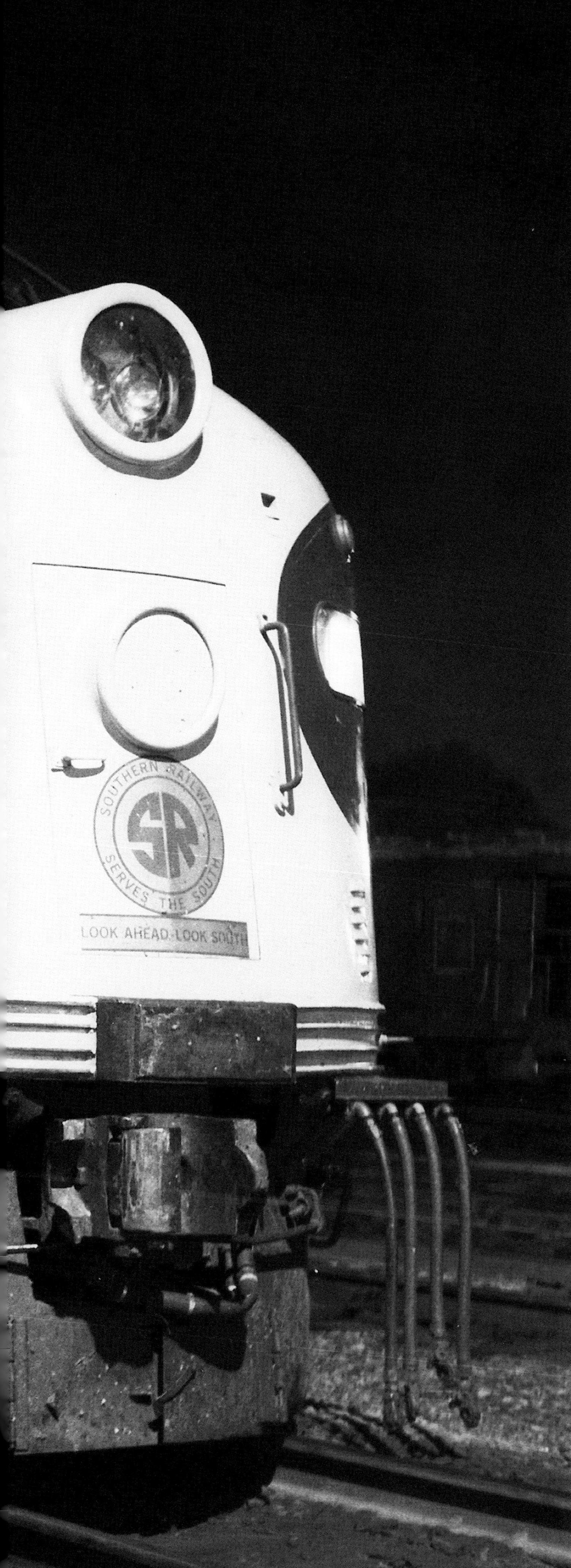

INTRODUCTION

This book is designed to allow the reader (and your author) the opportunity to experience, over and over again, the shear enjoyment of watching the evolution of the diesel locomotive on one of the most innovative, people-oriented, popular, prosperous and well-operated railroads in history: the Southern Railway System. At the outset, let me proudly admit that I am a Southern Railway fan—always have been and always will be. Indeed, from the time I began to remember "things," I was intrigued with this railroad that "served the South"—except for West Virginia only. Over time this intrigue grew to fascination and finally I was a loyal railfan of this unique road that, even during the era when most railroads were struggling financially to remain solvent, always seem to show a profit and continue expansion.

To many, the Southern was renowned for its meticulous care given to some of the most attractive and, certainly, colorful steam locomotives in raildom. This love the crews and mechanical personnel had for steamers (the last new steam locomotive purchased by the Southern was in 1928) helps to explain how their iron horses had continued operating efficiently for so long, even during World War II when the demands on the railroads to move people and war goods was enormous. In fact, WWII caused this forward looking railroad to delay their decision to completely dieselize their entire fleet of motive power, a goal that was finally achieved on June 17, 1953.

The Southern had been so impressed by the performance of General Motors' A-B-B-A FT combination of diesels in the late 1930's that it caused the road to make this momentous decision to place their future into the hands of the diesel.

By this time in their history, the Southern had reached the point that the road either had to purchase more modern steam engines or go with the diesel. Here the Southern began to earn its reputation as being farsighted in their thinking. They knew the diesel was the salvation of the railroads. Most other lines did not reach this conclusion until many years later and continued to purchase newer, more powerful steamers with such designs as 4-8-4's, 2-6-6-4's, 2-6-6-6's, etc.

The Southern had made the correct decision even though their love of the steam engine will exist until the merger with the Norfolk and Western in 1982. Still, this love did not cloud their practical side; it was the diesel or possible future ruination.

The Southern Railway System began operations on July 1, 1894, with the brilliant railroader, Samuel Spencer, as its first president. This creation came about as a result of the reorganization and consolidation of the Richmond & Danville Railroad System (also known as the Piedmont Air Line) and the East Tennessee, Virginia & Georgia (called the Kennesaw Route by many).

The new railroad, put together by J. P. Morgan & Company (New York bankers), came about as a result of the financial collapse and bankruptcy of both the R&D and ETV&G.

Even though the Southern was born in 1894, its roots go all the way back to 1833, when the South Carolina Canal & Railroad Company began operation with 136 miles of track (the longest railroad in the world at the time), stretching from Charleston to Hamburg, S. C. This company will eventually become part of the Southern's system as the new railroad began to expand.

Like many other railroads of the time, the Southern, which started life with more than two thousand miles of track, grew over the coming years through mergers, leases and acquisitions of other lines; however, unlike other roads, these acquisitions were allowed to retain their identity and corporate structure with their initials printed under the Southern's name (in small letters) on all the locomotives and cars. This growth had reached over 4,500 miles at the opening of 1895 and continued until June 1, 1982, when the Southern and Norfolk and Western merged to form the current Norfolk Southern Corporation.

Many of these lines incorporated into the Southern had such impressive and historic names as: Alabama Great Southern; Cincinnati, New Orleans & Texas Pacific; New Orleans &

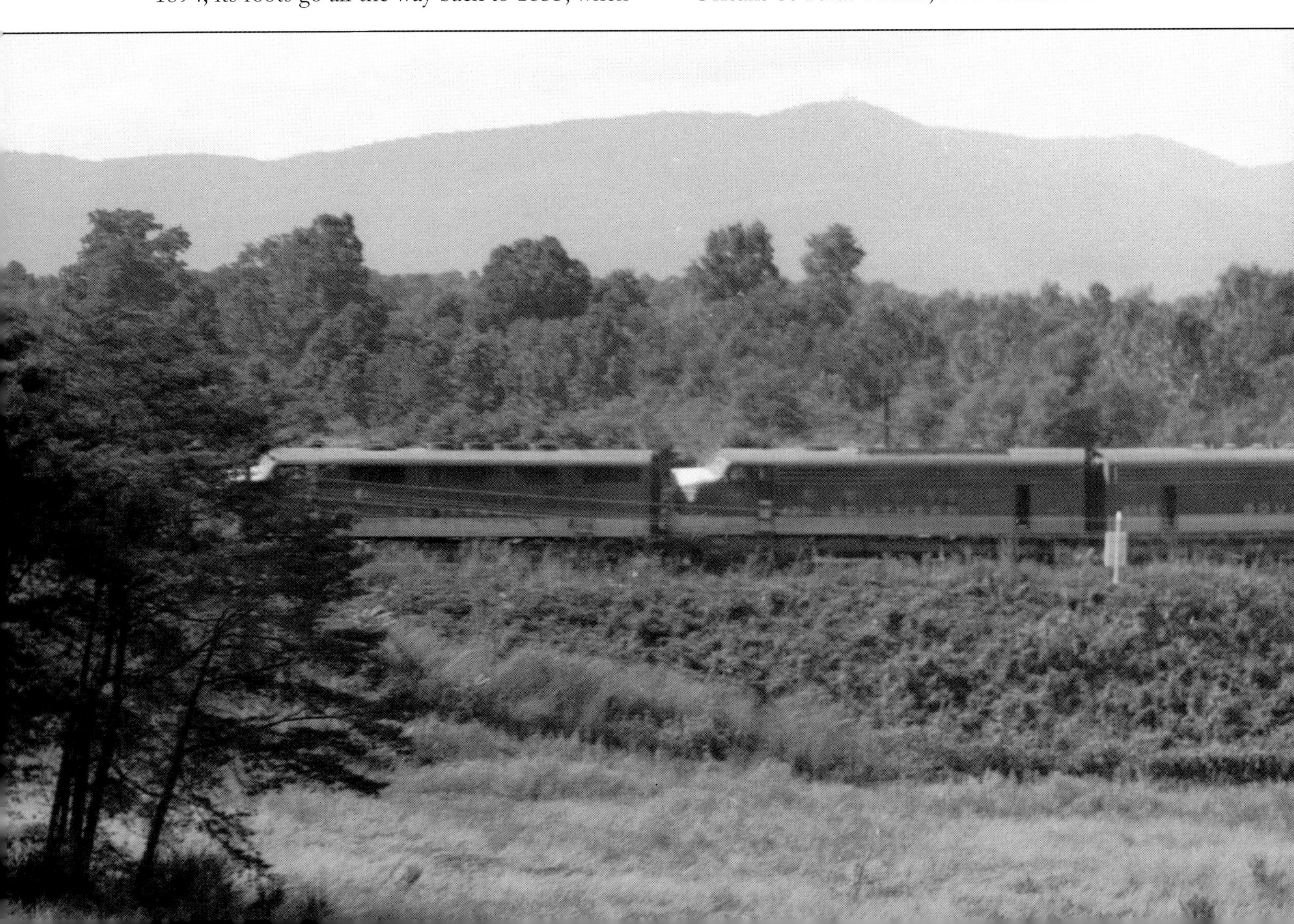

Northeastern plus many others. The Central of Georgia joined the "system" in June of 1963 while the old Norfolk Southern became part of the Southern family on January 1, 1974.

By the time of the 1982 merger with the N&W, the Southern had grown to 10,200 miles of track with 1,400 locomotives, 77,000 freight cars and approximately 21,000 employees. As a point of interest, the N&W had 7,900 miles of track, 1,400 engines, 87,000 freight cars and 22,000 employees. As a result, the newly created Norfolk Southern Corporation began operations with 18,100 miles of track, 2,800 diesels, 164,000 freight cars and 43,000 employees.

The 1982 merger came about as a result of the newly created CSX Corporation. In order to survive the potential competition of the CSX giant, the Southern knew it had to merge with a strong road that had the same philosophy and, preferably, an end-to-end meeting. The N&W met these parameters to a "T." True, the Southern had a flirtation with the Missouri Pacific in 1976 and the Illinois Central Gulf in 1979; however, the N&W proved to be the ideal partner in this marriage of two highly respected roads.

This book, this "labor of love," will cover the Southern's diesel development only. Even though I was able to photograph the vast majority of the numerous types of diesels used between 1960 through 1982, there were a few types I never encountered. In order to fill in these "gaps," I would like to thank such individuals as Tom Dixon, Leonard Rice, R. D. Sharpless, Bob's Photo Collection and Alco. Their kindness enabled this work to become a reality.

Now, find a comfortable place to relax, look through the pages of this book, reading each caption, and let your memory be reinforced when thinking of your experiences with the Southern Railway System under diesel power – enjoy!

Curt Tillotson, Jr.
May 1, 2003

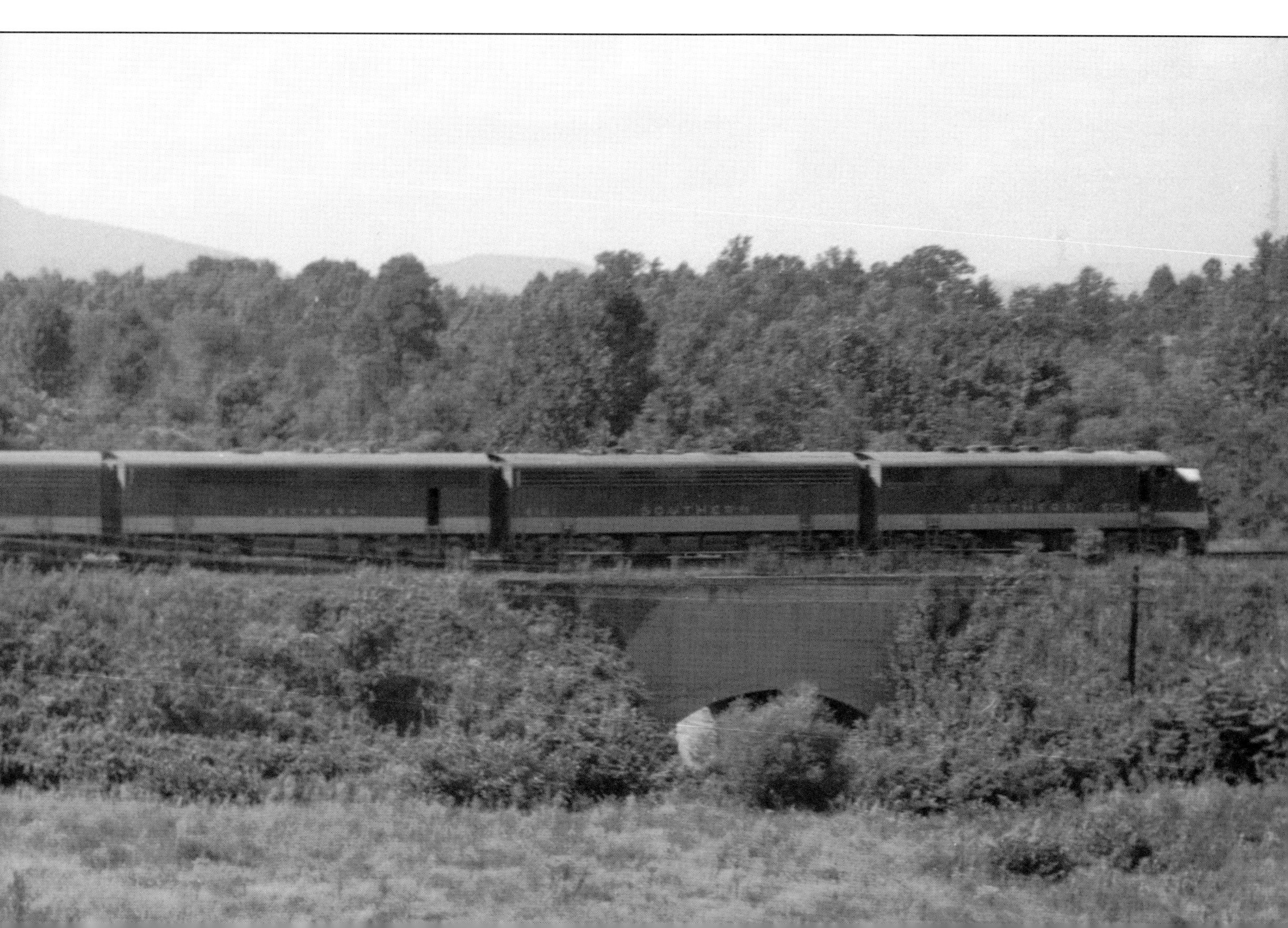

SOUTHERN RAILWAY DIESELS 1938-1982

St. Louis Car Company

Motorcars: 6 units
(No. 1-4, No. 40-41) – 750 h.p.

General Electric (G.E.) Switchers – 44 tons:

44 tons: 11 units (No. 402-403, 1950-1955; 6040; 6520 & 6840) – 350 to 410 h.p.
45 tons: 1 unit (No. 6841) – 300 h.p.
60 Tons: 7 units (No. 1, 15, 292, No. 300,301; 701, 703) – 600 h.p.

Alco & Baldwin Switchers

Alco S-1: 10 units (No. 6, 329, No. 2000-2001, 6000-6001, 2006 and 6500-6502) – 660 h.p.
Alco S-2: 39 units (No. 21, No. 23-24, 28-29, 332-335; 2208-2232 and 6057-6059) – 1,000 h.p.
Alco S-4: 2 units (No. 6074 & 6075) – 1,000 h.p.
Baldwin V0660: 2 units (No. 5 & 2005) – 660 h.p.
Baldwin DS-4-4-660: 1 unit (No. 12) – 660 h.p.
Baldwin VP100: 4 units (No. 22, 26, 27 and 2205) – 1,000 h.p.
Baldwin DS –4-4-1,000: 7 units (No. 36, 37, 2285-2289) – 1,000 h.p.
Baldwin S-12: 14 units (No. 311-314 and 2290-2299) – 1,200 h.p.

EMD Switchers

SW-1: 1 unit (No. 73) – 660 h.p.
SW-1M: 1 unit (No. 1087) – 1,200 h.p.
SW-1: 15 units (No. 1000-1014) – 600 h.p.
NW-1: 1 unit (No. 91) – 1,000 h.p.
NW-2: 71 units (No. 1016-1086) – 1,000 h.p.
NW-5: 1 unit (No. 2100) – 1,000 h.p.
TR-2A: 5 units (No. 1088-1092) – 1,000 h.p.
TR-2B: 5 units (No. 1093-1097) – 1,000 h.p.
SW-7: 35 units (No. 1098-1132) – 1,200 h.p.
SW-8: 1 unit (No. 1015) – 800 h.p.
SW-9: 11 units (No. 1133-1142) – 1,200 h.p.
SW-1500: 64 units (No. 67-83 and 2300-2347) – 1,500 h.p.
MP-15: 88 units (No. 2348-2435) – 1,500 h.p.

EMD Cab Units-Freight

FTA: 38 units (No. 4100-4127; No. 6100-6105 and 6800-6803) – 1,350 h.p.
FTB: 30 units (No. 4300-4319; 6150-6155 and 6825-6828) – 1,350 h.p.
F-2A: 4 units (No. 400-401; 6700-6701) – 1,350 h.p.
F-3A: 102 units (No. 4128-4206; 6106-6113; 6804-6806 and 6702-6713) – 1,500 h.p.
F-3B: 76 units (No. 4320-4384; 6156-6159; 6750-6755 and No. 6829) – 1,500 h.p.
F-7A: 76 units (No. 4207-4269; 6114-6120 and No. 6714-6719) – 1,500 h.p.
F-7B: 72 units (No. 4385-4429;6160-6183 and 6756-6758) – 1,500 h.p.

Alco & Baldwin Switchers

Alco RS-1: 7 units (No. 1-6 and No. 405) – 1,000 h.p.
Alco RS-2: 36 units (No. 1-4; 2101-2130 and No. 6206-6207 – 1,500 h.p.
Alco RS-3: 148 units (No. 5-10; 30-39; 108-119; 133-159; 2025-2062; 2131-2145; 6208-6239 and 6875-6882) – 1,600 h.p.
Alco RS-11: 1 unit (No. 11) – 1,800 h.p.
Baldwin DR5-6-4-1500: 8 units (No. 100 thru No. 107) – 1,500 h.p.
Baldwin AS-416: 14 units (No. 108-110; 1606-1613 and 1615-1617 – 1,600 h.p.

Fairbanks-Morse

H12-44: 4 units (No. 315-318) – 1,200 h.p.
H15-44: 5 units (No. 101-No. 105) – 1,500 h.p.
H16-44: 16 units (No. 2146-2155 and No. 6545-6550) – 1,600 h.p.
H24-66: 5 units (No. 6300-6304) – 2,400 h.p.

EMD Road Switchers

GP-7: 101 units (No. 8210-8213; No. 8216-8300) – 1,500 h.p.
GP-9: 24 units (No. 6245-6268) – 1,750 h.p.
GP-18: 26 units (No. 171-196) – 1,800 h.p.
GP-30: 120 units (No. 2525-2644) – 2,250 h.p.
GP-35: 76 units (No. 240-244; No. 2645-2715) – 2,500 h.p.
GP-38: 115 units (No. 2717-2822; No. 2879-2886) – 2,000 h.p.
GP-38AC: 56 units (No. 2823-2878) – 2,000 h.p.
GP-38-2: 257 units (No. 5000-5256) – 2,000 h.p.
GP-39X: 6 units (No. 4600-4605) – 2,600 h.p.
GP-40X: 3 units (No. 7000-7002) – 3,500 h.p.
GP-50: 90 units (No. 7003-7092) – 3,500 h.p.
SD-9: 6 units (No. 198-199; No. 203-206) – 1,750 h.p.
SD-24: 48 units (No. 6300-6347) – 2,400 h.p.
SD-35: 110 units (No. 2990, 2992-3099) – 2,500 h.p.
SD-40: 31 units (No. 3170-3200) – 3,000 h.p.
SD-40-2: 128 units (No. 3201-3328) – 3,000 h.p.
SD-45: 70 units (No. 3100-3169) – 3,600 h.p.

GE Road Switchers

U23B: 70 units (No. 3900-3969) – 2,250 h.p.
B23-7: 54 units (No. 3970-4023) – 2,250 h.p.
B30-7A1: 22 units (No. 3500-3521) – 3,000 h.p.
B36-7: 6 units (No. 3815-3820) – 3,600 h.p.
U30C: 5 units (No. 3800-3804) – 3,000 h.p.
U33C: 10 units (No. 3805-3814) – 3,300 h.p.

EMD Cab Units-Passenger

E-6A: 7 units (No. 2800-2802 and No. 2900-2903) – 2,000 h.p.
E-6B: 4 units (No. 2950-2953) – 2,000 h.p.
E-7A: 28 units (No. 801-810 and No. 2905-2922) – 2,000 h.p.
E-8A: 19 units (No. 6900-6916 and No. 811-812) – 2,250 h.p.

Alco Cab Units - Passenger

DL109: 3 units (No. 2904, 6400, 6401) – 2,000 h.p.
DL110: 3 units (No. 2954, 6425, 6426) – 2,000 h.p.
PA-3: 6 units (No. 6900-6905) – 2,000 h.p.

Slugs

40 units (No. 2460-2470; No. 2472-2487; No. 6021-6026 and No. 934-941

NOTES:
Many diesel units had their numbers changed over the years. The numbers used in this roster were original road numbers only.
A vast majority of the F-3's was upgraded to F-7 standards; many received steam generators and were used in passenger service as well.
Numerous F-7's were equipped with steam generators and sent into the passenger pool.
A majority of the E-6's was upgraded to E-8 standards.
A few E-7's were also given E-8 standards.

ABBREVIATIONS:
ALCO – American Locomotive Co.
GE – General Electric
GM/EMD – General Motors' Electro Motive Division
FM – Fairbanks Morse
H.P. – Horsepower

Bibliography

Alton, Lanier. *Southern Railway in Color*. Scotch Plains, NJ: Morning Sun Books, Inc., 1999.

Cheney, Fred D. and David R. Sweetland. *Southern Railway in Color.* Edison, NJ: Morning Sun Books, Inc., 1993.

Comstock, Henry (Ed.). "Southern Railway System Diesels," Railroad Magazine, Vol. 51, No. 3, pp. 114-119, April 1950.

Davis, Burke. *The Southern Railway, Road of the Innovators*. Chapel Hill, NC: University of North Carolina Press, 1985.

Drury, George (Ed.). *Historical Guide to North American Railroads,* Waukesha, WI: Kalmbach Publishing Co., pp. 406-410, 2000.

Noall, William (Ed.). TIES, Vol. 36, pp. 12-17, March-April 1982.

Nuckles, Douglas E. and Curt Tillotson, Jr., *Southern Railway System, A Pictorial Album.* LaMirada, CA: Four Ways West Publication, 1996.

Prince, Richard E., *Southern Railway System Steam Locomotives*. Green River, WYO: Richard Prince, 1970.

Reich, Sy (Ed.). *Diesel Locomotive Roster*, New York: Wayne Publication, p. 183, 1973.

Tillotson, Curt, Jr. *Classic Steam Trains of the South*. Lynchburg, VA: TLC Publishing, Inc., 1996.

Withers, Paul K. *Diesels of the Southern Railway 1939-1982*. Halifax, PA: Withers Publishing, 1997.

Withers, Paul K. *Southern, A Motive Power Pictorial.* Halifax, PA: Withers Publishing, 1987.

Young, B. E. (Ed.). TIES, Vol. 1, p. 12, August 1947.

Young, B. E. (Ed.). TIES, Vol. IV, pp. 9-10, August 1950.

Young. B. E. (Ed.) TIES, Vol. VII, pp. 4-8, July 1953.

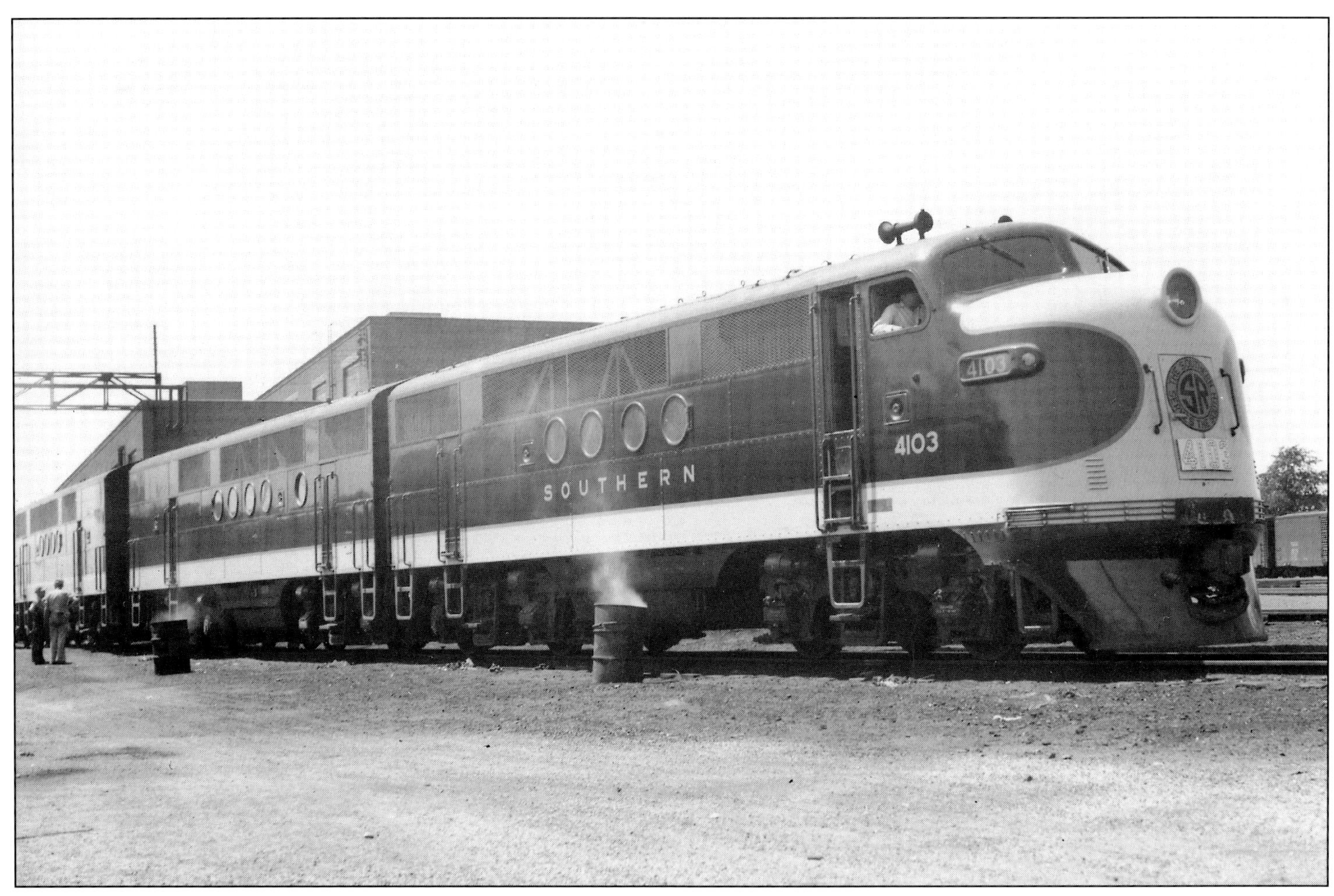

(Leonard W. Rice Photo , Tom Dixon Collection)

The time: June 13, 1946; the place, Alexandria, Va. yard; the situation: four GM FT model, Southern Railway diesel-electrics (in an A-B-B-A combination) are shown shortly after arriving in "Alex" with a through freight from Atlanta, Georgia.

General Motors' "steam terminators"—the FT's—had completed a feat that would have been impossible for the Southern's best steam power—a big, beautiful Ms-4 class 2-8-2 Mikado—to duplicate. No. 4103 and its three companions had traveled all the way from Atlanta to Alexandria (638 miles) and, by late afternoon, would return to Atlanta without a change of engines along the way and without any problems. Steam power, if pushed to its limits, could travel two divisions before being replaced by another locomotive. No. 4103 had passed through four divisions: the Charlotte (south and north ends), Danville and Washington, and would head back south over all four districts with little care and great money saving efficiency, one of the numerous advantages the diesel had over steam motive power.

Now, here is a mystery. When No. 4103 and its three companions arrived in Alexandria, the maintenance department wanted the FT quartet turned so that FTA No. 4112 (on the rear in this photo), which was up front on its trip north, to be the lead unit when the four FT's returned south with a mile-long freight. One of the other advantages diesels had over steam was that they could operate just as efficiently moving forward as backward. Yet, the boys at Alexandria wanted them turned (and they were).

Since the turntable could not accommodate all four engines together, the FT's were split into two units with each pair being turned. Then, as shown in this picture, they were re-assembled, fueled, and made ready for its southbound "adventure."

No. 4103 was built by GM on December 20, 1944; it was rated at 1,350 h.p. and produced 55,760 lbs. of tractive effort. This FT was rebuilt to an F7 rating (1,500 h.p.) at Spencer, N. C. on Nov. 6, 1953 and finally scrapped in Chattanooga, Tennessee on May 17, 1961. Running on 40" wheels, No. 4103 held 1,200 gallons of fuel, 180 gallons of lube oil and 20 cu. ft. of sand; its weight was 223,040 lbs. and this FT used Westinghouse 6EL air brakes.

I remember seeing the FT's in action on the Southern's hot Washington-Atlanta main line but I was far too young to consider taking photos of these magnificent, impressive and historic engines. But those wonderful scenes are still fresh in my mind and are reinforced by such photos as the ones appearing in this book.

Hail the King: 6100

Just before the start of World War II, the Southern faced a motive power dilemma. The last new steam locomotive purchased by the road was in 1928. Even with their renowned care, maintenance and love of the iron horses in their stables, "TLC" can only last just so long in keeping the passenger and freight trains moving efficiently with their current roster of steam power. The Southern knew it had to purchase new steam engines or look for an alternative form of motive power.

At this propitious moment in Southern's history, General Motors' Electro-Motive Division introduced the first road-freight diesel- electric engine ever built, doing so in 1939.

The FT ("F" for freight) model, with engine No. 6100, along with three helpers—two boosters (cab-less "B" units) and another "A" unit—represented the cutting edge of rail technology. Indeed, this quartet of FT's shook the rail world right down to its cinder-encrusted roots.

No. 6100 (a number given to this engine by the Southern) and its three other units spent a year, going from coast to coast, traveling over twenty different roads, accumulating eighty-three thousand miles and passing through 35 states, demonstrating just what its 5,400 horsepower and awesome tractive power could accomplish.

All railroads visited by No. 6100 were impressed with its power, low maintenance and reliability—none more than the Southern. The road that "Served the South" knew the FT was the answer to its motive power dilemma. In fact, after the 6100-led quartet of FT's were reconditioned by GM, following its coast to coast odyssey, the Southern purchased this set of revolutionary motive power on May 26, 1941.

GM had a huge success on its hands and the Southern knew it had acquired a part of the rail world's future, the power that would save it and all other roads from financial collapse.

After traveling over 2,000,000 miles, the Southern decided to donate No. 6100 to the National Museum of Transportation in St. Louis, Missouri, doing so on August 3, 1961, for the road realized the historic significance of No. 6100. In June of 1982, this remarkable engine which chased steam from the rails forever, was designated as a national historical mechanical engineering landmark and can be seen by the public to this very day, appearing in mint condition.

So the Southern not only donated Ps-4 (4-6-2) No. 1401—the prime example of its steam power—to the Smithsonian Institution in Washington, D. C., they also gave No. 6100 (diesel's first champion) to the facility in St. Louis as well – all of which enables us to take a look back in rail history.

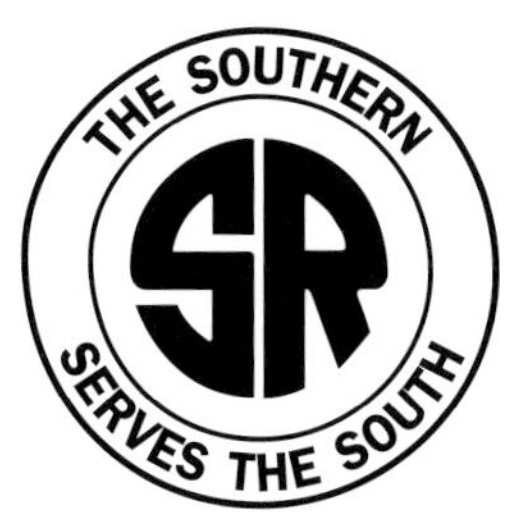

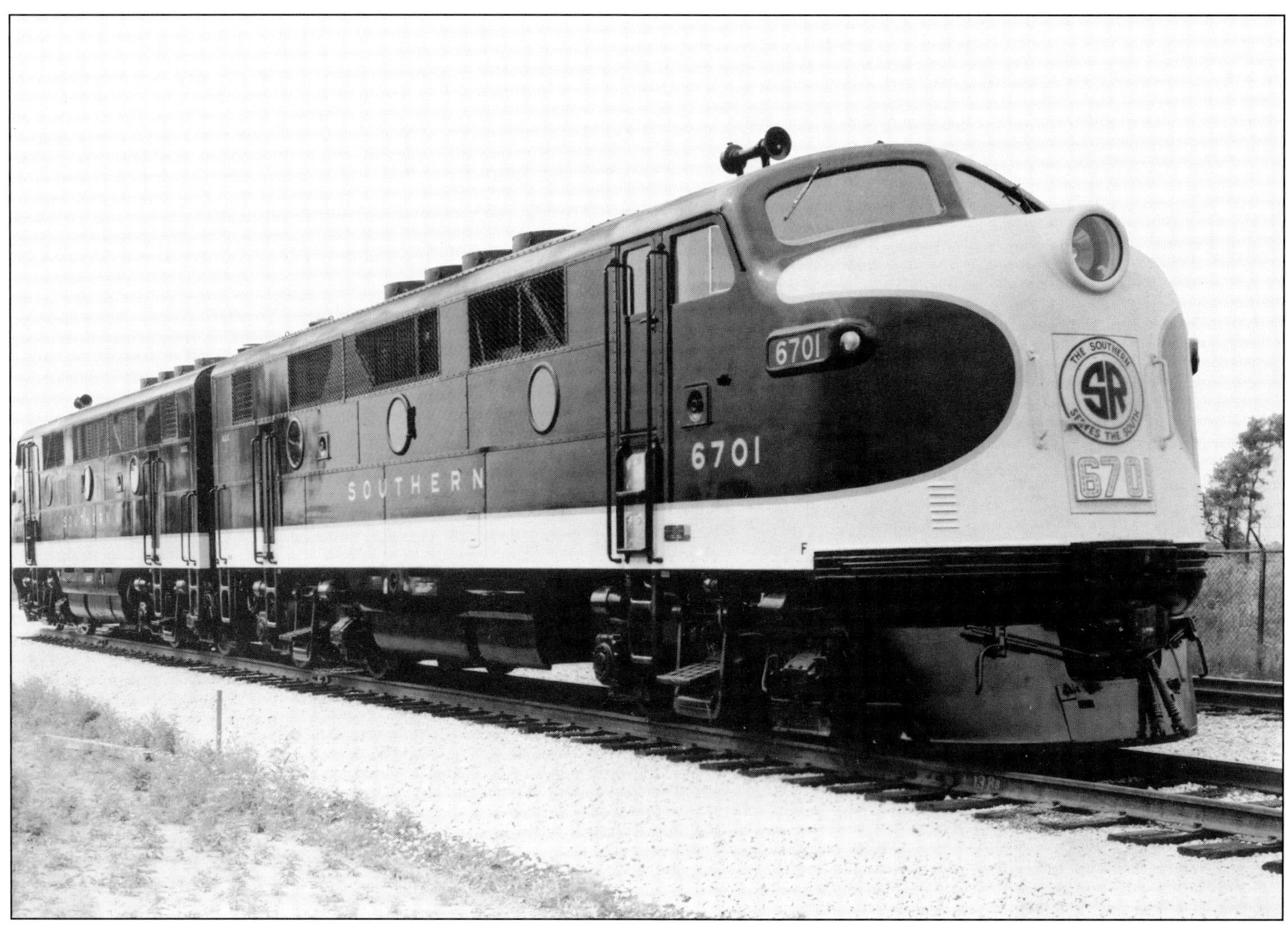

Here is a photo of a rare General Motors' built diesel-electric locomotive. The F2 was an interim model made while GM was phasing out production of their groundbreaking and successful FT model and beginning construction of the even more popular F3 series.

Only a few of the F2's were manufactured. The Southern purchased four of these "rare birds." Two, No. 400 and No. 401, went to Southern's subsidiary, A&EC (Atlantic & East Carolina) and the remaining pair – No. 6700 and No. 6701 – were placed on the AGS (Alabama Great Southern), another Southern subsidiary. No. 6700 & 6701 came equipped with a steam generator and could handle both freight and passenger assignments.

Even though the F2's were rated at 1,350 h.p. – the same horsepower as the FT's – there were several internal improvements that were not found on the FT's.

No. 6701, shown here in mint condition (and on excellent tracks), was purchased by the Southern in December of 1946. It produced 62,400 lbs. of tractive effort, weighed 249,500 lbs. and contained 1,200 gal. of fuel, 200 gal. of lube oil, 230 gal. of cooling water for its steam generator plus 16 cu. ft. of sand. It stood 15 ft. in height, 50'8" long and covered 10'7" in width. On April 14, 1951, No. 6701 was rebuilt to F7 ratings (1,500 h.p.) by the shop crews at Spencer, N. C. After serving the Southern for 26 years, this F2A was retired and traded to GM for a newer model on March 28, 1972.

Not much is known as to just where this photo was made in July of 1946. Since No. 6701 is in prime condition, it could have been photographed at GM's plant at LaGrange, Illinois or at an unknown location on the AGS.

The F2 was one of the few Southern diesel models I never saw; it reminds me of an F3A and, since the Southern used is for 26 years, it obviously served the road well even though there were only four units on its roster.

The new model sure looked beautiful and became even more attractive when that horrible sounding diesel horn was replaced by the soothing sounds of the air chime whistle.

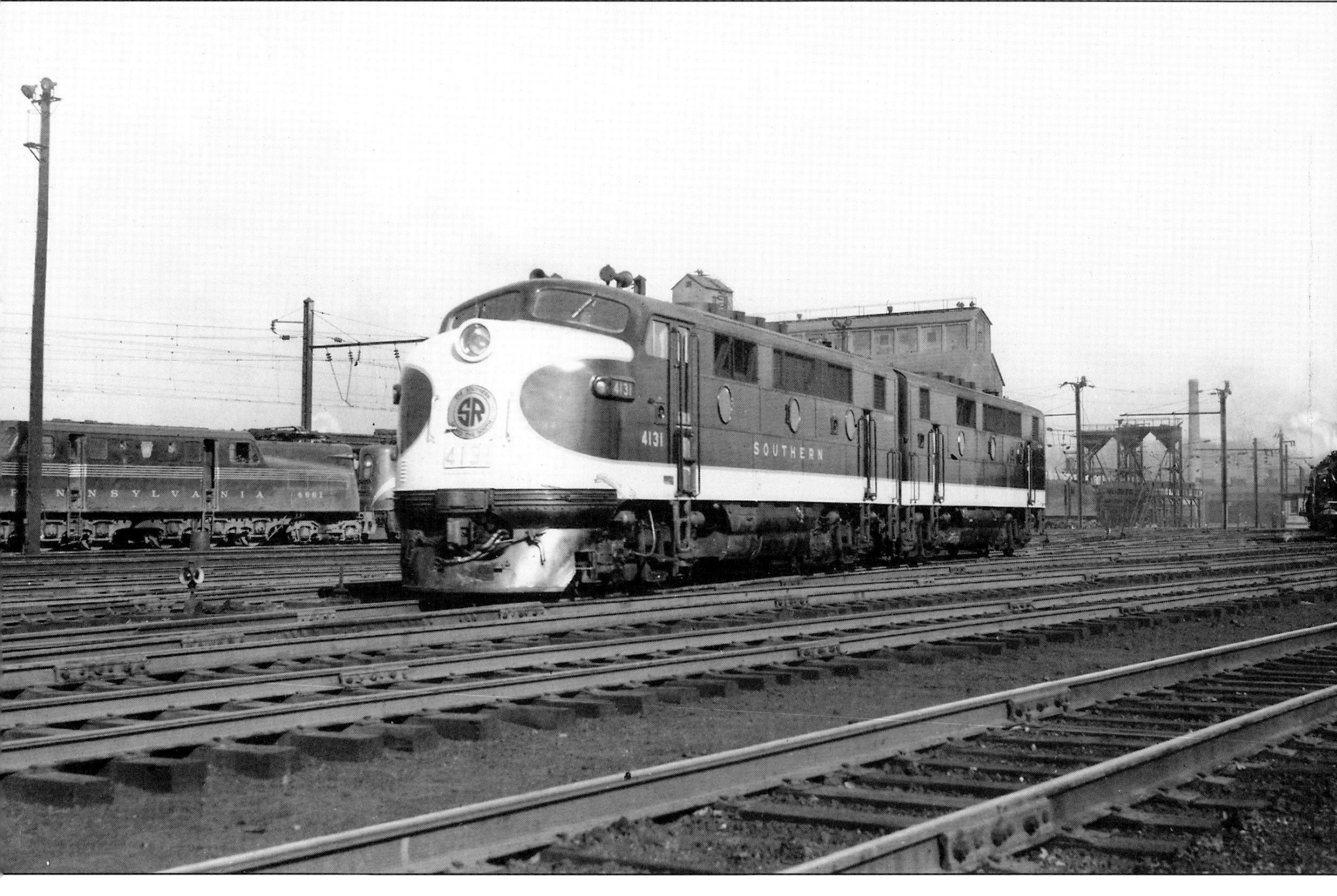

(By: Leonard W. Rice, Tom Dixon Collection):

This photo has it all: Pennsylvania's GG-1 electrics on the left, two green and gold colored Southern Railway Ps-4 Pacifics on the right, and in the middle, we find an A-B combination of GM/EMD-built, one-year-old, Southern F3 model diesel-electric locomotives.

Scenes such as this were commonplace at the Washington, D.C.'s Ivy City Terminal facility during the transitional years of steam to diesels.

All engines, be they electric, steam, or diesel, were washed after completing a run. During those days, railroads took a great deal of pride in the appearance of their locomotives. Today, "Mother Nature" usually washes the motive power. This practice of cleaning their engines helps to explain why all the power depicted in this January 24, 1947 exposure were so clean. Indeed, even the year-old F3's were washed as well as fueled and inspected after a trip from Atlanta, GA the night before. They are shown heading to Washington's historic Union Station to pick up another train and head back to Atlanta.

The F3 model diesels were so successful, even more so than their predecessors (the FT's), that the Southern purchased 102 F3A's and 76 F3B units. The F3A's were numbered in the following series: No. 4128-No. 4206 for the Southern proper; No. 6106-6113 (CNO&TP); No. 6702-6713 (AGS); and No. 6804-6806 for the NO&NE. Many of the F3's came from GM with steam generators, so they could handle either passenger or freight trains. This was the case for F3A No. 4131 and its unidentified "B" unit.

No. 4131, producing 1,500 h.p. was built in Nov. of 1946 (it was upgraded to F7 standards at Spencer, N. C. on 6/11/51); it's gear ratio was 61:16 and ran on 40" wheels. Weighing 253,100 lbs., No. 4131 could muster an impressive 63,300 lbs. or tractive effort. There was 1,200 gal. of fuel, 320 gal. of cooling water and 200 gal. of lube oil plus 16 cu. ft. of sand on board. The unit stood 15 ft. tall, 50 ft. 8 inches long and 10 ft. 7 inches wide. Dynamic brakes were installed in No. 4131 at Spencer on 3/1/56. Its steam generator was removed on Dec. 18, 1961 and the unit was finally traded to EMD on June 29, 1963, thus ending a 17-year career of working for the Southern. Needless to say, it did its job quite well!

Even though I never visited the Ivy City Terminal, after viewing this photo I feel I was there.

Thank you, Mr. Rice, for freezing this moment of rail history on film so that all of us can take a look back at this wonderful time for a railfan.

After the Southern decided to place their future on the diesel, they purchased examples of the internal combustion engines from different manufacturers – just to see what was available – such as Baldwin, the American Locomotive Company (Alco) and others. Baldwin and Alco had made a great number of the road's famous steam engines.

It did not take the Southern long to realize that the most efficient, low maintenance, reliable and less expensive diesels came from General Motors' Electro Motive Division (GM/EMD). In fact, for many years, even after the road had completely dieselized in 1953, Southern became a regular and loyal customer of EMD diesels.

Still, the other "foreign" diesels (non-GM) from Baldwin and Alco were interesting in both looks and performance. For example, shown here are representatives from Alco. The Southern purchased three Alco model DL109 "A" units and three DL110 "B" units. The "A's" were numbered: No. 2904 (for the Southern proper) and No. 6400 and No. 6401 for the CNO&TP, while the "B" units were No. 2954 (Southern) and No. 6425 and No. 6426 for the CNO&TP.

No. 6401 "A" and No. 6425 "B" are pictured here arriving in Bristol, Va. with (probably) No. 46, on a warm day in August of 1951. Within a few minutes, the Alco engines will be replaced by a Norfolk and Western streamlined, J-class 4-8-4 steam locomotive, which will ferry this varnish to Lynchburg, Va. where it will return to Southern rails to complete its journey to Washington, D. C. and points north.

No. 6401 was built in Feb. of 1941, had 2,000 h.p. and produced 55,290 lbs. of tractive effort. Its fuel capacity was 1,200 gal. and the DL109 also had 120 gal. of lube oil, 250 gal. of cooling water (all Alcos were factory equipped with a steam generator) and 20 cu. ft. of sand using 40" wheels with a gear ratio of 61:22, No. 6401 weighed 331,770 lbs. and in August of 1954 it was scrapped at Spencer, N. C.

The Alco passenger units were no matches for GM's E6's, E7's and E8's. They required more maintenance, spare parts were hard to come by and, from this railfan's point of view, they looked "out of scale" with their long body, "baby-faced" front, oversize headlight – it simply did not have the aesthetic appearance of GM's sleek, well-proportioned "E" units. As a result of all of its deficiencies, their career on the Southern was rather short for a diesel – only 13 years of service.

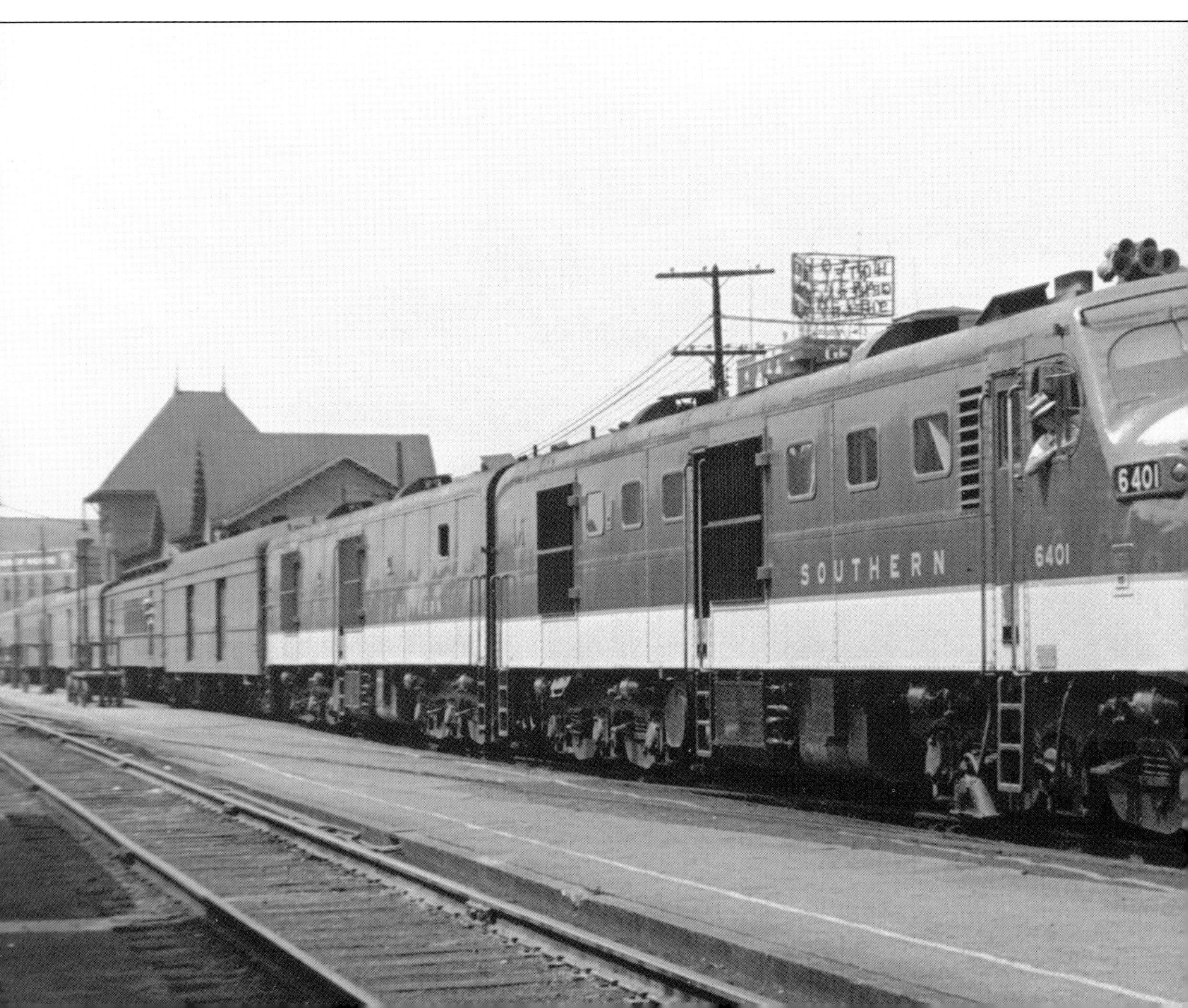

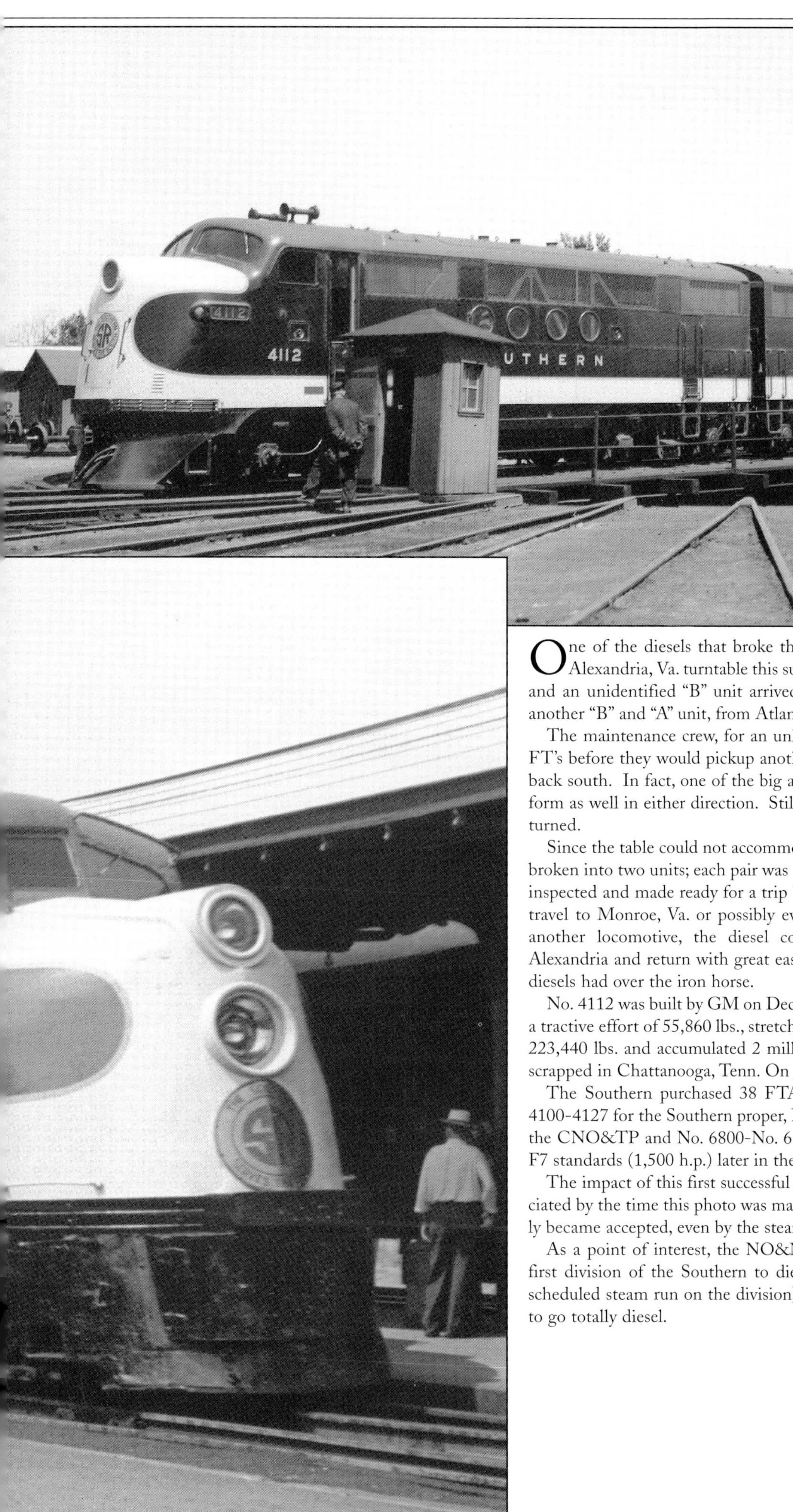

One of the diesels that broke the back of steam is shown on the Southern's Alexandria, Va. turntable this sunny July 13, 1946. GM's model FT No. 4112 and an unidentified "B" unit arrived in the area early this morning, along with another "B" and "A" unit, from Atlanta, Georgia with a long through freight.

The maintenance crew, for an unknown reason, wanted to turn the quartet of FT's before they would pickup another freight at nearby Potomac Yard and head back south. In fact, one of the big advantages of the diesel was its ability to perform as well in either direction. Still, the roundhouse boys wanted the four units turned.

Since the table could not accommodate all four engines at once, the quartet was broken into two units; each pair was turned and then reconnected, fueled, cleaned, inspected and made ready for a trip back to Atlanta. Unlike steam, which would travel to Monroe, Va. or possibly even Spencer, N. C. before being replaced by another locomotive, the diesel could make a round-trip from Atlanta to Alexandria and return with great ease—another one of the numerous advantages diesels had over the iron horse.

No. 4112 was built by GM on December 21, 1944, and produced 1,350 h.p. had a tractive effort of 55,860 lbs., stretched to 48'3" in length and 15' high; it weighed 223,440 lbs. and accumulated 2 million miles serving the Southern before being scrapped in Chattanooga, Tenn. On January 31, 1962.

The Southern purchased 38 FTA's and 30 FTB units; they were numbered 4100-4127 for the Southern proper, No. 6100 (the first FT) through No. 6105 for the CNO&TP and No. 6800-No. 6803 for the NO&NE. Some were rebuilt to F7 standards (1,500 h.p.) later in their career but most were scrapped by 1962.

The impact of this first successful road-type diesel-electric was not fully appreciated by the time this photo was made; however, the diesel's significance gradually became accepted, even by the steam loyalist crews. Boy, they look sharp!

As a point of interest, the NO&NE (New Orleans & Northeastern) was the first division of the Southern to dieselize, doing so on Dec. 26, 1948 (the last scheduled steam run on the division). The Washington Division was the second to go totally diesel.

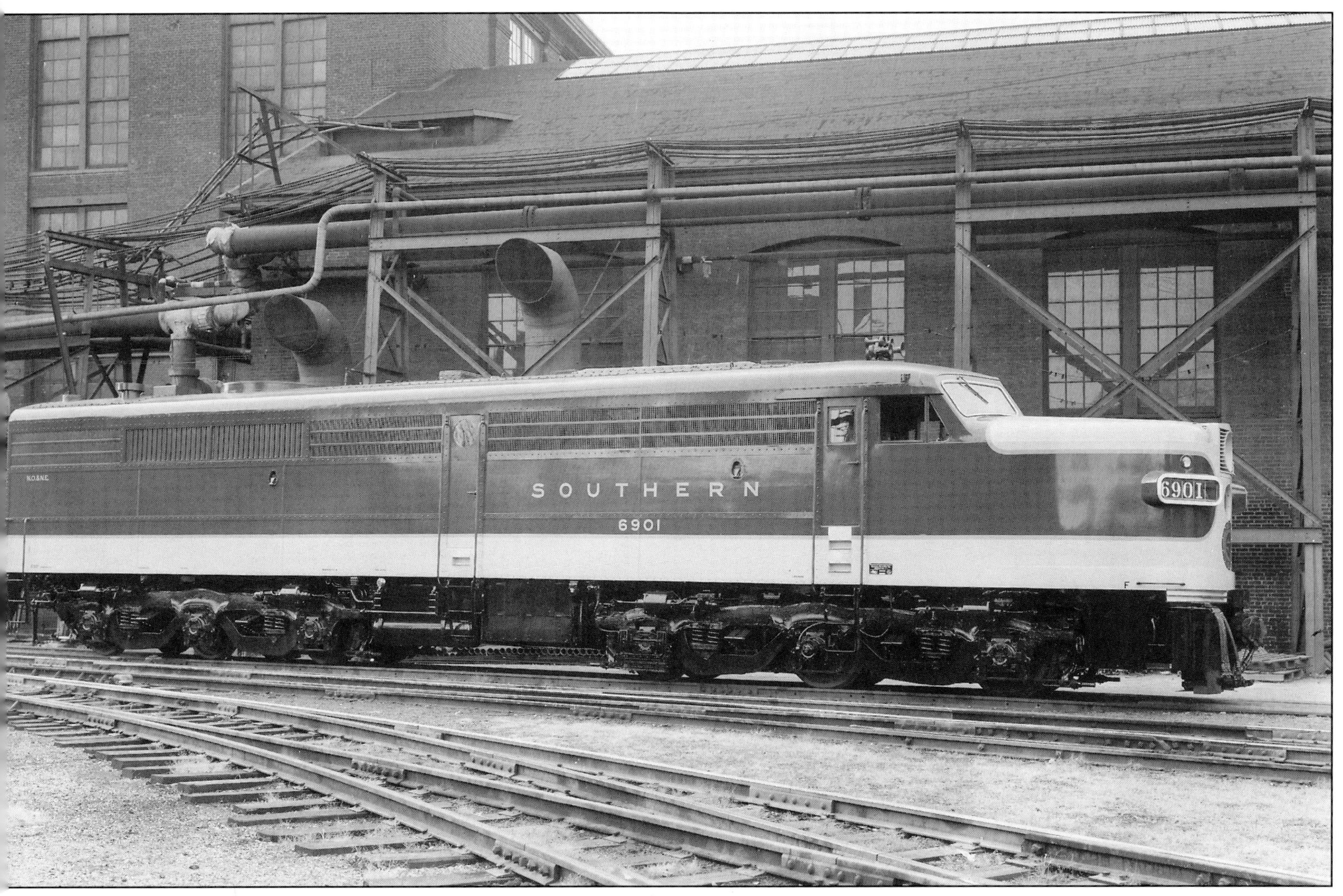

Even though the Southern experienced less than satisfactory performance of Alco's DL109's and DL110's, between 1941 thru 1954, the road tried another Alco passenger type diesel, the PA-3. In fact, about the time the Southern started scrapping the DL units, Alco PA-3's began appearing on the property.

The road purchased six units (No. 6900 thru 6905) and they were originally assigned to the NO&NE, although like most diesels they appeared in many other locations on the Southern during their life span – mainly west of the Appalachian Mountains.

PA-3, No. 6901, is shown just out of Alco's shops in Schenectady, N. Y. in Nov. of 1953, after receiving the most pleasing green, white and gold color scheme of the Southern.

Admittedly, the PA-3's really looked like main line passenger power when compared to the rather "homely" looking DL models. Indeed, many connoisseurs of diesels placed the PA's above GM's E-8A's in the "looks" department. Your author, on the other hand, consider them to be in second place, with the classic E-8A's as the most aesthetically pleasing diesels to grace the rails – the Ps-4's of diesel power!

No. 6901 had 2,000 h.p. (later raised to 2,250) and could produce 51,840 lbs. of tractive effort. Weighing in at 311,000 lbs. and running on 40" wheels, the dynamic brakes equipped PA had 1,200 gallons of fuel, 300 gallons of cooling water for its steam generator plus 230 gallons of lube oil and 22 cu. ft. of sand.

The 16-cylinder Alco 244-type engine of No. 6901 remained on the Southern until July 14, 1965 when it was traded to GM for a new EMD locomotive – 12 years of service for the road that "Served the South."

Even looking as good as they did, the PA-3's simply could not match the performance of EMD's "E's." Besides, by this time the Southern had grown used to the engines made at LaGrange, Illinois.

The classic looks of a diesel passenger engine! Motive power: Alco's PA-3 No. 6901.

Building and disposition dates: Nov. 1953 and traded to GM by the Southern on July 14, 1965.

Specifications: 2,000 h.p. (later increased to 2,250), 1,200 gallons of fuel, 300 gallons of cooling water, 230 gallons of lube oil and 22 cu. ft. of sand; produced 51,840 lbs. of tractive effort on 40" wheels, weighing 311,000 lbs. and dynamic brake equipped.

Remarks: Colored green, white and gold with the Southern's most famous symbol located below the grilled main headlight and second pair of lights – a classic passenger diesel, ranked by many with the smooth features of EMD's E-8A's for aesthetic appeal – one of six units (No. 6900 thru No. 6905) purchased by the Southern – it served the road for 12 years.

Closing Comments: Along with EMD's E-8A's, the PA-3's were among the most beautiful diesels which replaced steam from passenger assignments forever – a prime example of the old saying: "a picture is worth a thousand words."

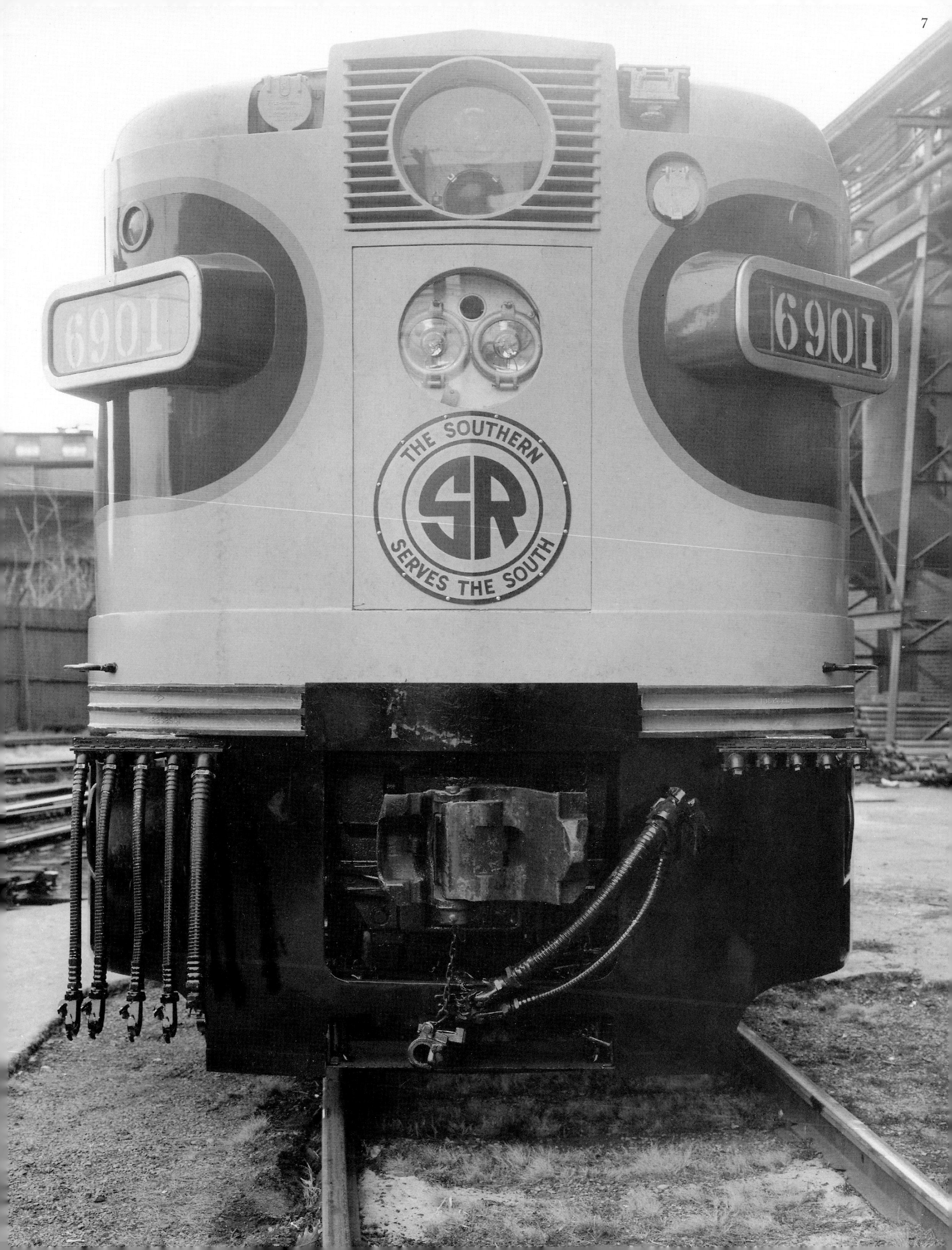
6901
6901
THE SOUTHERN
SR
SERVES THE SOUTH

E-6A

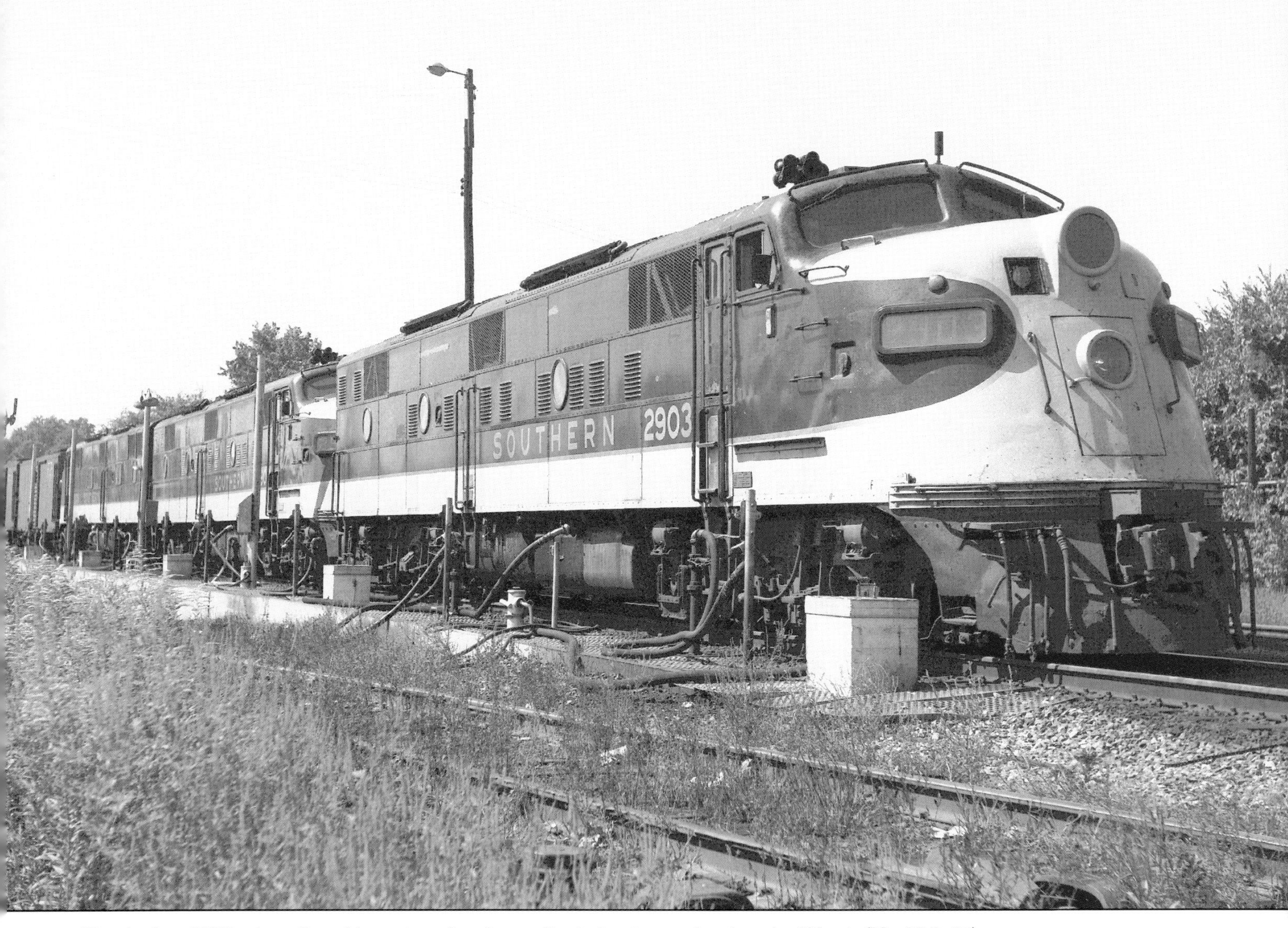

In the late 1930's, the rail world was introduced to a diesel-electric form of motive power made by GM's Electro-Motive Division. The Southern was especially impressed since it was at a point where the road had to make a major decision.

Even though the Southern was renowned for its steam locomotives, the newest steamer on their roster was purchased in 1928. As a result, the road had to purchase new motive power: steam, steam and diesel or diesels only. The performance of the historic FT models, No. 6100 and its three mates, convinced the road that their future would be tied to the diesel – complete dieselization, which was accomplished on June 17, 1953 (the demands of World War II delayed this goal).

In an attempt to use the public's interest in the new "streamliner" and have more passengers to use their trains, the Southern ordered enough Budd-built stainless steel cars to outfit two new "streamliners:" the "Southerner" (No. 47 & 48) and "Tennessean" (No. 45 & 46). To power their new trains, the road placed an order with EMD in Oct. of 1940 for seven E-6A's and four E-6B's (cabless units). The E-6A's that emerged from the builders were painted green, gold and white with the name, "Southerner" on both sides of the diesels which would power No. 47 & 48 and "Tennessean" on those assigned to No. 45 & 46. Eventually, a pair of E-6's (A&B units) would have the name, "Crescent" placed on the "A" unit (No. 37 & 38).

The seven E-6A's (No. 2800-No. 2802, No. 2900-No. 2903) were an instant success and before their retirement in 1967, they accumulated well over two million miles.

Here we have a rare scene captured on film: three E-6A's in Southern's black, white and gold colors (No. 2903, No. 2900 and No. 2902), powering No. 36, the "Washington-Atlanta Express," shown at rest in Danville, Va. in Aug. of 1966 (No. 2903 was built in May of 1941 – 25 years old!)

The streamlined "E's" had 2,000 h.p., carried 1,200 gal. of fuel, 16 cu. ft. of sand and weighed 306,420 lbs., producing 51,630 lbs. of tractive effort (the amount it pulled). It was also equipped to handle its trains well over 100 m.p.h. on 36" wheels.

No. 2903 was upgraded to an E-8A rating (2,250 h.p.) in Spencer, N. C. on June 2, 1953. Then the "old warrior" was retired in 1967 and sent to EMD on Aug. 31, 1967.

That long, tapered nose was a dead giveaway that this 23-car train (mostly head end cars) sitting in Danville, was one of the historic engines that helped to replace the famous and beloved Ps-4, 4-6-2's. The old E-6A's looked great; however, I would have preferred a Ps-4 on the point of No. 36.

A convenient boxcar in a nearby siding enabled me to make a portrait of a typical "passenger train at a station" shot during a time, before Amtrak, when the railroads actually tried to get the public to patronize their trains, even though ridership was decreasing at an alarming rate.

Southern's No. 33, the "Piedmont Limited," is shown at Danville, Va. this cold (25° F) Jan. morning in 1965. While the engines were being refueled, the engineer and firemen (yes, they still had firemen at this time) were outside, stretching their legs. They were also looking straight at me. I always wondered if they just wanted to see what I was doing (on top of a boxcar) or if they simply wanted to be in the picture.

Up front of No. 33 was the old "racer," E-6A, #2902, and much newer E-8A, #6912, handling 12 cars. That slant-nosed E-6A came from EMD in May of 1941 and was one of seven purchased by the Southern to power their two new, stainless steel streamliners: the "Southerner" and the "Tennessean." No. 2903 and 2903 were lettered, "Crescent," (No. 37 & 38), since this train was also remodeled at the same time. All E-6A's and four E-6B's were colored green, white and gold colors reminiscent of the beautiful Ps-4, 4-6-2's which ruled the mainline passenger runs for almost two decades.

The E-6A's were upgraded to E-8A specifications at Spencer, N. C. shops between 1953 and 1954, so #2902 had 2,250 h.p. at the time of this exposure, weighed 306,660 lbs. and produced 51,610 lbs. of tractive effort. The old "million-miler" was retired and returned to EMD on Sept. 6, 1967. It served the Southern well for 26 years.

What a great photo: the old E-6A and newer E-8A working together to move the "Piedmont Limited," one of the many passenger trains in the Southern's fleet, which was steeped in rail history.

I believe the crew from #2902 just wanted to be in this photo, frozen for all time in an era when railroading and railfanning was far more exciting (at least in my opinion).

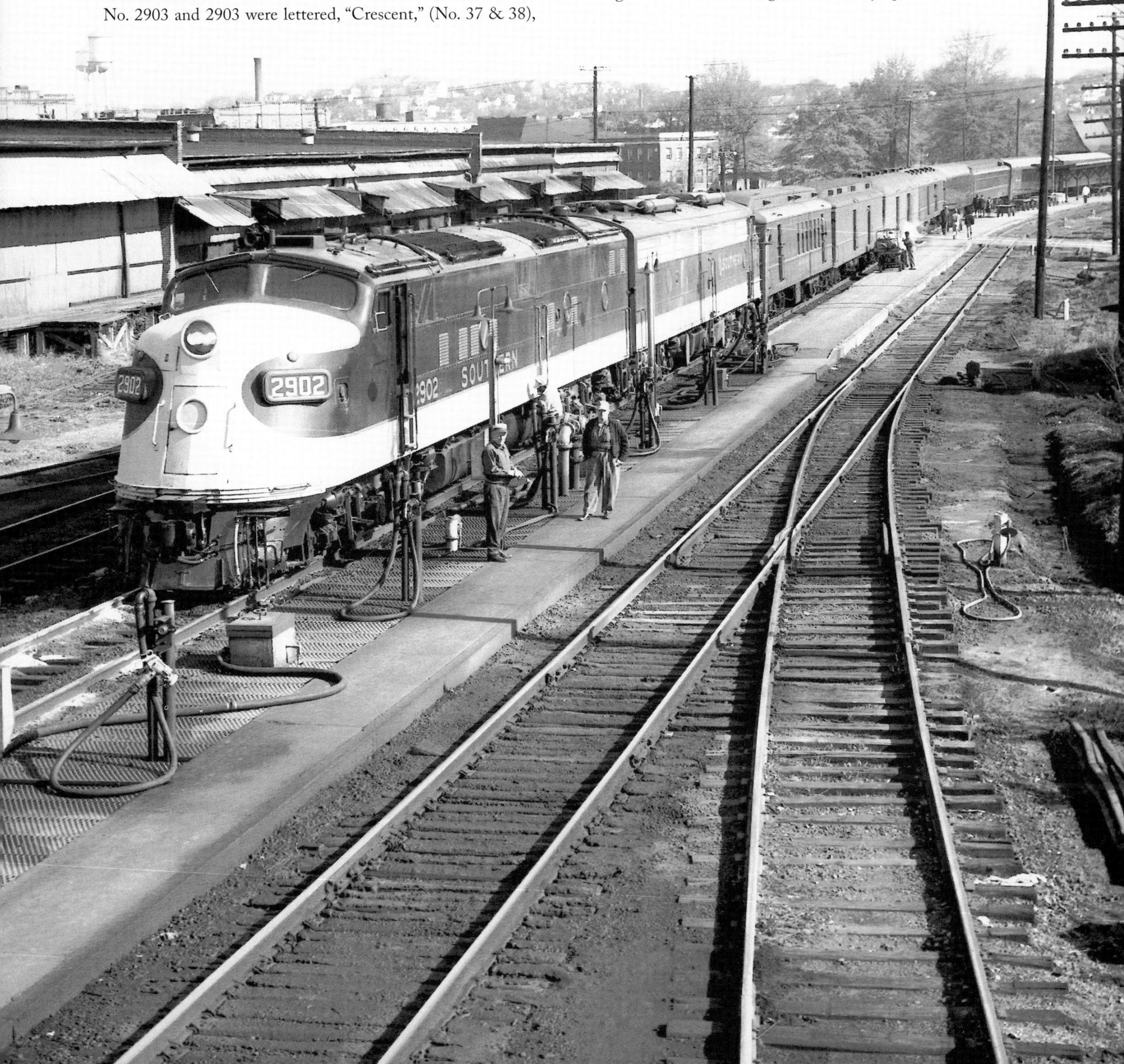

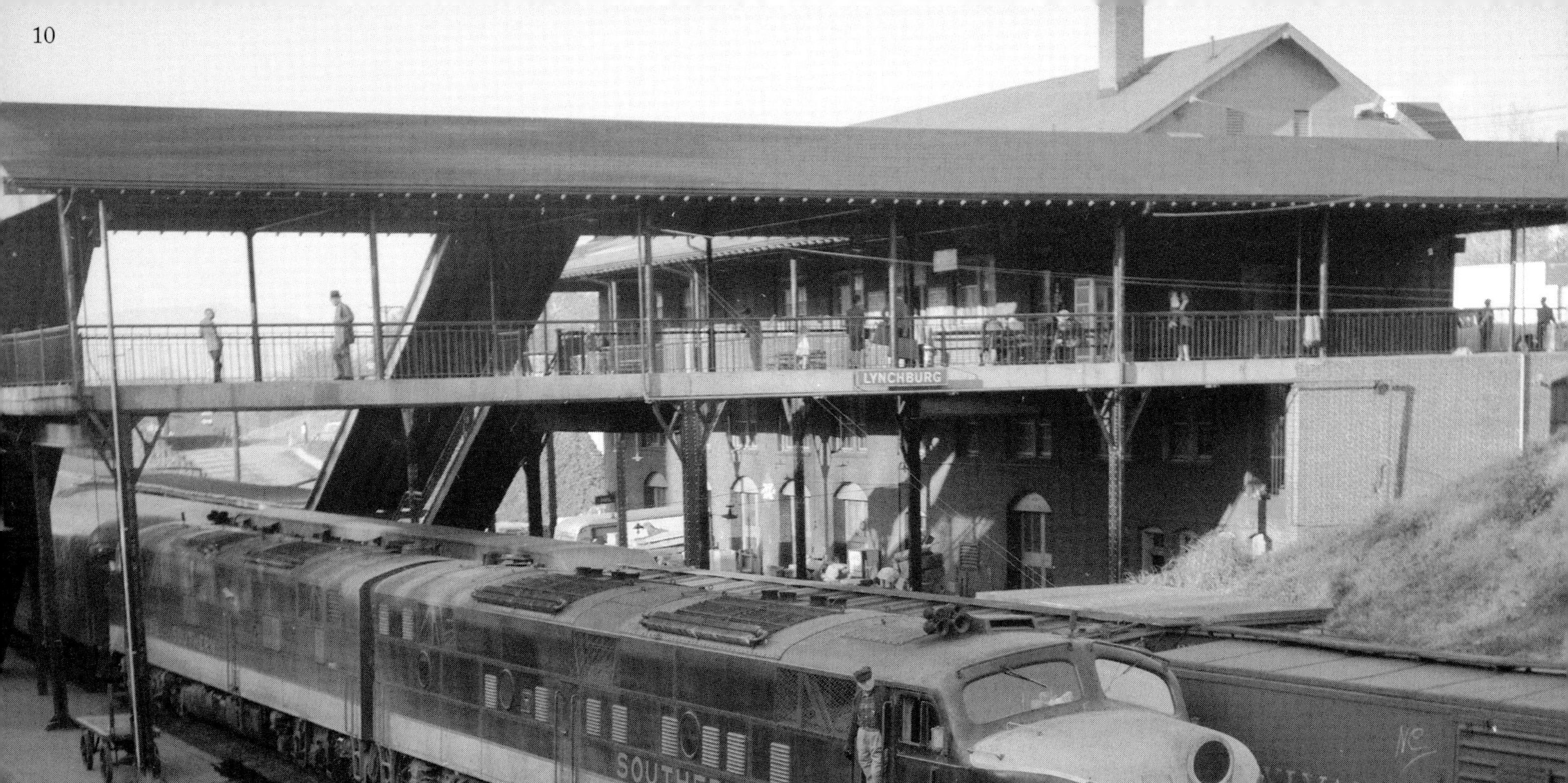

A classic locomotive, a classic station and an old "hogger" making a classic pose – all ingredients begging to be photographed. Fortunately, I was there and recorded the events that you can enjoy. The engineer standing in the door of his unit had probably pulled the throttle on more Ps-4 class steamers than he ever would on diesels before his retirement.

Kemper Street Station in Lynchburg, Va. was the place to be for watching big time railroading in action. A case in point was Southern's "Washington-Atlanta Express" (No. 35), shown here with 14 cars this Oct. day in 1963, pulled by the old, April 1941 built, EMD E-6A "warrior" (No. 2802) with an E-7A "youngster" (No. 2912). On the right of No. 35 was the "Tennessean" (No. 46), powered by two E-7A's.

When new, No. 2802 was painted green, white and gold lettered, "Southerner," since three sets (A and B units) were purchased to power Southern's new (1941) all Budd built stainless steel cars of their New York-New Orleans streamliner. The road purchased seven E-6A's and four E-6B's in 1941. Two sets were lettered "Tennessean" and, eventually, the remaining E-6A's were lettered, "Crescent."

At 21 years of age, the E-6A's were running out their remaining years on "plug" locals such as No. 35 (No. 2802 was retired in 1967). Their 2,000 h.p. was increased to that of an E-8A (2,250 h.p.) on Nov. 11, 1953 at Spencer, N. C. They still carried 1,200 gal. of fuel and No. 2802 weighed 305,660 lbs., producing a tractive effort of 51,610 lbs.

My family can be seen standing on the platform over the double track mainline (my dad was the first "watcher" on the left). Each autumn, we traveled from Oxford, N. C. to Lynchburg to see the beautiful colors of the season. Since I was driving, I would head straight to Danville, Va. and follow the Southern's mainline to Lynchburg. Then we headed east, following the N&W's mainline to Farmville, Va., then south to Keysville, Va. where we followed "my" line back to Oxford. I'm sure the colors were beautiful; however, I know for a fact that the train action was great!

F-3

In 1939, the Southern began obtaining large numbers of GM's Electro-Motive Division built FT diesel-electric locomotives. These "steam busters" were not only impressive in their performance but they were the wave of the future for the rail world as well. Each of the FTA's and "B" (booster) units produced 1,350 h.p. By 1946, EMD came out with the F3 models that were superior and more versatile than the FT's, with 1,500 h.p. per unit. Then, by 1949, the ultimate of the cab units, the F-7's made their appearance. The F-7's could out-perform both the FT's and F-3's and were easier to operate, more efficient and economical (and my favorite of all the freight units). The F-7's were so good, the Southern had nearly their fleet of 102 F-3's upgraded to the F-7 standards.

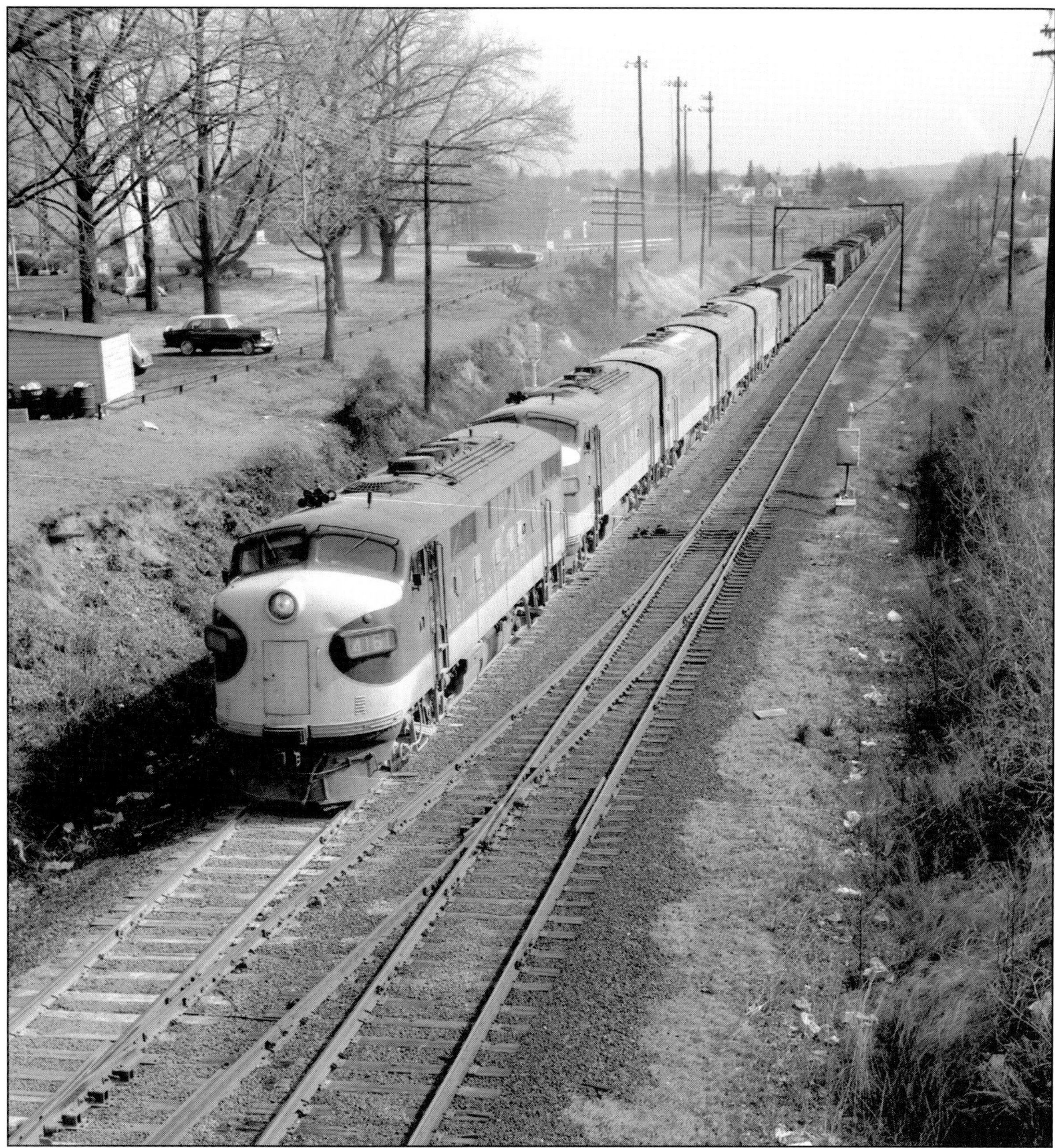

They were not as nimble as the "GP" and other road switchers but to me and the other railfans of my generation, there was nothing more beautiful than that "bulldog" front and streamlined car body of a group of "F" units working upgrade with a great deal of tonnage tied on behind. And the unique EMD sounds they produced while working at full throttle was an unforgettable occurrence – the "F" units represented railroading at its best!

Shown here, grinding up Cemetery Hill, south of Danville, Va. is F-3A, #4161 (upgraded to F-7 standards in July of 1952 at Spencer Shops), F-7A (#6114), two F-7B's (#4391 and #4409) plus an F-7A (#4226), pulling 186 cars (over a mile long) of through freight No. 57 (Potomac Yard to Atlanta) – all five units wide open at approximately 15 m.p.h., nearing the top of the hill while passing by the huge Dan River Mills textile plant. What a sight! What a sound!

The lead unit, the former F-3A, #4161, was built in Feb. of 1947, had 1,500 h.p., carried 1,200 gal. of fuel, weighed 245,560 lbs. and produced an impressive 63,300 lbs. of tractive effort. It was finally retired and returned to EMD in Oct. of 1971.

They were the most aesthetically pleasing freight units on the Southern and served the company well for almost 24 years. Five "F" units working upgrade with their throttles in "notch-8" – man, this was the type of railroading that put a smile on your face and a memory in your mind that would be with you throughout the rest of your life!

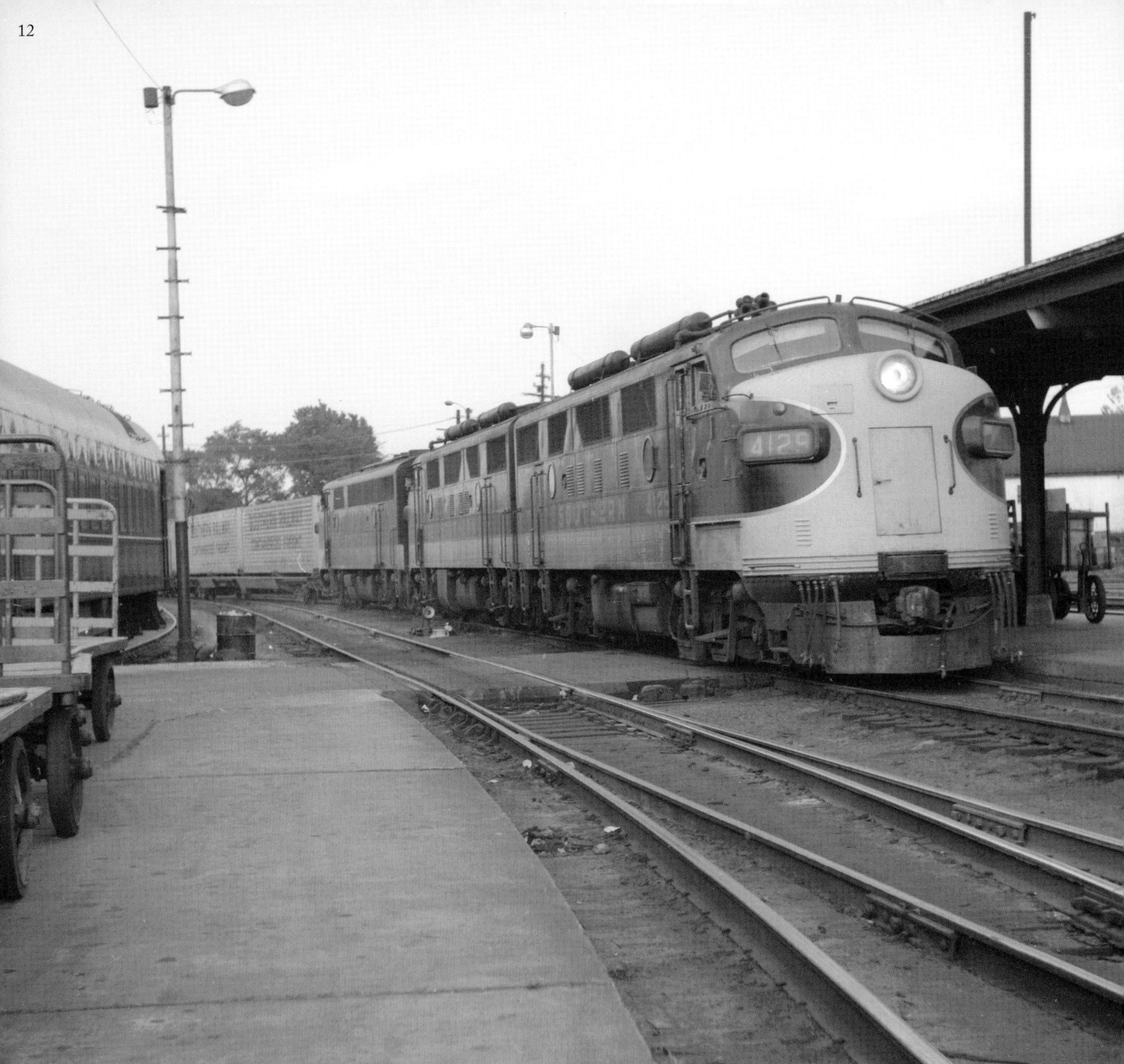

You are looking at one of the first solid piggyback trains operated by the Southern, approaching the beautiful passenger station in Greensboro, N. C. on a cloudy May 8, 1963 at 5:09 p.m.

The Southern called the train No. 23 but the sales department nicknamed it the COMAR Special – (Consolidated Motor and Rail). The "special" had three fast F-3A's on the point (#4129, #4167 and #4161) pulling 25 cars south this late afternoon.

Once the Southern was convinced that the piggyback business was a "look at the future," piggyback yards – big and small – began appearing all over the 8,000+ mile system. Within a few years, however, many of the smaller yards disappeared as the Southern consolidated them into fewer, larger piggyback facilities.

The F-3A, #4129, up front on No. 23, was built by EMD in Nov. of 1946, weighed 246,520 lbs., carried 1,200 gal. of fuel, had 1,500 h.p. and a tractive effort of 63,300 lbs. To increase its cooling water capacity from 230 gals. to 1,225 gallons, the road placed its air tanks on top of the locomotive. Its two single-chime horns were replaced by a five-chime "blower;" it was upgraded to F-7 standards on Oct. 18, 1952 at Spencer Shops and equipped with dynamic brakes on June 22, 1954. The dependable #4129 (part of 102 owned by the Southern) was returned to EMD on April 12, 1972.

I was ready to leave the Greensboro area after a successful day of railfanning when I heard a southbounder approaching. I hurried upstairs at the passenger station and reached the mainline just in time to "snap" a strange looking train – all piggyback – pulled by three F-3A's. Little did I know at the time that I was photographing the future of railroading this May afternoon in 1963.

When passenger business on the Southern began to decline and the old E-6's were making their last runs, the road began using more F-3's, F-7's and FP-7's on many of their remaining passenger runs. The "E" units – especially the E-8's – were found on the streamliners still in service such as the "Crescent," "Southerner" and a few others.

One of the non-streamliners, in this case No. 36, the "Washington-Atlanta Express," is shown just north of Lynchburg, Va.'s Kemper Street Station, headed by F-3A (#4133) and E-7A (#2921), pulling 21 cars (only 8 actual passenger coaches), this Nov. 3, 1963 at 4:40 p.m.

At one time, there were over 20 passenger trains that visited this area on a daily basis. Six of them: the "Pelican," "Birmingham Special" and "Tennessean" used the N&W from Lynchburg to Bristol, Va. before returning to Southern rails. You almost always found the E-6's, E-7's and E-8's as the motive power for these famous trains. With the aging of the E-6's and E-7's plus the drastic decrease in passenger revenue, however, trains were discontinued and no additional "E" units were purchased. Many of the "F" units had steam generators so they were employed on a more frequent basis.

F-3A #4133 was purchased by the Southern in Nov. of 1947 and continued in service until it was returned to EMD in Feb. of 1972, spending most of its life using its 1,500 h.p., 241,490 lbs. of engine weight and 63,300 lbs. of tractive effort hauling freight tonnage. Today, however, #4133 and its E-7A partner will help get No. 36 to Washington's Union Station.

I walked nearly a mile north of Kemper St. Station to find a good location to record the passage of 36. I believe I picked a good spot. What do you think? I also caught a southbound freight at this same area shortly after No. 36 went by, so all that walking paid off.

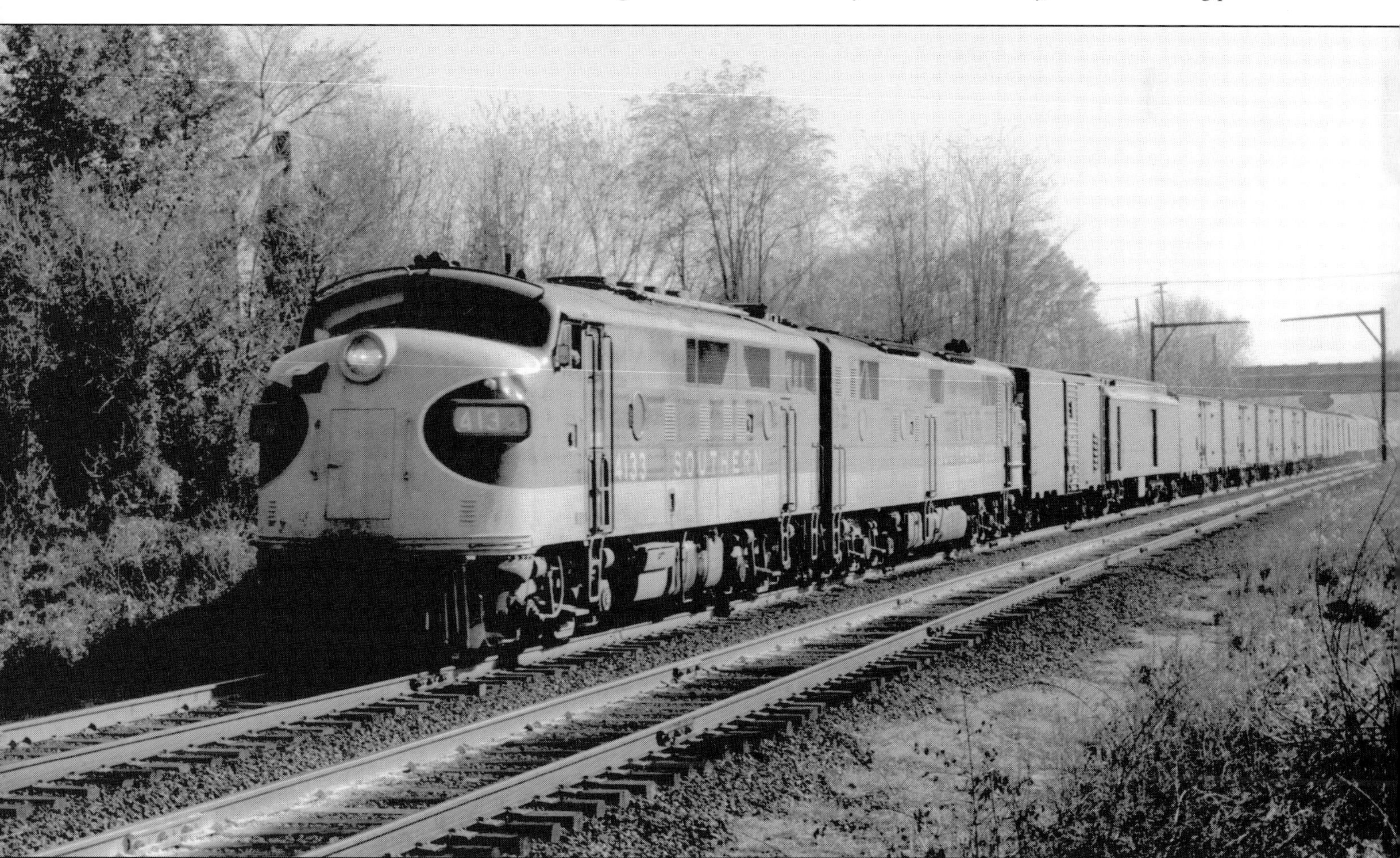

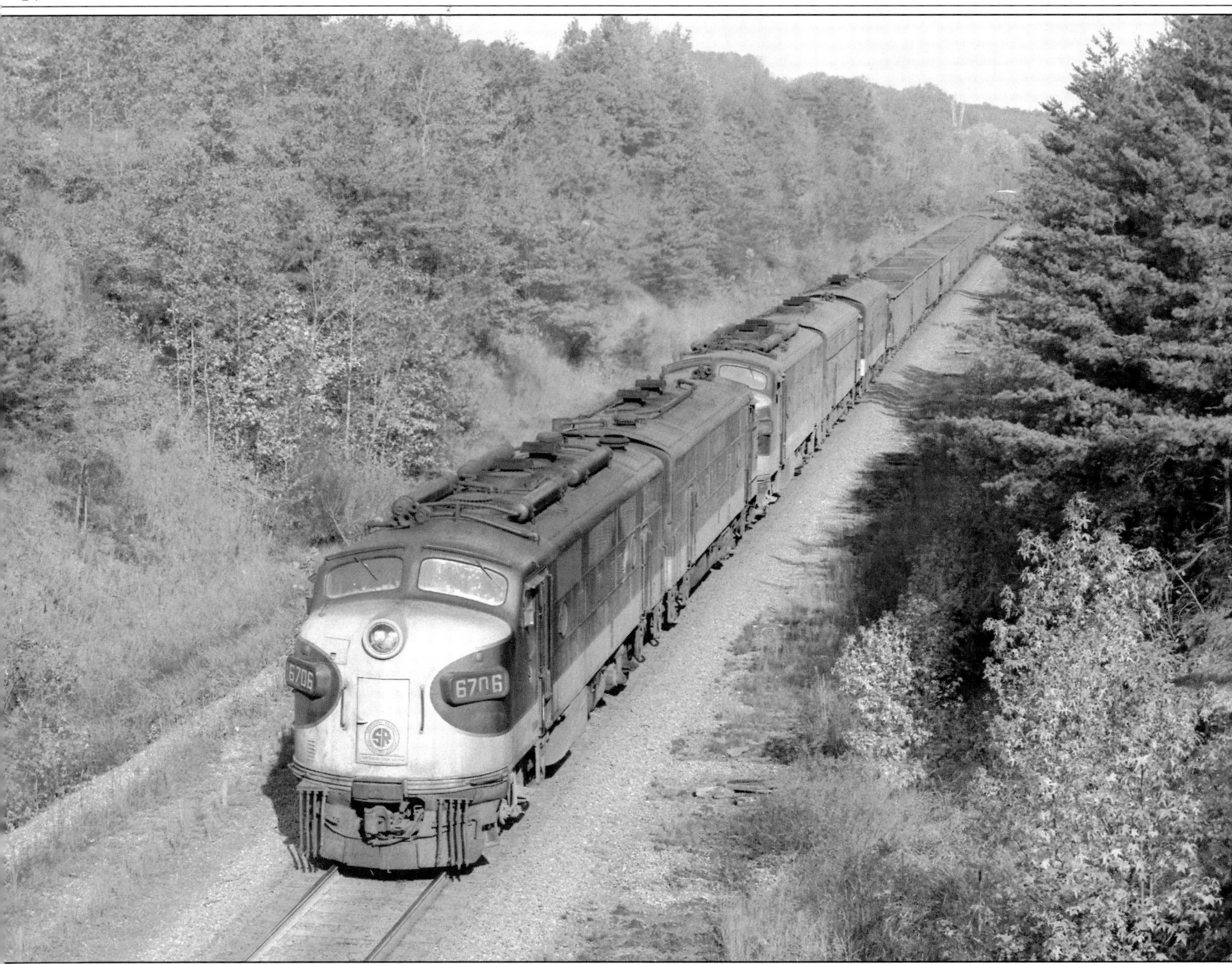

The date and time, Nov. 7, 1970, at 10:19 a.m.; the place, near Dry Fork, Va.; the situation, I was heading north out of Danville, Va. on U. S. 29 towards Altavista, Va. when my radio scanner made me aware of the fact that southbound 2nd No. 159 was heading my way. I hoped I could make it to Chatham, Va. to get an exposure of this Southern Atlanta-bound through freight; however, when I heard 2nd No. 159's engineer announced (over the radio): "Entering White" (a rail location), I knew I could not make it. As a result, I left the main road and headed west to a narrow bridge I knew of, which crossed over the Washington-Atlanta mainline. "White" was the beginning of numerous short, single track sections of mostly double track main. It ends at Fall, Va. which is located at the south end of the White Oak Mountain grade.

I made it to the bridge, got my camera's settings ready and then I heard the unmistakable sounds of a heavy freight approaching. So far, everything was going "according to Hoyle." Within the next few minutes, however, the ordinary would end and the unusual would begin – to my pleasant surprise.

By 1970, the mainline was being flooded with new GP-30's, GP035's and early SD, six-axle power, so I expected to find this type of motive power on 2nd No. 159. One problem, the engine sounds that I was hearing were not those of the GP's or SD's; it was a beautiful "growling" that I had not heard for a long time. Then my suspicions were confirmed when I finally saw the southbounder approaching my location: five "F" units! Five ""bulldog" nosed, streamlined freight units pulling 150 cars: (#6706, #6707, #4136, #4189 and #4170) – all F-3A's on a mainline freight in 1970?! I was very lucky to record such an occurrence during the twilight period of active cab units operation on the mainline. What a sound and, with that Southern symbol on its nose, what a beautiful sight!

No. 6706 – originally assigned to the AGS – was built by EMD in April of 1947, improved to F-7 standards in June of 1950 and given dynamic brakes in April of 1956 – all conversions being made at Spencer Shops. It had 1,500 h.p., weighed 247,300 lbs. carried 1,200 gal. of fuel and produced 61,800 lbs. of tractive effort. The air tanks were placed on top of the engine to increase its cooling water capacity from 230 to 1,225 gallons.

My trip to Altavista was delayed, for I had to get at least one more exposure of this rare and soon-to-be non-existence action. I had a feeling when I left home this morning that it would be a good railfan day for me. The five F-3A's on 2nd No. 159 confirmed my feelings. Just imagine how it used to be when the mainline was dominated by these streamlined freight engines – marvelous!

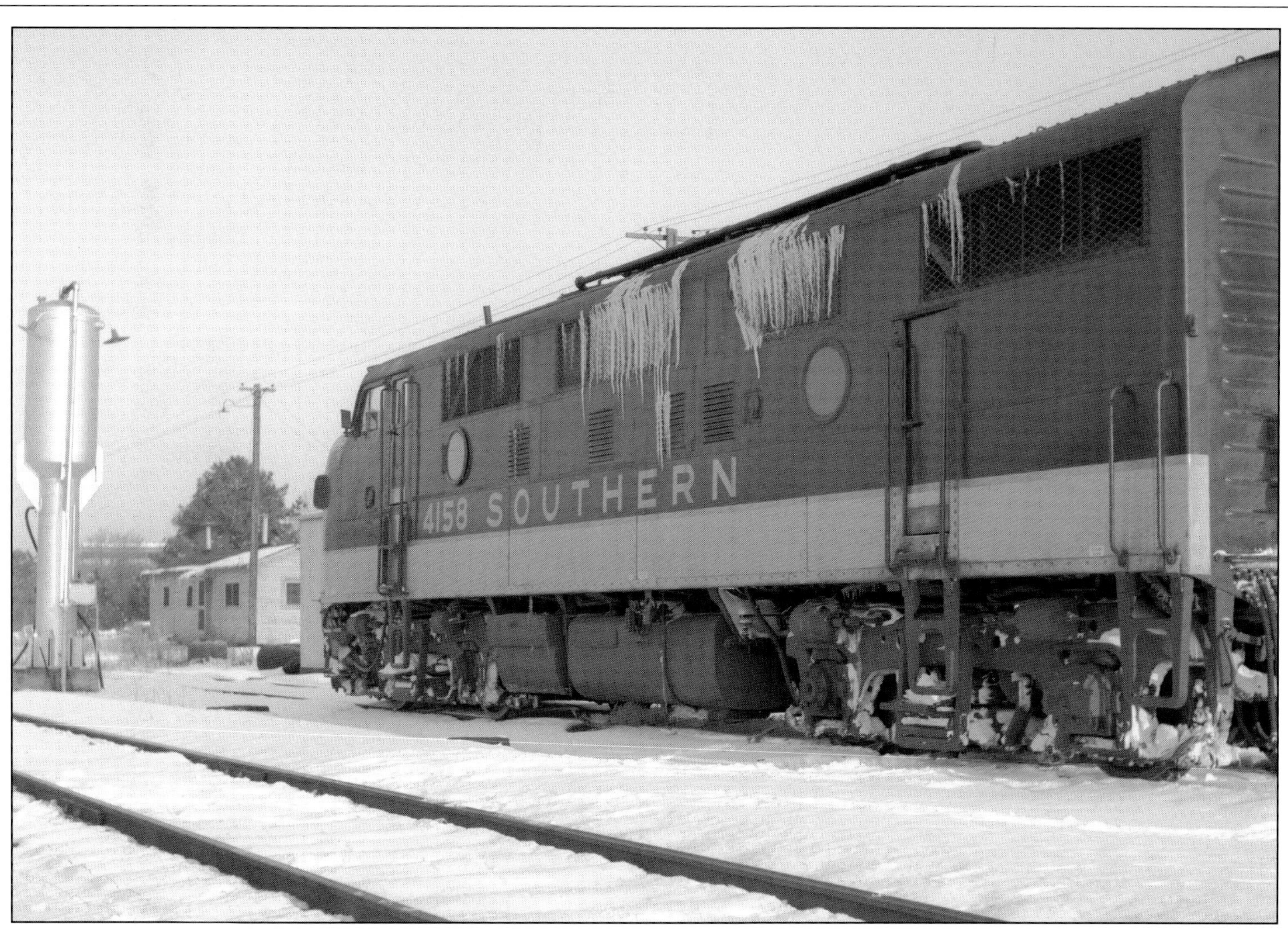

It was 25° F when I took this photo at the East Durham, N. C. ready track two days after a snow storm passed through the area, leaving nearly 10" of the "white stuff" on the ground – yes, we do have some hefty snow storms in my part of the "sunny South" from time to time.

You might wonder why this F-3A is not in action, moving tonnage and making money for the company. The Southern, like most roads, used their newest motive power on the mainline. No. 4158 was built in Feb. of 1947. By the time of this exposure (Jan 24, 1965, at 10:15 a.m.) newer GP-30's, SD-24's, SD-35's and other models had the major assignments on the mainline. As a result, the road found itself with a surplus of "F" units. As a result, the Southern assigned them to secondary and branch line service, replacing a great number of older RS-3's, GP-7's and similar models – even though they were never designed to do as much switching as these new duties required. It was really tough on the engineer when backing up and working industrial sidings.

This icicle encased F-3A was assigned to "my" line: the East Durham, N. C. to Oxford, N. C. – where it would make a round trip to Henderson, N. C. – when back in Oxford, it would continue working its way north to Keysville, Va. on a daily ex-Sunday schedule as No. 78 (the crew would put the F-3A to work at 11:30 a.m.).

These types of assignments were among the typical work the cab units had to face until retired. No. 4158 was returned to EMD on Sept. 22, 1973. Still, its 1,500 h.p., 249,280 lbs. of engine weight; its 1,200 gal. of fuel capacity and a tractive effort of 63,300 lbs., enabled it to work on "my" branch quite well. And until the GP-30's and GP-35's were replaced by newer power, the F-3A's and F-7A's ruled many such runs for over 4-5 years. Once the GP-30's and '35's were placed on branch line duties, the "F" units disappeared into rail history.

Man, let me get back to my car and cut the heater on "HIGH"! Brrrrr!

E-7

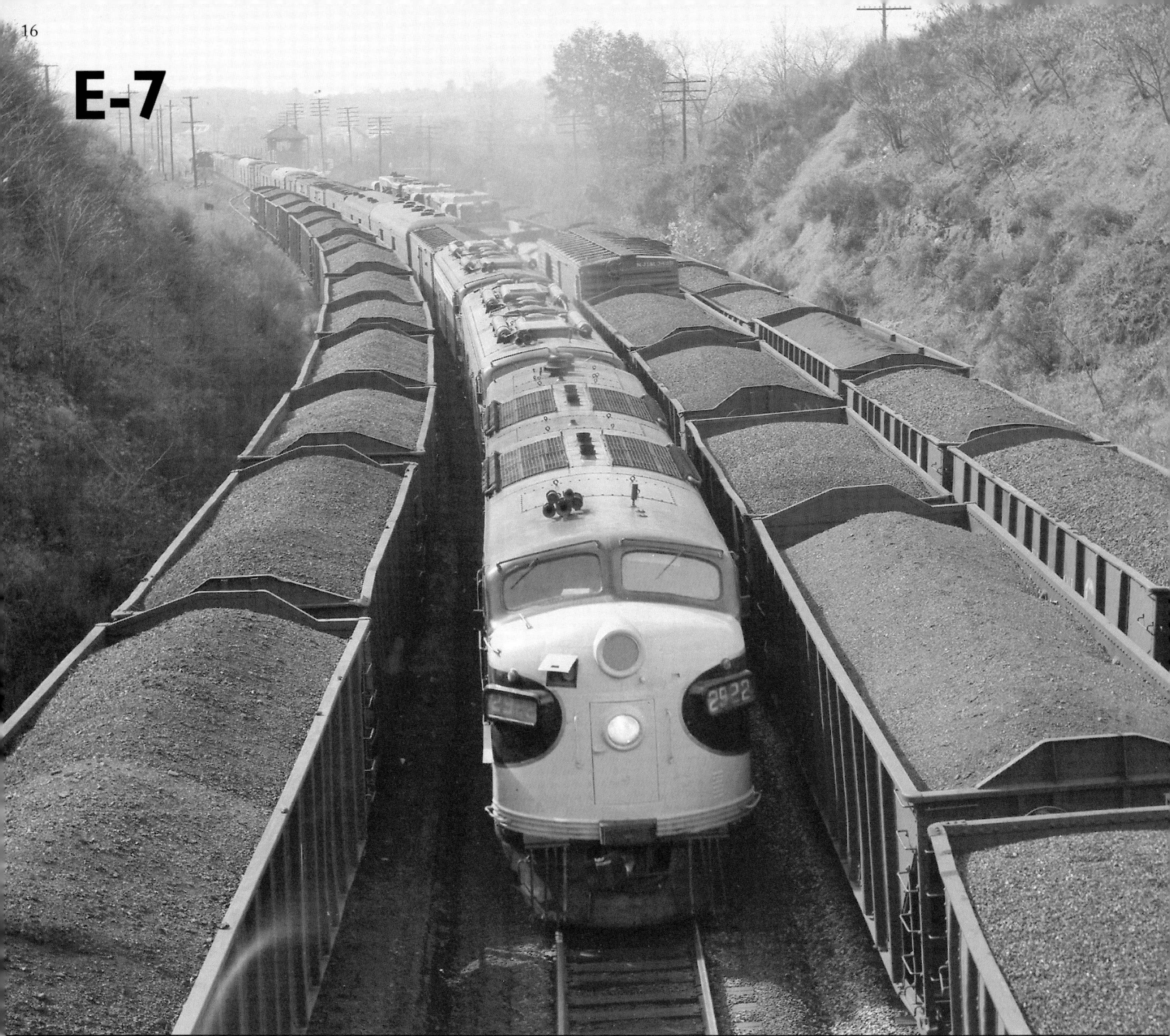

The coal business seemed to be a chief source of revenue for the Southern in Dundee, Va. area this Dec. day in 1964: both siding on either side of the double track, Washington-Atlanta mainline, were full of it; through freight No. 57 (on No. 2 track), pulling into the area with three GP-30's as its power, had a majority of coal in its consist of 135 cars (its engines are approaching Dundee Tower, shown in the background). However, on No. 1 track, heading north at an ever-increasing rate of speed, was No. 36, the "Washington-Atlanta Express," pulled by E-7A (#2922 and two E-8A's (#6908 and #2927), with 24 cars, shown passing through this "sea of coal" in the grand style of railroading during the 1960's.

Even though the old, 1941 built E-6A's were still performing well – all seven of them – they were beginning to show their age in both maintenance and cost. As a result, the Southern needed a passenger engine that was more fuel efficient and containing new and improved parts. The road had EMD built 18 E-7A's. The new models began appearing in service in 1946 and proved to be dependable and just what the road needed.

By 1949, they had #2905 through #2922 in their passenger fleet. Like most new power, the E-7A's were assigned to their premier passenger runs such as the "Southerner," "Crescent," "Tennessean" and others. By the time of this 1964 photo, however, the newer E-8's were handling these top jobs.

On this particular day, I got lucky since No. 36 had #2922 on the point. It was built in April of 1949, weighed 311,420 lbs., carried 1,200 gal. of fuel and with its 2,000 h.p. (eventually raised to that of an E-8 – 2,250), they had a tractive effort of 53,900 lbs., running on 36" wheels. They looked utilitarian when compared to an E-8, but they could get the job done and continued to do so until it was retired and returned to EMD on Sept. 20, 1968.

This was ironic yet beautiful scene: all that revenue making coal and a passenger train, with ridership decreasing rapidly and the company losing money as the American public's "love affair" with their automobiles taking them away from the far more efficient and safer mode of travel. Still, it was a thrilling event that unfolded in front of my camera this cold morning!

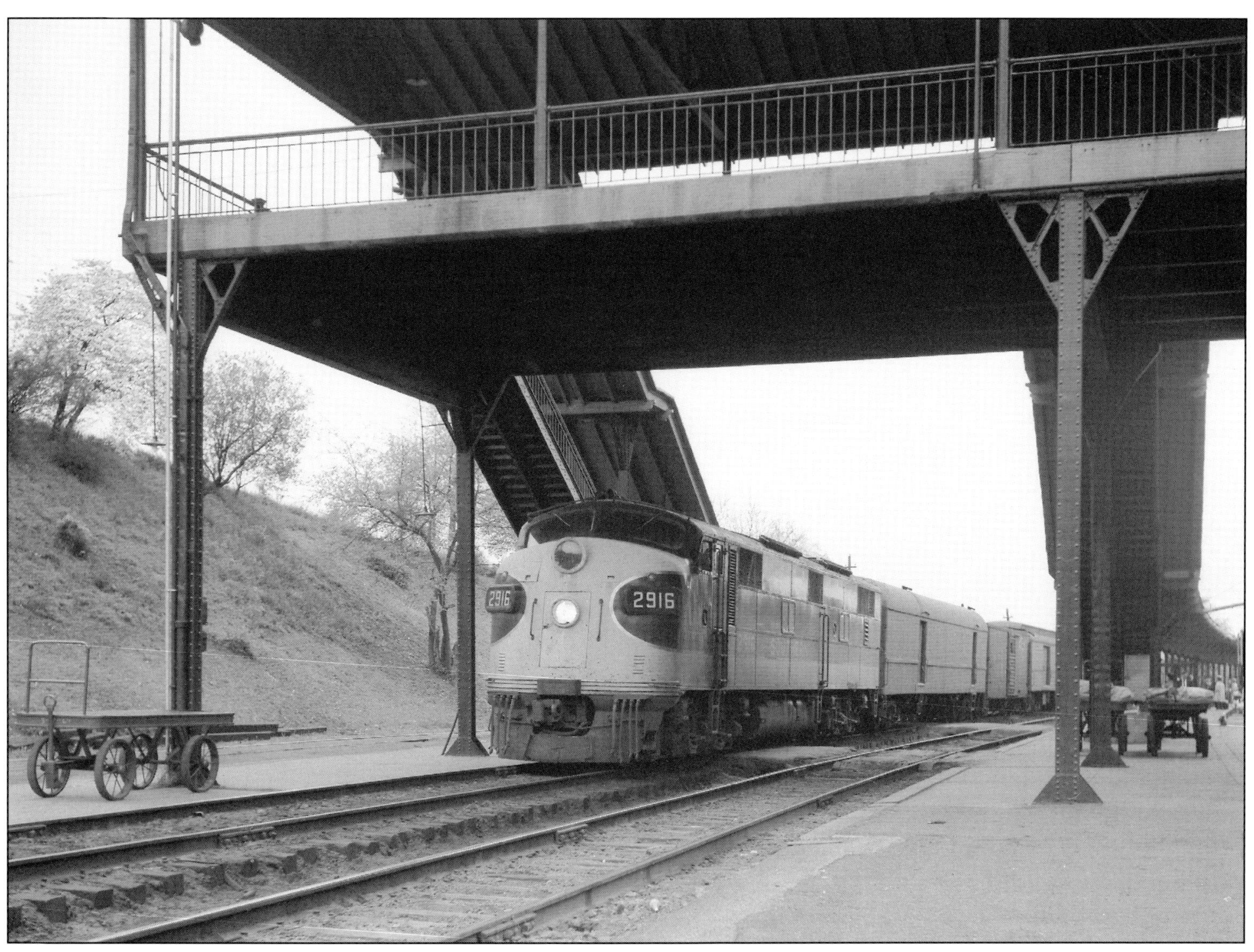

I fell in love with Southern's Kemper St. Station in Lynchburg, Va. on my first visit. In fact, on my introduction to Kemper St., I saw my first N&W Class J, streamlined 4-8-4. It had replaced a diesel on a Southern passenger train in Monroe, Va. – 8 miles north of Lynchburg. The steam giant would take the train to Roanoke and then to Bristol, Va. where the Southern would place a diesel back on the train and then carry it on to its destination. There were three such varnishes handled in this manner: the "Birmingham Special," the "Pelican" and the "Tennessean." So, long after the Southern had completely dieselized in 1953, you could still see active steam power at Kemper St. Station.

This day in May of 1964, we see an abbreviated No. 35, the "Washington-Atlanta Express, arriving at Kemper St. with E-7A #2916 pulling only 6 cars. By the mid-1960's, ridership losses had caused the Southern to prune its passenger fleet. By the looks of No. 35, it – along with its northbound counterpart, No. 36 – did not have long before being discontinued, as did other passenger trains as well.

No. 2916 came on the property from EMD in May of 1946 and continued moving the public until 1970 when, on Dec. 24, 1970, it was retired and returned to EMD. With 2,000 h.p. (eventually raised to 2,250), the utilitarian-looking E-7A produced 53,900 lbs. of tractive effort, riding on 36" wheels and carrying 1,200 gal. of fuel. It weighed 310,460 lbs. and had a pleasant-sounding five-chime horn on top of its cab.

This was the place to be in the early 1960's to witness several passenger and far more freight trains passing under the upper platform – especially the N&W steam locomotives arriving and departing.

Alas, today's Kemper St. Station is only served by Amtrak's "Crescent;" the upper platform has been removed and the facility is now a shadow of its former self. Yet, we have those wonderful moments, such as the one shown here, in our memories; and, as long as those and photos such as the one shown here continue to exist, we can still marvel at this grand structure that hosted so many trains, powered by both diesels and steam engines, for so many years. I still visit the station from time to time, but it's not and never will be the same.

After getting a new crew in Greenville, S. C., No. 34, the "Piedmont Limited," is shown nearing Duncan, S. C. on its daily journey from New Orleans to New York with its next stop being Spartanburg, S. C. No. 33 & 34 picked up and dropped off mail "on the fly" in several communities where it did not stop.

Today's No. 34 (July 6, 1964 at 1:40 p.m.) was powered by E-7A (#2919), FP-7A (#6140) and E-7A (#2916), pulling 12 cars at a good 65+ m.p.h. The three engines are working up a slight grade; and to keep the "Piedmont Limited" on time, we see a rare sight: an E-7A putting out exhaust fumes – an atypical occurrence for an E-7.

At the time of this photo, the Washington-Atlanta main was double tracked all the way. Today, with C.T.C. and microwave communications, the track on the right no longer exists. From Lyman to Taylors, S. C., it is single track territory; however, most of the mainline remains double tracked to this day – under the 1982 created Norfolk Southern's control. And Amtrak's "Crescent" is the only passenger service through this area (both streamliners pass through during the night hours – rats!). But the freights still rumble through with great frequency (thank goodness).

The twin-beam headlights, "tomato can" antenna and air-chime horns are among the most modern additions seen on the handsome E-7 up front. No. 2919 came from GM's Electro-Motive Division in April of 1949, weighing 311,960 lbs. and carrying 1,200 gal. of fuel, riding on 36" wheels. Originally, it had 2,000 h.p.; however, it was upgraded to E-8 standards and developed 2,250 h.p. Notice how much longer the E-7A looked compared to the FP-7A. The "E" was 68' long while the "F" unit was approximately 51 feet in length.

This E-7A was retired and returned to EMD on Dec. 24, 1970. But on this particular day, it was right where it should be:on the mainline pulling a passenger train whose name was steeped in rail history. I rode No. 34 on one occasion from Greenville, S. C. to Danville, Va. (where my family was waiting to carry me home). It was an adventure I shall never forget!

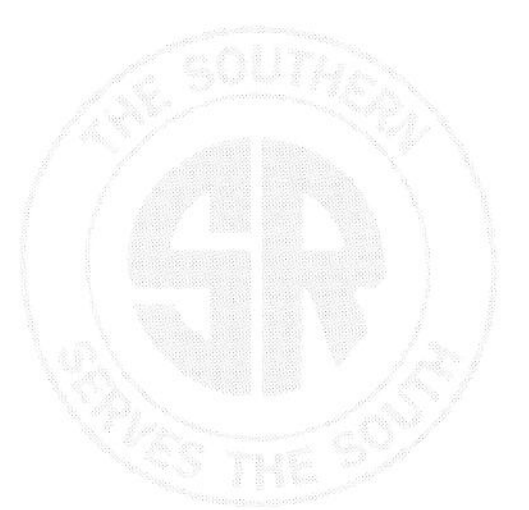

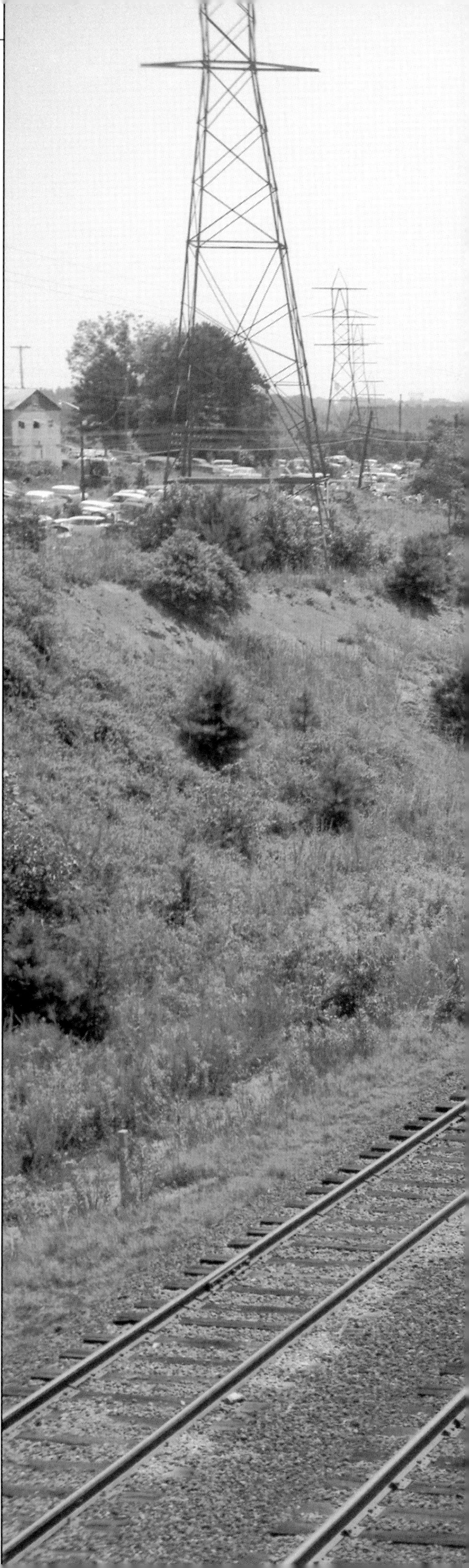

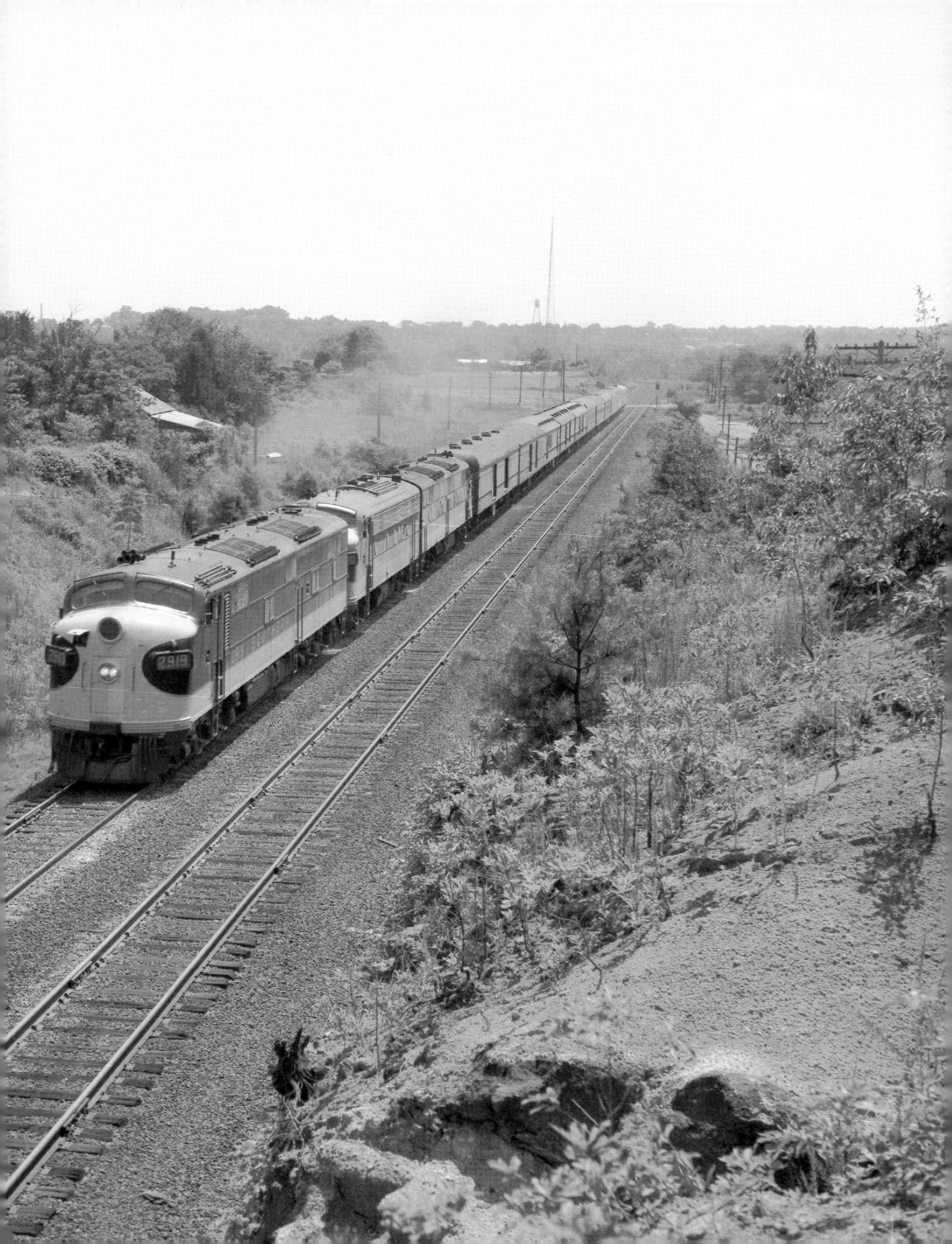
2919

E-8

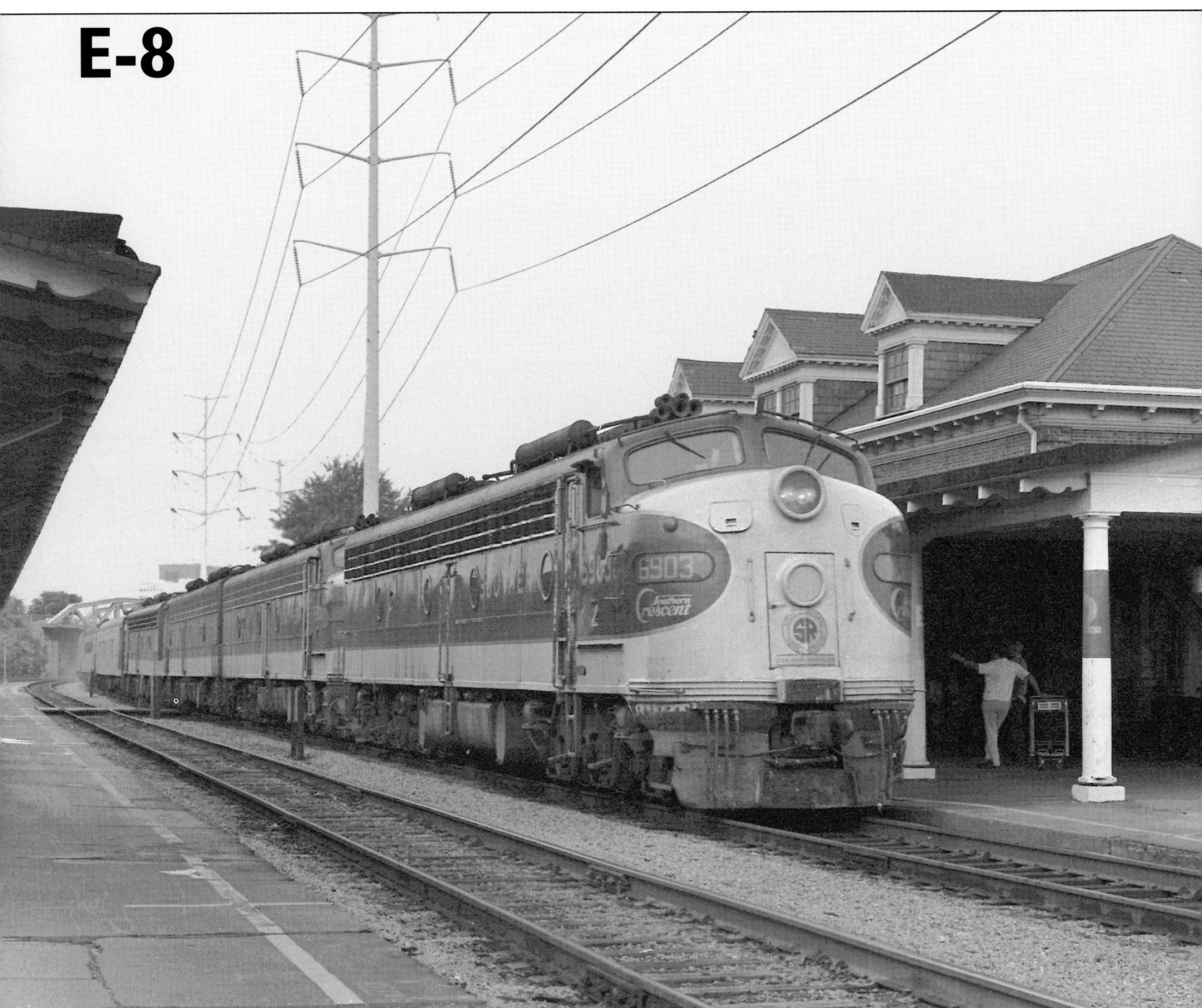

Even though the historic passenger station in Alexandria, Va. hosted up to 16 Amtrak trains each day – at the time of this photo – the two passenger trains that drew the attention of the railfans (and the public in general) were the non-Amtrak, luxurious and classic Southern Railway, north and southbound, "Southern Crescent," which ran between New York and New Orleans.

Shown here was No. 2, the "Southern Crescent" preparing for its daily stop at "Alex." On this partly cloudy morning (June 22, 1978-8:15 a.m.), the streamliner was powered by four, immaculately clean E-8A's (#6903X, #6900L, #6909R and #6901J), pulling 16 cars. Note that the columns on the front of the station made the decals of the different roads that used its facilities. As luck would have it, the lead unit of No. 2 was passing the column with the Southern symbol on it!

The E-8A's were among the most perfectly designed passenger diesel by GM, Electro-Motive Division (EMD). They were runners, quiet but powerful; they rode as smooth "as a Pullman" and the crews loved them. By this time, the Southern had only had two passenger trains keeping the shine on the rails of their Washington-Atlanta mainline: the "Piedmont" – No. 5 and No. 6 (powered by FP-7A's) and the long distance, famous No.1 and No. 2. To add that special touch and, hopefully, attack ridership, the Southern painted the E-8A's green, white and gold and placed the name, "Southern Crescent" under each number board in 1972. The resulting locomotives became known as the most beautiful passenger diesels to ever ride the rails!

No. 6903X, originally numbered #2926, came from EMD in Sept. of 1951 and was retired in 1979. Then it was sold to the New Jersey D.O.T. and renumbered #4333. It had 2,250 h.p., carried 1,200 gal. of fuel; it was 70'3" long, 10'7" wide and 14'10" tall. Weighing 334,039 lbs., it had a respectable 56,100 lbs. of tractive effort.

There were four tracks at the station: the two shown here were for passenger trains while the remaining two (on my left) were used by the freights going into and out of huge Potomac Yard.

Alexandria was the place to be if you loved trains, for the freight and passenger volume was almost unbelievable. Indeed, you needed two cameras, for on occasion you did not have the time to change film before another "visitor" passed through – paradise!

You are looking at one of the finest constructed diesel-electric locomotive models to emerge from EMD's La Grange, Ill. shops. It was designed to do one thing and one thing only: move the American public as fast, smooth and safely as possible to their destination; and the E-8A engines did just that!

Not only was the 2,250 h.p., 70'3" long "speedster" sleek and quiet, but it was powerful and the zenith of EMD's "E" series. The Southern enhanced its appearance by placing the air tanks on the roof so it could carry more fuel and cooling water between its trucks. This arrangement actually caused the engine to look more muscular. What could possibly make #2926, shown at Lynchburg, Va.'s Kemper Street Station, pulling No. 35, the "Washington-Atlanta Express" – along with fellow E-8A, #2923 – this late afternoon day in Aug. of 1962 with 16 cars, look better?

Believe it or not, the Southern did just that! In 1972, No. 2926 was renumbered to #6903 and painted green, white and gold. Then, as a final touch, the road had the name, "Southern Crescent," placed under both number boards. Then it and the remaining 17 E-8A's owned by the Southern were put into service pulling No. 1 and No. 2, the "Southern Crescent," between Washington and New Orleans (it went on to New York over the old PRR and eventually Amtrak). The new color scheme and the name of the streamliner actually did the impossible: it made the E-8A's even more beautiful! By the way, when the Southern added the Central of Georgia to its system in 1971, it inherited two E-8A's (#811 and #812). These two engines were not used on No. 1 and No. 2, however.

So, looking at #2926 at Kemper St. this quiet afternoon, who would have thought that in 10 years it would go through a metamorphosis and be turned into the "Cinderella" of passenger power and remain so until 1979 when it was retired and then sold to the New Jersey D.O.T., renumbered to #4333 and served for several more years, moving commuters to and from their jobs, day after day.

To me, this photo was among the best I made of this magnificent E-8A before it received its new colors and assignment and established its place in rail history forever. This was "Beauty at Rest!"

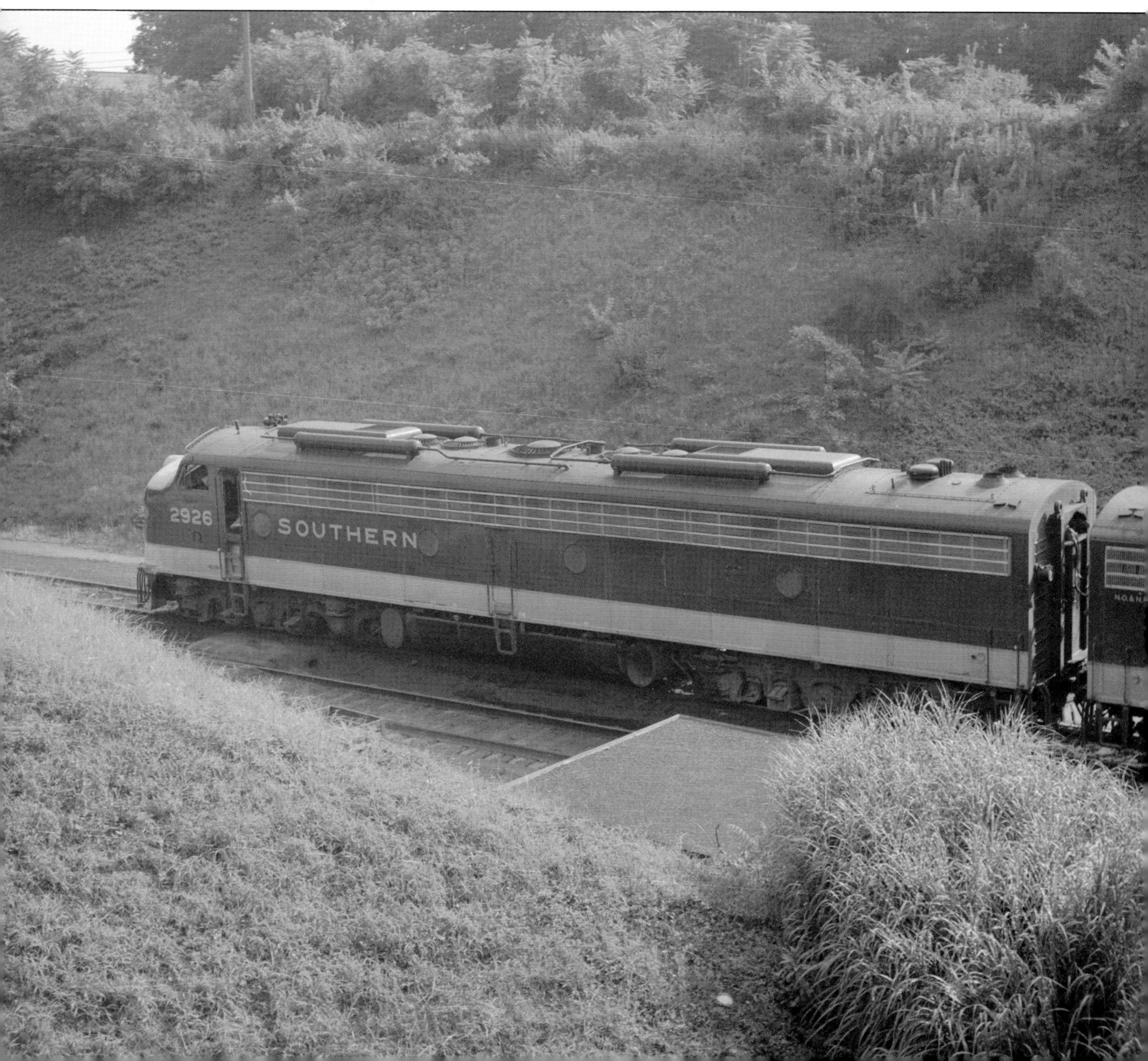

Before 1972, when the Southern painted their E-8A's green, white and gold, put the name – "Southern Crescent" – under each number board and assigned them to ferry their No. 1 and No. 2, the "Southern Crescent," on the Washington to New Orleans portion of the streamliner's New York-New Orleans run, you could find the E-8A's on many of the road's passenger trains. However, the Southern almost always had these beautiful diesels pulling two of their premier trains: the "Crescent" (No. 37 & 38) and the "Southerner" (No. 47 & 48).

Shown here are two black, white and gold colored E-8A's (#6914 and #2926) along with an E-7A (#2916), pulling 12 cars on No. 29, the "Peach Queen" – one of those "other" trains – just south of Greer, S. C. on a cloudy July 8, 1964 (11:15 a.m.) heading for Greenville, S. C. where a new crew will help No. 29 complete its journey from New York to Atlanta.

At the time of this photo, the Southern's mainline was double track all the way between Washington and Atlanta. However, when the road installed C.T.C., the road was able to cut several sections of their double track (and saved a bundle in taxes). In fact, the track hosting No. 29 is now gone! The mainline had single-track sections of 8 to 10 miles in length; then what the Southern called "long pass tracks," – sections of double track running, usually, 15-20 or more miles long.

Even from a distance, you could tell the difference between the utilitarian-looking E-7A as compared to the E-8A's with those air pumps on their tops and their streamlined, speedy looks. Indeed, the E-8A's were the ultimate diesel produced by EMD in their "E" series (for the Southern this consisted of the E-6's, E-7's and the magnificent E-8's).

No. 29's lead "speedster" was built in Dec. of 1953, weighed 331,350 lbs., had a tractive effort of 51,600 lbs. with its 2,250 h.p. No. 6914 was retired in 1979 and sold to the New Jersey D.O.T., renumbered to #4330 and hauled commuters for many additional years. However, the greatest moments in its life span was moving No. 1 & 2, in their green livery, and pleasing everyone who was lucky enough to see them in action.

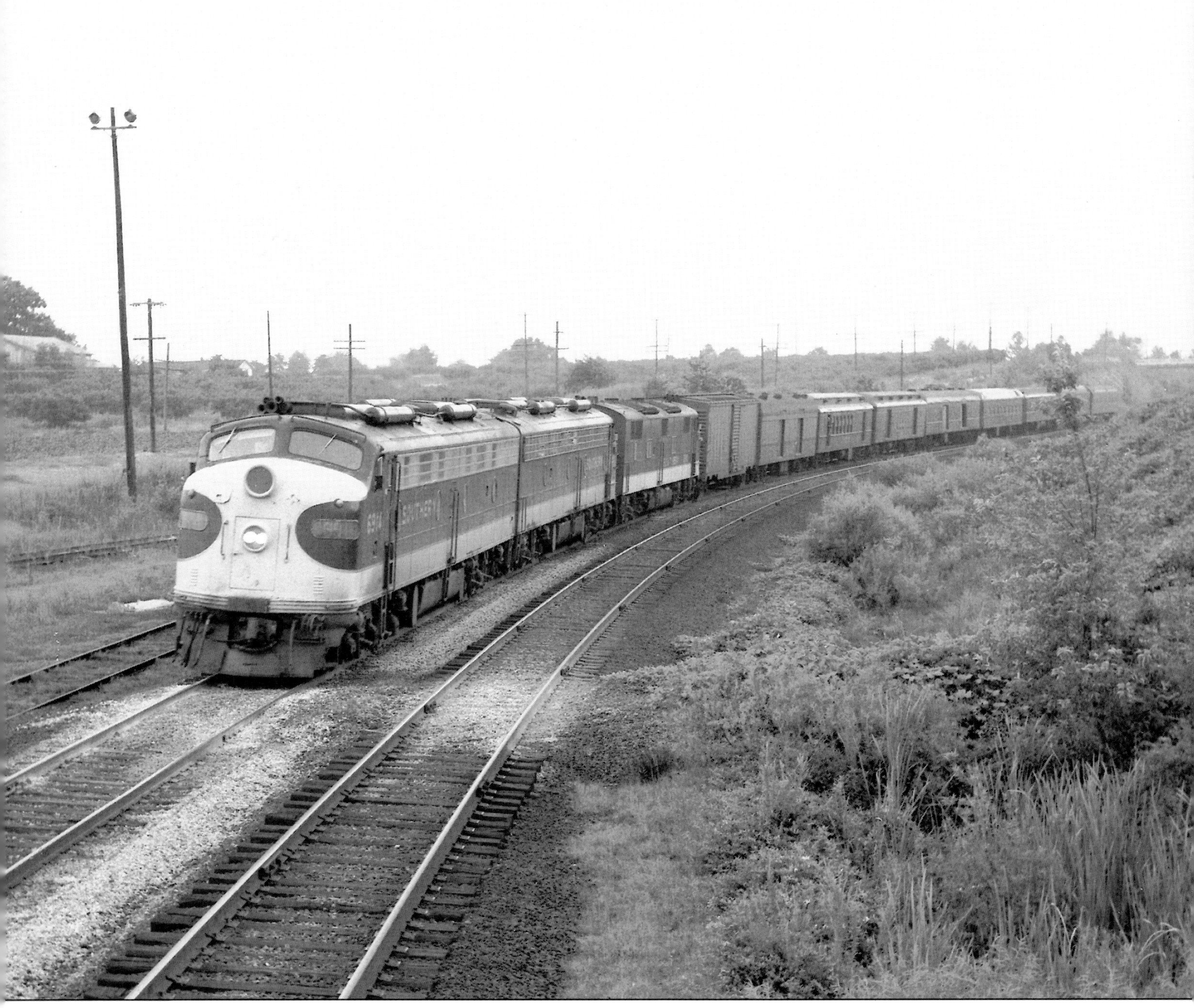

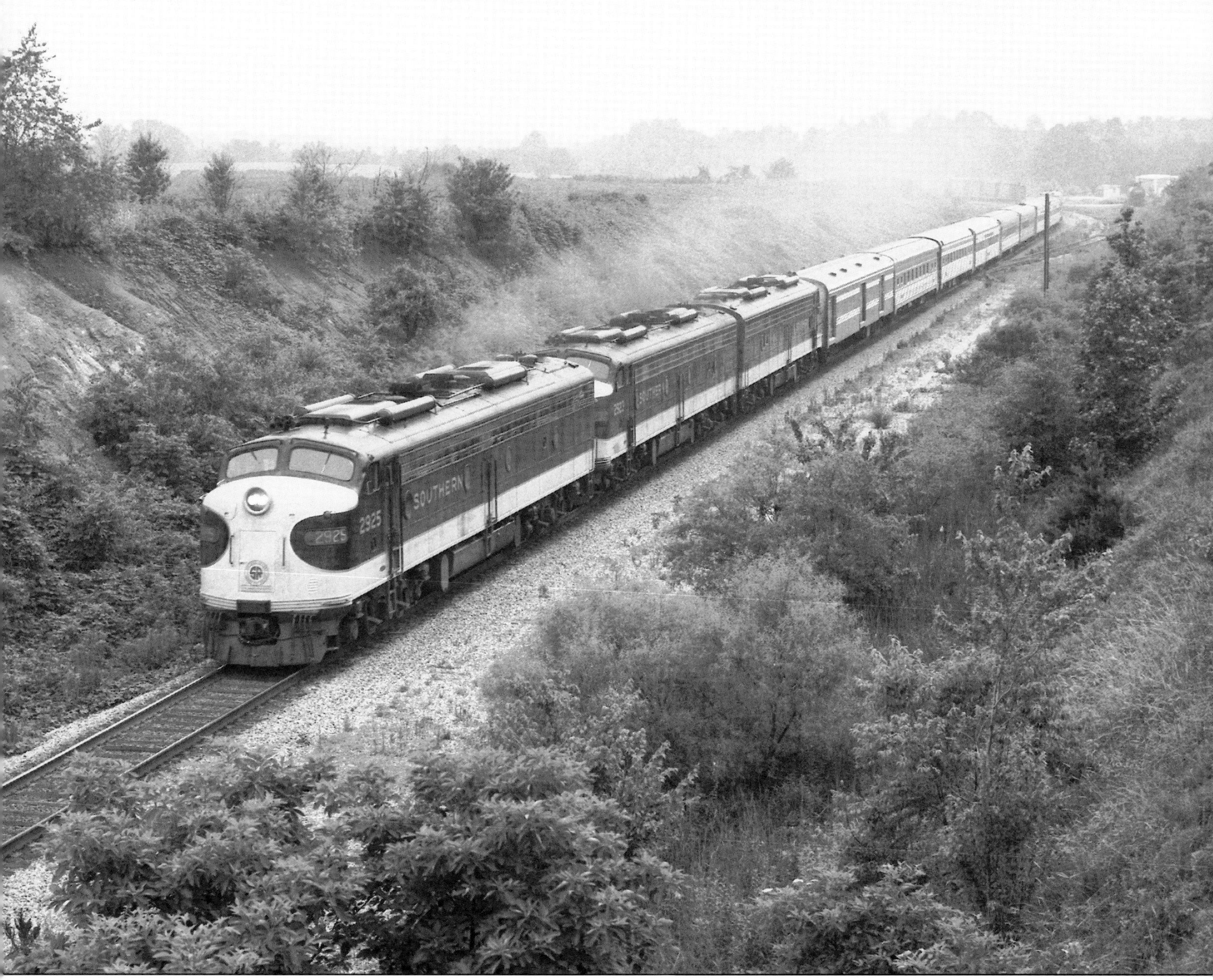

Whenever mom, dad and I traveled to Greer, S. C. to visit my dad's relatives, I always made it a point to be near the Southern's Washington-Atlanta mainline between 3:30 and 4:00 p.m. each afternoon, since the road's historic and classic No. 38, the "Crescent," passed through town at this time period with its sweet sounding air-chime horns "tied down" to protect the three main crossings in Greer. The immaculately clean E-8A's and its streak of stainless steel cars would pass through town at 45+ m.p.h. on its journey from New Orleans to New York. No matter how many times I witnessed this drama over the years, it was always the same: that period of anxiety of waiting, followed by the excitement of its passage and then the entire event of what had just happened was recorded in my mind forever.

One of those memorable encounters was recorded here on June 10, 1968 at 3:55 p.m. No. 38, with three E-8A's (#2925, #2923 and #6906) and 14 cars was shown approaching Greer, working upgrade at 60+ m.p.h. The three super-clean diesels were using their 2,250 h.p. in each unit to keep its train on time and showing a rare sign of exhaust, indicating the engineer had his three "charges" in notch "8," i.e., the throttles were wide open!

No. 2925 was built in Sept. of 1951 and painted black, white and gold with the air tanks placed on the top so it would have room for its 1,800 gal. of fuel plus cooling water. In 1972, its number was changed to #6902 and the E-8A was painted green, white and gold plus the name, "Southern Crescent," was placed under both number boards. No. 6902 and the other 17 E-8A's owned by the Southern were assigned to No. 1 & 2, the "Southern Crescent," and pulled this renowned and historic streamliner from New Orleans to Washington on its journey to New York. No. 6902 remained in this service until 1979 when Amtrak took control of the train. The 17 beauties were all retired in 1979 and #6902 was returned to EMD. The Southern never used the two E-8A's it inherited from the Central of Georgia in 1971. In fact, the two ex-C of G E-8A's - #811 and #812 – were also retired in 1971, not powering No. 1 & 2.

Our trips to Greer – each and every one – will always be with me, both being with my beloved family and the memories of the "Crescent" heading north each afternoon.

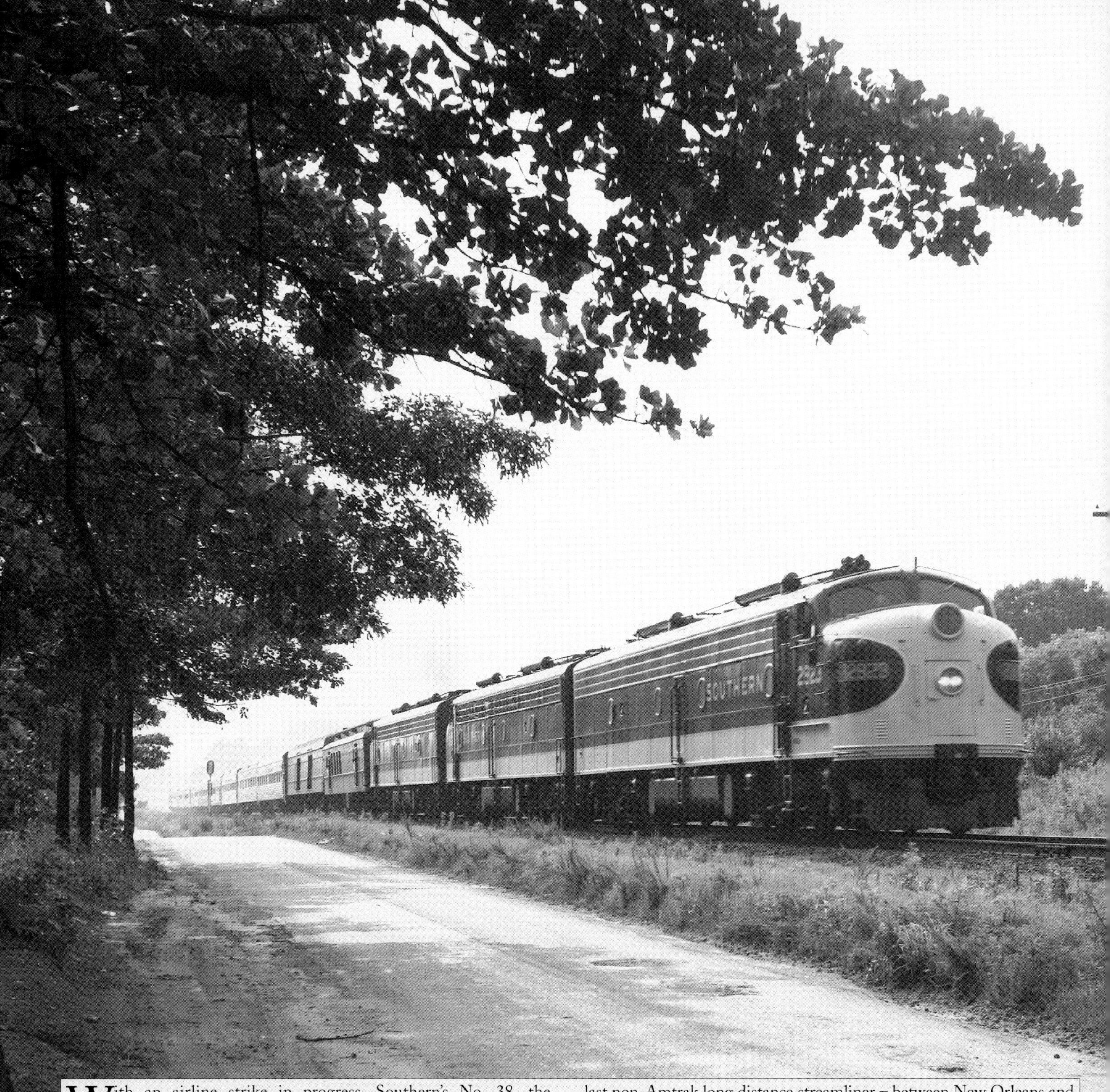

With an airline strike in progress, Southern's No. 38, the "Crescent," is shown passing through Greer, S. C. (my dad's hometown) with three, rather than the usual two E-8A's (#2923, #6914 and #2926) and pulling 14, rather than the usual 8 cars, all heading north on its daily New Orleans to New York, carrying a great number of passengers who would usually ride the planes (I bet they arrived at their destinations favorably impressed with the "Southern" hospitality they received this hot afternoon in July of 1966).

The lead E-8, #2923, had those pleasant sounding air-chime horns wide-opened as it passed through town at 45+ m.p.h. and now gaining speed, with its next stop being Spartanburg, S. C. This E-8 will have its number changed to #6900 and painted green, white and gold in 1972. It, along with the Southern's other 16 E-8's, had "Southern Crescent" painted under each number board and assigned to pull No. 1 & 2, this last non-Amtrak long distance streamliner – between New Orleans and Washington (and on to New York by Amtrak) – until 1979 when Amtrak took control of the entire train.

Once the Southern lost its last passenger train, they retired their regal-looking E-8's, which had 2,250 h.p., carried 1,800 gal. of fuel, weighing approximately 334,000 lbs. Thankfully, #6900 was saved and in Jan. of 1980, the Southern donated the green beauty to the North Carolina Transportation Museum, located in a place visited by #6900 on numerous occasions: Spencer, N. C.

The period 1953 through 1979 was highlighted by the passage of several Southern varnishes pulled by the most attractive passenger diesel ever built (at least in my opinion): the E-8A – it was truly a wonderful time for "us railfans."

FP-7

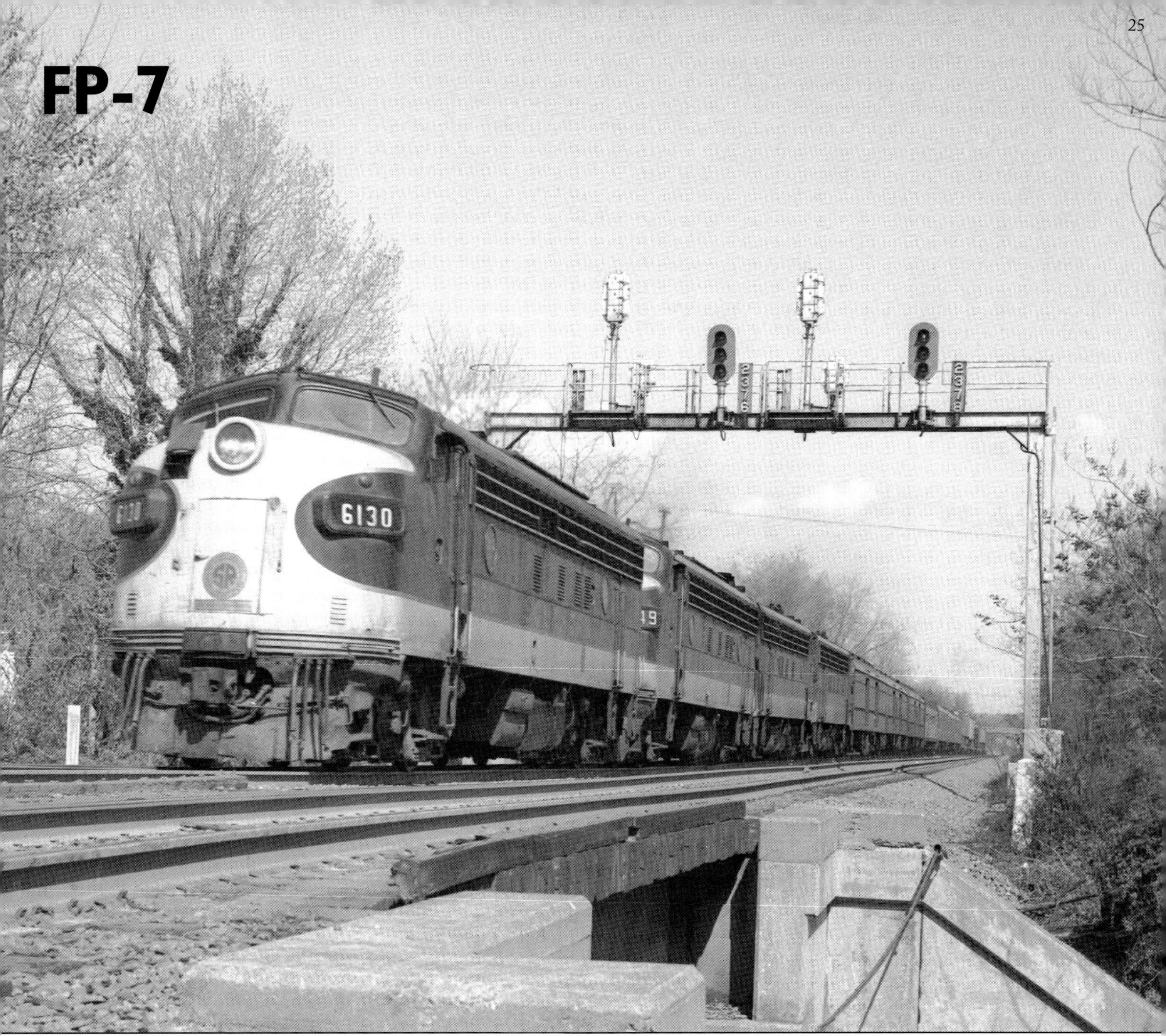

Southern's No. 5, "The Piedmont," is shown working up "Cemetery Hill" after a stop at Danville, Va. No. 5 was powered by four FP-7A's (#6130X, #6149X, #6143H and #6141R), pulling 19 cars (12 "piggy-back" car attached to its rear) this bright March 30, 1974 afternoon at 3:18 p.m. Unlike the southbound freights, this stiff climb did not present any problems for the 6,000 h.p. of EMD's FP-7A's although with those "pigs" on the rear, the four cab units were really "talking" it up in that beautiful EMD "F" unit roar – all at 35+ (and climbing) m.p.h.

As passenger train revenue began to decline during the period after the Korean War, the Southern did not purchase additional passenger power to protect their remaining varnish. Instead, the road decided to obtain a dual-purpose type of engine. Many of the F-3's had steam generators and could (and would) be used on passenger runs. However, the F-7's were superior in performance to the F-3's. As a result, in 1950 the road purchased 20 FP-7A's ("F"=freight, "P"=passenger) from EMD(#6130 through #6149).

The units met all the requirements of the Southern. No. 6130X was built in April of 1950, weighed 244,130 lbs., carried 1,200 gal. of fuel plus 1,750 gal. of boiler water and produced 61,000 lbs. of tractive effort. It, like the majority of its relatives, remained in service until the Southern joined Amtrak on Feb. 1, 1979. All but four of the FP-7's were considered to be surplus and retired.

The four remaining on the roster were: #6138, #6141, #6143 and #6149. They were painted green, white and gold in May of 1976 and used in excursion service. After the Southern-N&W merger in 1982, the now NS units had their numbers changed to: #3496, #3497, #3498, and #3499, respectively, since their old numbers were already in use by N&W's SD-40-2's. These four beauties were eventually retired in April of 1988.

No matter how many times I saw and photographed these FP-7A's taking on "Cemetery Hill," it was always a thrill watching those "bulldog nosed" cab units making those most recognizable EMD sounds and shaking the ground with their passage. Just look at the photo and you'll understand what I mean.

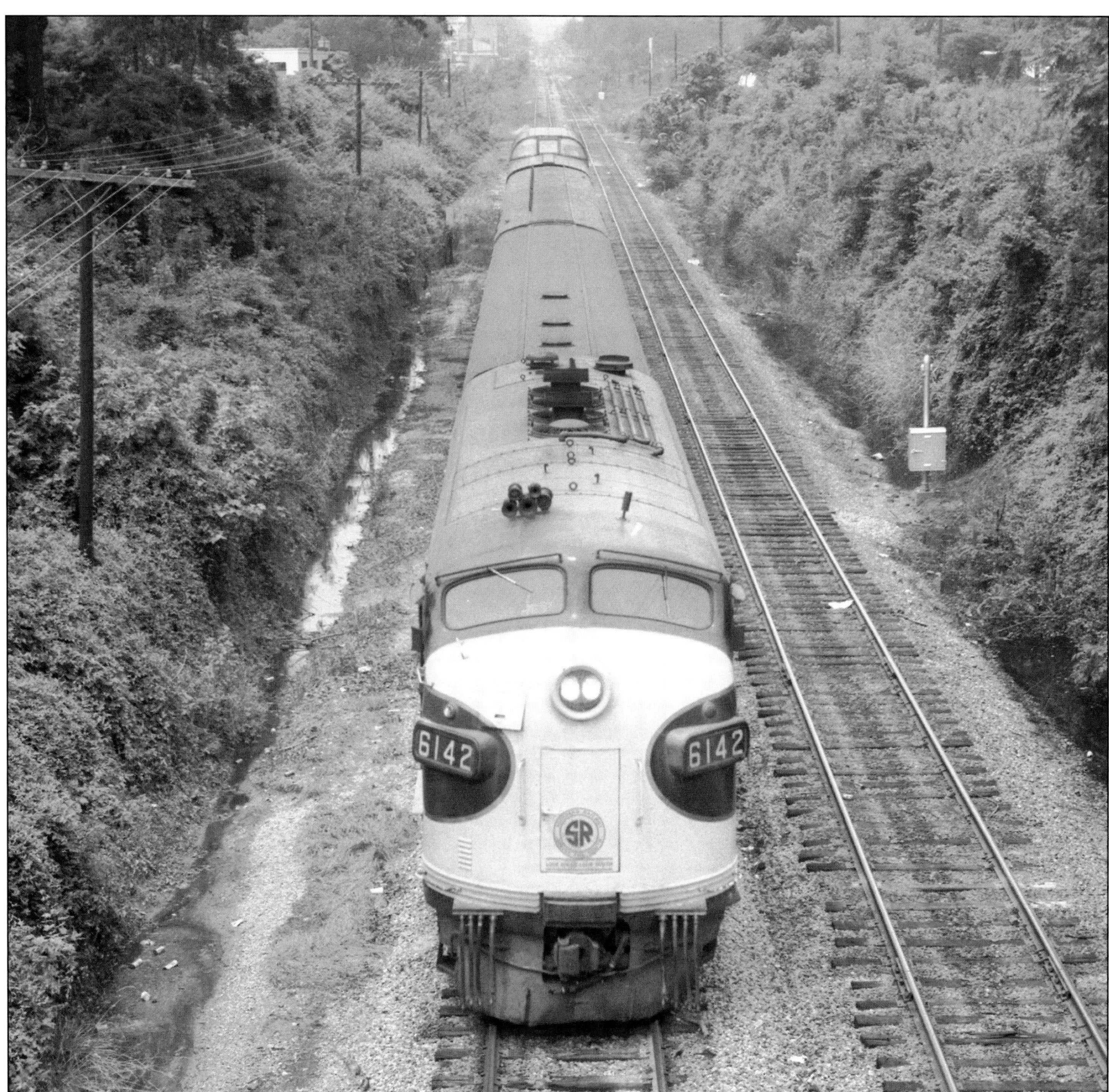

Coming into Salisbury, N. C. after a scenic run from Asheville, N. C. is Southern's No. 4 with Frank Clodfelter as engineer on the FP-7A (#6142), pulling three cars – including a "vista dome" on the rear of its consist – this June 1, 1974 at 1:40 p.m.

Even though only three cars long, No. 4 and its westbound counterpart, No. 3 – which will head back to Asheville later this afternoon – were well patronized by the public since the trains traversed some of the most spectacular scenery this side of the Mississippi River. Indeed, from Ridgecrest to Old Fort, N. C., it passed through seven tunnels, traveled over several grades and curves you simply had to see to believe. And with that dome car, you could witness this mountain majesty up close.

At one time the "Carolina Special," the "Asheville Special" and a local – in both directions – provided numerous opportunities for the public to view the wonders of "mother nature" on the Southern's Salisbury-Asheville line. And No. 3 and No. 4's time of existence was running out at the time of this exposure.

No. 6142 came from EMD in Nov. of 1950. It had 1,500 h.p., carried 1,200 gal. of fuel, 1,750 gal. of boiler water, weighed 244,270 lbs. and produced 61,000 lbs. of tractive effort. Standing 15' tall, 10'8" wide and 54'8" long, the FP-7A served the Southern until 1979 when the road joined Amtrak and it was declared surplus power and was retired. Only four FP-7A's remained on the system, even after the creation of the Norfolk Southern in 1982 (#6138, #6141, #6143 and #6147), but they were also retired – painted green, white and gold for excursion service – in April of 1988.

I rode the "Carolina Special" on one occasion; however, I always had a desire to travel this route in that dome car to get a clear view of the beautiful "Land of the Sky." Even though it was not to be, I can still imagine some of the sights I would have seen.

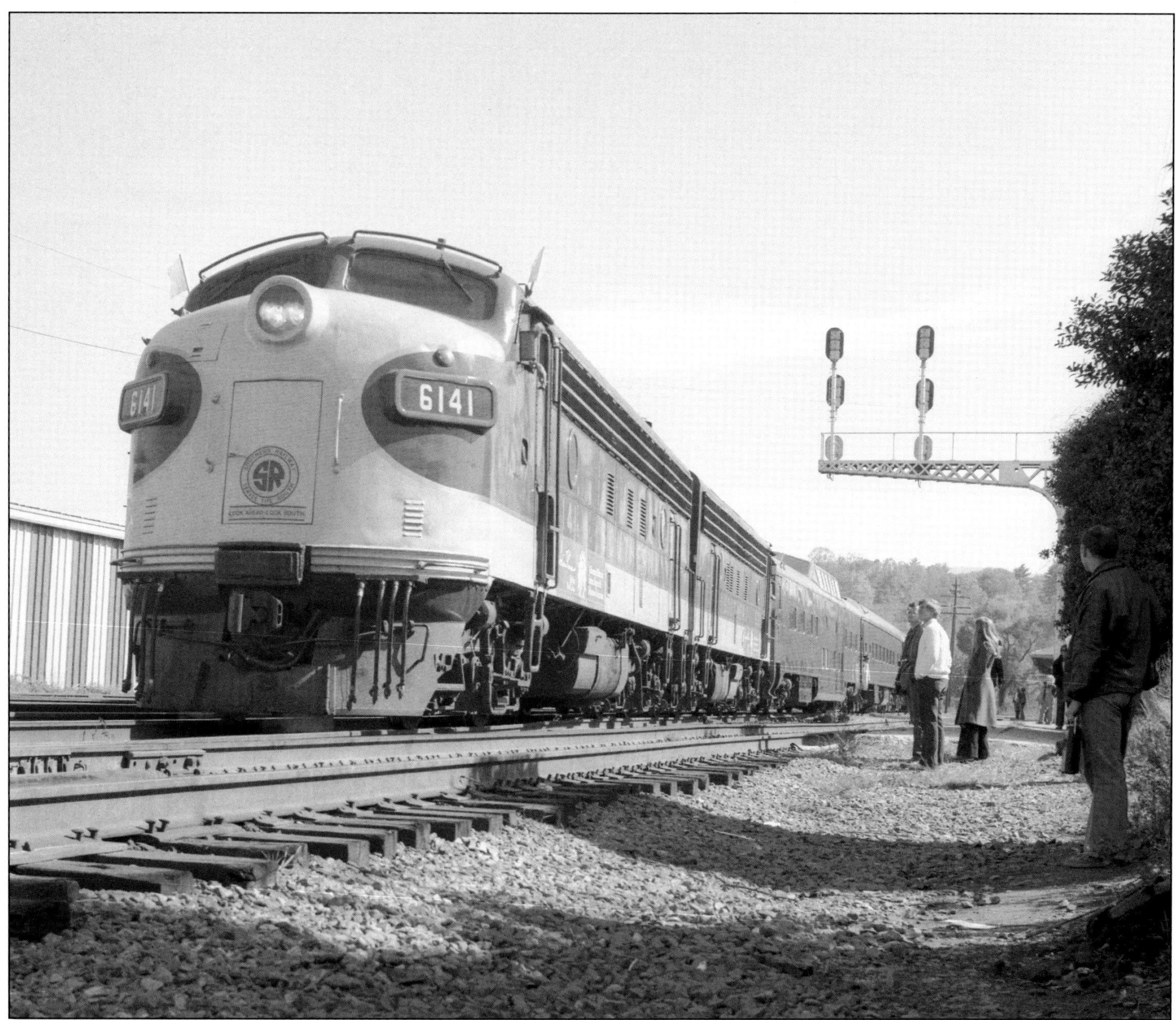

The Southern had 20 FP-7A's on their roster. They were mostly used in passenger service although by the time of this photo, July 24, 1976, E-8A's were always used on the road's main streamliner, the "Southern Crescent."

Four of the FP-7A's (#6138, #6141, #6143, and #6147) were painted green, white and gold in May of 1976 and used in excursion service. During the Bi-centennial year of our nation, the Southern placed two of these special beauties on an Asheville, N. C. (actually the station at Biltmore, N. C.) to Old Fort, N. C. round trip. This was one of the most scenic trips one could take east of the Mississippi River. FP-7A's #6141 and #6133 pulled the "Skyland Special" on this "mountain adventure," passing through seven tunnels and around curves you had to see to believe. The "Sky's" consist had opened cars, regular coaches and a domed car as well (7 total cars), so you could really see the beauty of the "Land of the Sky."

Its schedule called for the "Sky" to leave Asheville at 9:00 a.m., arrive at Old Fort, N. C. by 10:20 a.m. It departed from Old Fort at 11:00 a.m., rolling back into Asheville near 12:30 p.m. The family and I took the trip. I was in one of the open cars and almost "froze;" but I would take the same trip, in the cold mountain air, without hesitation!

The "Special" is shown back in the Asheville area at 1:05 p.m. after completing the round trip. Soon it would head to the ready track facilities to be readied for the next day's run. My old friend, Frank Clodfelter-engineer, historian, photographer and railfan-ran the two FP-7A's with a gentle hand on the throttle.

Once the Southern joined Amtrak on Feb. 1, 1979, all FP-7A's, except the four green and gold colored units, were considered surplus and removed from the roster. After the 1982 merger of the Southern with the N&W, the four FP-7A's had their numbers changed: (#6138 to #3496, #6141 to #3497, #6143 to #3498 and #6149 to #3499) because their original numbers were being used by N&W's SD-40-2's. The four beauties were finally retired in April of 1988.

Two green and gold FP-7A's, one of the most beautiful rides in America and Frank Clodfelter as your engineer: what more could you want? The "Skyland Special" was very popular and well patronized by the public while it ran. It surely provided several long-lasting memories for those who rode the "Sky."

Here is a scene worthy of being placed on the front of a Christmas card: snow on the ground, the public being carried to their homes for the holidays – all the ingredients necessary to qualify as a symbol for a Christmas-like scene were there. However, this exposure of Southern's No. 16, leaving Durham, N. C. on its daily Goldsboro, N. C. trip, was actually made on Feb. 29, 1964 at 8:25 a.m. – not Dec. 24th.

Two days prior to this action, a storm passed through the area leaving an accumulation of 10" of snow. With the temperature hovering near the 25° mark, not much of the snow had melted during those two days. As a result, No. 16 – pulled by FP-7A (#6143) with a three car consist – helped in creating this excellent example of winter railroading in the South. Yes, we do occasionally get a decent amount of snow in my part of the "sunny" South.

No. 16 had a New York to Raleigh, N. C. Pullman – the third car in the train. When No. 16 arrived in Goldsboro, it would be turned and then head back to Greensboro – as No. 13 – (picking up the Pullman in Raleigh) and making a connection with No. 38, the "Crescent," where the Pullman would be added to No. 38's train for its trip to New York. Many businessmen from the area would take the Pullman from Raleigh and/or Durham, do their paper work, have a good night's sleep and arrive in New York the next day. It was a popular arrangement until No. 13 & 16 were discontinued.

No. 6143 was a common sight pulling No. 16 and 13. The FP-7A was purchased by the Southern in Nov. of 1950. This particular unit had a most "colorful" career. When the Southern joined Amtrak in Feb. of 1979, all but four FP-7A's were retired. Then, in May of 1976, #6143, along with FP-7A's #6138, #6141, and #6147, were painted green, white and gold and all four were used in excursion service. They were very beautiful and became very popular among the fans. In 1982, when the Southern and N&W merged to form the current Norfolk Southern, the four FP-7A's had to be renumbered since four of the N&W's SD-40-2 series had their numbers. As a result, #6143 became #3498, #6138 became #3496, #6141 to #3497 and #6147 received the number, #3499. In April of 1988 – still painted green & gold – the four FP-7A's were retired after serving the railroad(s) for 38 years!

Look closely to the right of No. 16 – in the background. You'll see the first of three Seaboard Air Line RSC-3's getting a train ready for a run north to Henderson, N. C.

Yes, this was a scene – at least in my opinion – which would prove to be very popular on the front of a Christmas card!

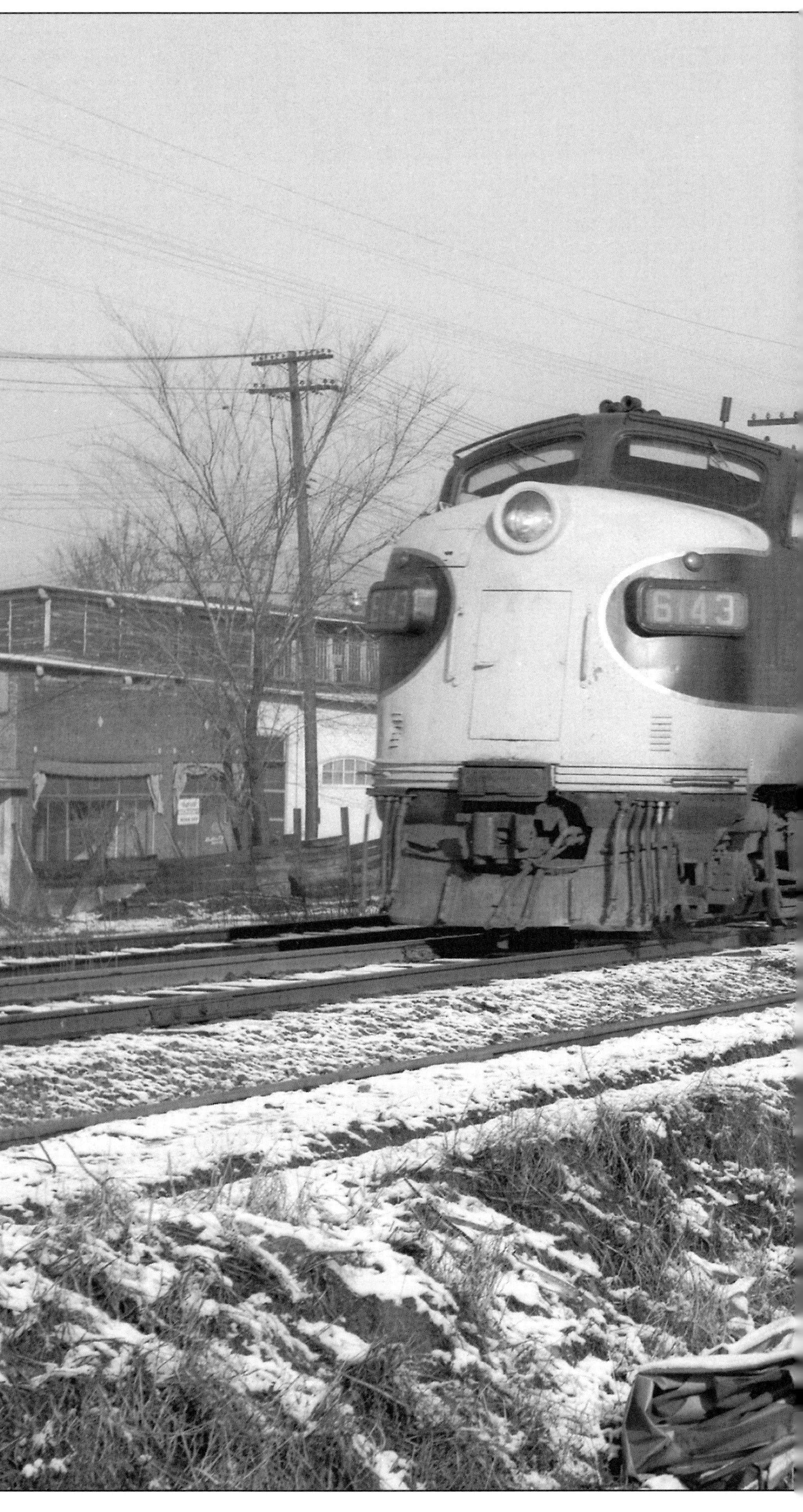

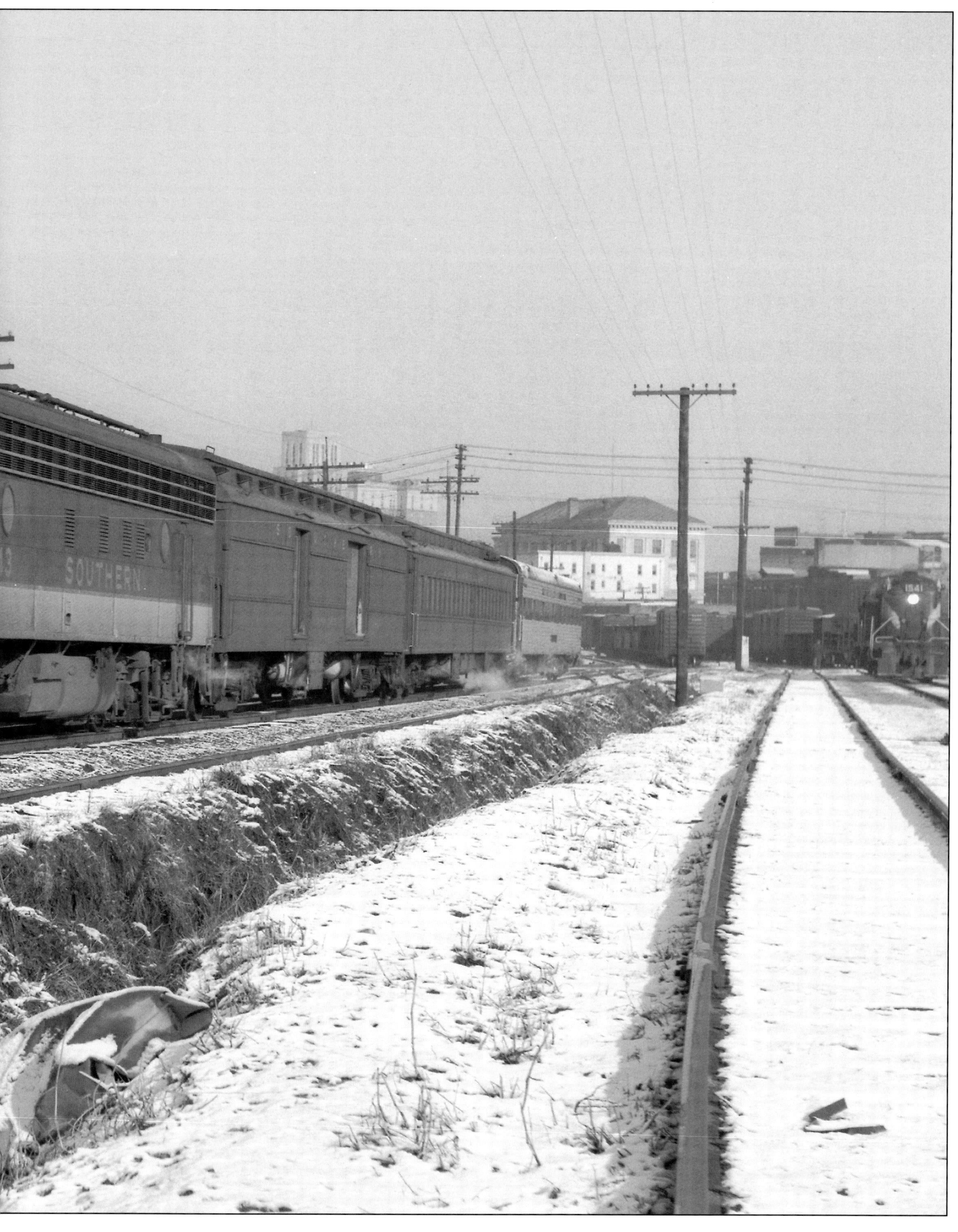
SOUTHERN
1541

GP7 AND GP9

On Jan. 1, 1974, the Southern Railway's ever growing system increased in size by 622 miles when they acquired the Norfolk Southern. One of the first noticeable changes made by the Southern was the removal of all the old NS, Baldwin-built road switchers. The road decided to keep the newer GP-18's and GP-38's; however, soon they would be painted black, white and gold, a long front would be applied to their short ends and they would be given new numbers.

When the Southern removed the Baldwins, they created a need for replacement motive power to not only meet the demands of the ex-NS customers but to help the big road create new traffic patterns as well. One problem: due to the NS's poor track – especially their branch lines – the replacement engines had to be both powerful enough but light in weight to keep the tonnage moving. The ideal locomotives that would fulfill these parameters would be the "GP" series of locomotives, especially the historic GP-7's, of which the Southern owned 101 units.

Shown, on June 24, 1974 at 9:34 a.m., was Southern's No. 25, the Raleigh-Fayetteville, N. C. round trip local leaving Raleigh with GP-7 (#8258R), A GP-38 (#2802R), and GP-38-2 (#5084X) pulling 46 cars, which had passed under the Hillsboro St. Bridge and nearing Boylan Tower (that's the SCL's mainline to the right).

No. 8258 (formally #2163) was purchased from EMD in April of 1951. In 1970-71, the Southern, in order to reduce the confusion caused by the great variety of numbers used for the GP-7's, renumbered them into the 8200 series. It had 1,500 h.p., weighed 241,100 lbs., had a tractive effort of 60,900 lbs. and carried 800 gal. of fuel. It continued making history for the Southern until it was returned to EMD in 1981 – 30 years of service!

This location was one of the good spots to catch NS and now Southern southbound trains in the Raleigh area. The GP-7's replaced the "F" units due to their superior versatility. They did not look as good as an F-7 but boy, could they work – in any assignment they received.

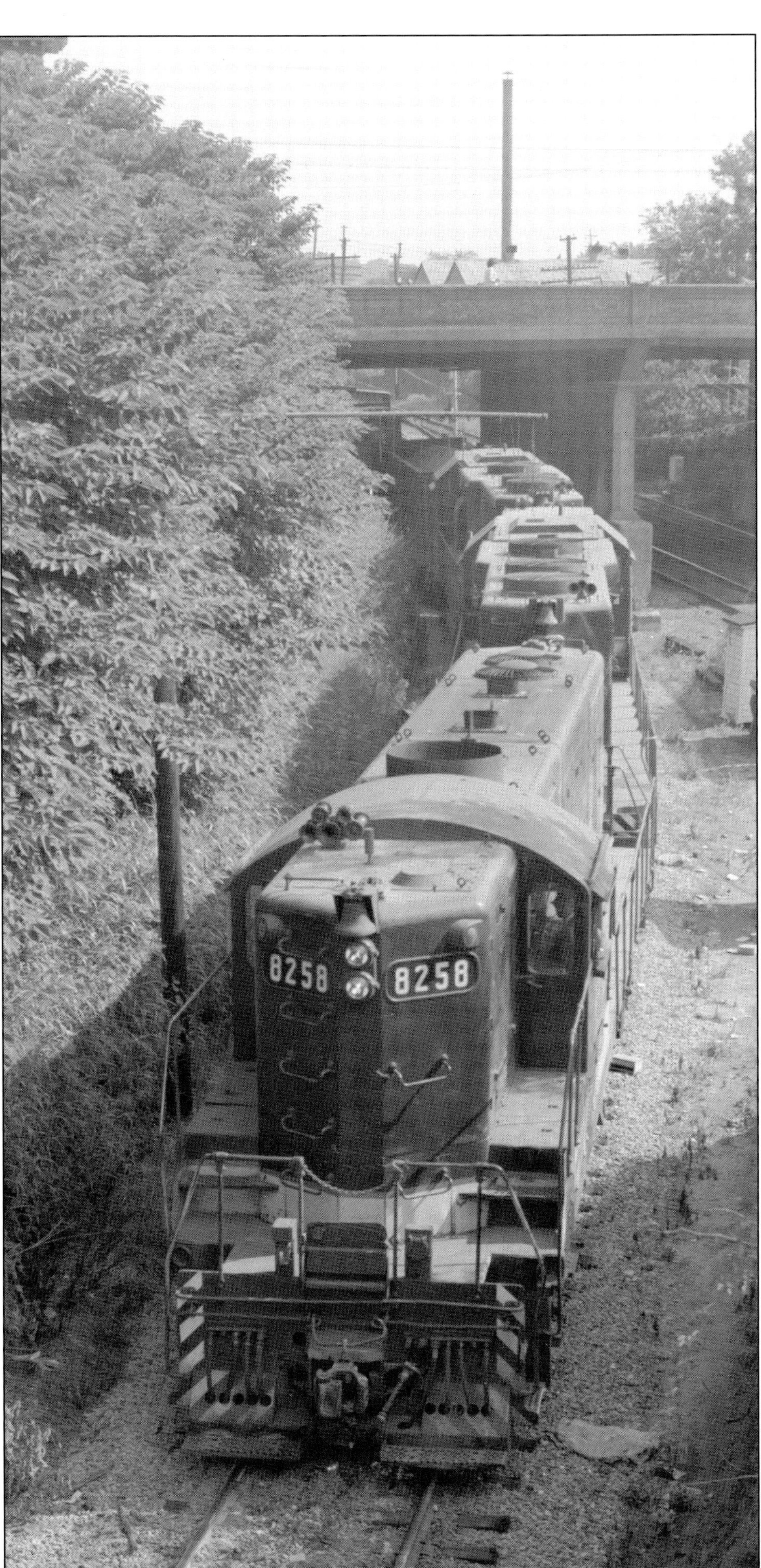

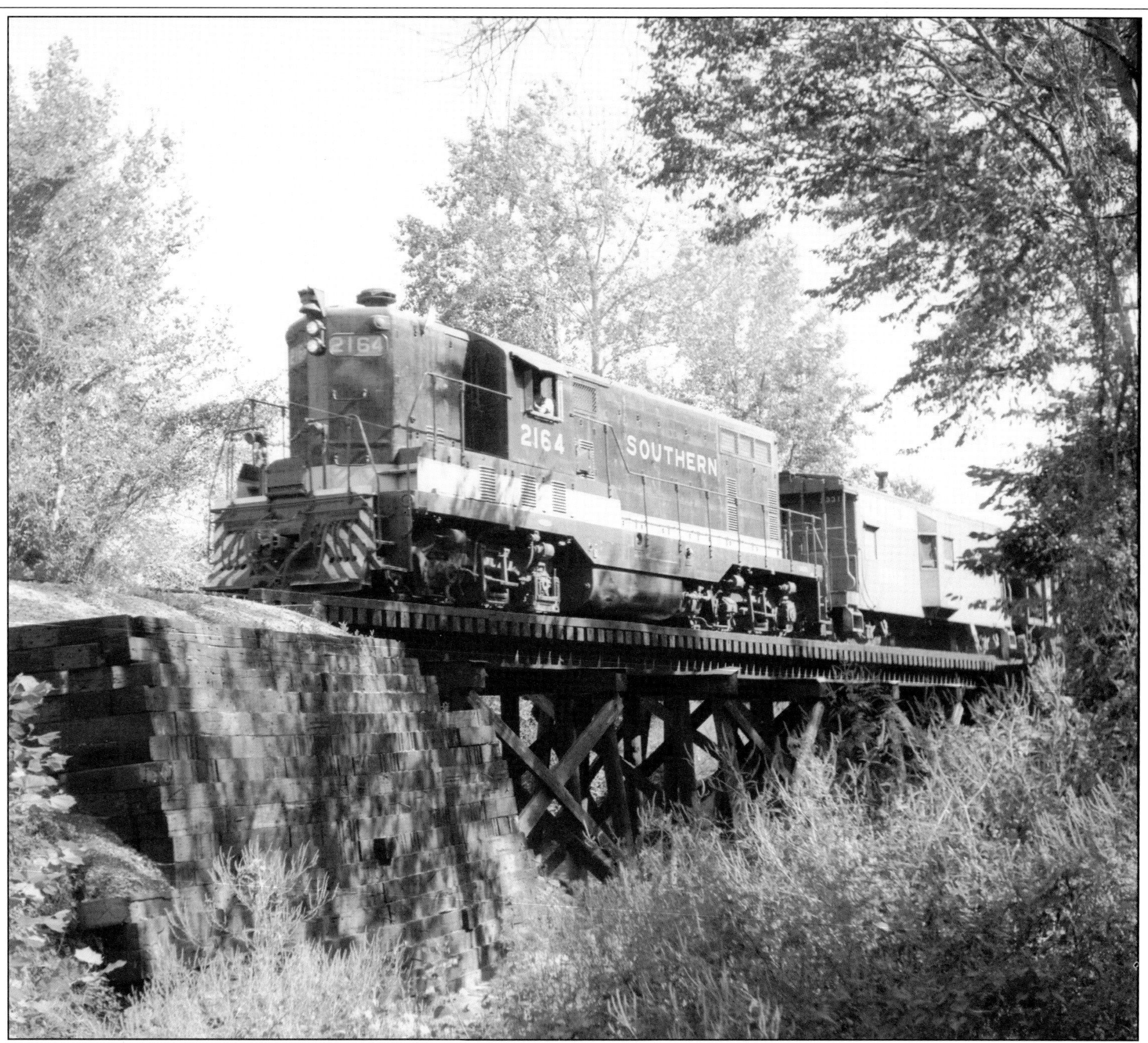

The GP-7's, along with their streamlined "F" brothers, helped remove steam from the rails forever. Then, due to its versatility, the GP's (General Purpose) even eventually replaced the "F" units as well (it was most difficult for an engineer in an "F" model faced with switching back and forward and/or running in branch line service).

The GP-7's could do it all. Operating in multiple units, they could handle mainline assignments, their work in the numerous yards was almost as effective as a regular switch engine and, with a steam generator, they could handle local passenger runs with great e´lan. However, their real value was in branch line service work which required a great deal of running forward and backwards, stopping and starting, working up and down grades and moving cars into and out of light-railed industrial sidings.

For branch line work they had the power – 1,500 h.p. – weight and tractive effort to fulfill the criteria such duty required. Shown here is a sample of a GP-7 in its elements. This was Southern's No. 78 which left East Durham, N. C. earlier in the day. Once in Oxford, N. C., (my hometown) #2164 (soon to become #8259) made a round trip to Henderson, N. C. Once back in Oxford, No. 78 continued working its way to its destination: Keysville, Va.

It was Sept. 4, 1964, at 2:10 p.m. as No. 78 crossed over "Fishing Creek" bridge with 21 cars heading north (my home was a few yards to the south of this location and it was my favorite place to be in order to catch No. 78 on film). No. 77 usually headed south to East Durham while No. 78 was on the Henderson Branch.

In the early 1970's, the Southern put all the different numbered GP-7's into the 8200 series. No. 2164 was built in April of 1951 and remained active until 1981. It was 56'2" long, weighed 242,570 lbs. and produced 60,900 lbs. of tractive effort. Quite often, the conductor would have the caboose tucked in behind the engine so he could do his paper work and then join the engine crew. Check that huge exhaust vent over the short end (where the "bathroom facilities" were located).

The EMD built GP-7's main competition were the Alco RS-3 model road switchers, with the GP-7's having 1,500 h.p. and the RS-3's mustering 1,600 h.p. Both were versatile and good engines. The Southern purchased 101 GP-7's and 148 RS-3's. EMD, in response to this stiff competition, introduced the GP-9 model in the mid-fifties. They had 1,750 h.p. – more "muscles" than the Alcos. The Southern ordered 24 of the GP-9's and never regretted this decision, for the '9's were as good as the GP-7's and had more horsepower.

Like the GP-7's, the GP-9's were assigned to many duties, jobs ranging from mainline, yard and branch line work. However, the '9's found their "niche" in branch line service – similar to the GP-7's. This particular GP-9, shown here, (#6246), heads local freight No. 78 out of Oxford, N. C. on the Southern's Richmond Division's East Durham, N. C. – Keysville, Va. line (including the Oxford-Henderson, N. C. segment as well) this March 19, 1965 at 3:30 p.m., pulling 18 cars. It s shown crossing "Fishing Creek" – a scene I captured from my location on the edge of Highway U. S. 15.

No. 6246 came from the EMD assembly line in July of 1955, weighing 252,760 lbs., carrying 800 gal. of fuel, 18 cu. ft. of sand and producing 61,400 lbs. of tractive effort (the amount it could pull). It was 56'2" long and had dynamic brakes added on June 23, 1962. It continued serving the Southern until 1982. The road actually installed Locotrol controls for "radio-train" operations in two GP-9's: #6250 and #6251.

Obviously, I had to wait until the winter season to make this exposure, for it would be impossible to capture such a scene when the trees were covered with thick leaves and the summer undergrowth as well. On the day I decided to get my "shot" No. 78 had a rare GP-9 up front – a lucky occasion since motive power on this line was usually RS-3's or GP-7's. I can only recall seeing four GP-9's on "my line, so I was fortunate to capture one on film, on the bridge, on its way to Keysville, Va. I believe my patience paid off. What do you think?

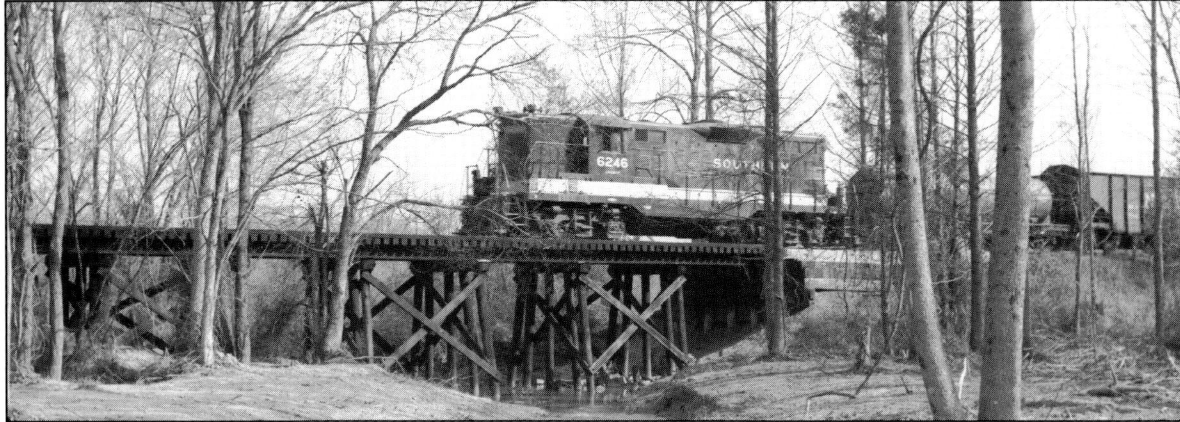

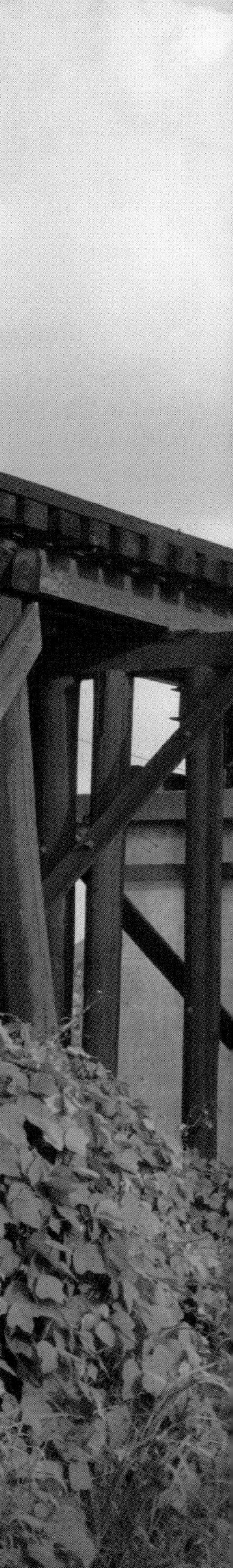

Just five months after the Southern added the Norfolk Southern to its growing family, it would be difficult to realize that – when looking at this photo – at one time, Baldwin-built road switchers, gray colored GP-18's and GP-38-2's – all lettered: Norfolk Southern – made this bridge rumble with tonnage as the old NS moved its trains in and out of their Glenwood Yard in Raleigh, N. C. About the only reminder of the NS days of operation was the lettering on the bridge shown here.

Southern's No. 25, a Raleigh-Fayetteville, N. C. round trip local freight, is shown here working upgrade this June 8, 1974, at 5:40 p.m., pulling 63 cars with all Southern motive power: GP-7 (#8255H) and two GP-38-2's (#5015J and #5070W). Within minutes, the local would pass by Boylan Tower where it would cross over the jointly operated (Southern – SCL) double track and head south over the former NS tracks.

When the Southern purchased the NS, they disposed of the old NS's Baldwin-built road switchers, painted the ex-NS GP-18's and GP-38's black, white and gold, put a full front on their short ends and assigned them new numbers. Until the ex-NS poor quality tracks were replaced with "big rails," the trains were powered by GP-7's and a few other "GP series, since their weight was not too great for the bad tracks.

This long bridge out of Raleigh remains a famous rail location to this very day. And huge six-axle power is the normal type engine used on the freights coming into and departing the capital city over this ex-NS structure.

EMD's #8255 came from the builders in April of 1951. It was originally numbered "2160." In fact, the 101 GP-7's in the Southern's fleet had so many different numbers, that the road renumbered the vast majority of these historic units into the 8200 series in 1970-71. With 1,500 h.p., 800 gal. of fuel, and weighing 252,760 lbs., it produced 61,400 lbs. of tractive effort. Indeed, it proved to be an excellent engine not only on the Southern but the rough tracks on the ex-NS as well. No. 8255 was finally retired in 1980 after doing all – and even more – that was asked of it.

Next to the Boylan Tower location, I would select the long bride leading to Glenwood Yard as my second most favorite place to be in order to capture the ebb and flow of Southern freights into and out of the yard – it was upgrade for the traffic leaving Glenwood and downgrade for the inbound movements. As a result, the bridge offered some of the finest rail action in the Raleigh area.

When looking at this photo, can't you hear the unmistakable sounds of three EMD "geeps" working upgrade with nearly a mile of tonnage tied on behind the last unit. And, with all that green colored kudzu below, it was a most scenic place as well.

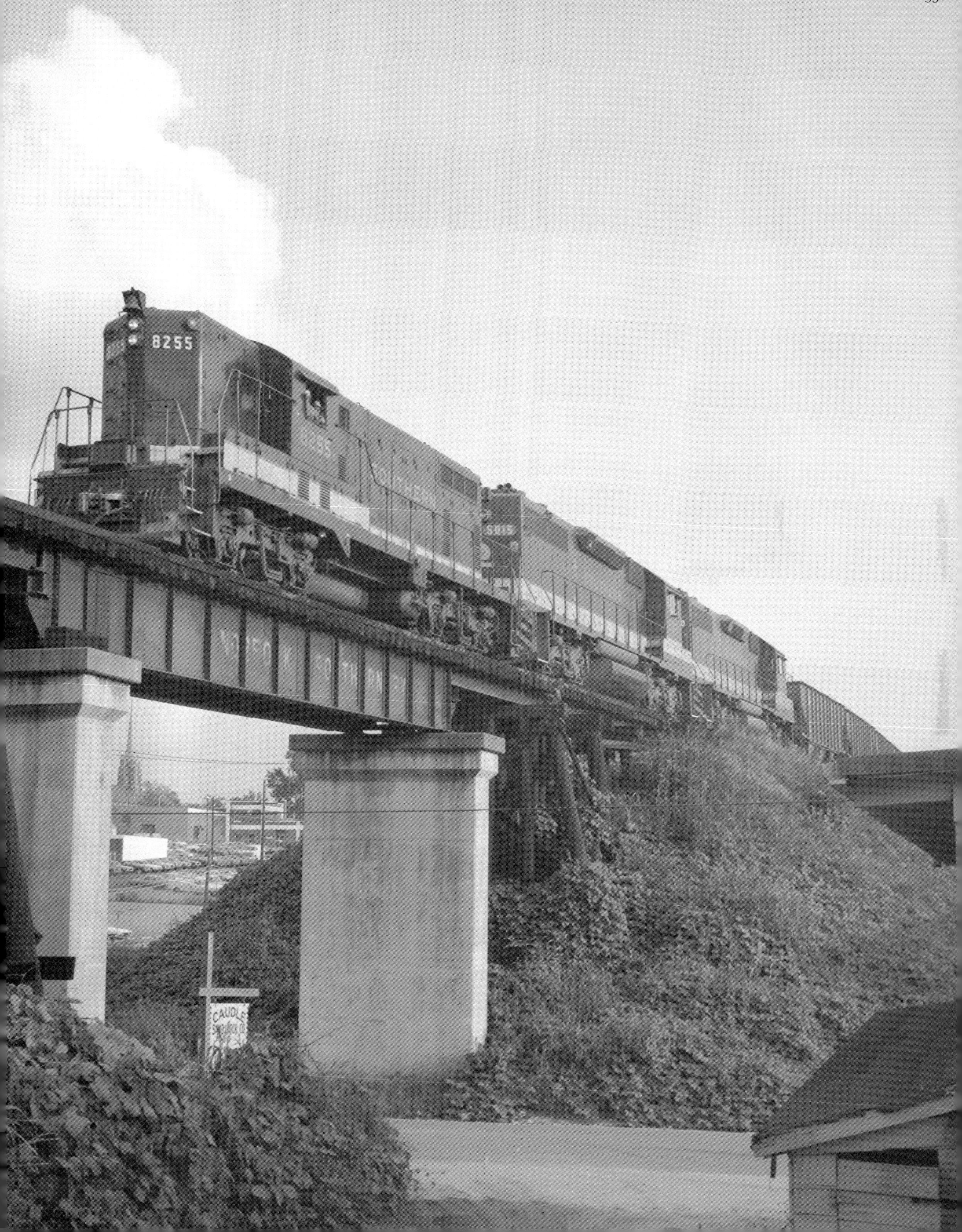
8255
8255
SOUTHERN
5015
CAUDLE

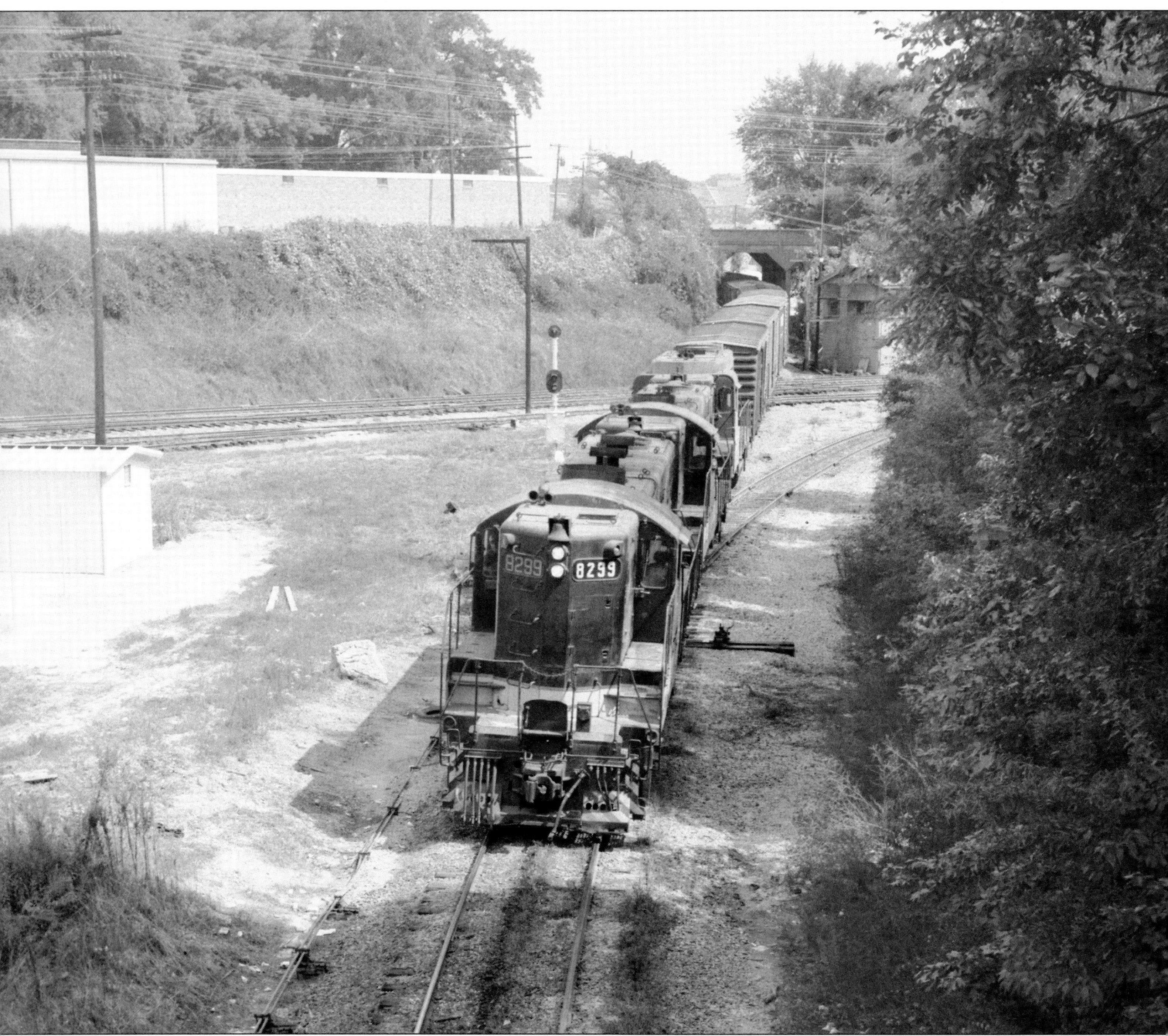

This is the place to be when you are in Raleigh, N. C. if you want to see and/or photograph rail action at its best: the Boylan Tower area or, since the tower has now been removed, the Boylan Bridge area.

For years, the tower (seen in the background) – actually owned by the old Norfolk Southern – protected the movement of trains in the area since you had the ex-NS's Norfolk, Va.-Charlotte, N. C. mainline crossing over the busy, jointly operated (Southern-SCL) double track. Even though at the time of this photo (Sept. 25, 1976, at 12:48 p.m.) automatic controls had been installed, you could still see the tower's rods on the left side of the track, rods operated by the tower's crews to control signals and switches around its area.

With nothing due in or out of Raleigh on the double track mainline, Southern's No. 25 was permitted to cross over the two tracks on its Raleigh to Fayetteville, N. C. round trip. Today's 45 cars were pulled by two GP-7's (#8299A and #8259K) plus a GP-30 (#2543T).

GP-7's #8299A (formally numbered #6541) and #8259 (#2164) were among the 101 units in the Southern's fleet of this historic EMD model. The vast majority of these engines were renumbered into the 8200 series in 1970-71 in order to consolidate the numerous numbers originally assigned to the '7's. They, along with their streamlined "F" units relatives, helped to give the steam engines the final push off the road for good – a job completed on June 17, 1953. No. 8299 was built in May of 1950 and continued in operation until 1981 when it was returned to EMD. It weighed 239,800 lbs. and produced 60,700 lbs. of tractive effort. The GP-7's were so popular that the Southern equipped #2181-#2189 (#8275-#8281) with Locotrol apparatus so they could be used in "radio-control" train operations.

This particular location was not used as often as the more popular Boylan Ave. Bridge for rail photography (on the right, behind the trees), so this gives you a different look at THE hotspot in Raleigh – not bad!

It was near 100° F when I made this photo (above) – on July 19, 1978 at 11:35 a.m. – of local freight, Extra 8237 South, leaving the busy complex at Chattanooga, Tennessee.

Look at all those tracks – all "big rail" mainlines. You might think this was the old PRR around Enola Yard near Harrisburg, Pa. Along with Atlanta, Chattanooga was one of the major hubs of the Southern. With lines to and from Cincinnati, Asheville, Atlanta, Birmingham, Memphis and Bristol converging on this single location, the rail traffic was tremendous. But, with all that action, there was a lull and suddenly this local freight, powered by two GP-7's (#8237A and #8236H) pulling six cars, "sneaking out" onto the multiple tracks in an effort to get its work done, to keep the local customers happy and keep the revenue rolling into the Southern's treasury department. It was such an incongruous sight: after witnessing all the long freights pulled by numerous engines passing through this area, to find this short local – all alone – doing its job.

During the period of 1970-71, the Southern renumbered all of its 101 GP-7's, which had originally been assigned several different numbers, into the 8200 series. No. 8237, on the front of the southbound local, came from EMD as #707 and #8236 was #709, both GP-7's formally owned by the 87-mile long Tennessee, Alabama & Georgia Railroad (TAG) which the Southern purchased on Jan. 1, 1971. EMD-built #8237 I in April of 1951 which had the usual 1,500 h.p. but carried 1,200 gal. of fuel rather than the normal 800 gallons. It weighed 245,332 lbs. and produced 60,043 lbs. of tractive effort; No. 8237 was retired in 1981, closing out a stellar career of 30 years.

It was so hot this particular day in 1978, I had to wipe the sweat off my face in order to avoid having sweat drop down into my camera's viewfinder. But, I got the shot, headed back to my air-conditioned car and waited for the mainline(s) to resume its normal action. That short local was truly an unusual sight on this big time rail scene, but I'm glad I recorded it as the Extra south began a long, hot day of work.

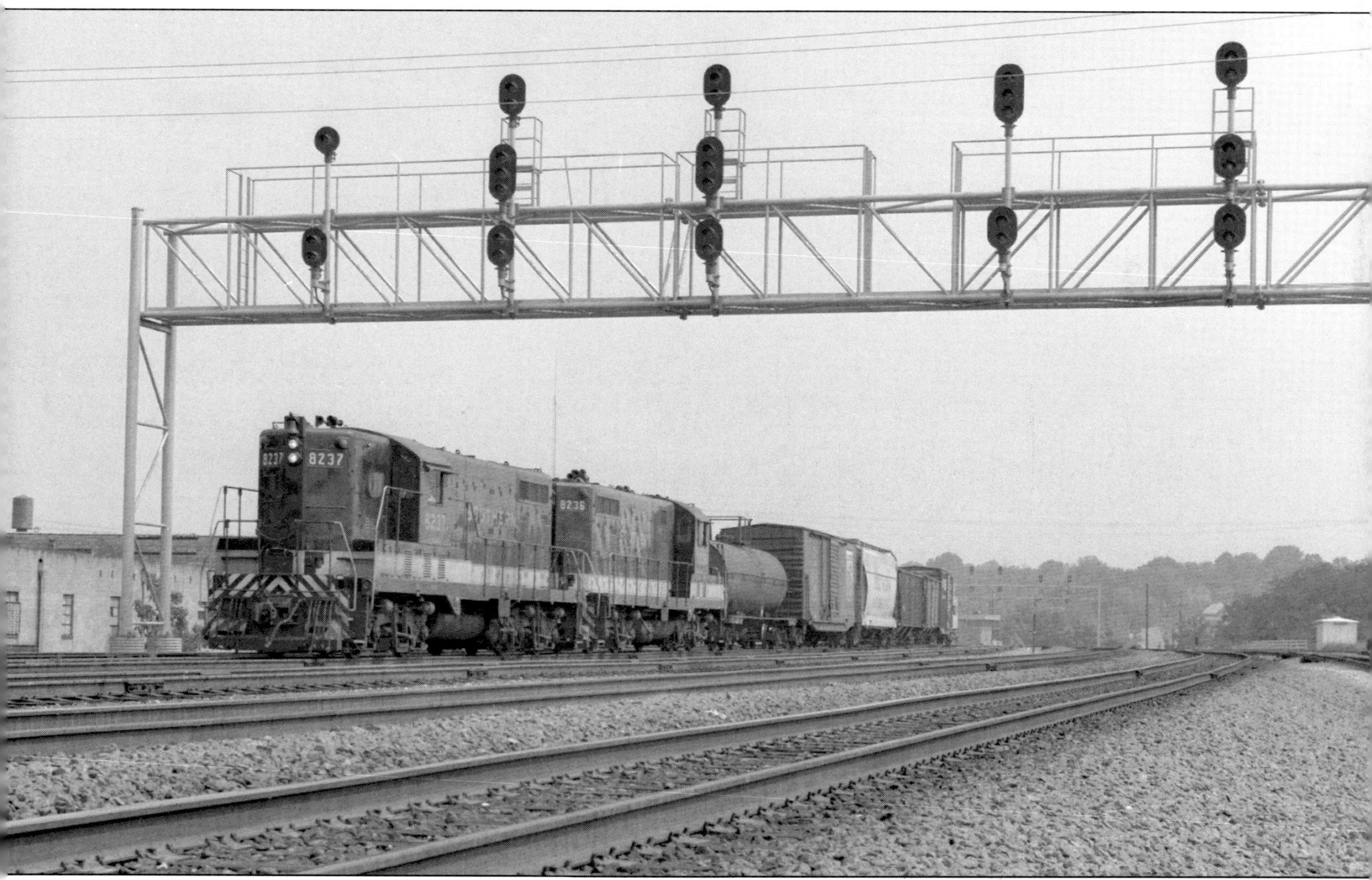

RS-3

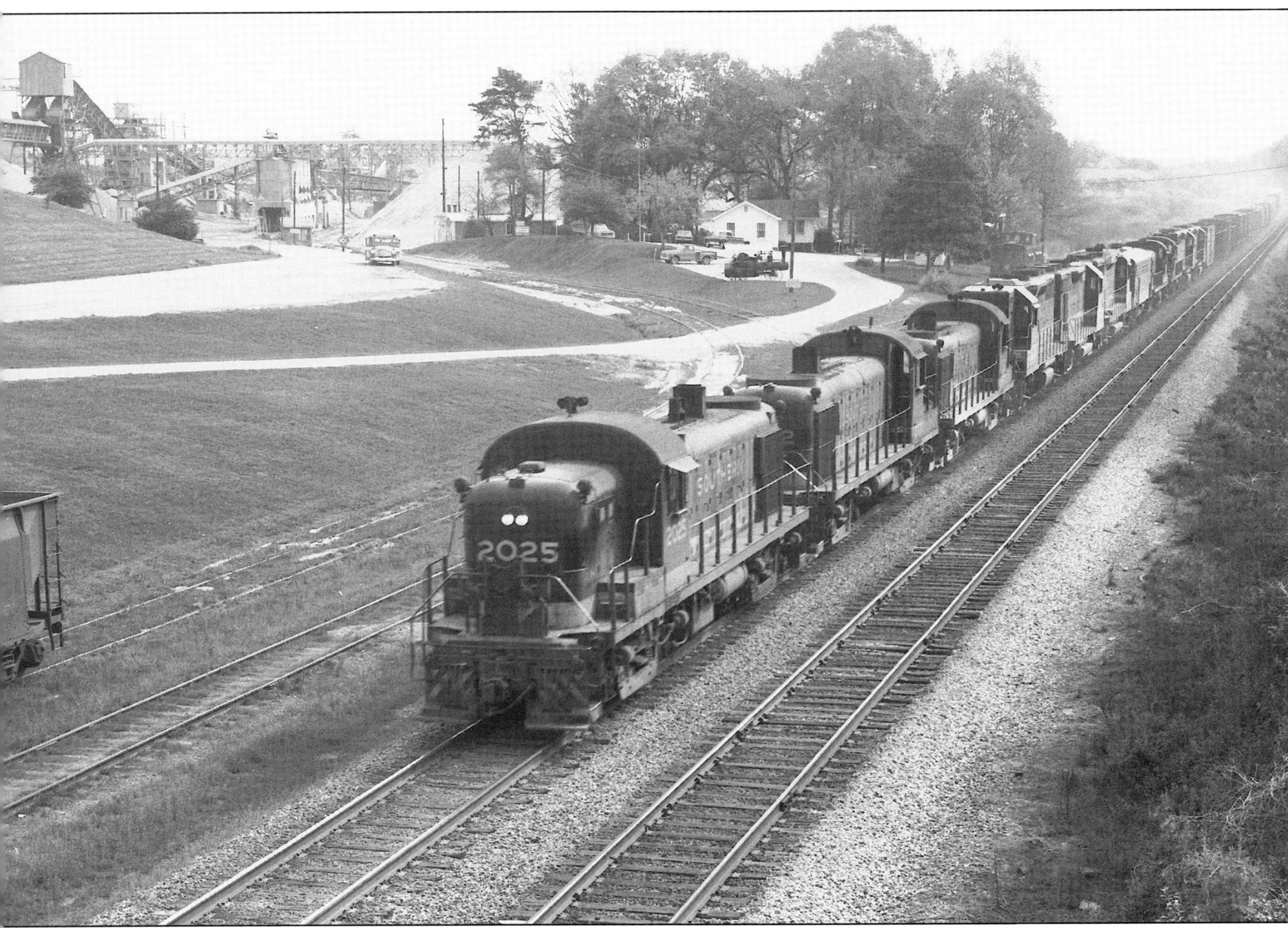

Was this a train carrying nothing but engines or a train actually hauling freight cars? That was the question on my mind as I looked through my camera's viewfinder at this atypical southbounder rapidly approaching me at 40-45 m.p.h.

As I passed through Liberty, S. C., heading north, I knew that Southern's No. 221 was due. As a result, I looked for a good location to photograph the Atlanta bound freight. Midway between Liberty and Easley, S. C. I found a perfect spot: it was near a rock quarry and there was a bridge passing over the double track Washington-Atlanta main-line.

Just as soon as I parked the family car and headed towards the bridge, I heard diesel chime blowing from the north. It was No. 221 – I made it! Within 2 to 3 minutes, I saw No. 221 coming around a curve, heading for a long straight stretch of good "running track." As I looked into my viewfinder, all I saw was engines, engines…engines, engines…engines, etc. In fact, I kept seeing engines until it was time to release my camera's shutter. After catching him on film, I counted 11 engines – yes, 11 engines, pulling 65 cars. So it was a freight after all – but what a freight!

It was April 22, 1973, at 9:20 a.m., and a record was being set for me. During the 40+ years of photographing trains, I had never seen one, in action, with 11 units: 3-R5-3's (#2025L, #2032K, and #2040T), GP-38 (#2786H), GP-35 (#2687H), GP-30 (#2550H), FP-7A (#6139A), 2 RS-3's (#6238A and #6236K) and 2 GP-38-2's (#5017X and #5026A) – Whew! Thanks goes to Mom and Dad for helping me get all these numbers.

If ever EMD had any effective competition for its most successful and historic GP-7, it was the Alco (American Locomotive Co.) built RS-3 – road switcher. The Southern realized these versatile and dependable engines were good. Indeed, they purchased 148 of these Schenectady (N.Y.) built locomotives. The RS-3's had 1,600 h.p. (the GP-7 had 1,500 h.p.). No. 2025 was built in April of 1952 and retired in 1976 (its trucks will eventually be used on EMD's GP-35 series); it weighed 242,200 lbs., carried 1,600 gal. of fuel, ran bi-directional and produced 60,500 lbs. of tractive effort. It could go anywhere and do anything the Southern asked of it.

Words escape me to adequately describe this scene: 11 engines (only the first three were "on line")! Once again, this is a prime example of the mystic of a mainline, i.e., anything at anytime!

Is this actually a passenger train? Yes, it was No. 29, the Southern's "Peach Queen," with 8 cars. Is that an RS-3 up front? No, it's an Also built RS-2 (#6206), followed by two RS-3's (#2058 and #2046) plus an F-3B (#4329).

It was very difficult to distinguish between Schenectady built RS-2's and RS-3's. The RS-2's had 1,500 h.p. (the RS-3's had 1,600 h.p.), #6206 weighed 242,900 lbs., was built in Aug. of 1949, carried 800 gal. of fuel and did not have dynamic brakes (the RS-3's were equipped with dynamics). It was retired in 1964 (traded to EMD on Dec. 25, 1964 – its trucks were used on EMD's new GP-35 models).

No. 29 was one of three south and three northbound passenger trains that stopped here in Greer, S. C. (my dad's hometown). The "Crescent" and "Piedmont Limited" picked up mail "on the fly," from the mail hoop shown on the right. By the way, the top of the building seen above the F-3B unit was part of my uncle's fertilizer and farm supply store. As a result, when we visited my dad's hometown, I spent as much time at my uncle's store as I did the local depot (just out of the photo on my left) to watch the action on the Southern's Washington-Atlanta main-line roll by.

No. 29, and its northbound counterpart (No. 30), often had freight engines in their power consist, sent from Spencer, N. C. to Atlanta's Pegram Shops for maintenance by this period of time (July 8, 1961, at 12:35 p.m.). No. 29's lead engine's green and gold color scheme and big headlight of #6206 dates this photo, for within the near future all such engines will be seen in black, white and gold colors plus they will be fitted with twin-beam lights. It did have a modern radio antenna, however (nicknamed a "tomato can" because of its shape).

Greer was a great location for a young man to observe and begin honing his photographic skills on "big time" railroading. Just within a "stone's throw" to my left was the Piedmont & Northern, a line that also brought me great joy two to four times each day during the daylight hours.

Today, however, Greer is located on one of the numerous short sections of single-track on the mostly double-track main, with No. 1 track (on the right) the only one remaining. Still, this photo shows the Greer I will always remember.

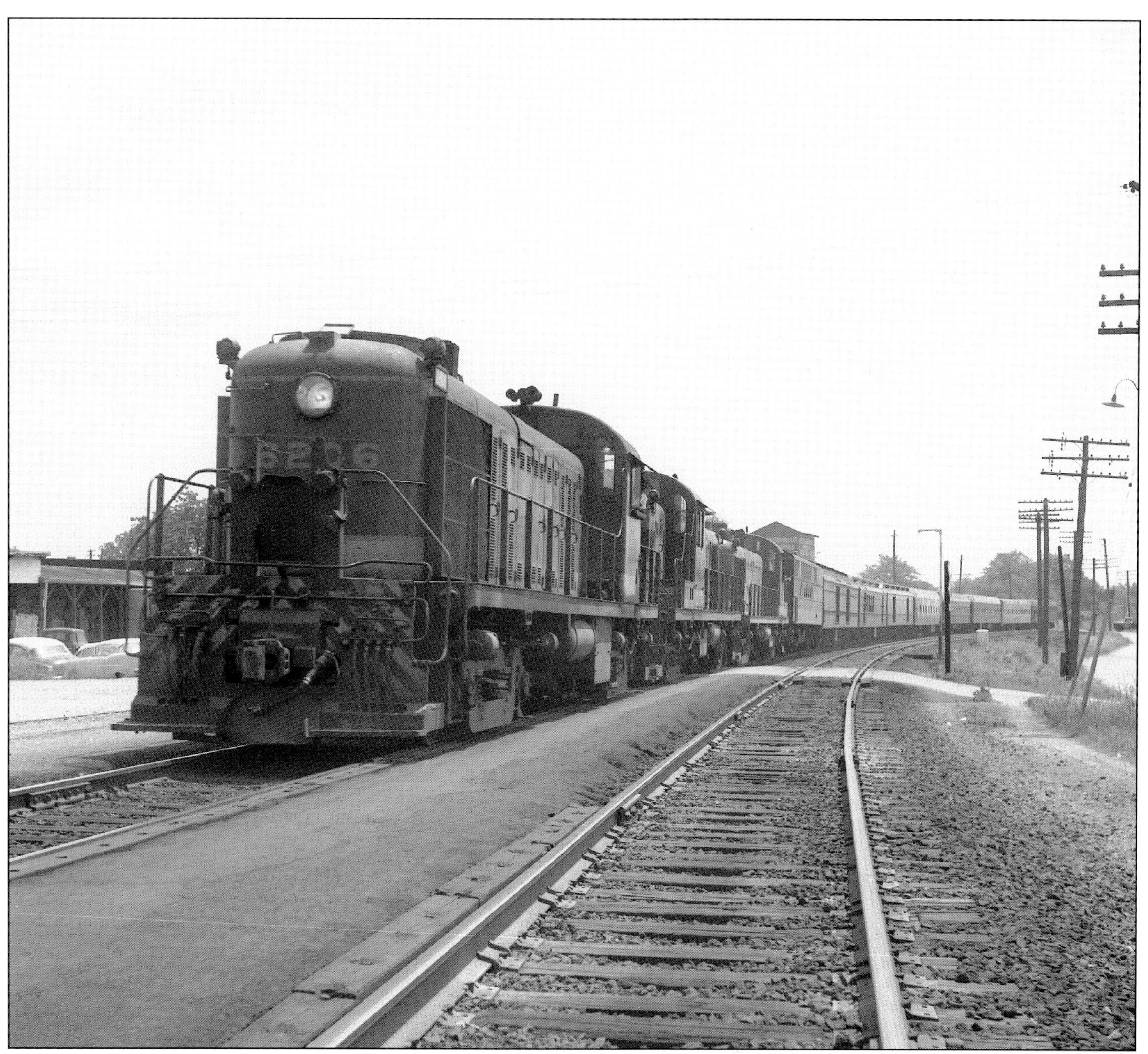

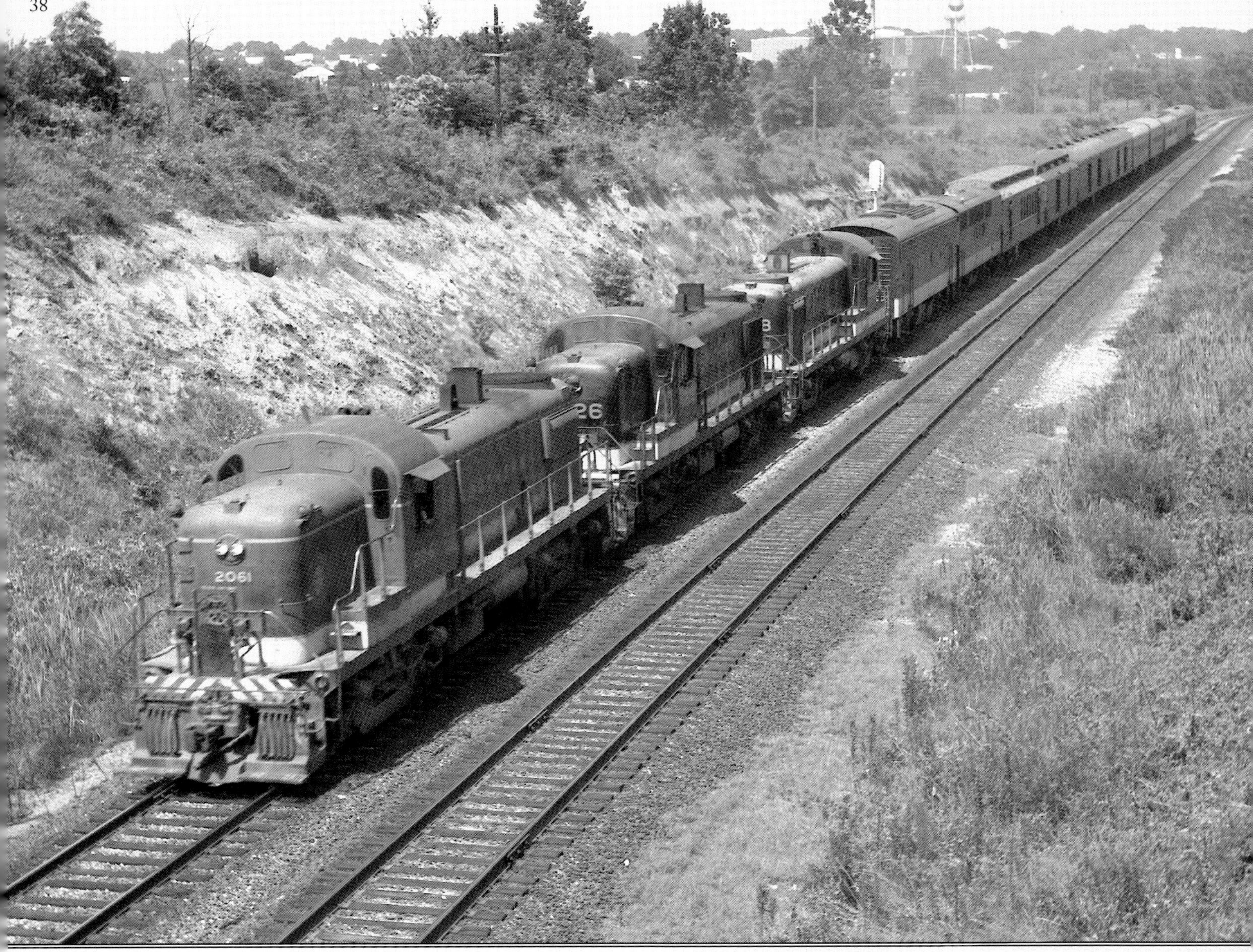
2061
26

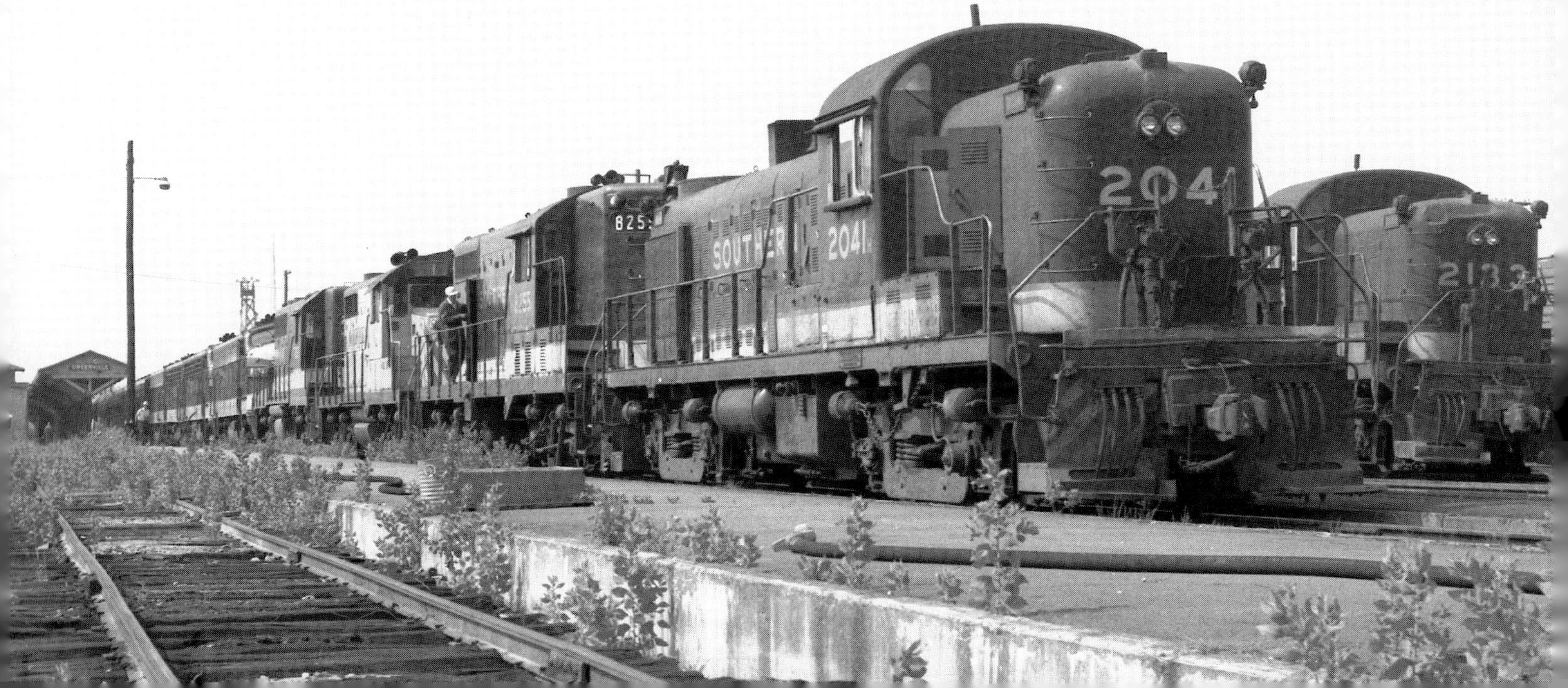
2041
SOUTHER
2041

It's 98° F, the sun's heat and the humidity were almost too much to bear, but it was a great day, for here comes Southern's No. 33, the "Piedmont Limited," shown between Greer and Taylors, S. C., with a mixed power combination, pulling 10 cars at 3:15 p.m., this July 12, 1962.

As the passenger business began to decrease, the Southern began to confine its major passenger power (their "E" units) to their streamliners such as the "Crescent," the "Southerner" and others. Such "lesser" trains such as the "Piedmont Limited," the "Peach Queen," et. al., had smaller power such as the FP-7A's and converted F-3's, plus the road used these passenger runs to ferry freight units that needed maintenance and/or inspection to and from Atlanta's Pegram Shops.

This photo is a good example of this power ferry policy, with No. 33's motors consisting of: three RS-3's (#2061, #6226 and #2041) and 2FP-7B's (#6757 and #6181). These engines will be in Atlanta before midnight and within a few days, they will be returned to Spencer where the units will be returned to their assignments.

No. 33 & 34 ran between New York and New Orleans; even though its name, the "Piedmont Limited," was steeped in rail history, it never achieved the status of the "Crescent," the "Southerner," "Royal Palm" and others. Still, for decades, it was well patronized by the public.

The "Piedmont Limited's" lead unit, No. 2061, was an Alco-built (June of 1953), 1,600 h.p. road switcher which carried 800 gal. of fuel (later increased to 1,600 gal.). It was a rival of EMD's highly successful GP-7. Indeed, the Southern was so impressed by the performance and versatility of the RS-3's, they purchased 148 units. No. 2061 was finally retired in 1976 when it was sent to EMD for a trade-in on a new GP-35.

When the RS-3's were plentiful and could be found in all types of service (they ruled "my line" – East Durham to Keysville – for nearly a decade), you tended to ignore them. After they were retired, however, I began missing their steam-like "belching" of smoke, the "chug-chug-chug" sounds and that utilitarian but effective shape. Even though I favored the GP-7's, I always had great respect for the tough RS-3's.

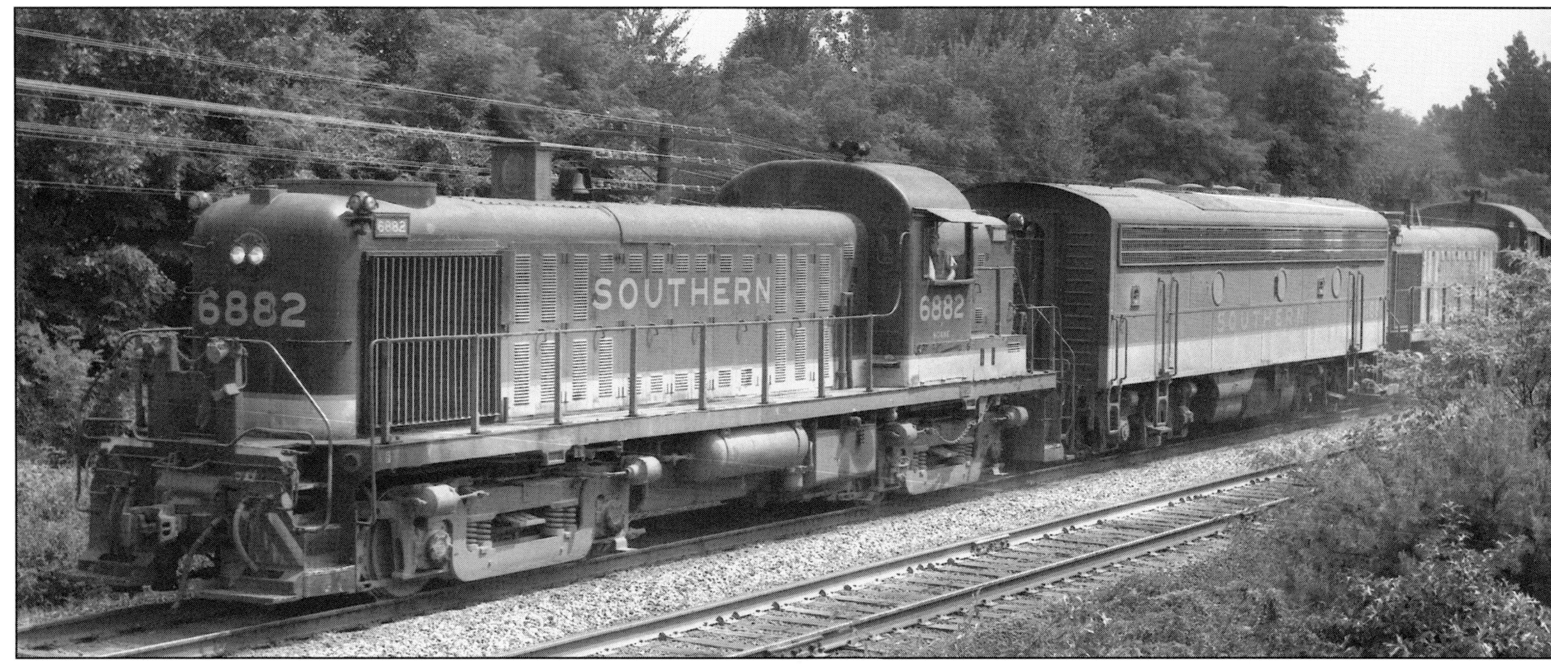

Southern's passenger train No. 6, the "Piedmont," is shown at the Greenville, S. C. station. Yes, it is a passenger train even though the first four engines were usually found pulling freights.

What a sight! We have an RS-3 (#2041H), a GP-7 (#8255H), ex-Norfolk Southern GP-18 (#1) and a GP-38 (#2885H – a former NS unit that had been painted black, white and gold, given a long, short-end and a new number – it was #2006 when working for the old NS) plus No. 6's usual four FP-7A's (#6134F, #6136R, #6149X and #6144A) – all pulling 31 cars (23 of them being piggybacks which were coupled to the last passenger car). A passenger train?! It appeared to be a freight with a few passenger cars placed into its consist!

The Southern ran freight engines on No. 5 & No. 6 that needed maintenance and/or inspection at Atlanta's Pegram Shops from Spencer, N. C. Some of the freight units are shown on No. 6 today (July 10, 1974 at 10:30 a.m.) heading back to Spencer where they will be removed from the varnish and returned to their regular assignments. No. 6 will complete its run to Washington behind the four FP-7A's.

The Greenville station was something else: a passenger station, yardmaster's office, division's office, dispatcher's office, track supervisor's headquarters, sale department and freight station -–all in one facility.

I'm sure you can understand why No. 5 and 6 were among the most favorite trains of the railfans between Spencer and Atlanta. Each day it was a new combination of motive power. However, today's arrangement of engines ranks as among the most unusual of them all. No. 2041H came from the Schenectady's plant in April of 1952 and remained in action for 24 years, being retired in 1976. It, along with the other 147 owned by the Southern, were worthy rivals of EMD's extremely successful GP-7's.

Even though I was there and photographed this menagerie of motive power, it's still hard to believe it actually happened. By the way, the 23 "pigs" brought the Southern more revenue than the passengers on board No. 6, I'm sad to say

RS-11

After completing my military obligations (in the days of the draft), I secured a position in the Research Triangle Park (south of Durham, N. C.) in an effort to save enough funds so I could complete my college requirements for my BA degree (which I did in 1967).

Each morning on my way to work from Oxford to the Park, I would go by the west end of the East Durham Yard to see if there was any action on the Southern's busy Greensboro-Goldsboro, N. C. line.

I believe it was a Monday morning (7:30 a.m.) in the early part of July of 1963 when I crossed the tracks on my way to work. When I looked to the west, I saw through freight No. 82 stopped next to the ready track area. On occasions, I would see No. 82, but this particular morning there was something different. The lead engine had a pair of "ones" painted on its nose, front and rear, under the cab windows; and the diesel was not lettered, "Southern," but instead it had "Carolina & Northwestern" (part of the Southern's family) on its sides.

Parking my car, I grabbed my camera and used ten of the twelve exposures on the roll of film. Why so many shots of the same train? I had found the rarest of the rare diesels on the road. The Southern owned hundreds of diesels belonging to dozens of different models; however, there was only one - only ONE - Alco-built RS-11, numbered #11. This "endangered species" of diesel in the great sea of Southern engines was in front of me! It was to be swapped for the RS-2 (#2103) – seen on the right – and, to my great delight, the "double ones" would operate on "my" line (Durham-Oxford-Henderson-Keysville, Va. branch) for two weeks!

RS-11 (#11) came from Alco as basically a RS-3 with an updated carbody in March of 1956, worked for the Southern until, on June 11, 1973, it, along with several older engines, was traded in to GE for a batch of new U-23B's. General Electric sold the RS-11 to the Chicago & North Western (on Dec. 22, 1973) and renumbered to #4651. The historic engine was finally retired on Aug. 9, 1983.

It had 1,800 h.p., carried 1,200 gal. of fuel, weighed 242,800 lbs. and was 56'11" long; however, it did not have dynamic brakes.

Even though this was a Monday, it was a good day – one I shall always remember.

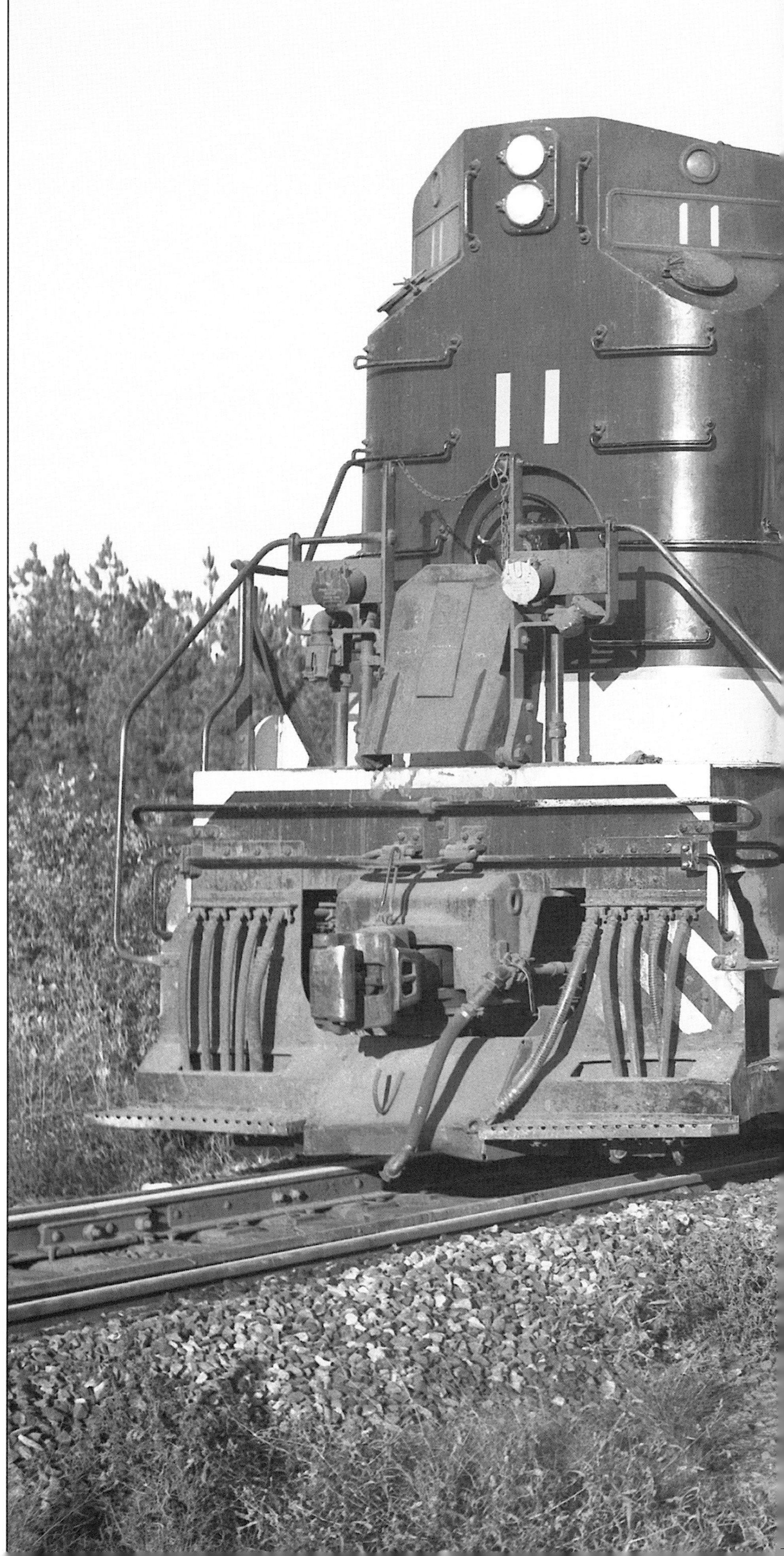

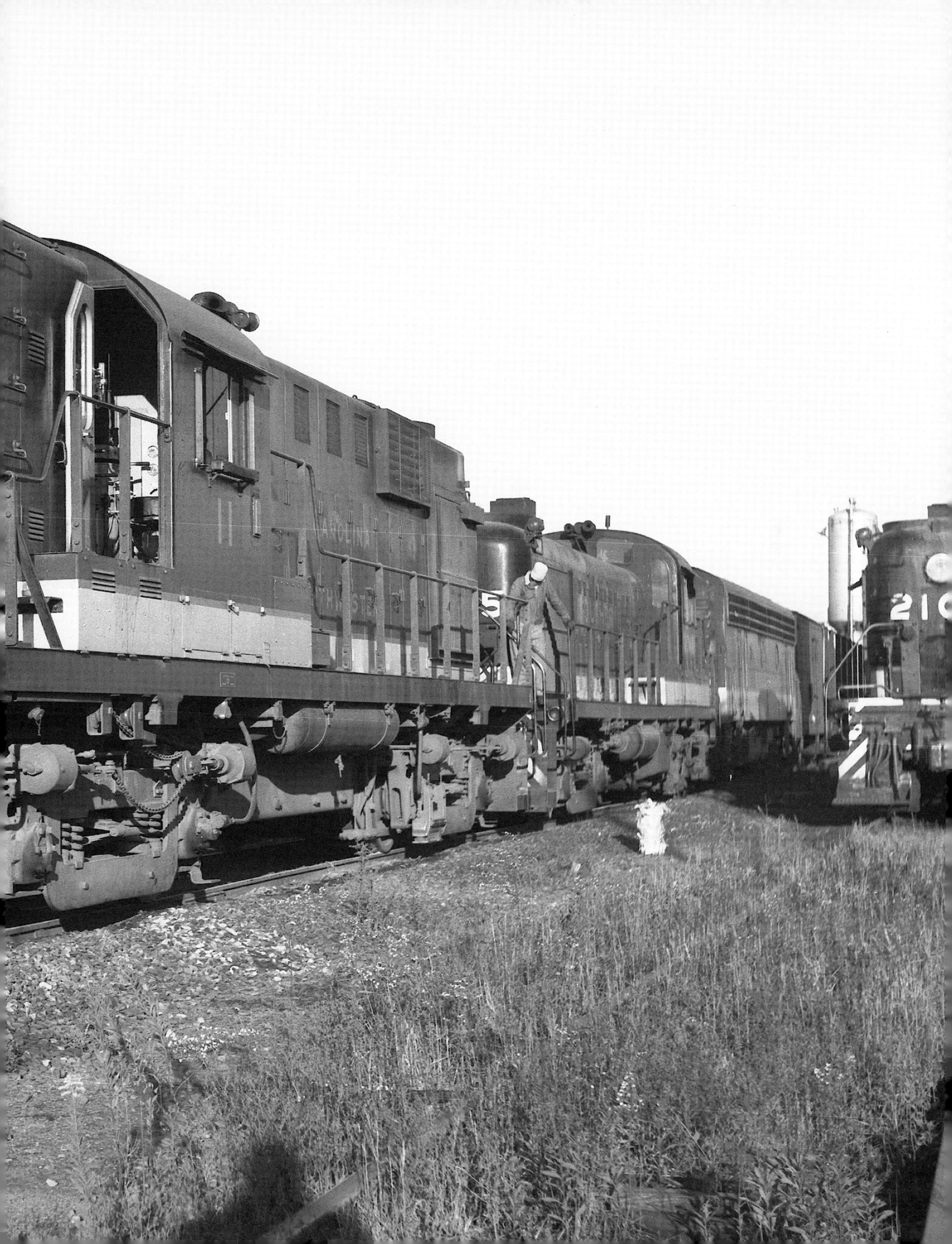

GP30

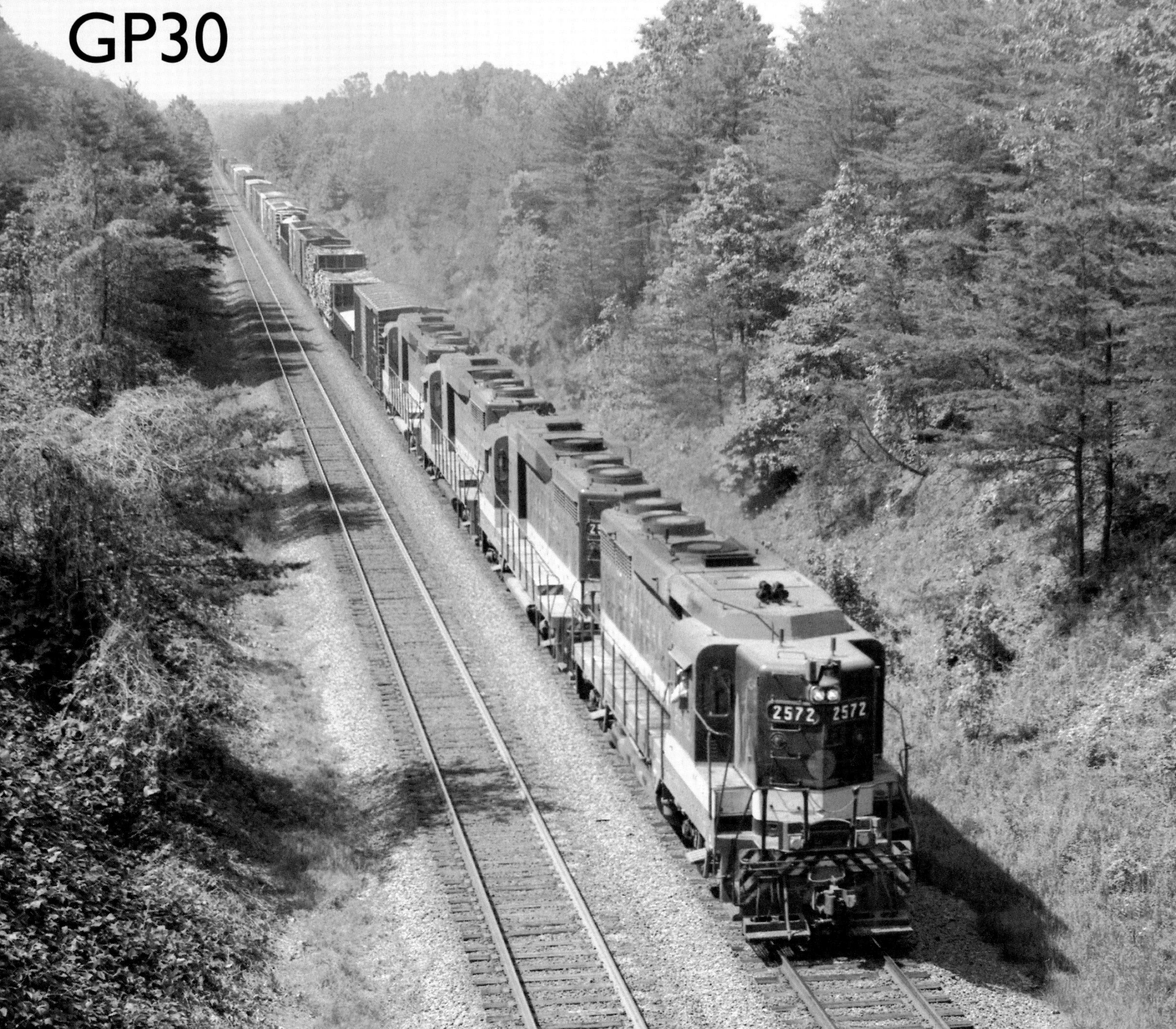

The Spencer, N. C. – Monroe, Va. district crews on the Southern's Washington-Atlanta mainline nicknamed this long stretch of straight, level beautiful track in the Chatham, Va. area the "race track." This remains a most appropriate nickname since you have nearly four miles of smooth, "arrow-straight," double track where an engineer could make great time with his train. There was even a double crossover on this "race track" where a slower freight could be passed by a faster train – both going in the same direction – without delaying either movement.

I'm standing on the U.S. 29 highway overpass north of Chatham as Southern's No. 158 (Atlanta-Potomac Yard) goes under me at a good 50+ m.p.h. with four GP-30's proving the power (#2572A, #2542X, #2626A and #2620J), pulling 121 cars this June 3, 1972 at 9:40 a.m.

It was quite a sight, seeing a pinpoint of light far to the south, watching as it grew larger and larger until I could see that No. 158 had four '30's up front and a lengthy train – all passing under me at a good speed – producing a dramatic moment that would be hard to forget. I always made it a point to photograph all the steamers in excursion service at this location.

By 1972, newer power had appeared on the mainline which, for almost a decade, the GP-30's dominated, and you began to see less '30's. Looking at No. 158 this day, you would think these 2,250 h.p. engines still ruled the main.

No. 2572A, weighing 247,200 lbs. and carrying 2,600 gal. of fuel, began its work on the Southern in Oct. of 1962 and continued until June 1, 1982; then it served the NS until Dec. of 1990. So, the Southern, which had 120 units in their GP-30 fleet, truly got their money's worth out of these powerful four-axle locomotives.

This location remains an ideal place to capture both north and southbound trains on the mainline – at speed. Just be careful since there is little distance between the edge of the bridge and the 60+ m.p.h. highway traffic right behind you. Still, it's a great place to be in order to see and capture on film some great rail action!

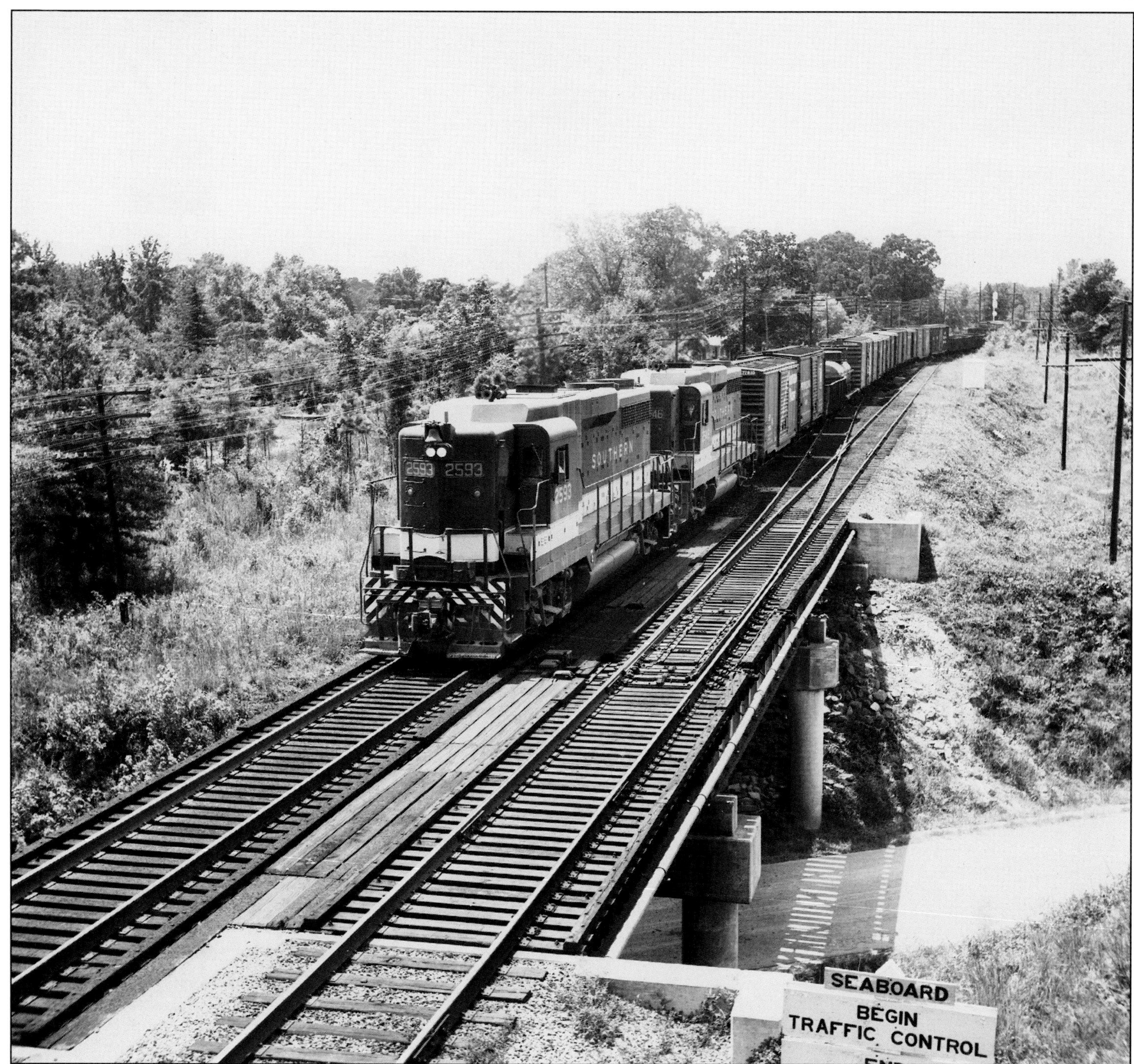

The Southern and Seaboard jointly operated an 8.1-mile section of double track between Cary, N. C. (in the background) and Raleigh, N. C.'s Boylan Tower. Once in Cary (coming from Raleigh), the Southern would turn to the right (in this photo) and head west to Greensboro, N. C. while the SAL turned south towards Hamlet, N. C. and Miami (this was part of their Richmond-Miami mainline).

At the time of this photo (Sept. 9, 1965, at 11:15 a.m.), the Southern ran No. 64 from East Durham, N. C. to Goldsboro, N. C. and No. 65 from Goldsboro to East Durham (they usually met in Selma, N. C. where the road crossed the ACL's double track mainline). Shown here is No. 64, entering the double track to Raleigh and points east, powered by two, still new, GP-30's (#2593 and #2546) carrying 82 cars. Behind me was Southern's through freight No. 83 waiting for No. 64 to clear the area so it could head to Greensboro and down the Washington-Atlanta's mainline to historic Spencer, (N.C.) Yard. I took this exposure while standing on a signal pole – something I would not do today. Still, I managed to get a good portrait of Southern action on the Raleigh – Cary main. The sign at the bottom of this photo indicated the SAL used C.T.C. In fact, the Seaboard was one of the roads to use C.T.C. (from Richmond to Miami) to avoid having to install double track – especially between Richmond and Hamlet – to handle an increase in train volume. Its farsightedness really paid off, for C.T.C. was the wave of the future in railroading.

Engine No. 2593 was only two years old at the time of this photo (coming from EMD in Oct. of 1963) and continued working until the NS retired it in Oct. of 1990 – 26 years of service. It's 2,250 h.p. on four axles, with an engine weight of 250,112 lbs., made them ideal units for all forms of service, be it main, secondary (like here) or branch lines – including yard work as well. It truly demonstrated just what its designation, "GP," stood for: General Purpose.

Even though this was a scary position I selected, I'm glad that I did, for it gives the fans a most interesting look at the west end of this busy section of double track which is still in use to this very day, by the Norfolk Southern and CSX.

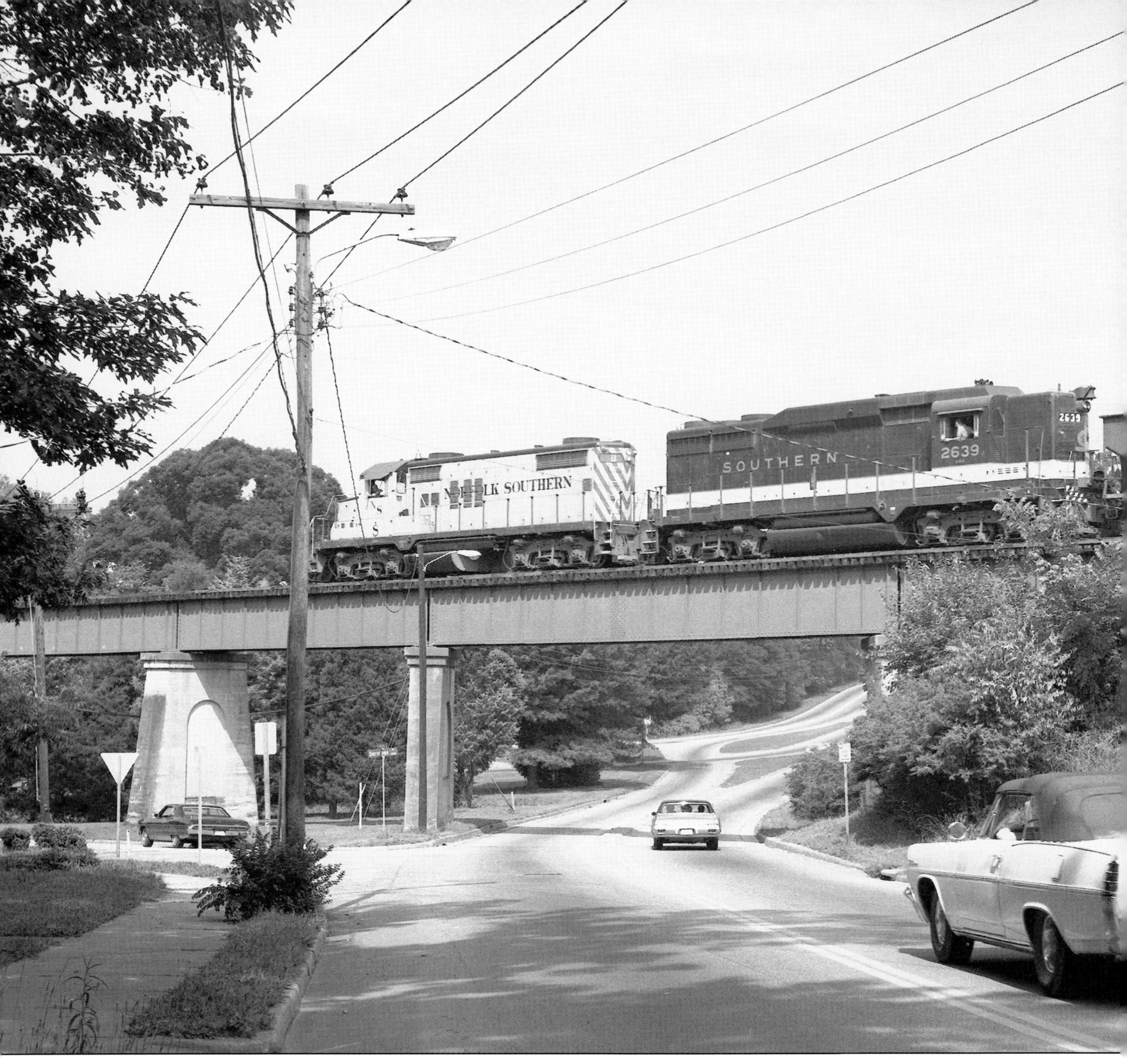

The Southern grew by 622 miles on Jan. 1, 1974, when the road acquired the old Norfolk Southern. One of the changes occurred when the Southern had all the NS Baldwin-built road switchers removed. Then, they not only painted the ex-NS GP-18's and GP-38's into Southern black, they gave all of them a full front short end along with new numbers. For a few months after the takeover, however, one could find old NS colors and Southern's mixed together pulling trains in the Raleigh, N. C. area and on through freights between Raleigh and Spencer (N.C.) Yard.

An example of this mixture of motive power and color schemes is shown here as we see Southern's No. 25 leaving town on its Raleigh-Fayetteville, N. C. round trip with ex-NS GP-18 (#8) and Southern's GP-30 (#2639J) carrying 58 cars this June 1, 1974 at 10:11 a.m., crossing the beautiful, historic and much photographed Boylan Heights' Bridge – part of the former NS's Norfolk-Charlotte mainline – Western Blvd. Is shown under the bridge. The color contrast makes for a most interesting portrait. Soon #8 will be colored black, white and gold, it will have a full front short end and will sport a new number. In the case of No. 8, the GP-18 will become Southern's #187.

No. 2639J, which will be the lead engine on its return trip to Raleigh, was a product of EMD's class of 1963 (Oct.). It had 2,250 h.p. (No. 8 only had 1,800 h.p.); it carried 2,600 gal. of fuel, weighed 250,380 lbs. and the GP-30 (one of 120 owned by the Southern) was among the tallest diesel models on the road's roster: 16'3" tall, 56'2" long and 10'9" wide. It continued in service until retired by the current NS in Feb. of 1990 (No. 8, a.k.a., #187, was retired in March of 1985).

I always considered this location, just south of Boylan Tower, to be among the most photogenic in the Raleigh area. Unfortunately, most traffic over the structure comes through during the dark hours. As a result, this photo was unique not only because it had NS-Southern power working together, it was made during daylight – not bad!

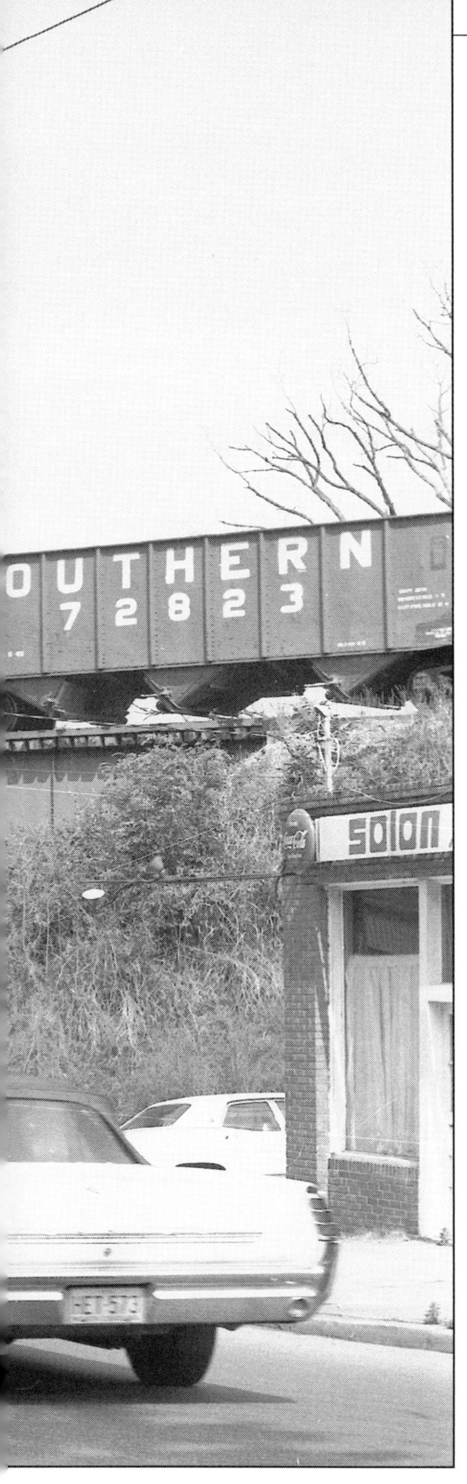

Southern's Three Trademarks

During its existence (1894-1982), the Southern Railway System had three symbols that represented this unique entity.

From its inception in 1894, the trademark used by this new road consisted of the letters "SR" with an arrow passing through them from left to right (Figure #1).

The most recognized symbol came about as a result of a "doodle!" The late L. E. Jeffries, former vice president and general counsel of the Southern, was riding on a passenger train in 1915 when, to help pass the time away, he took a half-dollar, placed it on a "doodle" pad and encircled the coin with a pencil. He then took a quarter, placed it inside the circle he had just made and drew another circle; finally, Mr. Jeffries put the initials "SR" within the center of the double circles. Next, he put "The Southern Serves the South" in the space between the circles and, as they say, the rest is history (Figure #2). This circle trademark first appeared in Southern's September 1915 timetable and was used until the late 1950's and early 60's when, inexplicably, the Southern removed the beloved symbol from all engines, cars and other equipment.

Finally, after realizing the error of this action, they returned to their trademark in the mid to late 1960's. However, the symbol was different. It had the usual circle within a circle, the letters "SR" in the center and the slogan "The Southern Serves the South" within the two circles; but the new trademark also had "Look Ahead, Look South," placed under the familiar circle (Figure #3).

This addition, in your author's opinion, enhanced the beauty of the symbol which represented this great road until the 1982 merger, which resulted in the Norfolk Southern using a horse, a "thoroughbred," as its trademark.

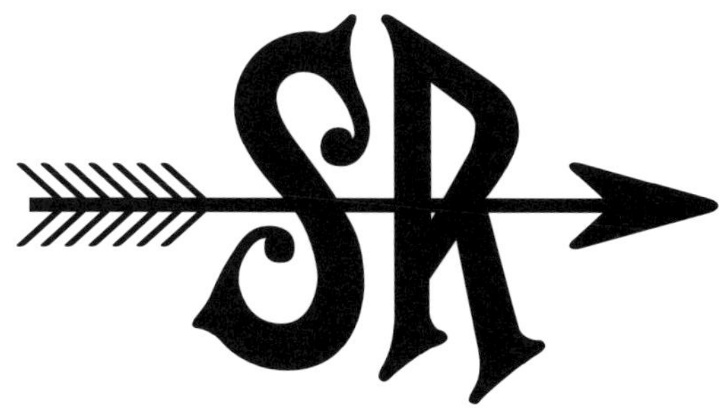

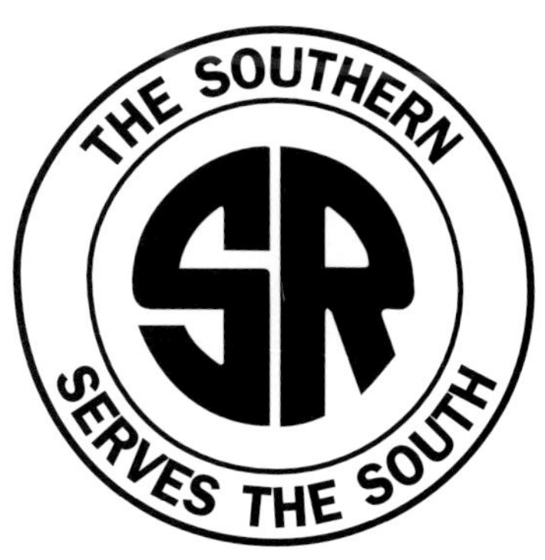

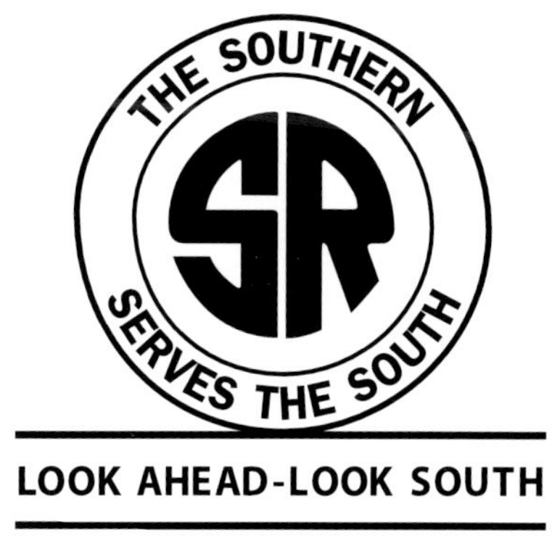

GP35

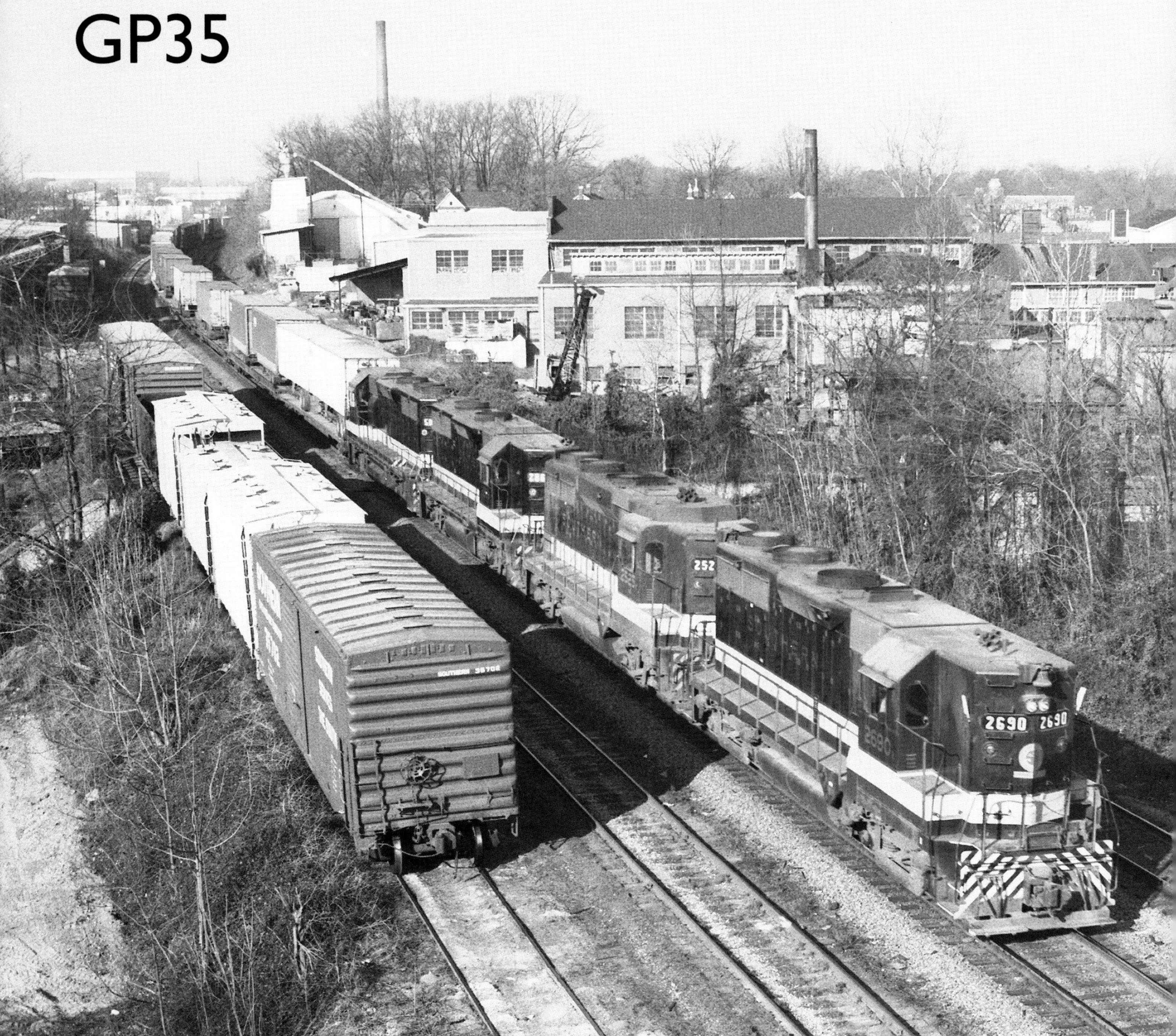

After picking up a long cut of "hot" piggyback cars from Pomona Yard, Southern's No. 222, a.k.a., the "three deuces," is shown nearing downtown Greensboro, N. C. on March 9, 1974 at 9:20 a.m. Within minutes it would pass the Eastern Division headquarters' building where the dispatcher was following its movements on his C.T.C. board.

No. 222 was the fastest northbound piggyback on the Washington-Atlanta mainline. In fact, its speed came close to rivaling that of the "Southern Crescent" – which passed through the area during the night hours.

Today's power for the fast "pig" was: GP-35 (#2690R), GP-30 (#2525K), GP-38AC (#2869R) and GP-38-2 (#5009R), carrying 76 cars. Note the "grimy" looks of that GP-30 as compared to the other cleaner units. The "boys" at Potomac Yard will have to give it a bath to keep it looking good enough to meet the "Southern standards" of appearances.

The 3rd track from the right was used by trains using the Greensboro-Sanford, N. C. line as well as several switchers going to and from uptown where a small yard was located – all in an attempt to avoid delaying movements on the double-track mainline.

No. 222, running as Extra 2690 North, had a combined 8,750 h.p. to move its long, priority train at near passenger train speed. Leading the quartet of engines was GP-35, #2690R, which was assembled at EMD in March of 1965 and, with 2,500 h.p., was the most powerful unit in the consist. It weighed 257,480 lbs., carried 2,300 gal. of fuel, and 40 cu. ft. of sand and, unlike most Southern diesels, its short end was designated as the forward position.

No. 222's passage was the highlight of the day for it was fast, superior to all other trains; and besides, I could get two exposures of him: one at south Pomona and again, leaving the yard for its expedited trip to "Pot Yard." It was truly a photo of railroad's future in action, NOW!

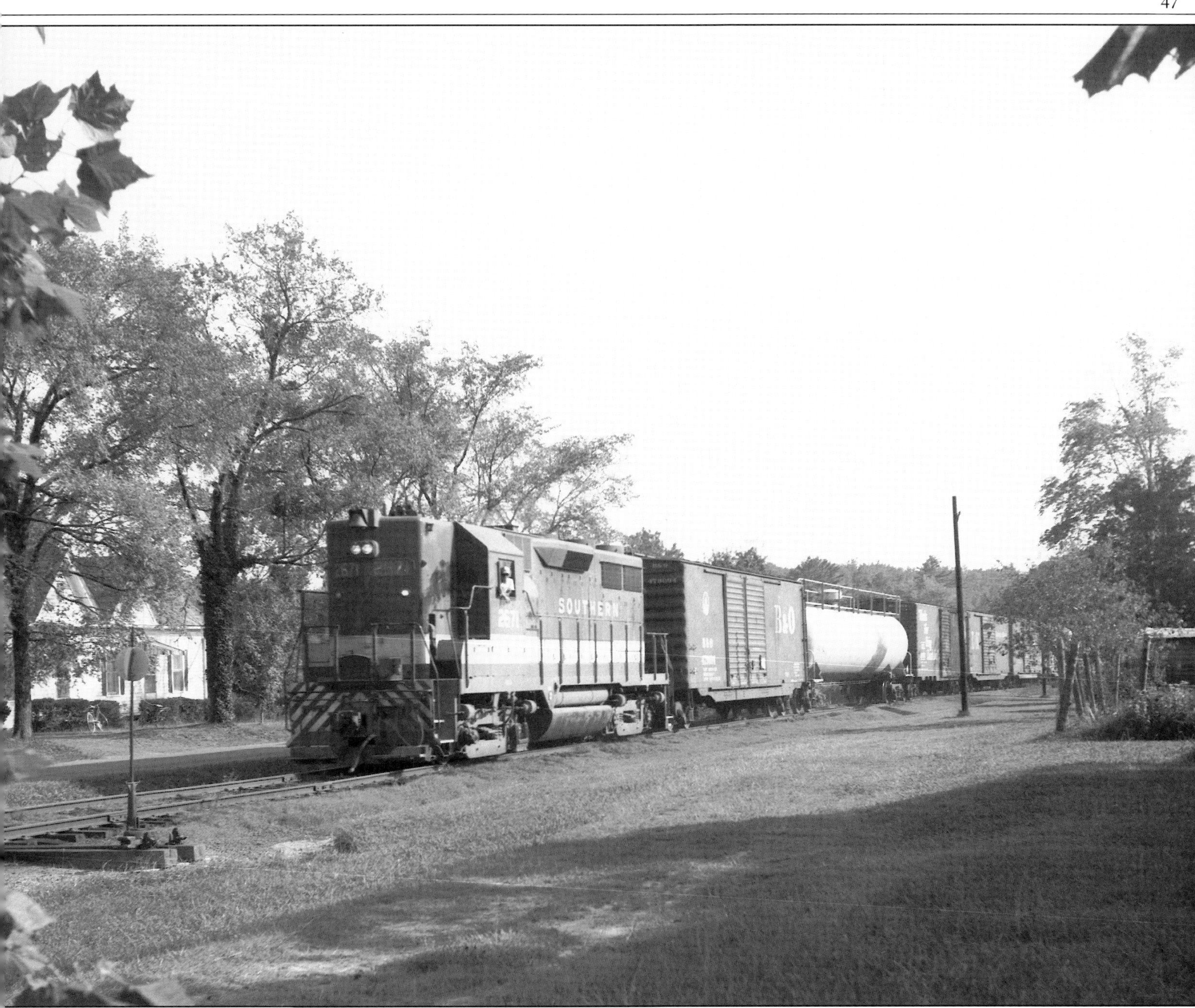

Shown here is Southern's daily ex-Sunday local freight No. 78 entering my mom's hometown of Stovall, N. C. on Nov. 14, 1967, pulled by GP-35 (#2671) with 24 cars at 3:10 p.m., on its journey from East Durham, N. C. to Oxford, N. C. (my hometown) where it will make a round trip to Henderson, N. C. and then travel on to Keysville, Va. where it would connect with the Southern's Richmond-Danville, Va. line – the progenitor of the road that "Served the South." No. 78's counterpart, No. 77, usually passed through Oxford on its way to East Durham while No. 78 was on the Henderson branch.

For several decades, my grandfather was section foreman and he and his crew were responsible for the track's condition from Stovall to the Virginia State line (10 miles to the north). And Stovall was the location of my first train ride. My grandmother and I took the mixed freight to Durham, 42 miles away. It took us nearly four hours to reach our destination where mom, dad, and two aunts, who went on by automobile, waited for us. We spent almost two hours working the three huge tobacco-processing plants in Oxford. And talk about coincidences, on my historic day, my Uncle Ernest was the engineer on the handsome 2-8-0, #400, with its driver rims painted white. What an adventure for this six-year old lad!

The GP-35's, like the GP-30's, not only proved very impressive on the main and secondary lines, they were ideal engines for branch line service as well. With all their power, they could handle long trains on the up and down, light rail lines owned by the Southern.

No. 2671 was only two years old at the time of this photo, coming from EMD in Feb. of 1965. It's 2,500 h.p. and 255,020 lbs. of engine weight plus 2,300 gal. fuel capacity and 40 cu. ft. of sand proved to be perfect motive power for such lines as the Richmond Division East Durham-Keysville run. Both the GP-35's and GP-30's were two of the few models in which the Southern designated the short end as the forward position. The Southern and N&W were the only two 1st class roads to use a full front, short end on all their diesel models.

This was an ideal portrait of Southern railroading with the regular train passing through a small, quiet and friendly community, offering it access to the busy, loud and "foreign" outside world. The station was just a short distance to my left.

Yes, this type of shot was among my slow, carefree exposures where I had nothing to worry about except to record the "event of the day" in Stovall.

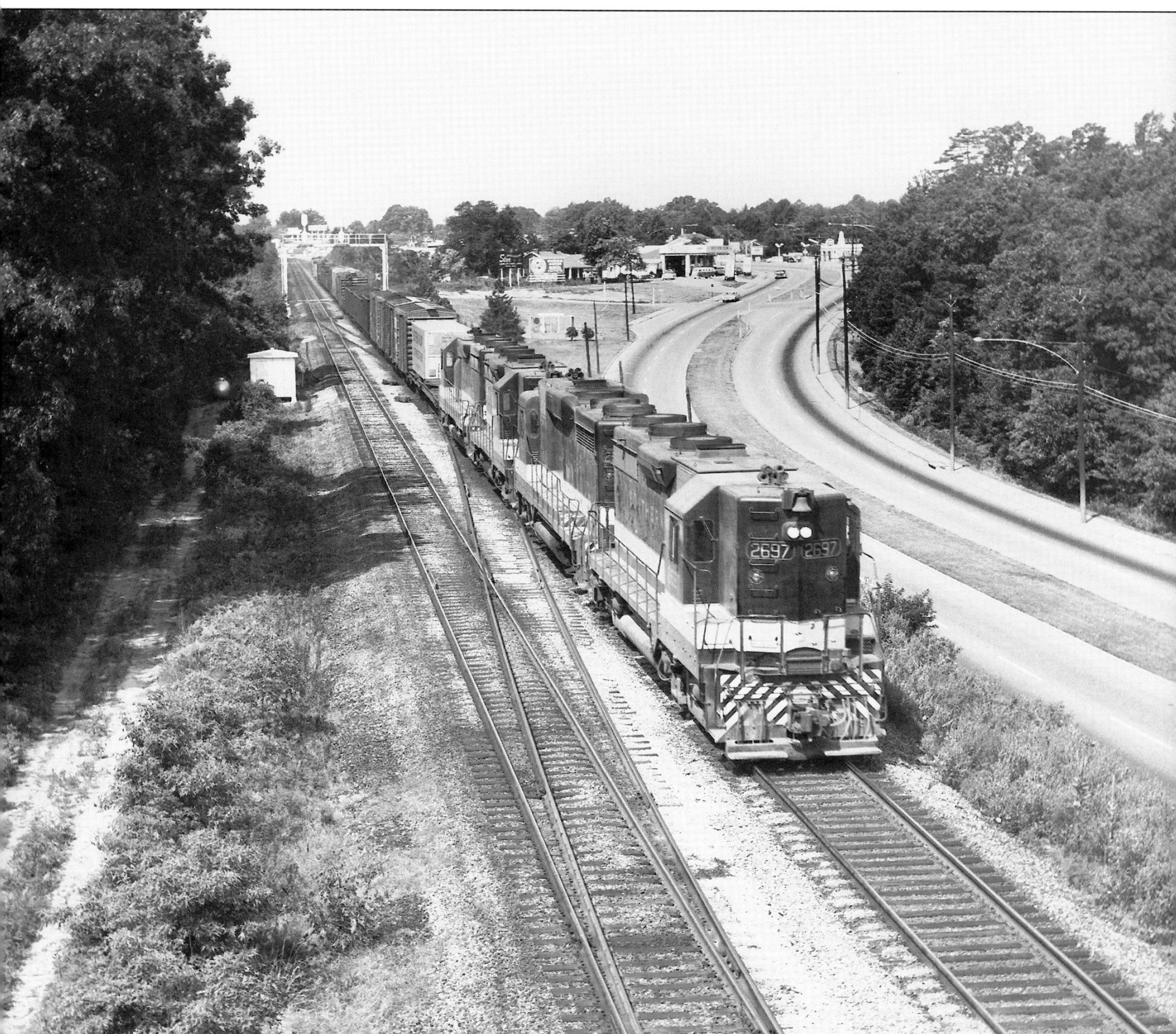

With centralized traffic control (C.T.C.), continuous railed double track, microwave communications and a double crossover, you have a modern, most efficient piece of railroad, one that could accommodate a vast number of trains in a smooth fashion without any delays.

This description of superior railroading fits the scene shown here south of Danville, Va. at a rail location known as "Bentley," while Southern's No. 58 passed through behind GP-35 (#2697), GP-30 (#2553) and two additional GP-35's (#2671 and #2690) pulling only 26 cars. After leaving the Danville-Dundee area, No. 58's consist would swell to 125 cars. This would make the Potomac Yard- bound freight's encounter with the grade on White Oak Mountain far more interesting than just handling 26 cars.

With highway U.S. 29 on the right, Bentley was an area to be since the double crossover was frequently used on a daily basis with faster trains being placed on a track that would enable it to go around a slower freight. And, at Bentley, the trains going to and coming from the old Danville & Western, which enters the Washington-Atlanta mainline at Stokesland, Va. (just around the curve behind No. 58) use Bentley in order to be on No. 1 track (on the left), if possible, so its northbounders could enter the yard at Dundee or for a southbound freight to be on No. 2 track in order to enter the former D&W territory for a trip west out of Stokesland.

The date and time of this action was July 12, 1966 at 1:15 p.m. and No. 58's lead locomotive, #2697, had been in service since March of 1965 – a year old. The '35 was more powerful than the popular GP-30 (2,250 h.p.), with 2,500 h.p. and carried 2,300 gal. of fuel; with its 16 cylinders and 257,320 lbs. of engine weight, the '35 produced approximately 51,600 lbs. of tractive effort. It continued in service until May of 1989.

On my numerous visits to the Danville area over the years, I never hesitated to "stay awhile" at Bentley to record the rail action between the double signal bridges at the double crossover which enabled me to capture on film, railroading at its best!

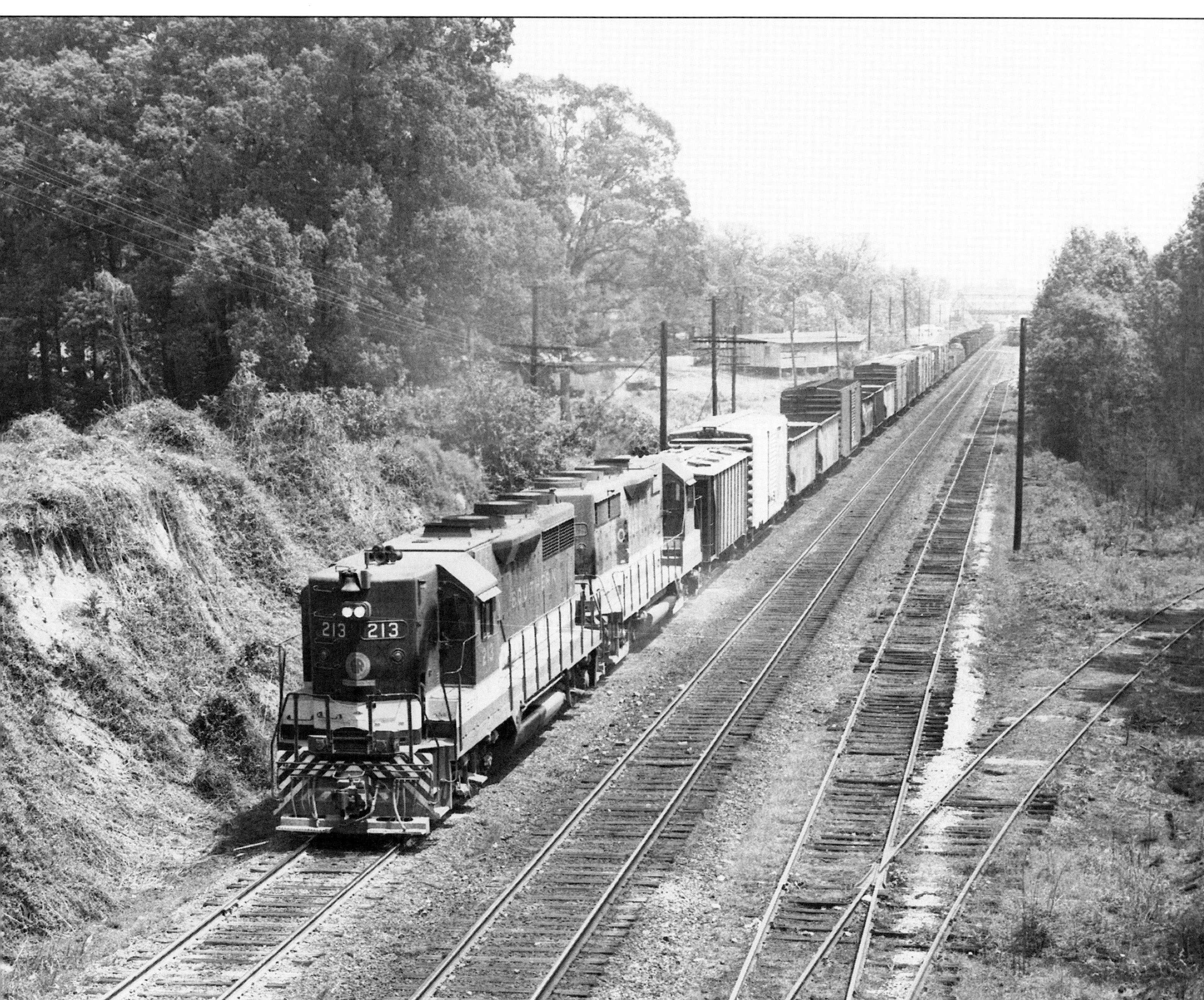

For 8.1 miles from Raleigh, N.C.'s Boylan Tower (seen in the far background) to Cary, N. C., the Southern and the SCL jointly operated a double track section of tracks. For the SCL, it was part of the old Seaboard Air Line's Richmond-Miami mainline; for the Southern, it was part of their Greensboro-Goldsboro, N. C. line. At the time of this photo, the line averaged 25-30 trains per day. Today, this segment is jointly run by the Norfolk Southern and the CSX, seeing 6 Amtraks and between 12 and 14 freights.

For almost half the distance on this double track, between Raleigh and Cary, it presents a fairly stiff grade for all trains leaving Raleigh. Southern's No. 83 (Raleigh to Spencer Yard via Greensboro, N. C.) is shown starting out of Raleigh and up this challenging climb. No. 83 is passing the N. C. School for the Blind (on my right) and nearing both Pullen Park and the campus of my alma mater, North Carolina State University, this June 1, 1971, at 2:12 p.m. Since my dormitory room faced the tracks, I am amazed that I received my BA degree in History because of those numerous, joyous distractions that passed by my window, day and night.

Usually No. 83 rated three units; however, on this particular day there were only two engines available: two GP-35's (#213 and #2715), to move its 95 cars. They did not break any speed records but the combined 5,000 h.p. got the train up the hill and on to its destination.

No. 213 was one of the five GP-35's obtained from the Central of Georgia in 1971 when the C of G was incorporated into the Southern's "family." It will soon be renumbered to #243 and help complete the 76 units owned by the Southern (#240-#244, #2645-#2715). Besides producing 2,500 h.p., it weighed 252,760 lbs. and carried 2,300 gal. of fuel. It moved tonnage from Dec. of 1963 until May of 1989.

This bridge plus the one over the double track at the east part of N.C.S.U. campus were great locations for photographing trains, both leaving and entering the Raleigh area and remains so to this very day.

Boy, for such usually quiet engines, the two "35's shown here were really "talking it up" as it "tackled" the grade. As a point of interest, the second engine in the power consist of No. 83, #2715, was the last GP-35 purchased by the Southern.

This was a great day to be a railfan

GP-38

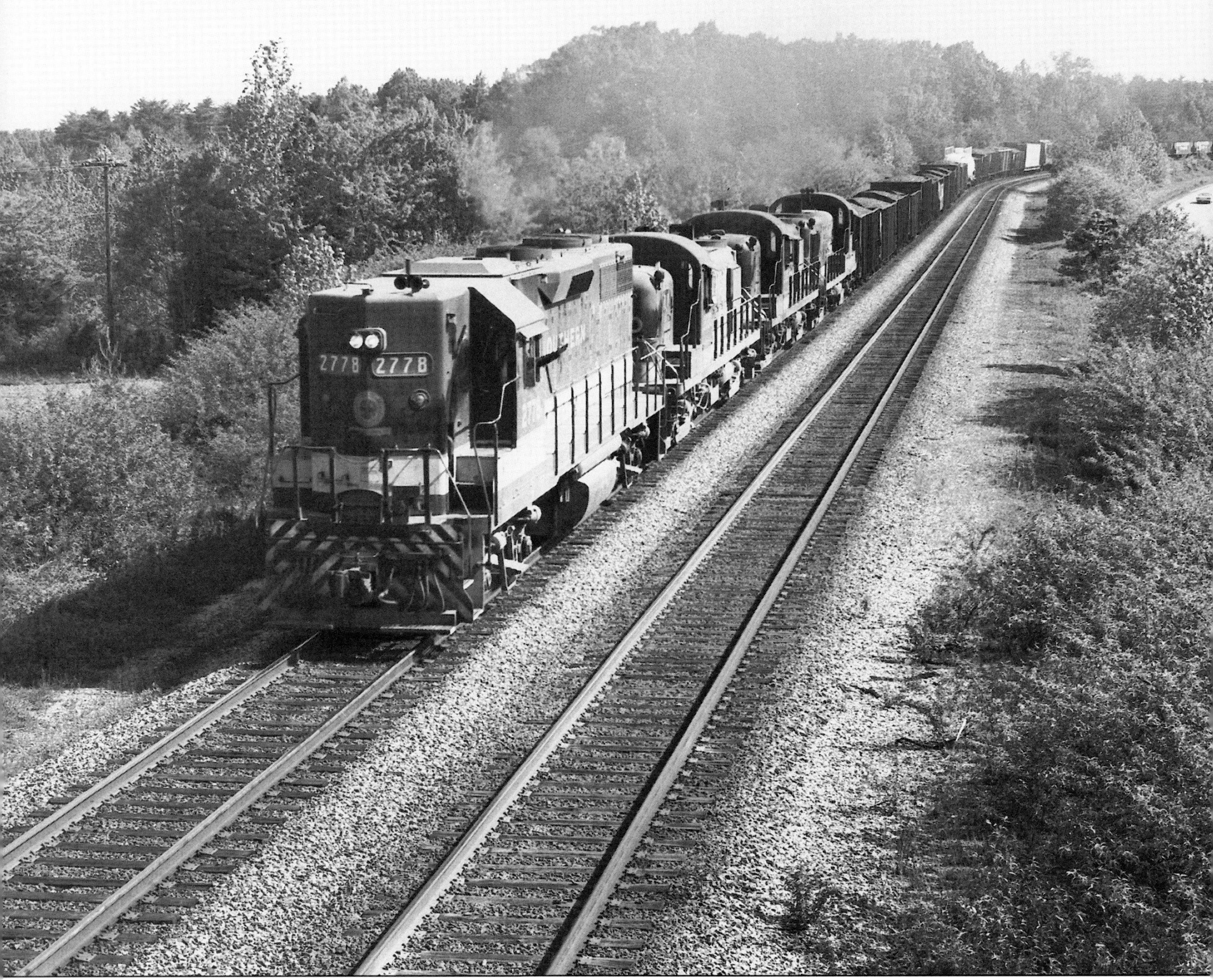

The new and the old are shown as a team, moving tonnage (135 cars) at a brisk pace, on the Southern's Washington-Atlanta mainline near Swann, N. C., this May 6, 1972, at 9:15 a.m.

What a combination of motive power used to ferry 1st No. 159 from Potomac Yard to Spencer Yard: a Jan. 1970, EMD built GP-38 (#2778X) ahead of three older RS-3's (#2030L, #2025L and #2040L). The GP-38 was just two years old while the Alco-GE's had at least 20 years of service accumulated. Yet, the young and old were getting the job done.

GP-38 (#2778X) had 2,000 h.p., weighed 242,845 lbs., had 1,700 gal. of fuel. It was 59 ft. long, 15'5" high and approximately 11 ft. wide. It is still piling up mileage, but now for the Norfolk Southern-EMD built them well!

The GP-38 series (GP-38AC and GP-38-2's) were as successful as the record setting of GP-7 and GP-9 models. They were easy to handle, reliable; and the '38's could pull whatever they were assigned: coal drags, through freights, piggybacks as well as locals and they even excelled at yard work. They were truly general purpose locomotives.

Can you imagine my surprise when, looking through my camera's viewfinder, I saw "just another GP-38;" but, behind #2778X were three RS-3's all together! Incidents such as this go toward explaining why a mainline remains so interesting: you never know what to expect when the next train approaches!

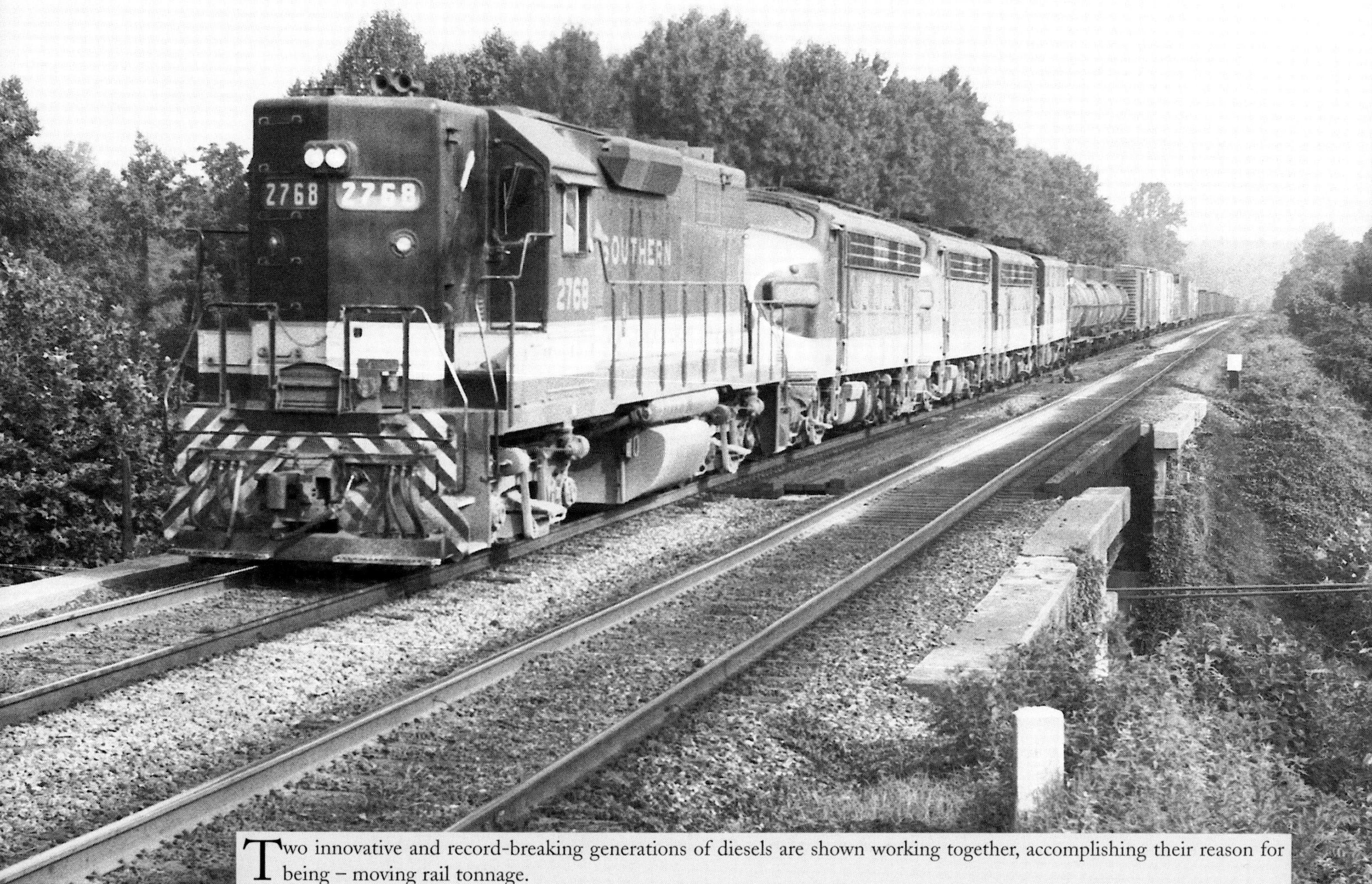

Two innovative and record-breaking generations of diesels are shown working together, accomplishing their reason for being – moving rail tonnage.

Shown in this Aug. 21, 1971 (9:22 a.m.) exposure was a nearly two-year-old GP-38, heading four – at least 21 year old – F-7A's, pulling 116 cars on Extra 2768 South, nearing Dundee, Va. on Southern's Washington-Atlanta mainline.

Even though I am an F-7A, E-8A fan and wished the four "bulldog nosed" F units had been up front of this "cleanup" train, I must admit the GP-38 "youngster" on the point was good. However, what a contrast in locomotive styles: the modern, rather blunt looking utilitarian design vs. the streamlined, esthetically pleasing look of the "old-timers."

The Extra South was referred to as a "cleanup" train because it would help make room in all the yards it passed by, so more inbound traffic could be accommodated. The extra was a yardmasters' "dream come true" and such a train almost always had a most interesting motive power combination. Extra 2768 South was no exception to this unofficial rule, that's for sure!

GP-38 (#2768) came from EMD's LaGrange, Ill. Plant in Nov. of 1969, bringing 2,000 h.p. vs. the F-7A's 1,500 h.p.; the '38 weighed 242,825 lbs. and carried 1,700 gal. of fuel. It was 59 ft. long (the F-7A stretched to a length of 50'8"). By the way, behind the GP-38 were four F-7A's (#4244, #4231, #4191 and #4129).

During the early 1970's, you could occasionally find a few old "F" units roaming the mainline rails they knew so well. Most, however, spent their last years working secondary lines and even local freights. Even "my East Durham, N. C.-Oxford-Henderson-Keysville, Va. Line's motive power were "F" units for over three years, before they all became a part of rail history, except for a few that were preserved (thank goodness).

The future and the past together. It was a wonderful scene!

GP-38-2

After almost two decades, the Southern finally decided to upgrade "my" line: East Durham, N. C. – Keysville, Va. To accomplish this task would require thousands of crossties, ton of ballast, spikes, etc. – all before the track crew arrived with all their amazing equipment.

One of the many ballast trains involved in the rehabilitation is shown here, north of Clarksville, Va., heading toward Keysville and the Southern's Richmond-Danville, Va. line which it will use to get to the quarry for another load of ballast.

The 64 empty ballast cars are being pulled by GP-38-2 (#5037T), GP-38AC (#2860L) and two GP-38-2's (#5076L and #5088A), preparing to pass under the U.S. 15 highway overpass. You can barely see it, but in the far background is Kerr Lake and a new 27-pier supported bridge which this extra had just crossed. The lake is not only the main supply of water for many towns, it is also a delight for boaters, fishermen and vacationers as well.

The date was July 8, 1982 (a month after the creation of the Norfolk Southern as a result of the merger of the Southern with the N&W) and by Oct. the upgrade project was completed. As a result, the speed limit increased to 35 m.p.h. (up from 25) on the entire 88-mile long line.

Leading this impressive Extra North, at 11:25 a.m. with the temperature at an unbearable 94°F (I had to wipe the sweat off my forehead before looking into my camera's viewfinder), was GP-38-2, #5037T. This excellent General Purpose was built by EMD in March of 1972 and was using all of its 2,000 h.p. to move the northbounder up a slight grade. It carried 2,600 gal. of fuel, weighed 247,920 lbs., rode on Blomburg type "M" trucks and part of the 257 units owned by the Southern. For some unexplainable reason, it did not have that impressive Southern symbol on its "nose."

The GP-38-2 series was among the most successful models purchased by the Southern; they could do it all: mainline, local and yard assignments -–as well as pulling ballast trains. The crews loved them since they were easy to operate and very reliable.

This fine exposure made the tremendous heat bearable. I hope you will agree with my feelings concerning a great example of rail action.

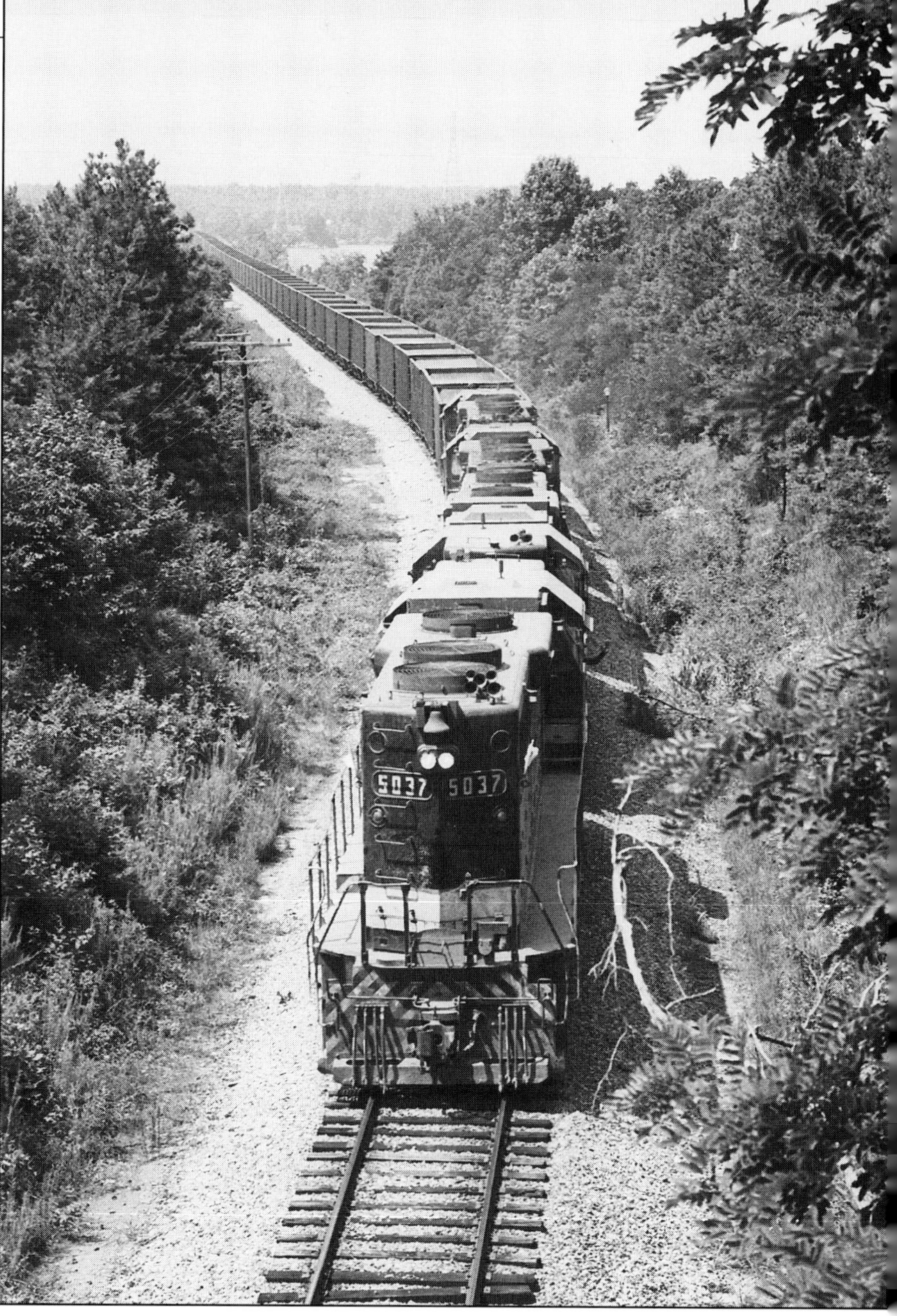

Local freight No. 21 is shown crossing the Grassy Creek Bridge – part of the huge Kerr Lake area – at 1:05 p.m. on its regular round-trip from Keysville, Va. to Oxford, N. C. (U.S. 15 is shown on the left). Yes, this WAS a local freight, headed by GP-38-2, #5108R, not a helper engine for a passenger train.

True, this Aug. 5, 1981, was not an ordinary day for No. 21. The Southern decided not to run its excursion train to Durham, N. C. where it would be used on several railfan trips in the eastern part of the state. Instead, they had local freight No. 21 tow the two FP-7A's (#6143H and #6138H), with their 15 cars, to Durham. As a result, No. 5108R not only had two green, gold and white colored passenger engines, 15 passenger cars plus 15 freight cars (on the rear) heading south. What a sight. What a wonderful sight!

The excursion train was left in Oxford where the East Durham-Oxford round-trip, night freight (No. 17 & 18) would take the varnish on to Durham; No. 21 would head back to Keysville as No. 22, working all the way. I believe its crew enjoyed this unusual occurrence almost as much as yours truly.

No. 21's motive power was the old reliable GP-38-2, #5108R – part of 257 units owned by the Southern (#5000-#5256). No. 5108R was created in Jan. of 1974 and continues to move tonnage to this very day (for the Norfolk Southern). This EMD model had an impact on the Southern – and other railroads – as great as the GP-7's and GP-9's since they could handle any and all assignments: mainline runs, local freights and they even excelled in yard work as well. With its 247,695 lbs. of weight and 2,000 h.p., #5108R could do it all, with less fuel and maintenance plus the crews were very comfortable with the 5000's. It held 2,600 gal. of fuel, 72 cu. ft. of sand and had a pair of sweet-sounding Nathan P-142 horns and that impressive Southern symbol put the crowning touch to a quite handsome and yet rugged engine.

I followed No. 21 on this particular day from Chase City, Va. to Oxford on "my" line, and it was a most enjoyable experience since I was the only railfan there. The entire adventure was mine and mine alone – great!

You might be interested to know that this same bridge supported the weight of smoke-belching steam locomotive's driving wheels of both #4501 and #722 during those glorious and sorely missed steam excursion years. Each engine made three trips over "my" line. Believe me, during those wonderful excursions, I was definitely NOT alone.

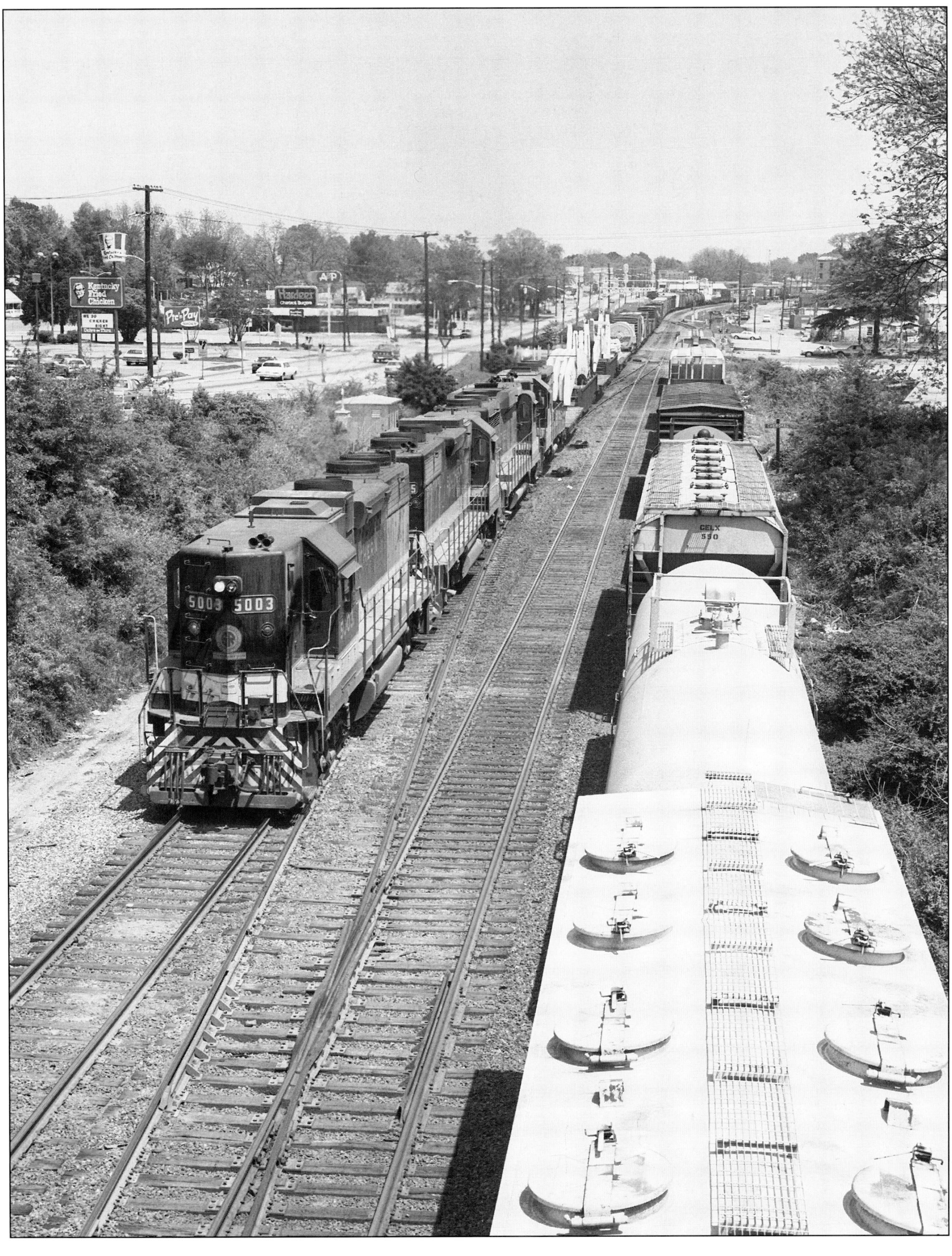
Kentucky Fried Chicken
Pre-Pay
5003 5003
GELX 550

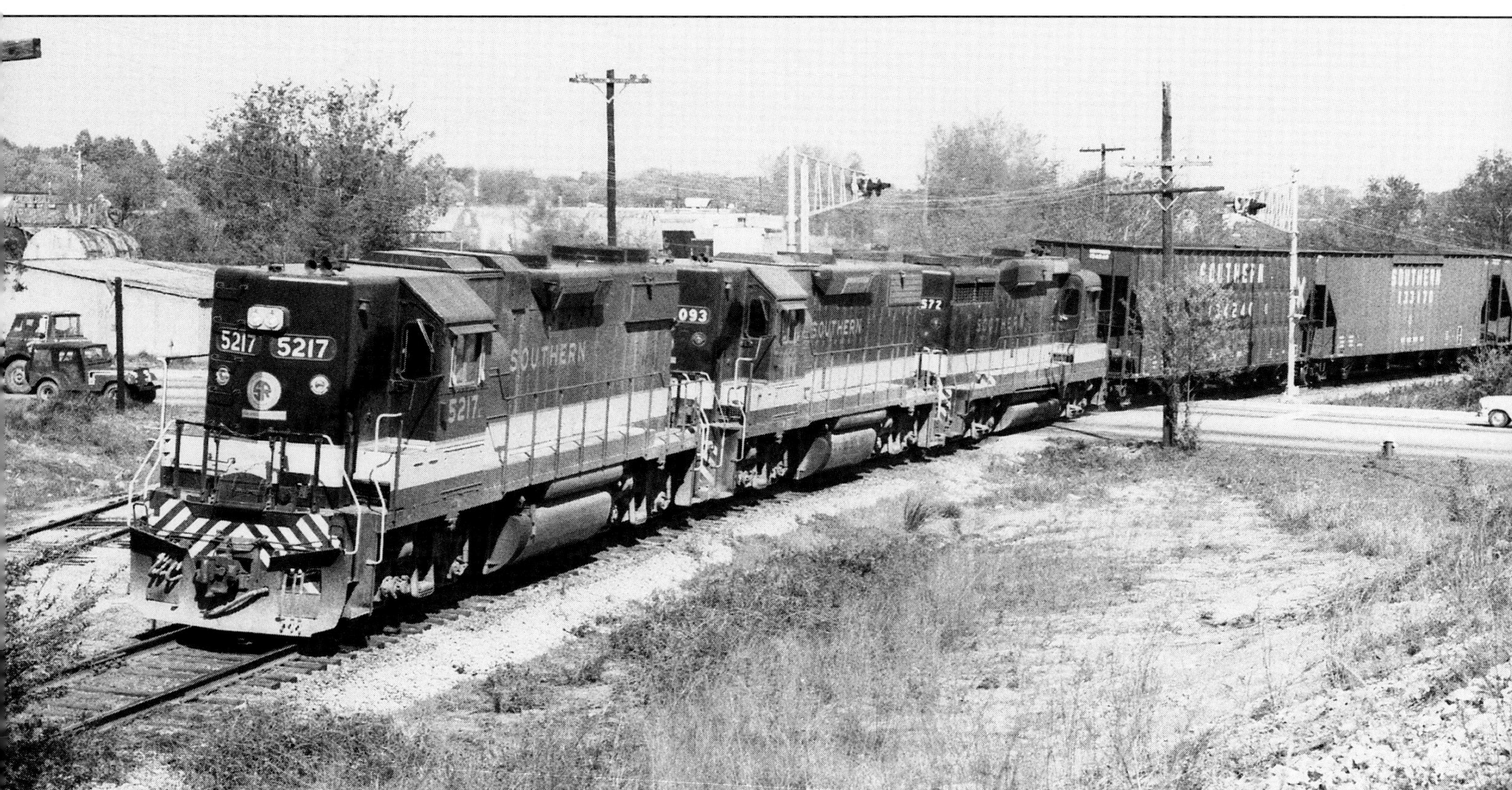

After collecting cars from Asheville, N. C. (down Saluda Grade) and the Washington-Atlanta mainline at Haynes Yard, No. 172 heads east towards Columbia, S. C.'s Andrews Yard and then on to the coast at Charleston, S. C.

No. 172, shown in south Spartanburg, S. C., had just left the Southern's double track mainline at Beaumont (a railroad location) with 94 cars pulled by two GP-38-2's (#5217L and #5093A) plus GP-30 (#2572R) at 9:16 a.m. this April 9, 1977, on a continuous rail, well-kept line which, today, carries a great number of overseas-bound automobiles. This used to be called the "Route of the Carolina Special" – an historic passenger train that ran from Charleston to Cincinnati, Ohio and then to Chicago, Ill. over the NYC.

The lead engine (#5217L) was equipped with the very effective snow-plow "cowcatcher," which was placed on all GP-38-2's from #5167 through #5256, and it had a fuel capacity of 2,900 gallons (up from 2,600 for #5000-#5138). Built in Jan. of 1977 (3 months old in this photo), it had a pair of Nathan five-chime horns, weighed 248,809 lbs., mustered 2,000 h.p. and held 72 cu. ft. of sand. The beautiful EMD unit – part of the 257 purchased by the Southern – now wears a "thoroughbred" on its nose rather than the impressive Southern symbol. Of all the GP-38-2's owned by that road that "Served the South," only ten have been retired. It was among the most numerous second-generation model on the Southern's roster for a good reason: the '38-2's could do it all. It was dependable, fuel-efficient, required little maintenance and could fulfill all assignments with elan – and the crews loved them.

Spartanburg was a great rail town with the Southern's Washington-Atlanta mainline, as well as the Charleston-Cincinnati line. Add to this the Clinchfield, the SCL (former ACL) and the Piedmont & Northern. It's a location all railfans need to consider when picking places to find GREAT rail action!

Gaffney, S. C.: another town that was split—right down the middle—by a busy railroad (in this case, it's the Southern Railway's Washington-Atlanta mainline). Add to these interesting ingredients a scenic bridge ("just made" for rail photography) at the south end of the community plus a double crossover (called "Cherokee" by the Southern) and you truly have a railfan's delight.

As evidence to prove my last statement, look at this photo of Southern's No. 155 passing through town on its way to Atlanta and points south, powered by GP-38-2 (#5003X), GP-38AC (#2865K), GP-30 (#2546A) and GP-35 (#2707W) with 159 cars this April 19, 1981 at 12:05 p.m. What a beautiful sight!

No. 155 worked most areas bypassed by the priority freights. Its next stop will be Spartanburg, S. C.'s Haynes Yard, then Greenville, S. C. where it will not only set off and add cars to its train but will have a new crew added to take it on to Atlanta.

Even though the southbounder was a marvelous adventure for me, I noticed that most of the town's citizenry hardly noticed No. 155's passage since it was one of at least 25-30 trains that visited Gaffney day and night, seven days a week. I don't believe I could live in a town like Gaffney, for I would go broke from purchasing and having processed so many rolls of film! I would try to see and photograph all of them. Why? I am a railfan – always have been and always will be (and proud of it)!

The lead engine, running in the crew's preferred, short end forward position, was #5003X: built by EMD in Jan. of 1972, had 2,000 h.p., carried 2,600 gal. of fuel, 72 cu. ft. of sand; weighed 248,910 lbs., stood 15'3" tall and was 59'2" long. The engineer had that good sounding pair of Nathan P-142 horns "tied down" as it led No. 155 through town at 25-30 m.p.h. It still moves tonnage today, garbed in the color scheme of the Norfolk Southern.

Living next to a busy mainline must be wonderful, if you like trains. Maybe it's good that I live near a branch line, for I doubt if I could accomplish very much else because of the great rail action tugging at me to not only see but record on film all of the train movements. As a result, I think I would prefer to visit such locations, for it's truly a "Shangri-La" for railfans!

GP-38AC

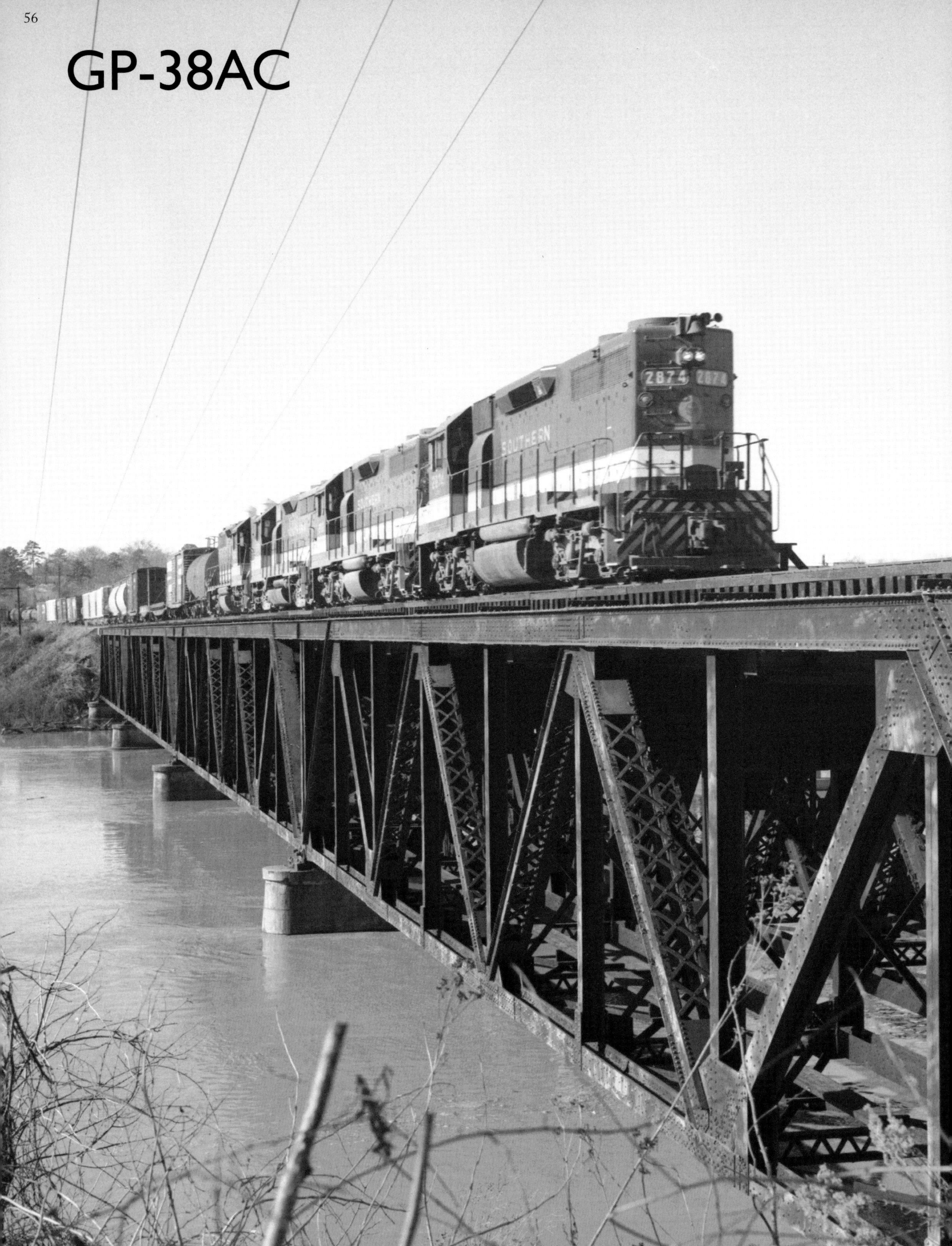

From Raleigh, N.C.'s Boylan Tower to Cary, N. C. (7.9 miles) a jointly operated (Southern-SCL) double track section of tracks accommodated a great number of trains. For approximately five miles from Boylan, all westbounders had (and still have) a stiff grade to face before reaching Cary where the Southern headed west to Greensboro and their mainline, while the SCL turned South to sunny Miami.

Wide-opened at nearly 25 m.p.h. and making those wonderful sounds that only EMD engines could produce when working at their maximum capacity, Southern's No. 83, headed by three-month-old GP38AC (#2859) and a GP-38 (#2755) — all pulling 76 cars, this Dec. 11, 1971 at 12:35 p.m. — was photographed from the West Raleigh Bypass bridge as it roared through Method, N. C. — a suburb of Raleigh — on its way to Spencer Yard via Greensboro, N. C.

The excellent performance and versatility demonstrated by the GP-38 impacted the rail world, including the Southern, much as the GP-7 and GP-9's, the models that helped to "put the last nail in the steam engine's coffin." The '38's could do it all with their 2,000 h.p.: piggybacks, through and/or local freights (even on the point of local passenger trains) as well as yard work.

The GP-38's, of which the Southern owned 115 units, were outstanding; however, the big road felt they could perform even better and more economically. The crews at EMD's plant at LaGrange, Ill. Produced the GP-38AC series in mid-1971. They immediately proved to be able to meet each and every one of the Southern's parameters: the '38AC's had a larger fuel capacity (2,600 gal. compared to the '38's 1,700 gal.), it had an "AC" main generator instead of the usual "DC," the difference being that the "AC" generators proved more reliable and did not have the "DC's" brushes. This change enabled them to require less maintenance. In fact, the GP-38AC came very close in matching the most successful of the '38 series: the GP-38-2.

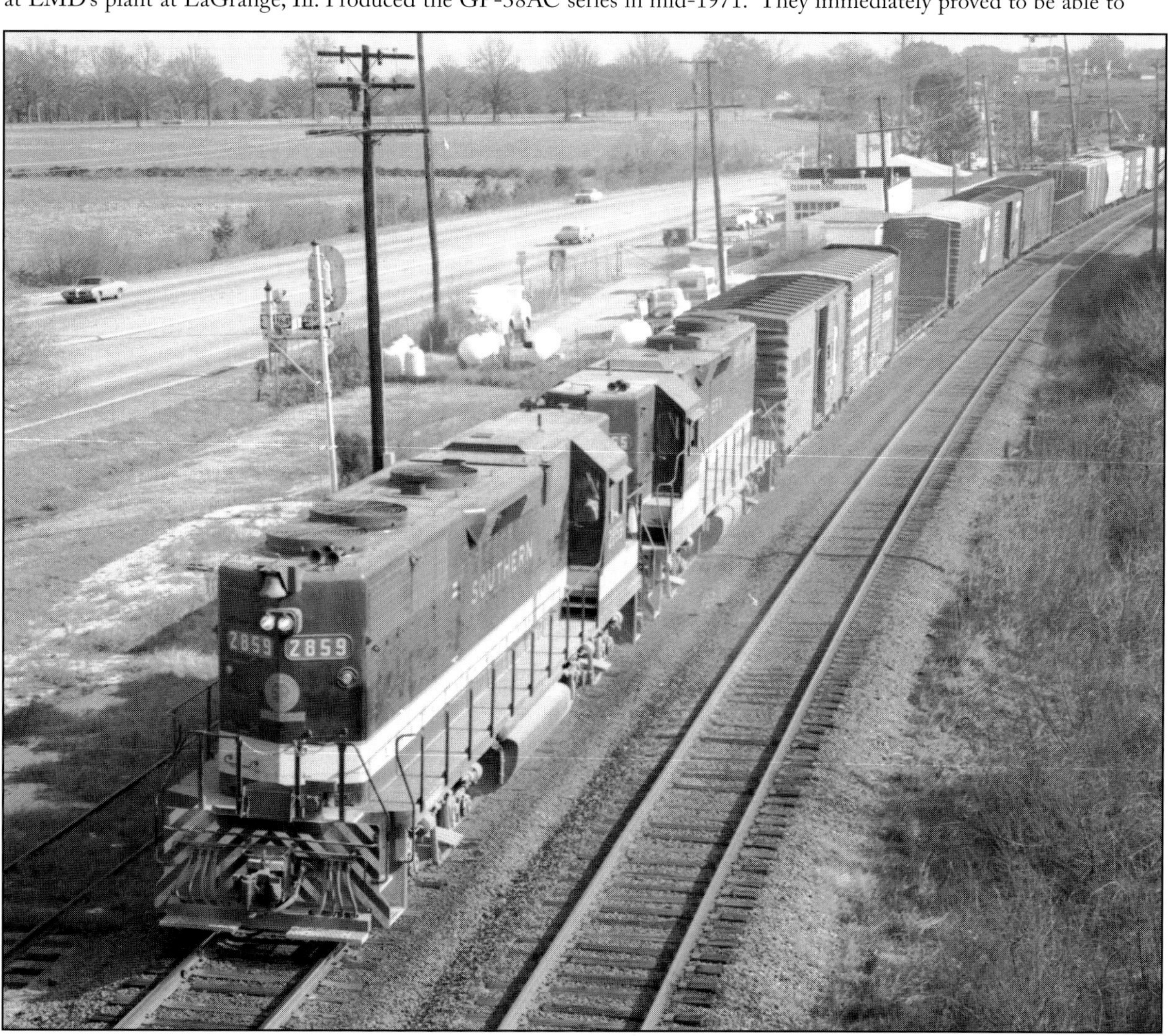

Even though the "18-wheelers" were passing close behind me at 60+ m.p.h., I'm glad to have risked "life and limb" in order to have recorded this most dramatic scene of rail history on film. By the way, I would NOT do this today!

After leaving Spencer (N. C.) yard, Southern's Potomac Yard bound through freight, No. 158, "takes to the air," as it crosses the busy double track bridge over the Yadkin River at a good 40+ m.p.h. with 126 cars pulled by: GP-38AC (#2874L) and three GP-38's (#2761L, #2804X and #2810K) – all on the hot Washington-Atlanta mainline this Dec. 28, 1973 (11:43 a.m.).

The GP-38AC on the point, #2874L, was built in Sept. of 1971, weighed 247,760 lbs., had 2,000 h.p., carried 2,600 gal. of fuel and 72 cu. ft. of sand. It was 59'2" long and 15'6" high. No. 2874L is still in service today; however, it is on the 1982 created Norfolk Southern's motive power roster.

The '38AC was an improvement on the highly successful GP-38 in at least two areas: it carried more fuel and sand (the '38 only held 1,700 gal. of fuel and 56 cu. ft. of sand) and it's more efficient "AC" main generator was superior to the GP-38 "DC" device since it required less maintenance and was far more reliable as well. Indeed, the GP-38AC was said by many "in the know" to have been an almost match for the most successful of the '38 series: the GP-38-2.

Between April and September of 1971, the Southern, through a trade of many old F3's, acquired 56 of the GP-38AC's (#2823 through #2878); and they proved to be so effective and durable that they are still active today, but with the Norfolk Southern and not the Southern.

This was a great spot to spend some time if you were a railfan and/or fisherman, for it was possible to catch some eatable fish from the old Yadkin; and, in between bites, you could watch (or photograph) a parade of trains passing over the big and impressive structure which, to this very day, remains a great location for all railfans (and fishermen as well).

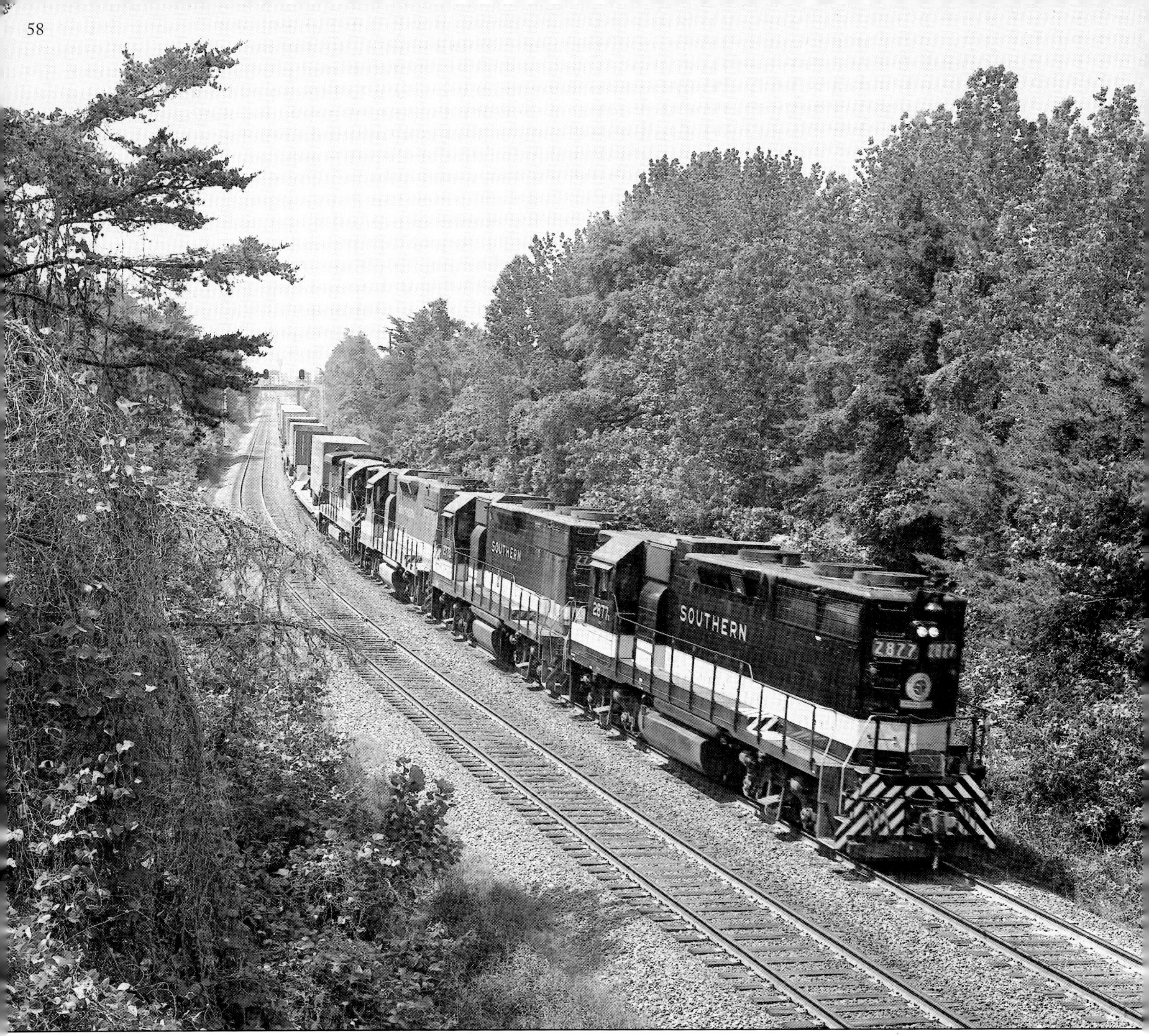

EMD's sales department boasted to the Southern that their '38 series of engines would meet all the big roads' demands of operating with great reliability and economically. The builder's promises proved to be factual, for the GP-38's and their two successors, the GP-38AC's and GP-38-2's could, and did, it all on the Southern, pulling everything from piggybacks to doing yard work in a most effective manner.

A prime example of this EMD phenomenon's abilities is shown here at Shelton, N. C. on May 23, 1981, at 11:20 a.m. The usual GP-50's were not available to power one of the Southern's hottest trains on their Washington-Atlanta mainline: No. 222-a.k.a., the "Three Deuces-a solid Atlanta to Alexandria, Va. piggyback. As a result, the 61 "pigs" were pulled by GP-38AC (#2877), GP-38 (#2773), GP-38AC (#2872) and a "stranger": a GE-built B23-7 (#4003) on the rear. The high priority piggyback arrived in Alexandria on time!

Coming downgrade at a good 50-55+ m.p.h. and approaching the Virginia state line, No. 222 is shown passing one of my favorite locations for rail photography: well-maintained double track, a signal bridge in the background, a scenic setting and an elevated curve. Yes, this was the place to be in order to record the ebb and flow of mainline action on film.

The lead engine was the Sept. of 1971 built GP-38AC (#2877) which had 2,000 h.p., weighed 247,160 lbs., carried 2,600 gal. of fuel plus 72 cu. ft. of sand. With their more efficient "AC" main generator, it was so reliable that it remains in service today, hauling trains for the 1982 created Norfolk Southern.

Wouldn't it be great to spend the entire day at this spot, "shooting," southbounders growling and sanding upgrade and the northbounders with their dynamic braking system "screaming" in keeping the mainliners under control. It is still a good place to visit to this very day in order to witness the passage of the many trains of the Norfolk Southern.

This is a true portrait of modern railroading in action!

EMD placed the letters, "GP" in front of its four-axle models. This designation stood for, "General Purpose," meaning the diesels could be used in most of the different services required by the railroads. For example, this GP-38AC, #2824 – shown passing through Wellford, S. C. – could be found pulling piggybacks, through and/or local freights; it could also be most effective as a yard engine as well.

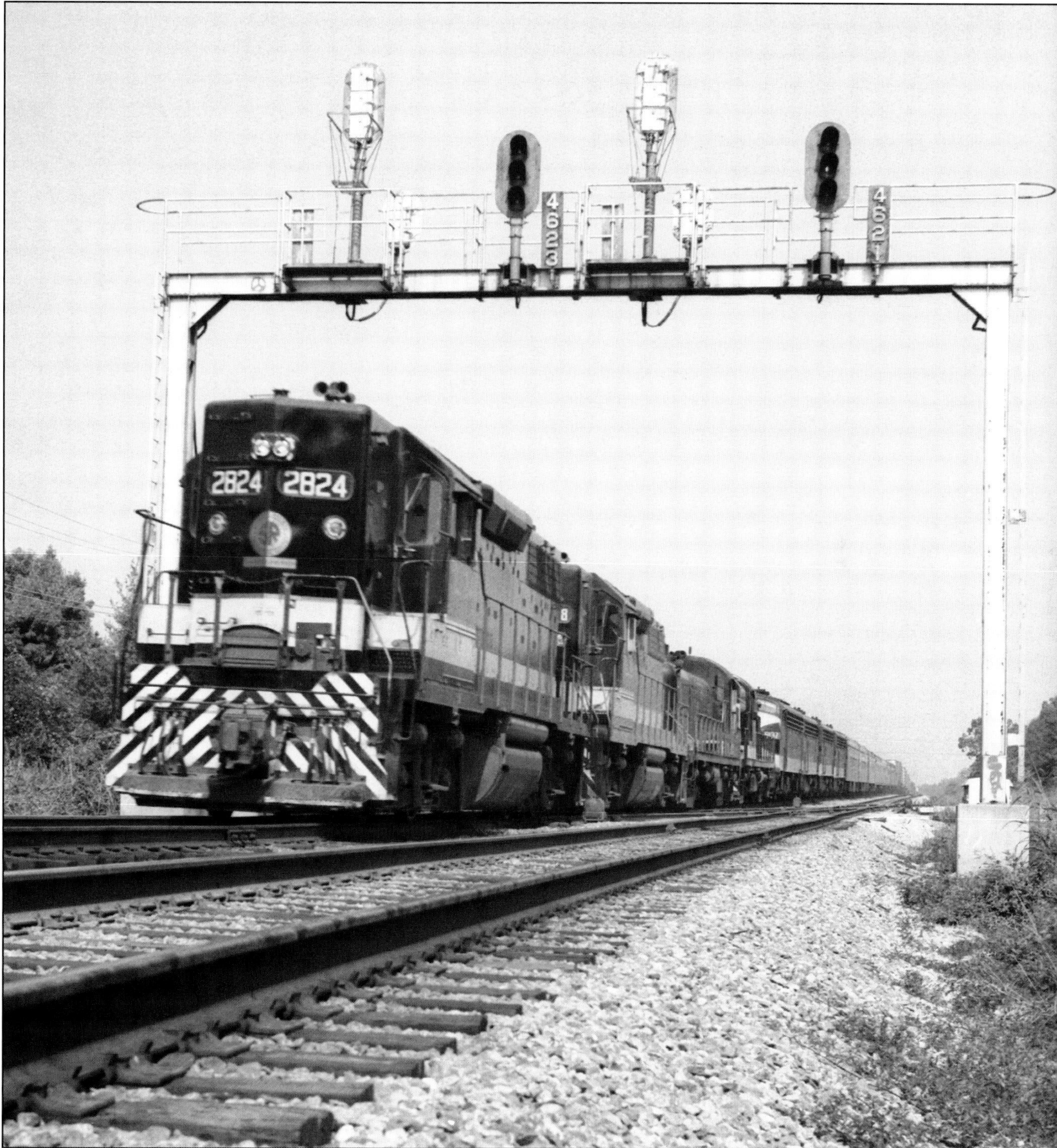

In this photo, made on Aug. 24, 1972, at 10:05 a.m., however, the term "GP," was stretched somewhat to include heading a passenger train! On this particular day, GP-38AC (#2824F), along with another GP-38AC (#2828H), two Alco-GE RS-3's (#2032F and #2043W) plus the more appropriate four FP-7A's (#6137K, #6130X, #6147J and #6140W) was on the point of the "fast" (60+ m.p.h.) moving, Atlanta to Washington passenger train, No. 6 – Southern's "Piedmont" – which had 8 passenger and 28 "hot" piggyback cars: what a sight!

Can you imagine the Atlanta and Greenville, S. C. crew's reaction when they reported to their stations in order to carry No. 6 north on the Washington-Atlanta mainline and, instead of finding the usual FP-7A's on the front, they had two GP-38AC's and two RS-3's ahead of their beloved and beautiful passenger units.

Actually, the four "freighters" were being brought to Salisbury, N. C. after receiving a "checkup" at Atlanta's Pegram Shops. When No. 6 departed the Salisbury area, it would be powered only by the four FP-7A's. On numerous occasions, the Southern would send freight power for inspection to Atlanta on No. 5 and get them back on No. 6, so this was not as an uncommon sight as you might have thought.

No. 2824F came on the Southern's property in April of 1971 and remains in service today (for the Norfolk Southern). It was actually a more effective and economical model than the popular GP-38 and its success lead to the development of the renowned GP-38-2 series.

On this particular Aug. 1972 day in Wellford (south of Spartanburg, S. C.), however, it was just me and No. 6 with its atypical motive power arrangement. It was a moment I will never forget. I hope you will enjoy my luck, my special few seconds.

GP-50

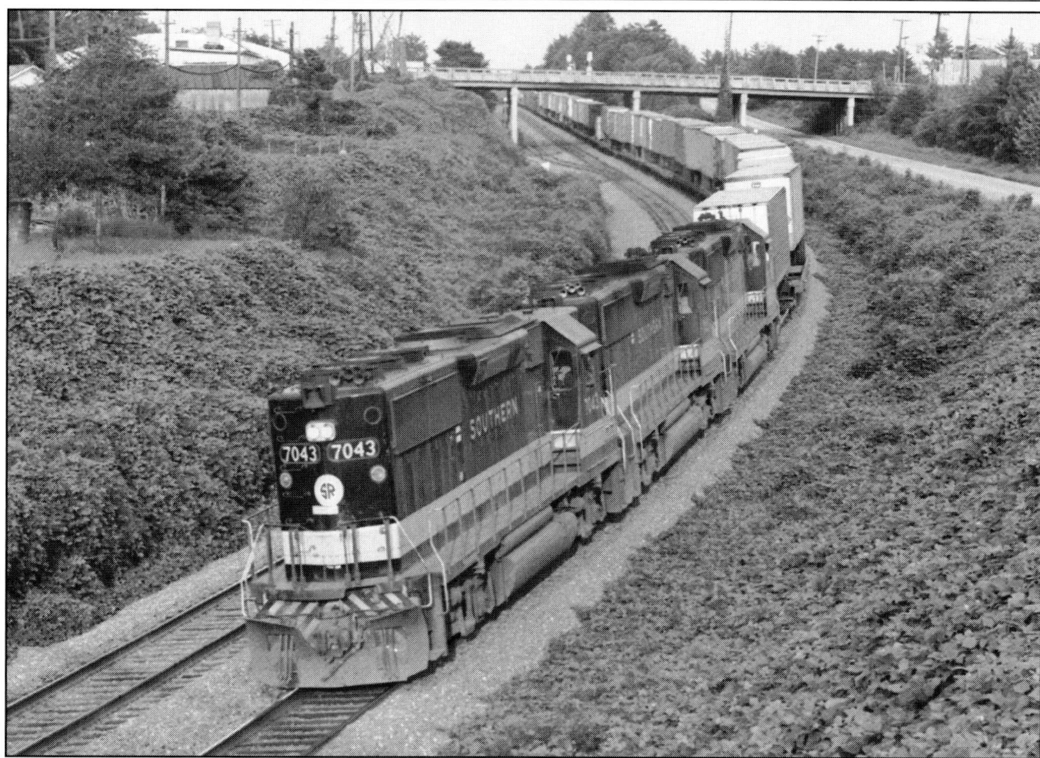

With the rapidly setting sun, I knew that I had an opportunity to photograph one last train before the daylight disappeared and what a photo it turned out to be!

Among the hottest, solid piggyback trains on the Southern (now Norfolk Southern's) Washington-Atlanta mainline was No. 219. This "pig" train had stopped at the Greenville, S. C. station to get a new crew, then it picked up a cut of "pigs" and headed for Atlanta and points south.

With the light fading fast, I went to a location in south Greenville where I knew that I could get an exposure. Within a few minutes, No. 219 started moving. With three GP-50's up front pulling 71 cars this August 31, 1985, at 6:50 p.m., I photographed this streak of piggybacks, now doing 40+ m.p.h., an increasing, as it passed through a "sea of kudzu" – I made it! The photo captured mainline railroading at its best with three '50's doing what they were designed to do, pulling the one commodity for the railroads that was growing with a rapid pace: piggybacks.

By the late 1970's the Southern had decided to use six-axle power on their fast freights and piggybacks. However, when EMD sent them three of their GP-40X's (#7000-#7002), the road was so impressed with their performance, they placed an order for 90 of the GP-50's (#7003-#7092).

The '50's exceeded even what the boys at EMD's plant at LaGrange had promised. No. 219's lead GP-50, #7043J (built in Oct. of 1980), had 3,500 h.p., a high adhesion capability, carried 3,500 gal. of fuel, weighed 255,752 lbs., had 30 cu. ft. of sand, snowplow "cowcatchers," a pair of Nathan five-chime horns; it was 59' 2" long, over 11 ft. wide and 15' 8 1 /4" high.

The GP-50's could make time and yet move a great deal of tonnage. They were quiet, rode as smooth as a "Pullman" and beloved by the crews; for over a decade, they held the top assignments for both the Southern and now the Norfolk Southern. In fact, all units are still moving tonnage with efficiency. Indeed, to this day, I never heard a crewmember say anything bad about the "7000's" – they were and remain that good!

Boy, I'm glad I had just enough light to make this exposure, when the '50's were in their prime, for it not only performed beyond expectations, it looked great as well!

With the arrival of nighttime, I had to use my flashgun to capture on film No. 219, pulling into Greenville, S. C. this July 21, 1982 (8:45 p.m.) with 68 cars. The solid piggyback train will get a new crew here at the station, pickup "hot" piggyback cars and then head towards Atlanta, Ga. Arriving there near midnight.

Tonight's No. 219 had three powerful and popular GP-50's (#7037L, #7043J and #7062J) at the head end. No. 219 was also part of the daily "parade" that passed by this beautiful facility which was not only a passenger station but also housed: the division headquarters, the C.T.C., dispatcher's office, the freight station, yardmaster's office, etc. The term "parade" was used by both the Southern (now Norfolk Southern) employees and railfans alike, to indicate that between 6:00 and 10:30 p.m., at least four southbound and three northbound trains (including the "Crescent") passed this location on the Washington-Atlanta mainline. In fact, several families from Greenville and the surrounding area, came to the station to watch this wonderful train after train after train performance.

GP-50 #7037L (built in Oct. of 1980) was one of 90 ordered by the Southern to haul their priority freights and piggyback trains. With their 3,500 h.p. and excellent adhesion qualities, they truly made the Southern proud. In fact, for almost a decade the GP-50's which are still in operation today – handled all the top assignments for both the Southern and Norfolk Southern and completed them with great efficiency.

Alas, today the station no longer exists. The Norfolk Southern replaced it with a more "modern" facility – without a shed. The passengers getting on and off the "Crescent" better hope the weather is good, for if it was raining, they'll surely get wet – as will the train crews.

Yet, nighttime railroading remains exciting even though now, in Greenville, you have to get yourself under an umbrella – along with your camera and flashgun – in order to try and make an exposure in bad weather.

Progress, on occasion, is not always as good as some say. Still, we have photos, such as this one, to remind us what it was like before the "progress attack!"

"Radio" Trains

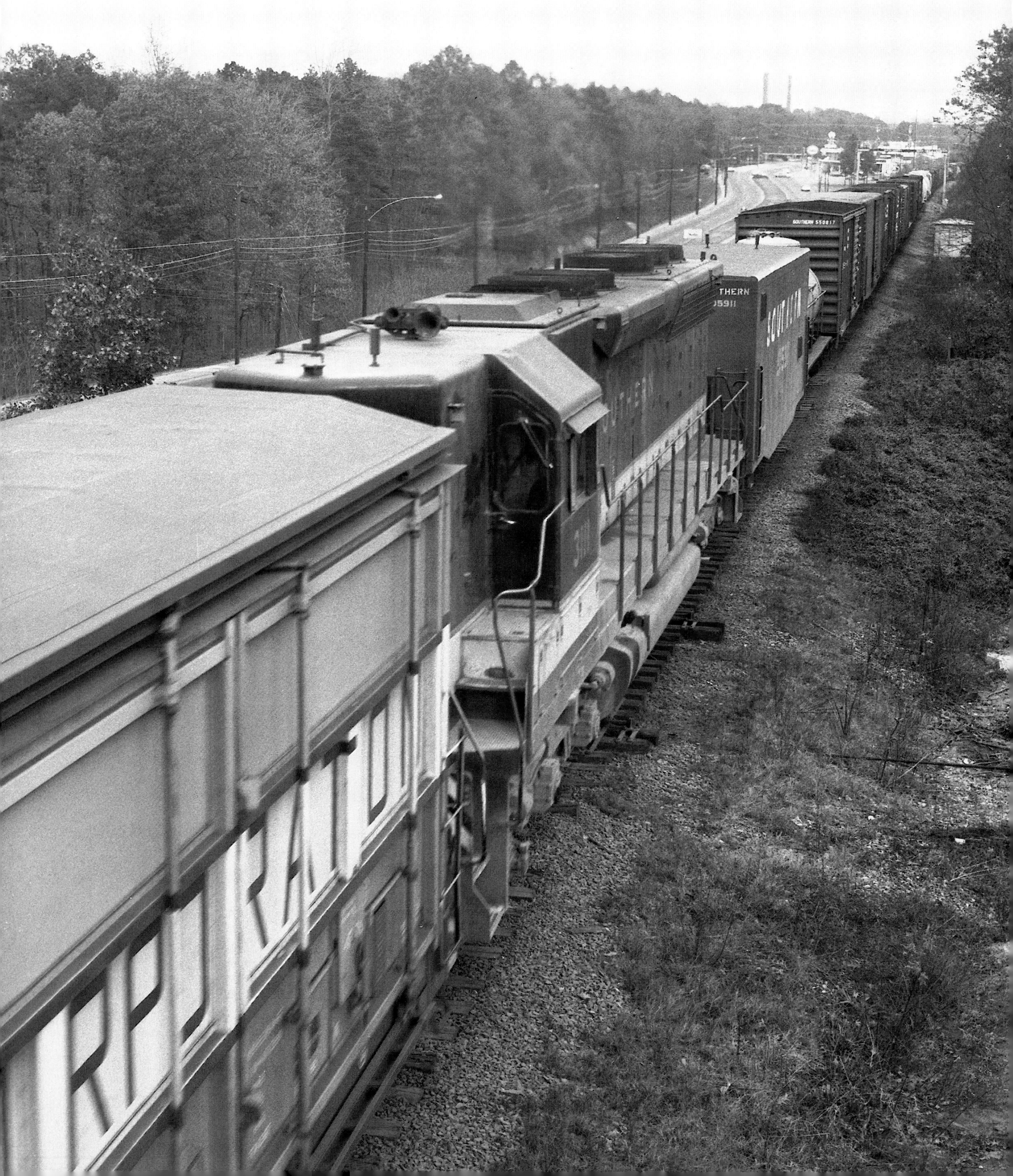

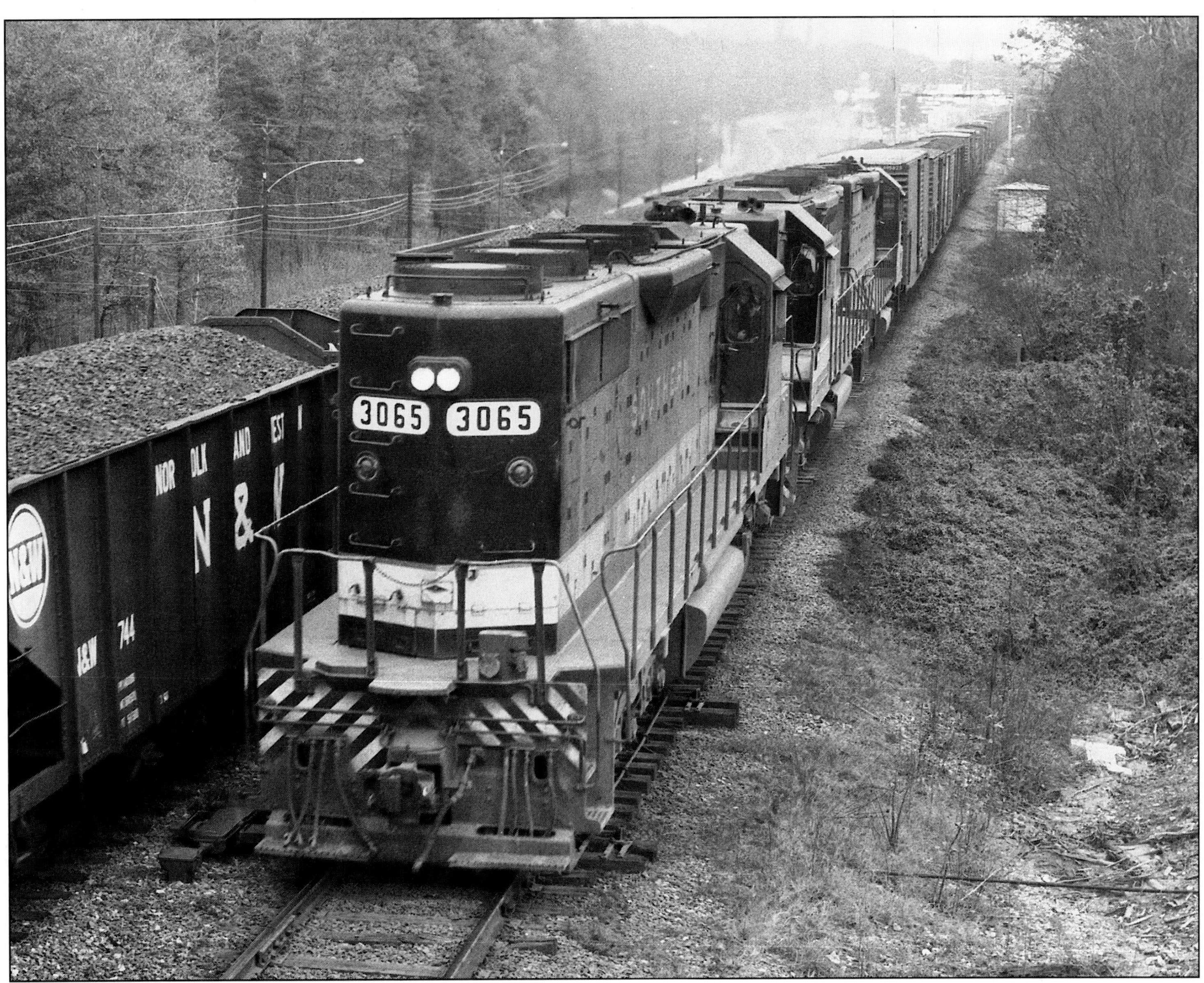

Here in this photo, which was taken on Dec. 5, 1971, at 2:25 p.m. south of Danville, Va. is a portrait of modern railroading at its best in 1971: a "radio train" shown passing a slower moving coal train at a double crossover (the area is called "Bentley") on the mostly double track Washington-Atlanta mainline of the Southern Railway, which was protected by centralized traffic control (C.T.C.) and automatic block signals. In fact, every piece of high tech communication and equipment available was being used to get all trains-both No. 153 (running from Potomac Yard to New Orleans, La.) as well as Extra 4223 South (five "F" units and 78 cars of coal shown on the left, heading for Spencer Yard) to their destinations as fast and safe as possible with as little cost as necessary.

The Southern, which at this time, was rapidly building a reputation as being one of the most innovative and successful railroads in the United States, used C.T.C. to run the faster No. 153 around the coal train, without delaying either train. They used "radio control" technology on its high priority freights (and, eventually, on coal trains as well). For example, the engineer on No. 153, located in the lead engine, could control the movements of another diesel, or diesels, which were placed in the middle of his train an engine without a crew (sometimes called a "slave unit(s)")-by using radio control technology. His movements of the throttle, brakes and other devices were instantly sent by radio signals to a radio signal receiver car, which was coupled to the "slave" engine(s), and the un-manned unit(s) responded to the engineer's actions even though he was a mile away. This procedure made the middle engine(s) both a pusher and puller, thereby reducing the stress placed on the car couplers and keeping the air brake pressure high throughout the entire long and heavy train. The modern equipment reduced delays and increased the safety factor; it also saved the Southern and its customers a great deal of time and money and made it a more dependable and safer road to use.

The engine units equipped with the radio control equipment could be identified in two ways: there were more radio antennas placed on top of its cab and the number boards had a white background with black numbers-just the opposite of those diesels not so equipped.

With every modern device and method of procedure being used, No. 153 will make it to New Orleans without delays. Today's hot shot was powered by: SD-35 (#3065A-equipped with the radio control machine), SD-40 (#3184F) and SD-35 (#3095F) with SD-45 (#3111H) located almost a mile back in the train, running in front of the radio receiver car, helping move the 148 cars without a person on board.

Watching one of these trains pass by with the engines in their normal location and then, suddenly, another engine or engines-without a crew-roaring by, was almost as unusual as having a train pass you with one of more engines not making a sound-something called a "slug."

Railfanning: it's GREAT!

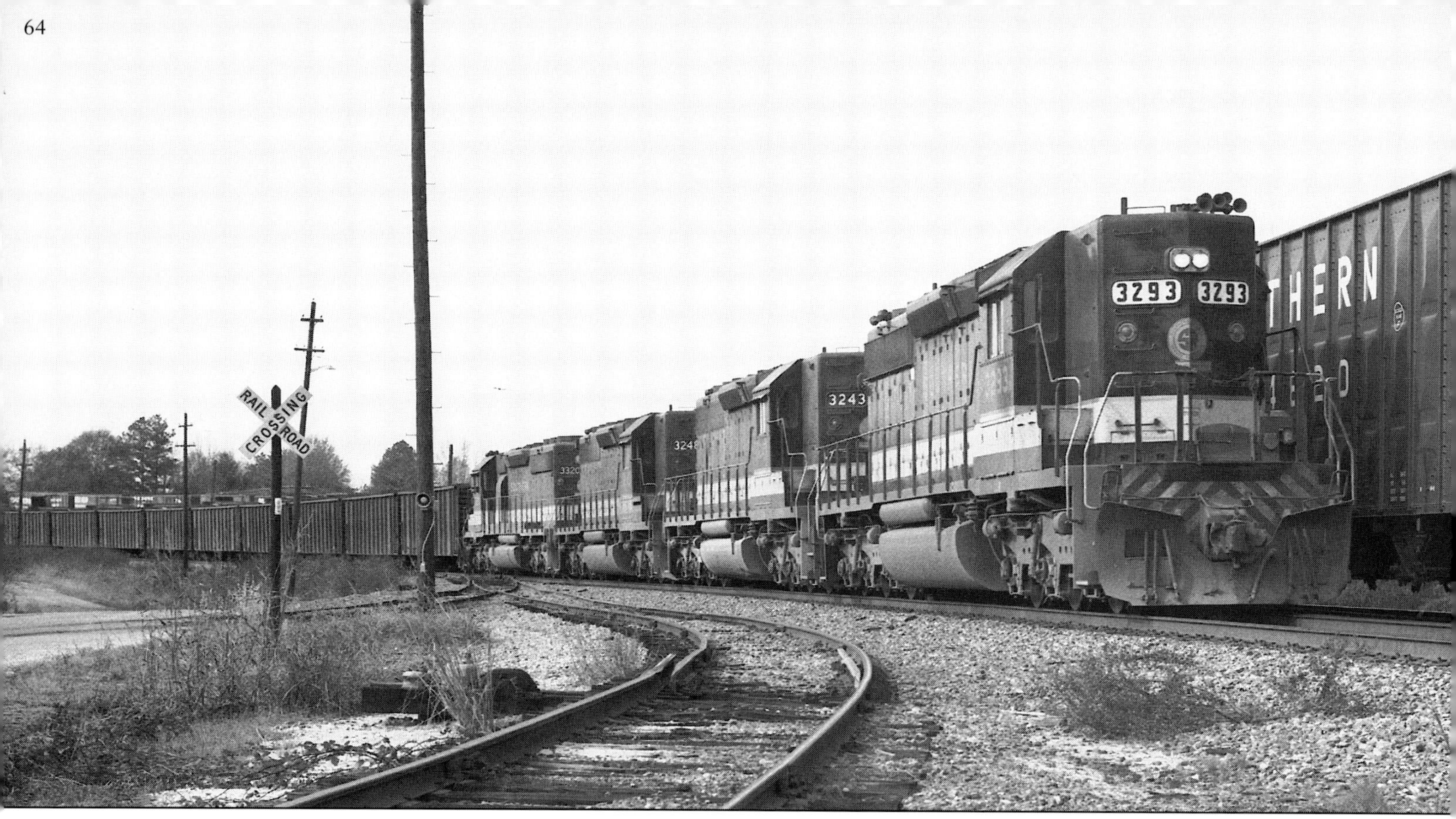
RAIL ROAD
CROSSING
3293 3293
3243

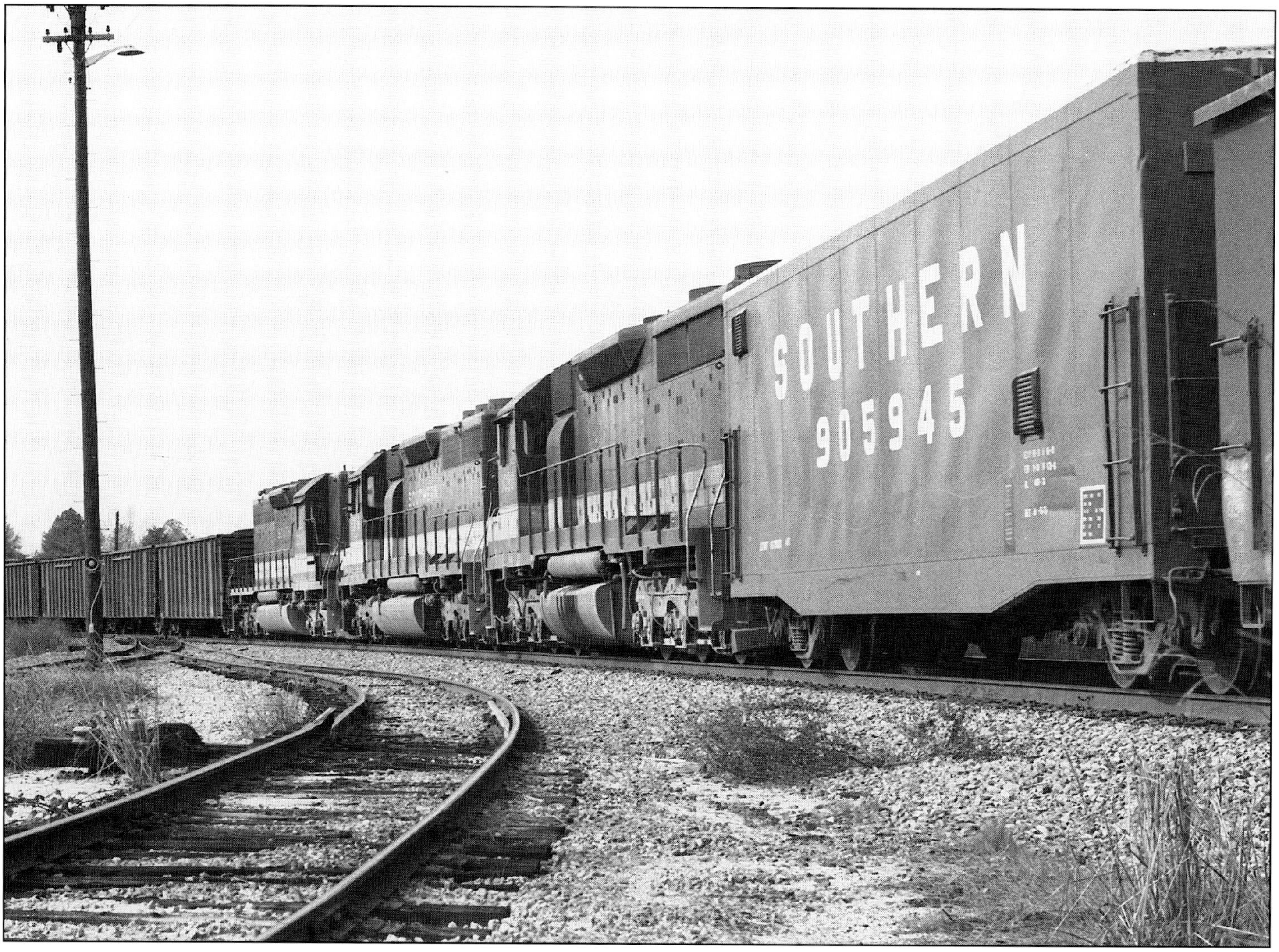
SOUTHERN
905945

When operating a long, heavy train in mountainous territory, you need as much motive power as possible. This surplus of power was required not only to conquer the many grades your train would face but this power, especially the diesel's excellent dynamic braking abilities, was needed to keep a train under control as it descended these obstacles and, thereby, avoiding a disastrous "runaway" event.

There is no better example of this procedure in action than the Southern Railway's 76 mile long line from Spartanburg, S. C. to Asheville, N. C.-a route made famous by the awesome 4.7% Saluda Grade (for every 100 ft., the track rises 4.7 ft., giving a 4.7% grade).

Train No. 172-a solid, radio control coal train (note the number boards on the lead engine which had a white background with black engine numbers-one of the indications that this engine was equipped with radio control devices)-is shown entering Spartanburg's Haynes Yard after a successful trip down Saluda Grade. Up front was four, six axle SD-40-2's (#3293W, #3243J, #3248H and #3320X) and, in the middle of the 110-car train, were three radio control engines: SD-35 (#3090W), SD-40 (#3176L) and SD-40-2 (#3250W) plus radio receiver car #905945. Once a new crew was added and the last two front engines removed at Haynes, No. 172 would enter the Washington-Atlanta mainline this Nov. 22, 1980, at 1:20 p.m. and head north to its destination of Belmont, N. C. (south of Charlotte), the location of a huge, coal powered, electricity generating plant. Actually, the local railroaders and fans called No. 172, the "Belmont Turn."

With the dynamic braking and radio controls, long and very heavy trains like No. 172 could make it down Saluda Grade with ease and when No. 171 goes back to the mines for more coal, it will be able to climb Saluda much better than a non-radio control train. This is another example of high tech railroading in action, not to mention that it created a marvelous sight to behold (and record on film).

The Blast vs. The Air Chime

On June 17, 1953, a heavy Mikado (2-8-2) of the Southern Railway System, No. 6330, pulled into Chattanooga, Tennessee. After a brief ceremony, photos and speeches, the 1926 Alco built Ms-4 went to the engine terminal where its fire was extinguished. Southern's President Harry A. DeButts was heard to say, "It took us 123 years to put out that fire."

This last regularly scheduled steam powered run on the Southern resulted in this progressive road becoming the first major American railroad to completely dieselize. As a result, a great deal of the romance of trains disappeared, along with No. 6330's fire.

The stack talk, the smoke, the flashing rods of driving wheels were all gone. Also missing were the melodious sounds of the steam locomotive whistle.

That blast of a single air horn of the diesel proved too offensive to the ears of the crews as well as the public, especially those individuals living near the tracks, those who grew up listening to that beautiful sounding steam powered whistle on the "iron horses" they were so used to.

President DeButts was well aware of the annoyance produced by the diesel air horn and he did something to rectify this situation. Even he admitted missing the steamboat whistle. The solution of this problem was the development of the Air-Chime whistle.

Robert E. Swanson, Chief Inspector of Railways for the Government of British Columbia (Canada), who had 25 years of experience in designing multi-toned steam whistles, used a wire recording to capture the sounds of a Canadian Pacific Locomotive blowing its whistle. With the help of laboratory instruments, it was discovered that the blend of musical notes and harmonics made the steam locomotive whistle so appealing.

Eventually, this blend was reproduced with a set of six specially shaped horns operated by compressed air. Further research led to the development of a five-tone, a three-tone and even a one-tone horn - all sounding like steam locomotive whistles.

Southern's Charles M. Kimball, Assistant Vice-President (Safety) was most interested in this development. As a result, the Southern invited the Nathan Company (who, by this time had Mr. Swanson on its payroll) to come south to help the Southern eliminate the horrible "blatt" of its diesel horns.

The Nathan and Southern researchers met at the Alexandria, Va. yard to create the most pleasing and yet warning signal for its ""growlers." Lt. Charles Benter, retired director of the United States Navy Band, would also add his expertise on creating a harmonious whistle. The people in the Alexandria area heard the sounds of whistling (some soft, loud, near and far) for three days!

Finally, after 204 tests, a five-tone Air-Chime whistle was developed for road freight and passenger diesels as a result of a combination of five musical notes: "C-sharp," "E-natural," "G-natural," "A-natural," and "C-sharp"—sounds that had a wonderful, far more "carrying" and penetrating effect than the old single horn used on the early diesels.

The new Air-Chime whistle had an immediate and positive reaction from both railroaders and the public. Later, not only Nathan, but also the Leslie Tyfon multi-tone air horn and Westinghouse Pneuphonic (3-bell) horns were also used by the Southern.

Eventually, even the diesel bell was made to sound more like one from a steam locomotive. Indeed, the only steam sound the Southern could not create for their diesel engines was to make them go "choo-choo-choo!"

SD-24

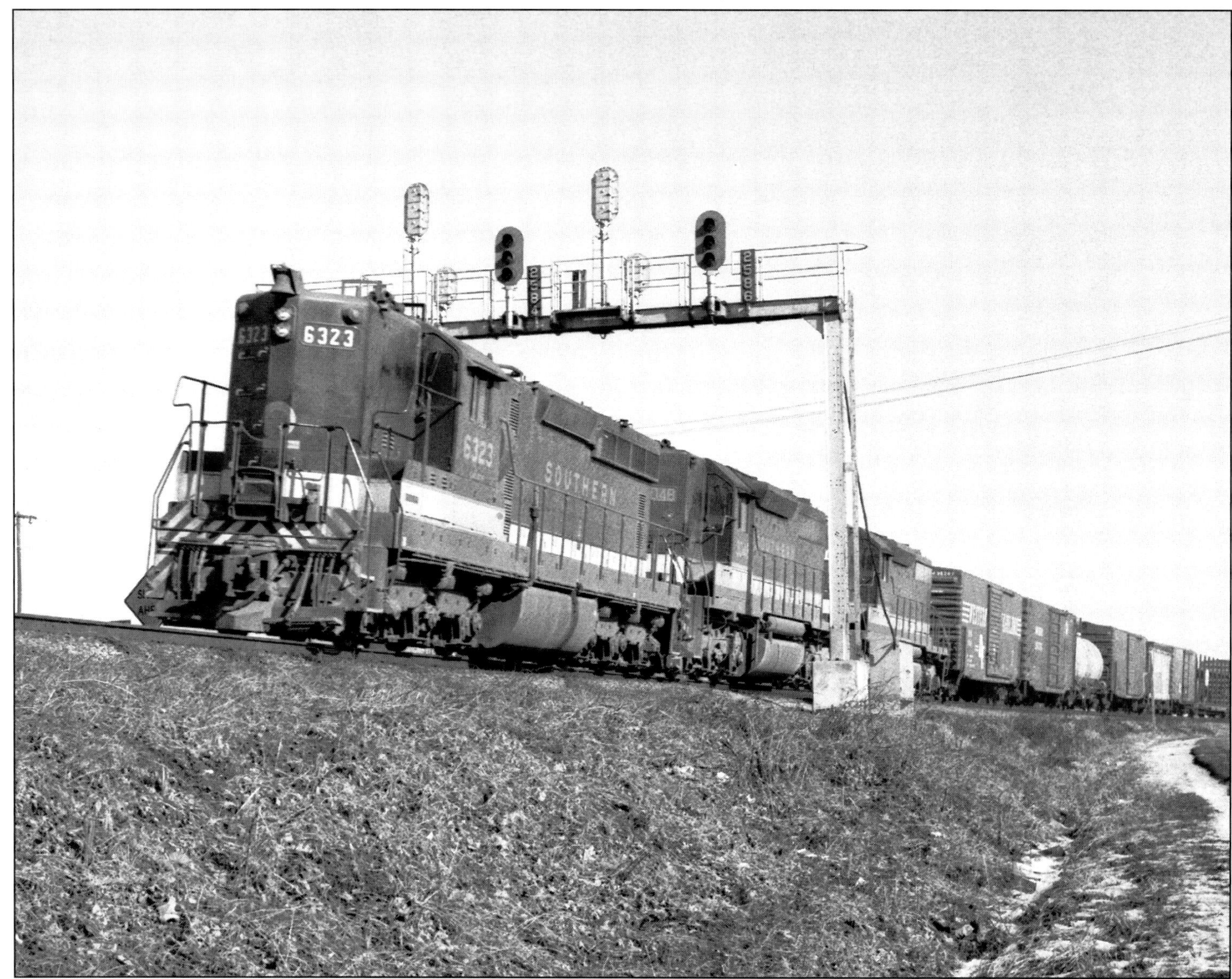

A snow storm passed through the area two days before this photo was taken; evidence of the storm could still be seen on the ground next to the Southern's Washington-Atlanta mainline which was hosting through freight No. 159, shown passing under a signal bridge on its approach to Reidsville, N. C., this cold Feb. 6, 1971 at 10:00 a.m.

Today's No. 159 was powered by SD-24 (#6323) and two SD-35's (#3048 and #3065), pulling 126 cars – all at 40+ m.p.h. The big six-axle SD-24 up front came from EMD in Feb. of 1960. It had an impressive 2,400 h.p., weighed a hefty 375,860 lbs. and carried 3,000 gal. of fuel. To me, #6323 appeared to be an extra large GP-7, with six rather than four axles. It was 60' 8" long, 16' 1" tall and 10'8" wide and the Southern purchased 48 of these first EMD built, successful six-axle, powerful and handsome engines (#6300 through #6347).

The difficulties of moving tonnage on the Southern's CNO&TP (Cincinnati, New Orleans and Texas Pacific) – especially on a segment called the "Rat Hole Division," because of the numerous tunnels, sharp curves and stiff grades in that area. As a result, the road decided to use a six-axle model that EMD said could do the job. The SD-24's were able to eliminate most all of the problems on the old "Rat Hole."

The Southern discovered that the "mountain maulers" could also make good time with heavy tonnage on their other mainlines as well, so the '24's handled most of the road's priority freights until the arrival of the SD-35's in 1965.

No. 6323 and most of its fellow SD-24's were retired in 1978 with Precision National (a locomotive leasing company) buying most of them. The Southern purchased 48 of the new SD-40-2's to fill the motive power void left by the retirement of the huge, powerful, successful and handsome engines.

You could tell that #6323 had served some time on the CNO&TP by looking at the icicle breaker in front of its air chimes, put there to protect the horns from the icicles hanging down from the tunnels.

I always had a grudging respect for the SD-24's and felt very fortunate in catching them on the front of several mainline freights prowling the rails of the Southern. With the bell on top, the ice breaker in front of the horns and that impressive Southern symbol, the SD-24's looked - and sounded - like a great deal of power placed inside a car-body that gave it the appearance of a handsome working locomotive.

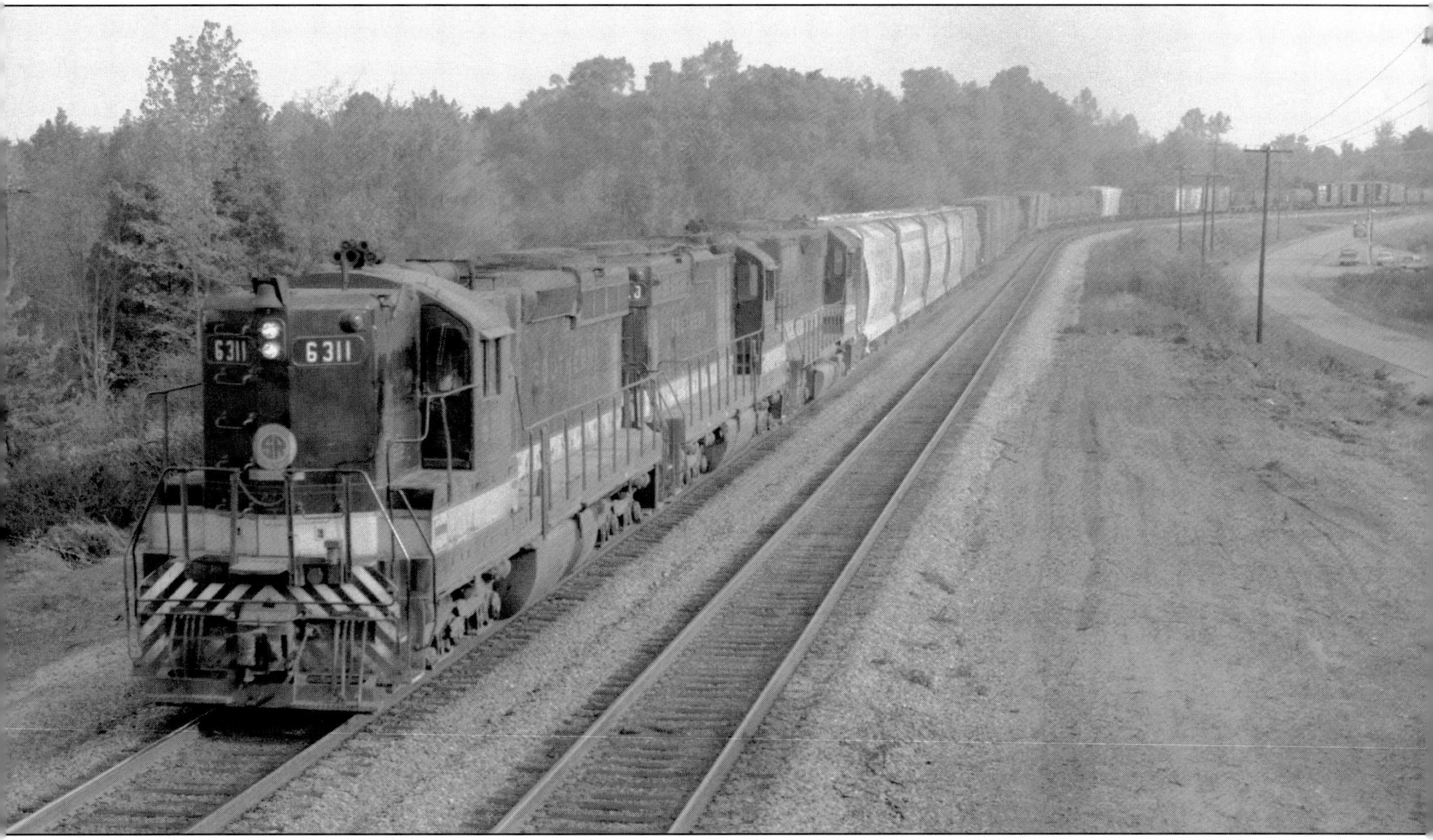

I was hanging onto the side of the signal bridge at Swann, N. C. as 1st No. 159 approaches me at a good 50 m.p.h. with two huge SD-24's (#6311L and #6328X) and an equally powerful SD-35 (#3028W), pulling 145 cars on the Southern's hot mainline between Washington and Atlanta.

Even high off the ground, I could still feel the ground trembling as a result of the fast passage of over a million pounds of locomotives heading south by yours truly and his camera. Fortunately, with all this action going on, I remembered to release my camera's shutter at the right time this Oct. 26, 1974 at 9:05 a.m. What a wonderful way to start a railfan's day!

No. 159 ran in three sections this particular day, but only the first one had SD-24's, which were slowly being replaced by the more powerful SD-35's. In fact, within four years (1978), No. 6311 and #6328 would be retired.

The SD-24's were very successful and the right diesels at the right time for the Southern. With 2,400 h.p., weighing 378,810 lbs. and carrying 3,000 gal. of fuel, they could produce an impressive 93,700 lbs. of tractive effort – just what the road needed.

At Swann, the mainline dropped down to one track for approximately 10 miles, but it went back to double at Sadler, N. C. (just north of Reidsville, N. C.). Even with C.T.C. and microwave communications, the mainline remains most double tracked to this very day (under Norfolk Southern).

This was an excellent location for rail photography: a super clean, double track main, little traffic on old U.S. 29 (on the right) and it was just me and 1st No. 159 enjoying a morning together – one we all can enjoy over and over again with this photo to show fans just what it was like.

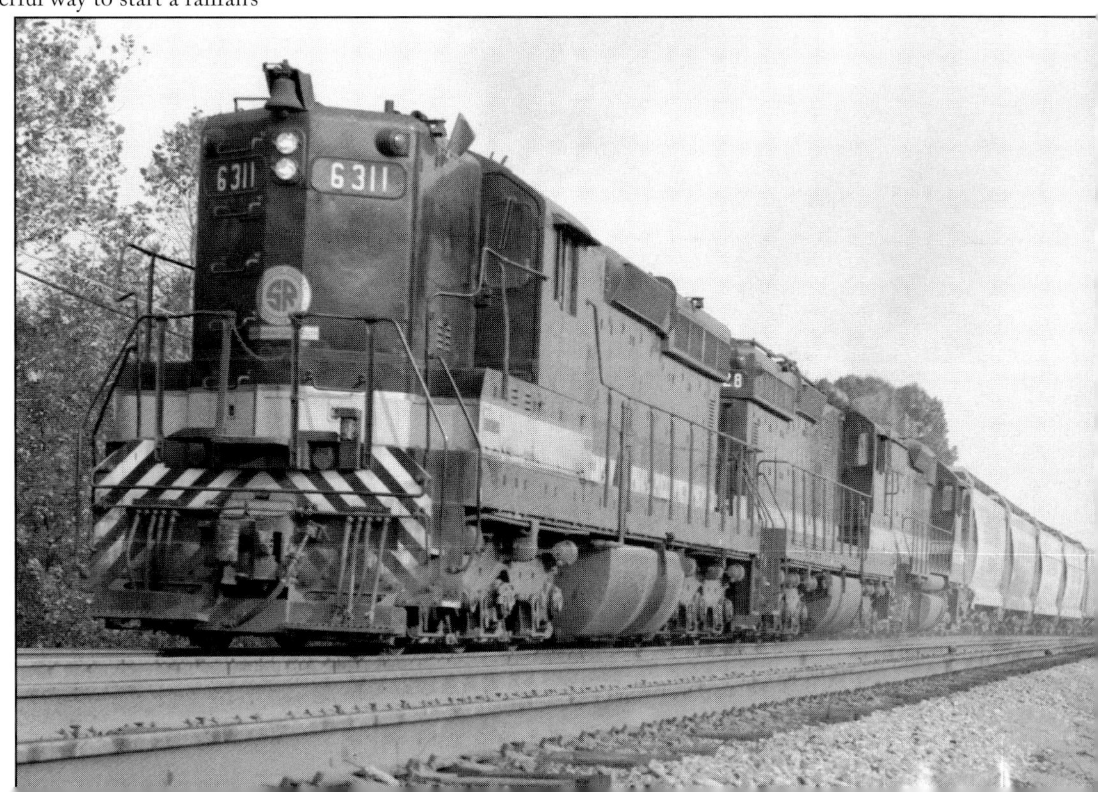

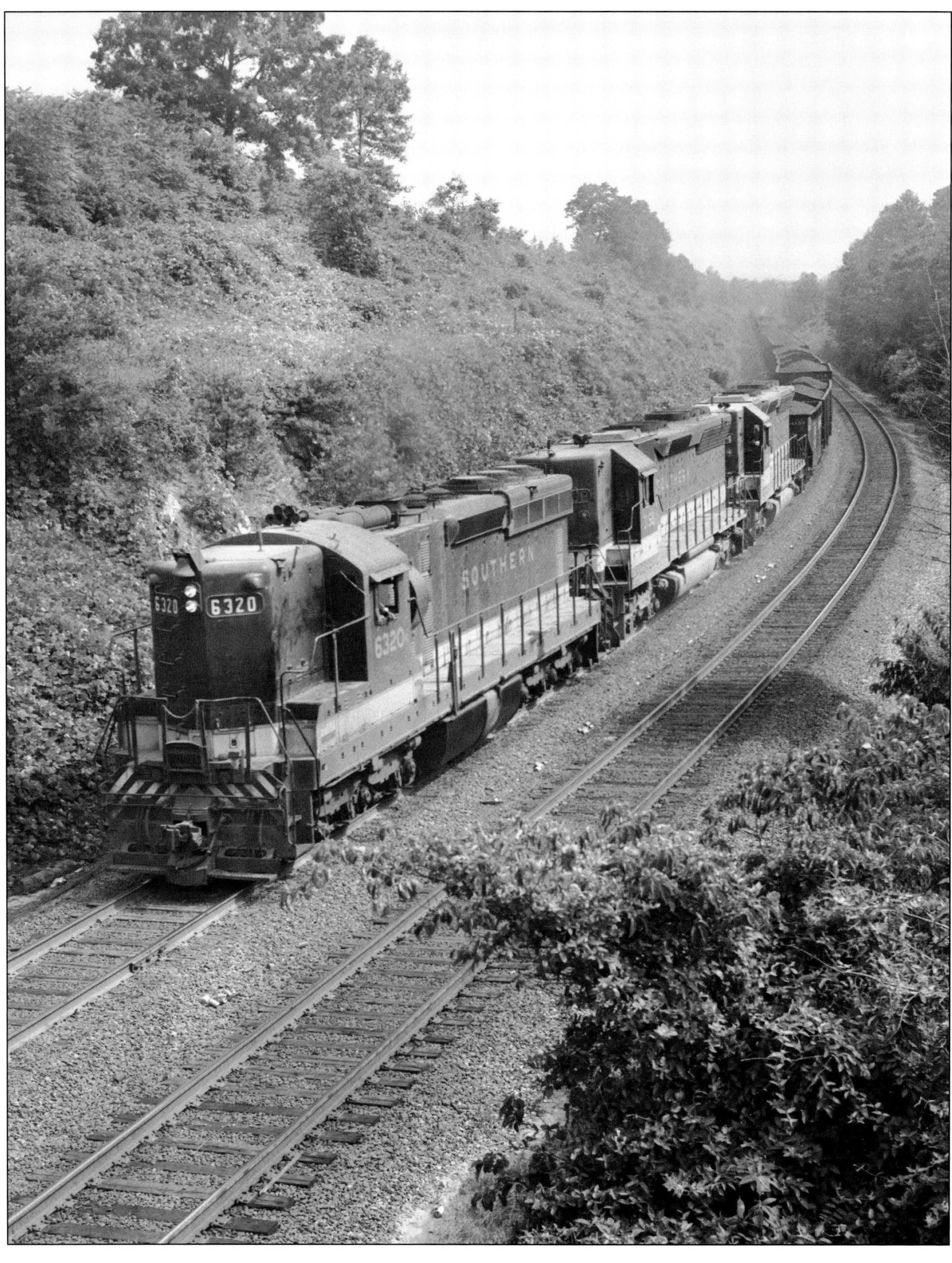
6320
6320
SOUTHERN
6320

Talk about power! An SD-24 (#6320R –2,400 h.p.) and two SD-45's (#3158J and #3164F – each having 3,600 h.p.) are really "talking it up" as they work upgrade at Motley, Va. after getting 85 cars of coal from the N&W connection in the Altavista-Hurt, Va. area, heading south on the Southern's Washington-Atlanta mainline as 1st No. 159, this July 15, 1972 at 10:30 a.m.

These three six-axles went north from Spencer, N. C. Yard to Altavista as a "caboose hop", i.e. three diesels and a caboose, in order to pick up this long cut of coal left for the Southern by the N&W. Knowing the amount of tonnage waiting for them in Altavista and the curves and grades the train would face heading south, the motive power dept. picked these three "big boys" to do the job.

This highway bridge I'm standing on at Motley was an ideal location to photograph heavy tonnage trains, like 1st No. 159, working upgrade. This photo should be evidence enough to support my opinion. I must admit, however, I was not sure what power was on the point as I heard the train approaching. Within a minute or so, while looking in my camera's viewfinder, I knew this was my lucky day, for up front was a handsome SD-24 working "all out" with two "brutes" – the most powerful diesels on the Southern: the mighty, 20 cylinder SD-45's. The #6320R had been working for the road since Feb. of 1960 and would continue doing so until 1978 when all 48 of the '24's were replaced by the then new SD-40-2's.

I got a great photo of this memorable event but I wish I had a tape recorder as well. Even though the old saying, "one picture is worth a thousand words" is true, if you add the sounds of this event, it would create a situation worthy of an "Academy Award" for dramatic railroading in action. Even though fairly quiet engines, all three SD's were "roaring" as 9,600 h.p. was at work – about 15-20 m.p.h. on a superb piece of double track. As a point of interest, 1st No. 159 would be up to 45+ m.p.h. within five miles!

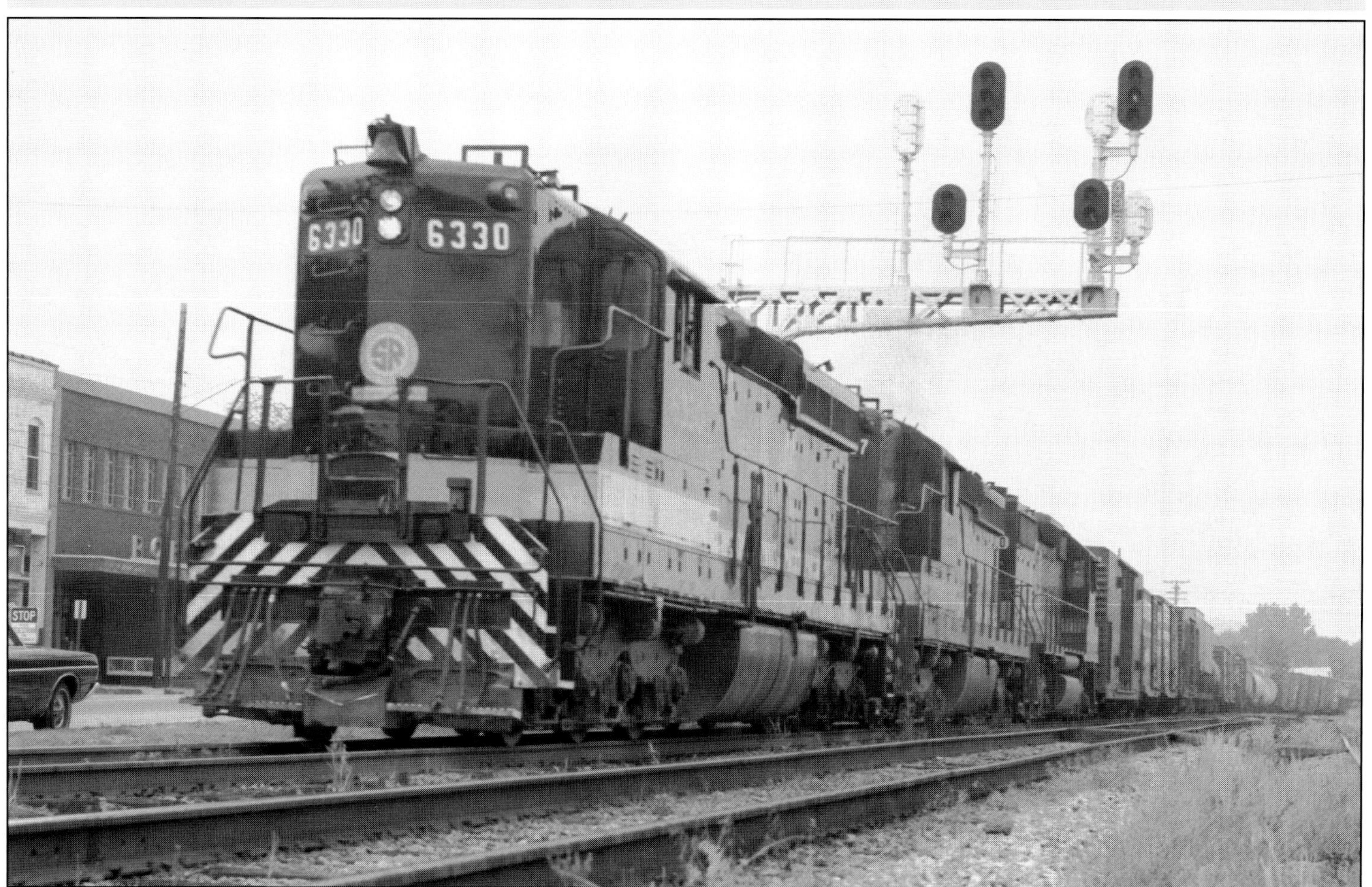

With the rain falling and the inside of my umbrella propped on top of my head, I photographed No. 168 passing through Easley, S. C., pulled by two SD-24's (#6330L and #6337A) and a big SD-35 (#3050H) – with 132 cars this June 19, 1973 at 12:01 p.m.

Easley was another one of those wonderful towns, which was split in half by the Southern's busy Washington-Atlanta mainline. The cantilevered signals shown here were what I called: "friendly train indicators." Their normal signal color was yellow, so, if one went red in color, you knew a train was approaching the area from behind it; if a light went green in color, it indicated that a train was coming towards it. If one went red and the other went green – all at the same time – I went looking for a bridge, so that if both trains appeared at the same time, I had a chance to photograph both of them. However, if I was at ground level, one could block off the other from my camera.

Within approximately 11 miles, No. 168 will be in Greenville, S. C. where this Atlanta crew will be replaced by the Spencer, N. C. crew, so this particular group of railroaders were preparing to finish their assignment for the day.

At least, #6330L got a wash job – thanks to "Mother Nature." The 2,400 h.p., Oct. of 1959 built, six-axle engine carried 3,000 gal. of fuel, weighed 378,690 lbs. and produced 93,700 lbs. of tractive effort. It was part of 48 units (#6300-#6347) owned by the Southern; all were retired in 1978 – many were sold to Precision National (a locomotive leasing company). They will be remembered for their dependability; power and good looks.

Even though the rain caused me problems, they were soon forgotten because, with the help of my "trusty" umbrella, I caught a huge "clean" SD-24 on the front of a northbounder passing through Easley. It was a good day!

SD-35

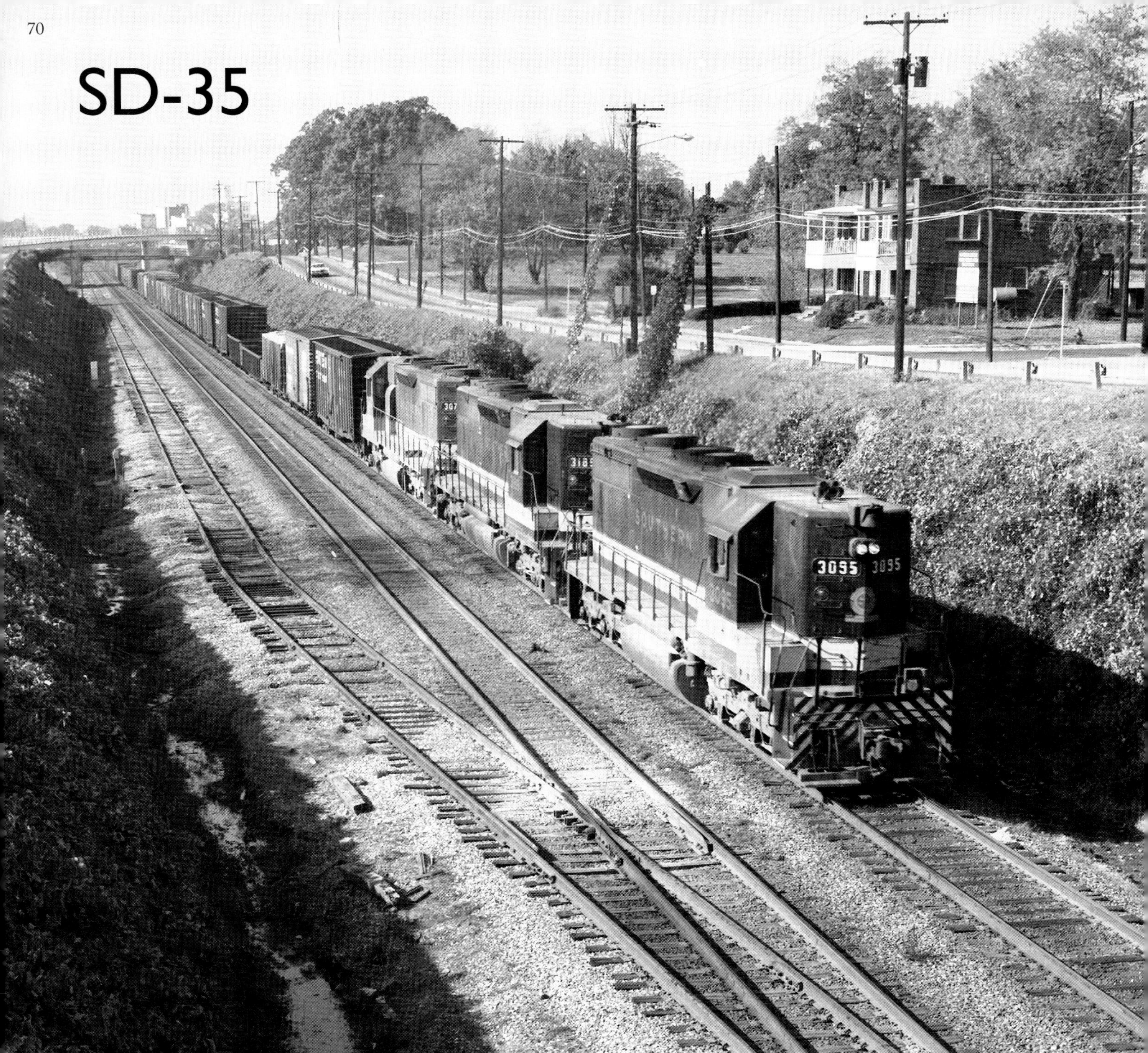

Passing through High Point, N. C. – the "Furniture Capital of the World" – No. 158 is fresh out of Spencer, N. C. Yard and on its way to Potomac Yard. Its first stop will be Greensboro, N. C.'s Pomona Yard (just 11 miles to the north). No. 158, pulled by SD-35 (#3095T), SD-40 (#3189W) and SD-35 (#3077L) – with 154 cars – was approaching Hoskins (a rail location) where the mainline goes to single track for nearly 8 miles before returning to double track once more.

No. 158 was a favorite train for the yardmasters between Spencer and "Pot Yard," for its stopped at most of their yards, getting and leaving cars. They especially enjoyed the arrival of the northbounder, for it helped make room for more cars from other mainliners in their yards. So, No. 158 did not break any speed records. Instead, it was a "cleanup" movement and its crew will really earn their wages this day (Nov. 2, 1974 at 10:30 a.m.)

A train such as No. 158 needed ample motive power to not only move their tonnage rapidly on the mainline to avoid delaying other, priority freights but to pull and push long cuts of cars into and out of the several yards it will work. So, No. 158's 8,000 h.p. will help get its miles freight to its destination.

Engine #3095, built by EMD in Dec. of 1965, carried 3,000 gal. of fuel, operated with 16 cylinders (which required two 48" and one 36" radiator cooling fans). It was 60'8" long and had 2,500 h.p. – the same as its smaller, four-axle cousin – GP-35. It weighed 372,365 lbs. and did so well the Southern eventually had 110 of them in service. No. 3095 was finally retired by the Norfolk Southern in March of 1986, after serving 21 years – EMD built them to last!

The pedestrian bridge which I was standing on was an excellent location to photograph both north and southbound rail action. Unfortunately, today the bridge is fenced in on both sides and it is almost impossible to get shots of the many trains that pass through. Our society has changed so much that today we now have to protect the trains from the public!

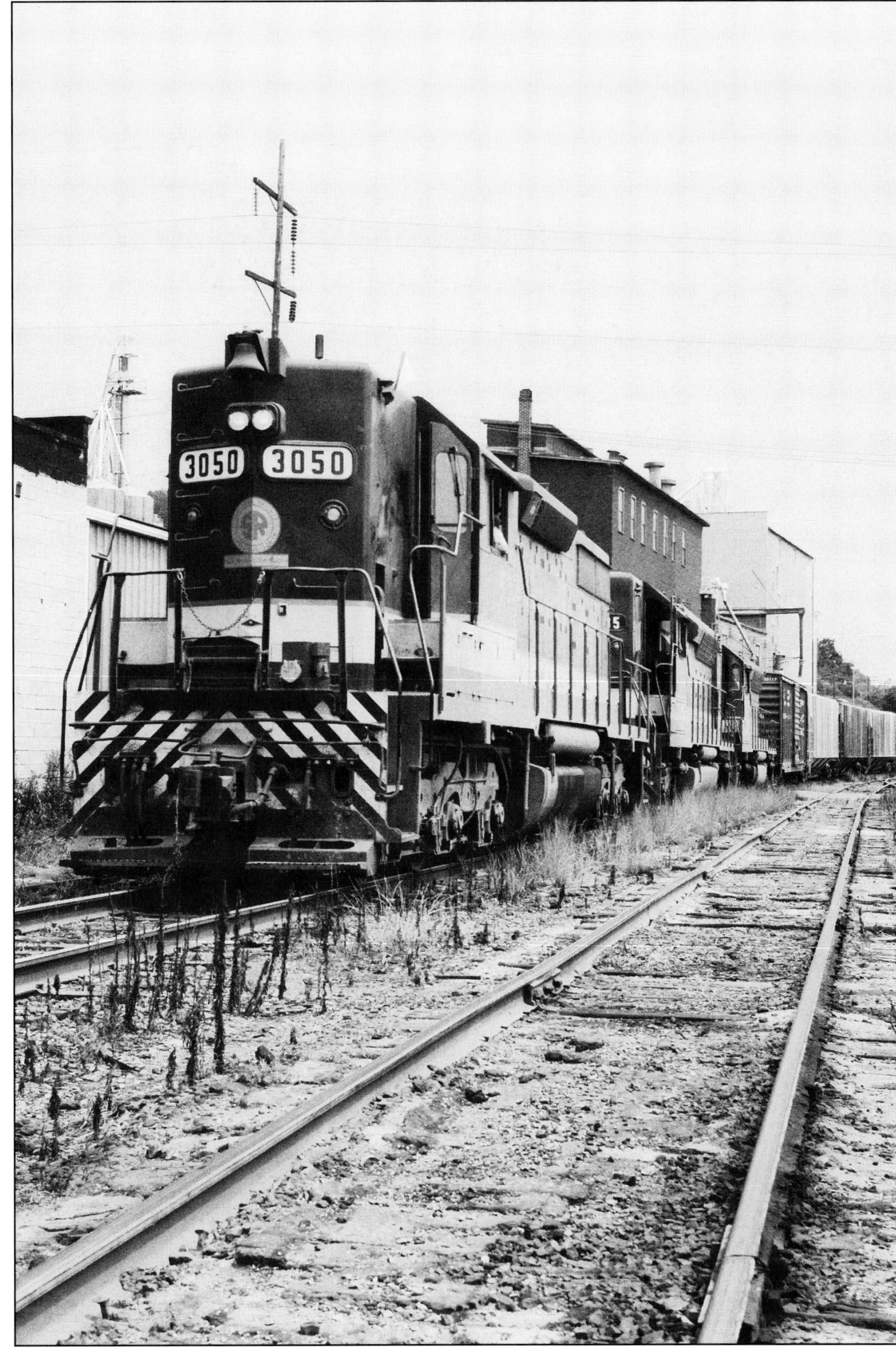

For years, the Southern had relied on four-axle diesels to move their trains. However, as the horsepower increased with the arrival of new models, such as their GP-30's (2,250 h.p.) and GP-35's (2,500 h.p.), a problem developed. It was discovered that their powerful GP-30's and '35's developed slippage difficulties when working at full throttle. As a result, the units could not take full advantage of the power they had.

Remembering the success of their six-axle SD-24's which had very little slippage and used all of their 2,400 h.p. in both the hill country and made good time working the mainline as well; because of these factors, the Southern ordered SD-35's from EMD in 1965, containing the basic specifications of their GP-35's. Almost immediately, the road noticed a great improvement in the pulling power and almost no slippage of their SD-35's even though the '35's had the same horsepower (2,500) as the GP-35's.

The Southern was so impressed with the SD-35's performance, they eventually owned 110 units in their motive power fleet (#215 and #216 – former C of G engines whose numbers were not changed - #2992 through #3099). They held 3,000 gal. of fuel and 40 cu. ft. of sand; the '35's were 60'8" long, stood 15'8" tall and were 10'4" wide. The Southern even put Locotrol apparatus into 39 SD-35's (#3000-#3012, #3050 through #3075) and ran them in "radio-control" train service for many years.

Shown here is one of the SD-35's equipped with Locotrol (white background on their number boards with black colored numbers). No. 163, running as Extra 3050 West, is pictured ready to depart Asheville, N. C. for Knoxville, Tenn. via Morristown, Tenn. The through freight, pulled by SD-35 (#3050H) and two SD-45's (#3135F and #3136X) with 113 cars, was ready to leave the "Land of the Sky;" however, the dispatcher decided to hold No. 163 until an eastbound extra from Knoxville arrived in Asheville Yard. The extra east (using the tracks I'm standing on) arrived within ten minutes after I made my exposure this July 23, 1976 at 3:08 p.m. Then, with ease (and no slippage), No. 163 left town, crossed over the French Broad River and headed west into the mountains.

No. 3050 was built in Nov. of 1965 and continued in service until March of 1985, when the Norfolk Southern retired a large part of the SD-35 fleet. It weighed 377,050 lbs. and the Southern actually designated the short end of the SD-35 as the forward position. However, they were operated bi-directionally.

This photo was the first one I ever made on the Southern's old Tennessee Division. What an introduction: two through freights within 20 minutes. Not bad!

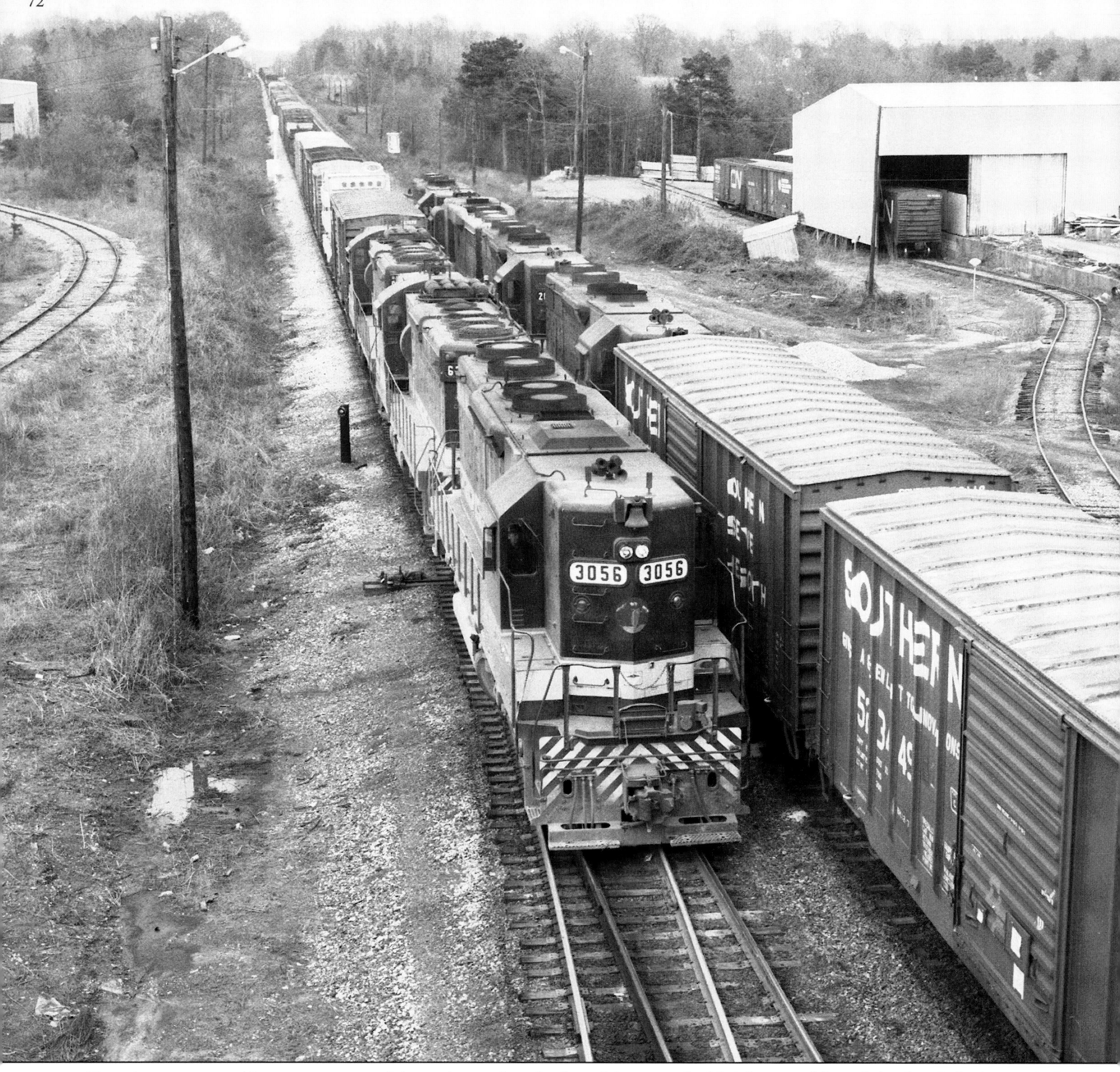

One in, one out – this was a common sight at the north end of Spencer (N.C.) Yard. On this partly cloudy day – March 30, 1975, at 4:45 p.m. – I had just photographed 1st No. 142 (on the right) heading north towards Potomac Yard with four GP's and 110 cars. After I took the photo, I looked back to the north to watch the northbounder picking up speed when I saw 3rd No. 159 approaching the yard. Fortunately, I had one last unexposed frame on the roll of film. As a result, I got lucky: one in and one out!

The 3rd section of No. 159 pulled by SD-35 (#3056X – one of the 39 '35's equipped with Locotrol equipment which would enable it to operate "radio-control" trains) and two SD-24's (#6323A and #6300W) with 87 cars.

Even though this was a common occurrence, the south end of Spencer Yard was the place to be, for not only did you have trains to and from Atlanta, you had freights to and from Columbia, S. C. plus you had tonnage from the Asheville line entering and leaving the yard. Normally, on a visit to Spencer, N. C. – from 9:30 a.m. until 5:00 p.m., I would average seeing and photographing 20 or more trains. Indeed, I always looked forward to my trips to the Spencer – Salisbury area even though it required a 2 hour drive from home, down Interstate 85 which was always loaded with drivers who should not have been allowed on this dangerous road.

Weighing 376,290 lbs., carrying 3,000 gal. of fuel and, with its 16 cylinders, producing 2,500 h.p., No. 3056's life span ranged from Nov. of 1965 through March of 1985. The Southern got its money's worth from the 110 SD-35's it once owned.

Photographing such a scene was thrilling and it will remain with you as long as you retain the ability to remember. Again, I got lucky!

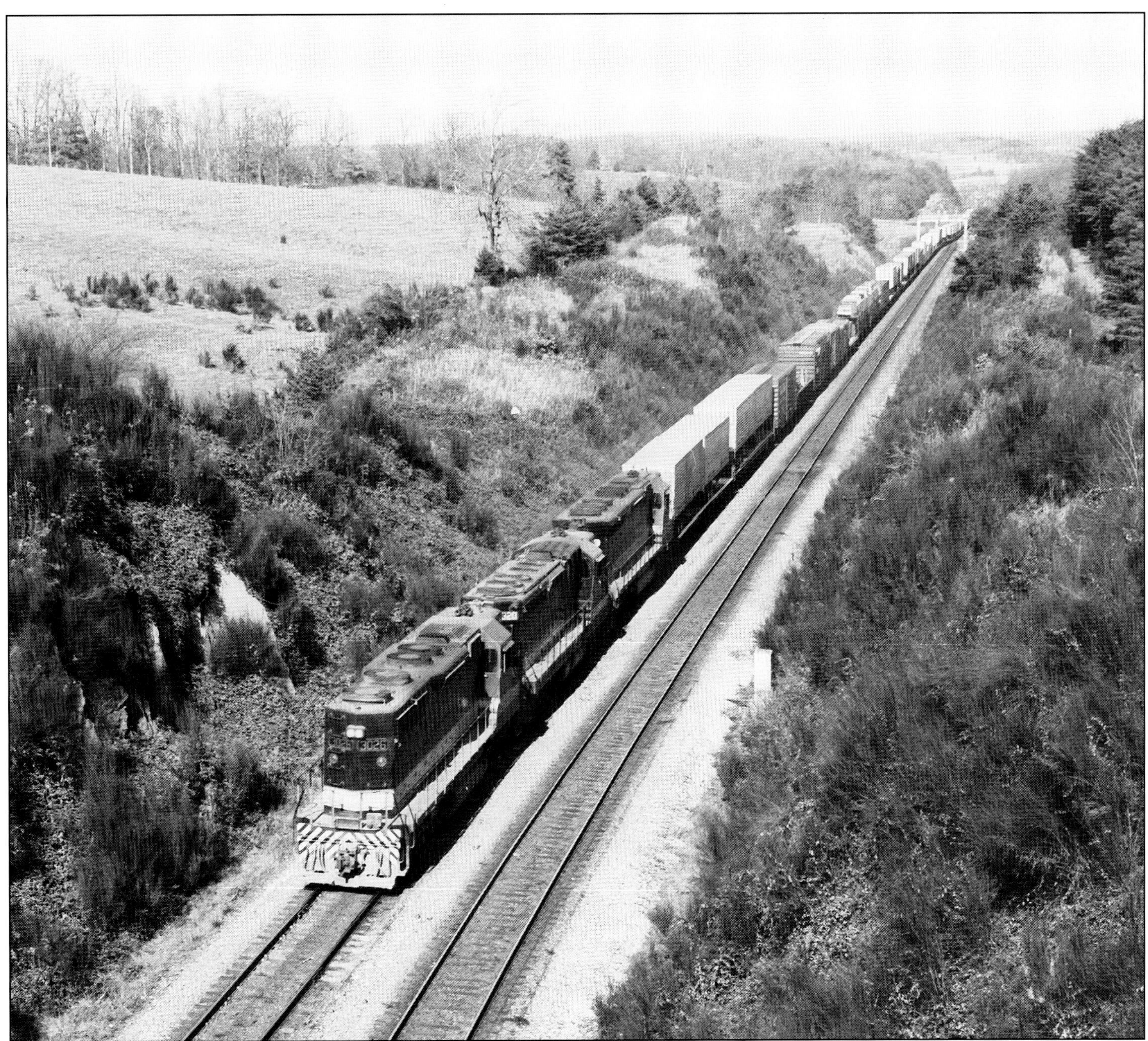

Just north of Altavista, Va. are a series of large and tall hills. In order to keep their Washington-Atlanta mainline as grade free as possible, the Southern made a deep cut through these obstructions. These cuts not only enabled their line to remain level, it also gave a railfan photographer a great location to record rail action in a most scenic area – but only in late fall and the winter seasons. During the spring and summer months, there is simply too much undergrowth and snakes!

This vantage point enabled me to catch Southern's hottest southbound piggyback entering a segment of double track just south of Deal (a rail location). Today's No. 19 had SD-35 (#3026), SD-24 (#6320) and a huge SD-45 (#3127) as its motive power, pulling 62 "pigs" at a good 55+ m.p.h. (Nov. 19, 1969, at 12:32 p.m.). Deal was located 5 miles north of Altavista and hosted 25-30 trains per day.

The power combination for No. 19 represented the three most successful early six-axle diesels on the Southern, the SD-24's showing that even a six-axle unit could make good time in the mountains, as well as on the mainlines in flatter areas; the SD-35's demonstrated that it could eliminate the slippage problem faced by its four-axle relative, the GP-35, and take full advantage of its 2,500 h.p., while the massive SD-45 was the powerful giant of a locomotive the Southern wanted to really move the tonnage and free up extra units that could be used on other trains.

The SD-35 heading No. 19 today (#3026) came from EMD in Nov. of 1965 and worked for 21 years, moving several million pounds of tonnage until retired by the Norfolk Southern in March of 1986. Of the three six-axles, the SD-35 was the only model whose short end was designated as the forward position by the Southern; however, it was operated bi-directionally although, like all SD-s, the crew preferred the short-end-forward position so they would have a better view of the tracks ahead.

It took me a good 20 minutes to reach this position but the time spent in climbing was worth it, for not only did I get a shot of No. 19, approximately 15 minutes behind No. 19 was No. 153 as this hot freight was passing by, northbound No. 158 was slowly moving forward on No. 1 track, hoping the dispatcher would allow it to enter single track at Deal without stopping (No. 158 did not have to stop). So, my visit to the "hill" was worth the effort. I hope you will agree with me.

SD-40

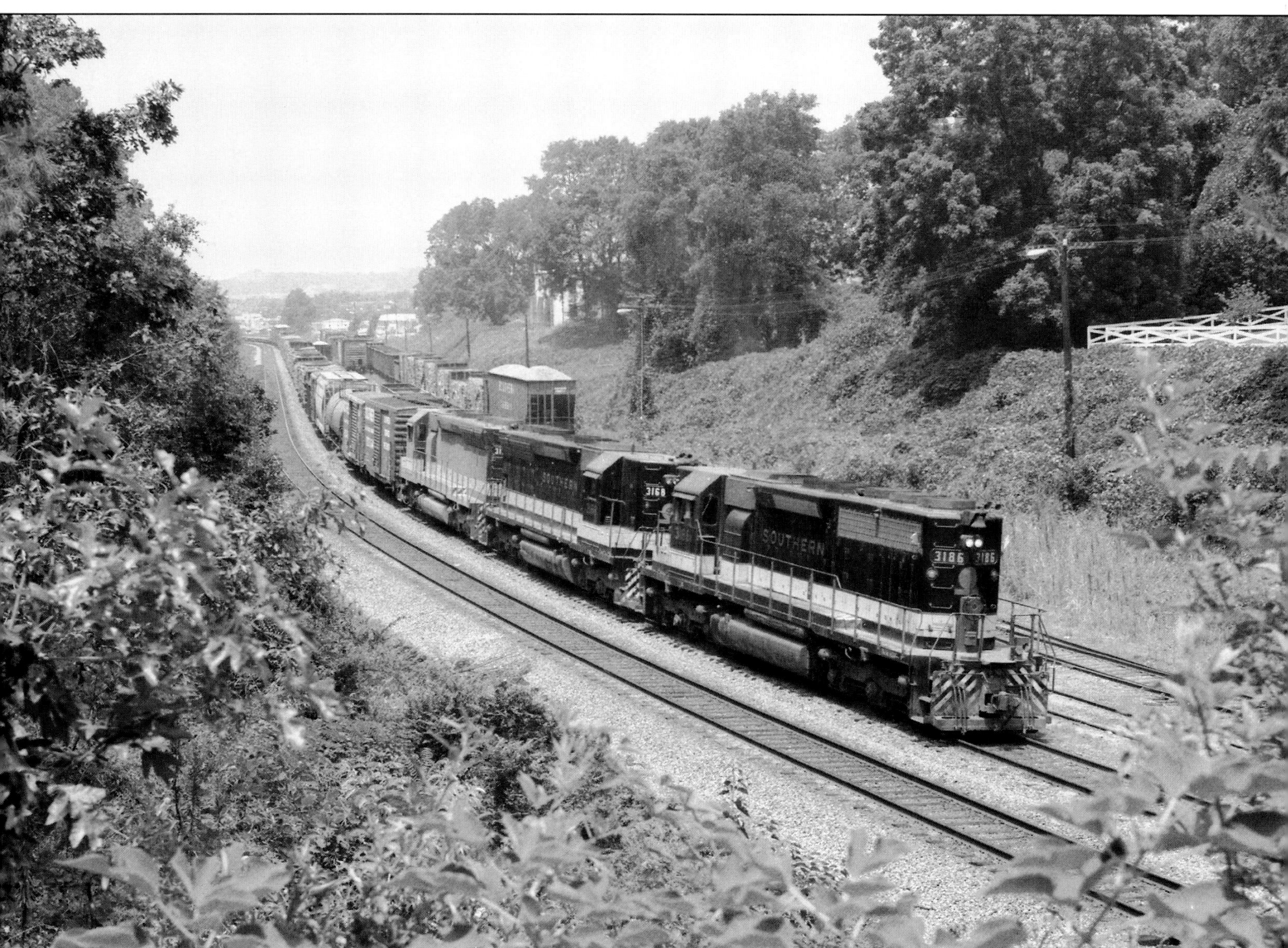

Talk about a scenic location to record rail action!

Once or twice a year Mom, Dad and I would visit relatives at both Greer, S. C. (my dad's hometown) and Seneca, S. C. To reach our family member in Seance required crossing a bridge which passed over the Southern's Washington-Atlanta mainline, part of Seneca yard and the branch line from Belton-to-Seneca-to-Walhalla, S.C. In the early 1960's, I happened to cross this bridge just minutes before Southern's No. 38, the "Crescent" was due, so I parked nearby and within minutes, a long line of stainless steel cars pulled by two super clean E-8A's, rounded the gentle curve and passed by my camera. My resulting photo turned out to be among the best I made of this luxurious train with the historic name.

Every year after this "encounter," I always recalled this beautiful location which, to me, was an ideal spot for rail photography. With this in mind, on July 22, 1976, at 1:15 p.m., I passed over this same bridge shortly after noticing a nearby signal go "green," indicating a northbounder was on the way. Stopping the family car (under a shade tree-it was 98° F), I walked onto the bridge just in time to see Extra 3186 North approaching, pulling 136 cars with a big SD-40 (#3186K) and two even larger SD-45's (#3168H and #3128K). Yep, I made another (at least in my opinion) portrait of modern railroading in action.

It was ironic to find this extra north with this power combination, for the Southern's SD-40's (and the improved SD-40-2's) would eventually replace the powerful SD-45's. Even though the 3,600 h.p., 20 cylinders SD-45's could pull any and all the tonnage a yardmaster tied onto it, the '45's used a little more fuel and required more maintenance than the Southern desired. As a result, they ordered a batch of SD-40's from EMD. These SD-40's were actually built on the SD-45's frames, but had only 3,000 h.p., 16 cylinders; however, they were more fuel-efficient and required far less maintenance than the massive SD-45's.

Between 1971 and '72, the Southern purchased 31 of the SD-40's (#3170-#3200). No. 3186X, on the point of the extra north, was built in Dec. of 1971, held 4,000 gal. of fuel, 72 cu. ft. of sand, weighed 375,360 lbs.; it was 65'8" long, 15'8" high and 11' wide. It proved to be one of the most versatile "SD's" ever built, not only on the Southern but most other roads as well – the "GP" of the six-axle family. No. 3186 remains in service today, but for the Norfolk Southern, and its short end is now considered the forward position for running (thank goodness).

This location will always remain one of my favorite spots for taking rail photos for not only northbounders but southbound trains as well, since the attractive Seneca Station can be seen on the northside of the bridge.

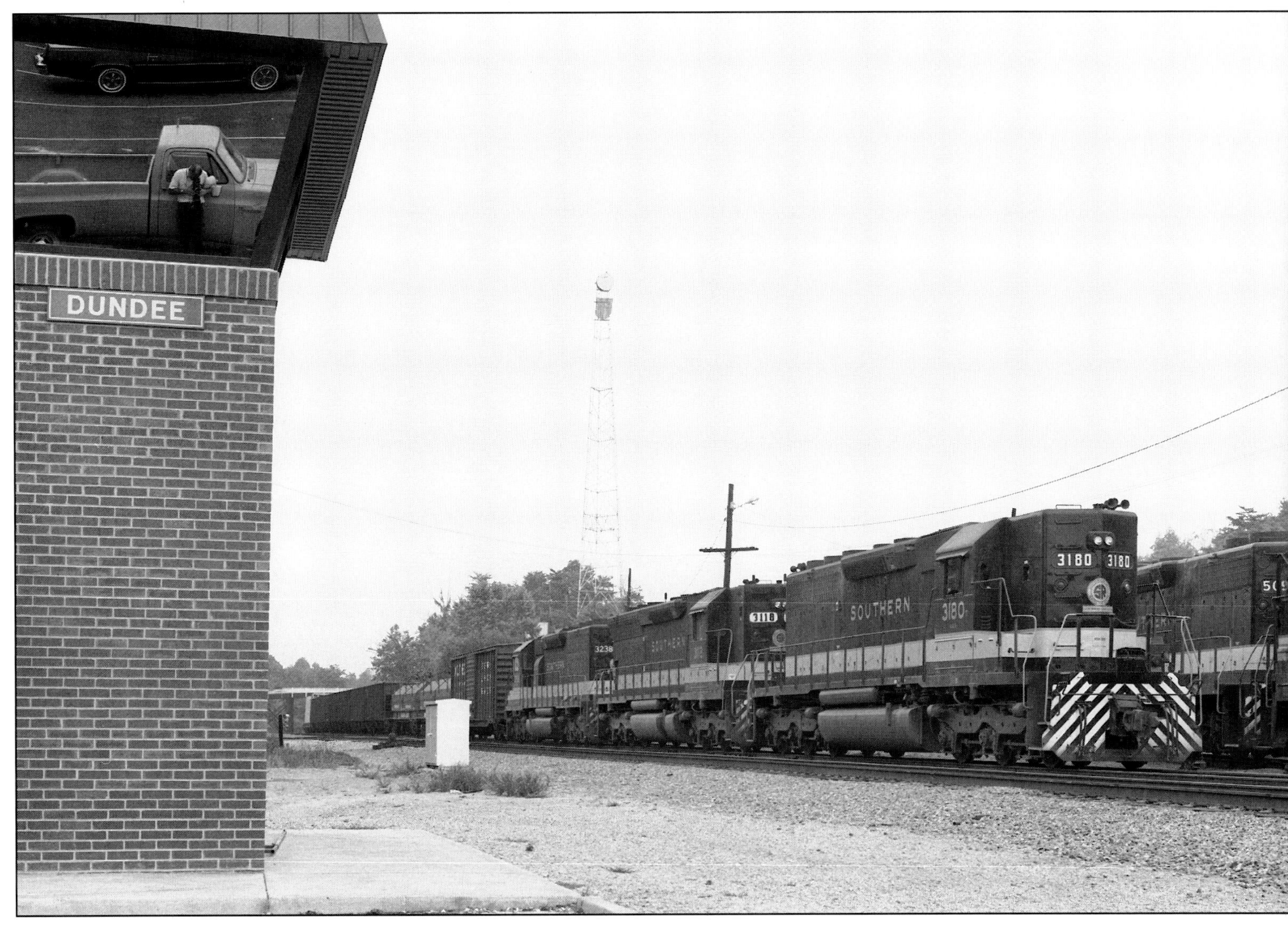

Little did I know that I was taking a photograph of myself while making an exposure of Southern's No. 159 pulling into Dundee, Va. this hazy and hot Aug. 27, 1981, at 2:26 p.m.

Unbeknownst to me, my appearance was reflected, crystal clear, on the angled windows of Dundee Tower (upper left), so now I know how I appeared when I released the shutter of my Rollie while recording SD-40 (#3180T), SD-45 (#3118T) and SD-40-2 (#3238J), lugging in 145 cars on its Potomac Yard-Spencer Yard journey. The Dundee Yard engines-seen on the right-(GP-38-2 #5098X and U-23B #3927F) would head south a short distance so that No. 159 could leave and pick up cars from the yard.

The two most successful EMD "SD" series, the SD-40 and SD-40-2's, are shown bracketing the huge SD-45 which they helped to eventually replace. Even with their phenomenal power, the '45's used too much fuel and their 20 cylinders needed far too much maintenance for the Southern's requirements. As a result, the road felt it was better to lose 600 h.p. and gain a more fuel efficient, 16 cylinder locomotive that would require less maintenance (the SD-45's had 3,600 h.p. while both the SD-40 and SD-40-2's had 3,000 "horses"). Because of these facts, between 1971 and 1972, the Southern purchased 31, SD-40's (#3170-#3200) and almost instantly the road realized that THIS was the engine for their future (they also obtained 128 of the SD-40-2's as well).

No. 3180 came out of EMD's LaGrange, Ill, plant in April of 1971, weighed 376,129 lbs., carried 4,000 gal. of fuel, 243 gal. of lube oil, 254 gal. of cooling water and 72 cu. ft. of sand. They were so successful that all but three – (#3181-retired) and (#3191 & #3198 both wrecked and scrapped), are still moving freight today for the Norfolk Southern.

Wow, so that's how I appeared when "snapping" a photo. As a point of interest, that was not my vehicle directly behind me. My "beauty" was that shiny black Pontiac "GP," i.e. Grand Prix-not General Purpose-in the background.

Have you ever experienced such a similar situation?

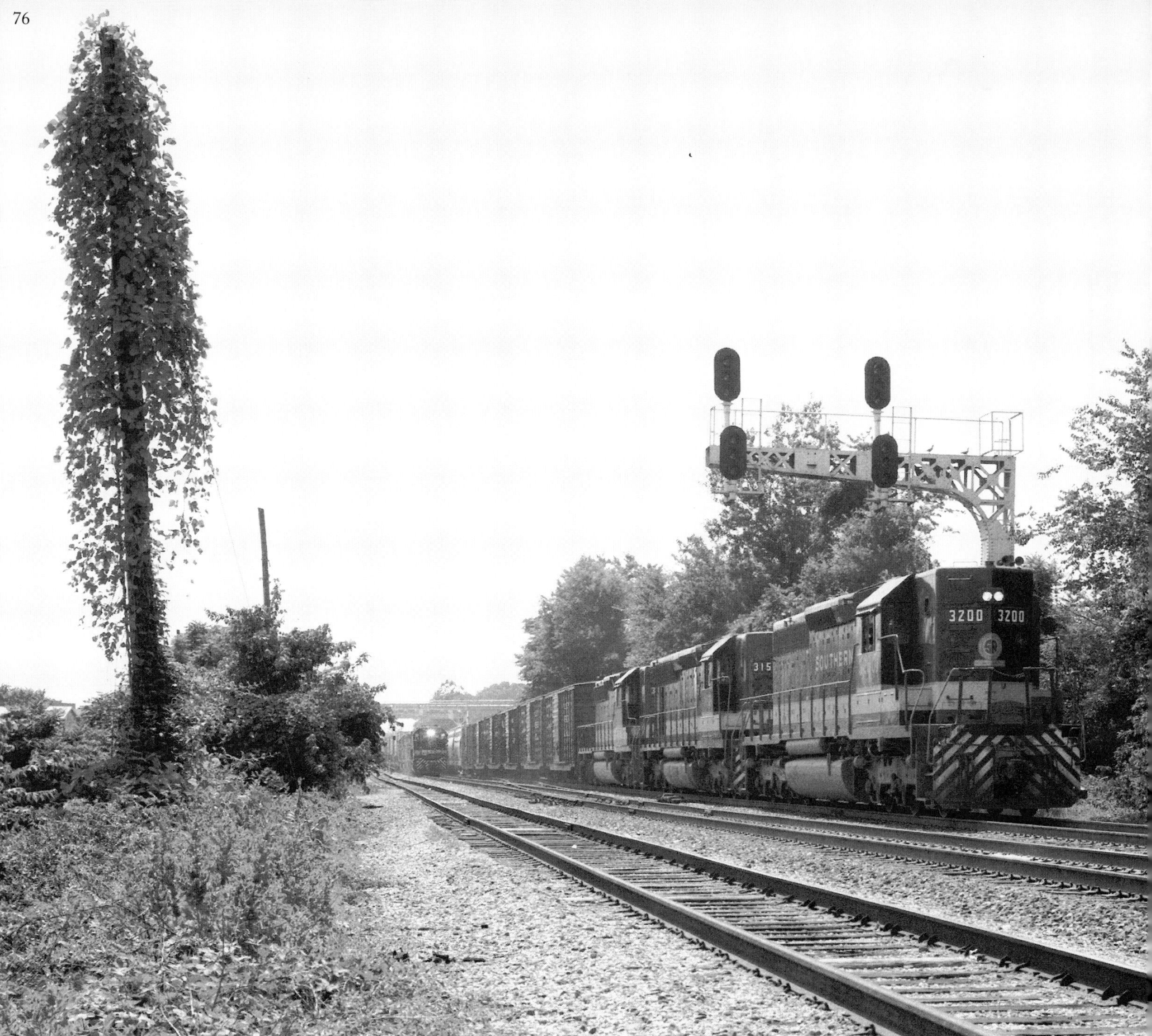

A portrait of modern railroading in action: centralized traffic control (c.t.c.), automatic block protection, double track, microwave communication, continuous-"ribbon"-rails, a double-crossover. You name it and it could be found in this scene on the Southern's Washington-Atlanta mainline.

The place: Greensboro, N. C.; date and time: July 9, 1981 at 3:30 p.m.; trains shown: No. 118, on the right, passing No. 156, in the background – both freights heading for Potomac Yard in Alexandria, Va.

The dispatcher watching these two trains on his c.t.c. board, was located in the Eastern Division headquarters found in the building on the west side of the Elm St. crossing – two blocks behind your photographer. Since No. 118 was running a few minutes late, the dispatcher decided to run it around No. 156. Both freights should arrive at their destination by midnight. The Eastern Division dispatchers controlled all mainline trains between Salisbury, N. C. and Alexandria.

No. 118, led by SD-40 (#3200-last of the SD-40 series), had help in moving its 95 cars of high priority freight with a huge SD-45 (#3159F) and SD-40-2 (#3276J). No. 3200J came from EMD in Jan. of 1972 and with its 3,000 h.p. and engine weight of 376,920 lbs., it continues in service only today it's with the Norfolk Southern. In fact, the fuel efficiency and less maintenance needed by the SD-40's and SD-40-2's would soon remove the larger and more powerful-but "fuel hungry"-SD-45's as the major mainline six-axle power. The SD-40 and '40-2's would be the main SD's moving the priority trains for almost two decades.

On many occasions, I came to this double-crossover area (called "Elm") to witness and photograph such scenes as this; and it never ceased to amaze me how all the modern equipment enabled the uninterrupted movement of so many trains. In fact, it was much like me operating my O-gauge model Lionel trains in my attic at home.

"Elm" was a good place to observe and/or photograph railroading in the modern style-no doubt about it!

SD-40-2

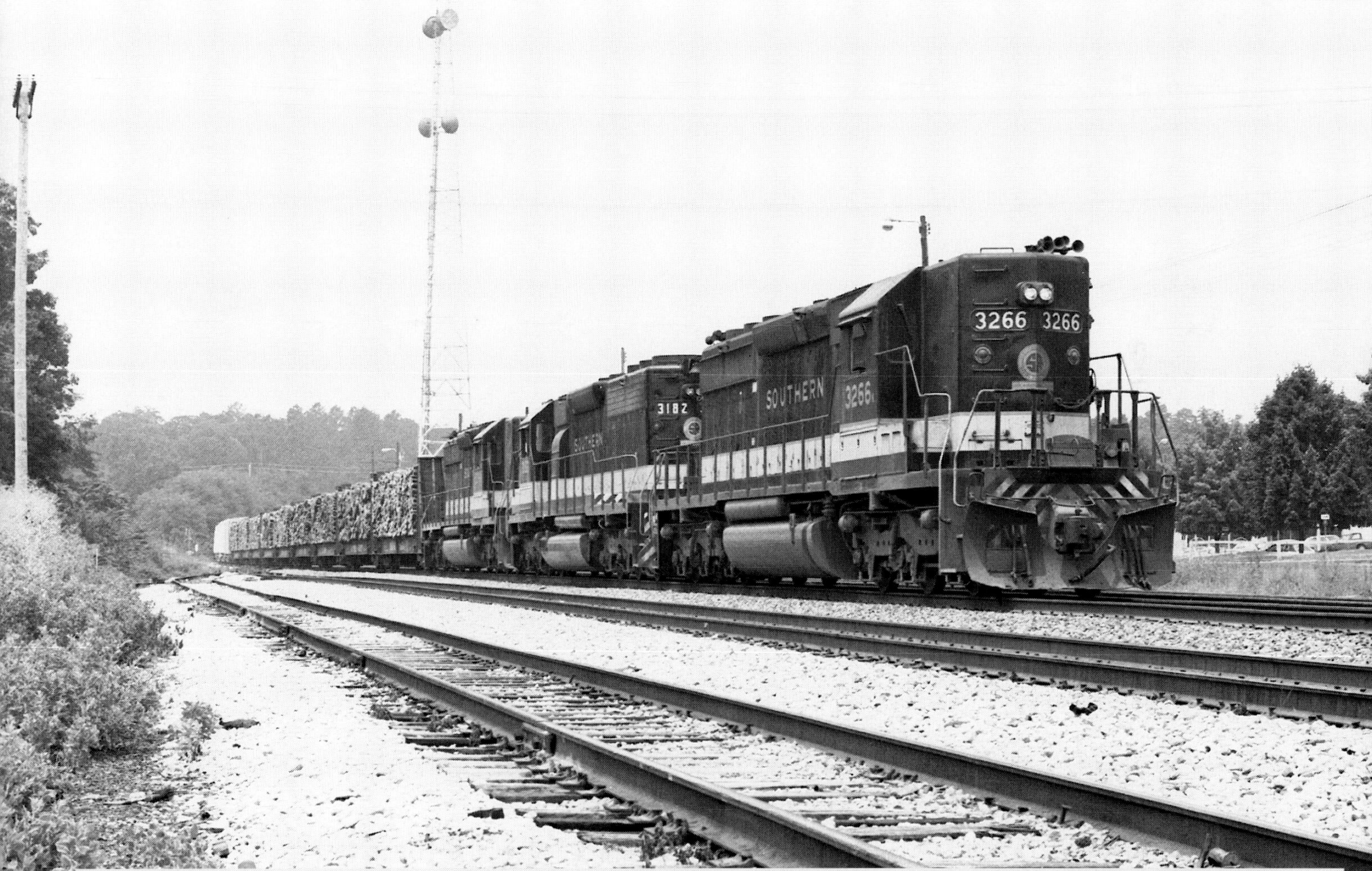

It was 101°F this July 15, 1983, as Norfolk Southern (formally Southern) No. 142 arrived in Seneca, S. C. at 12:40 p.m. I had a decision to make: should I leave my cool, comfortable car to photograph this Spencer (N.C.) yard-bound freight or just watch as it worked the yard? Obviously, I decided to "take the heat" in order to "freeze" this moment in rail history for others to see. Some would call me a "crazy" railfan. I would prefer the term "dedicated" railfan. In fact, after looking at this photo over the years, I am convinced that I made the correct decision to record this Washington-Atlanta action in this scenic and friendly town on this super hot day – you can bet that I did not stay outside very long!

The track on the left of the double track main was part of the ex-Southern (now NS) branch line from Belton to Walhalla, S. C., which passed through town and made a connection with the mainline.

No. 142's motive power: SD-40-2 #3266X, SD-40 #3182J and SD-40-2 #3291H, contained two of the most successful EMD models in their catalog, the SD-40 and newer SD-40-2 (because of the improvements included in their second series, EMD gave them a "dash" 2 suffix). The SD-40-2's proved to be so dependable and durable it really caught the fancy of the rail world. The Southern purchased 128 of the versatile motors (#3201-#3328) – all made between Dec. of 1972 and April of 1979.

No. 3266X (No. 142's lead engine) left the shops at LaGrange, Ill. In Jan. of 1978. It had 3,000 h.p., carried 4,000 gal. of fuel and a pair of Nathan five-chime horns. Its bell was placed at the top of the long end and it had that very effective snowplow "cowcatcher" on both ends. Weighing 374,216 lbs., No. 3266 continues in service today, now for the Norfolk Southern. Although not as powerful as the SD-45's, the '40-2's were more fuel efficient and required less maintenance – two items that really caught the Southern's interest.

They were used over most of the 10,000+ mile system and were "at home" on coal drags, through freights, piggybacks and any other assignments they were given AND they were quite photogenic as well. Wouldn't you agree?

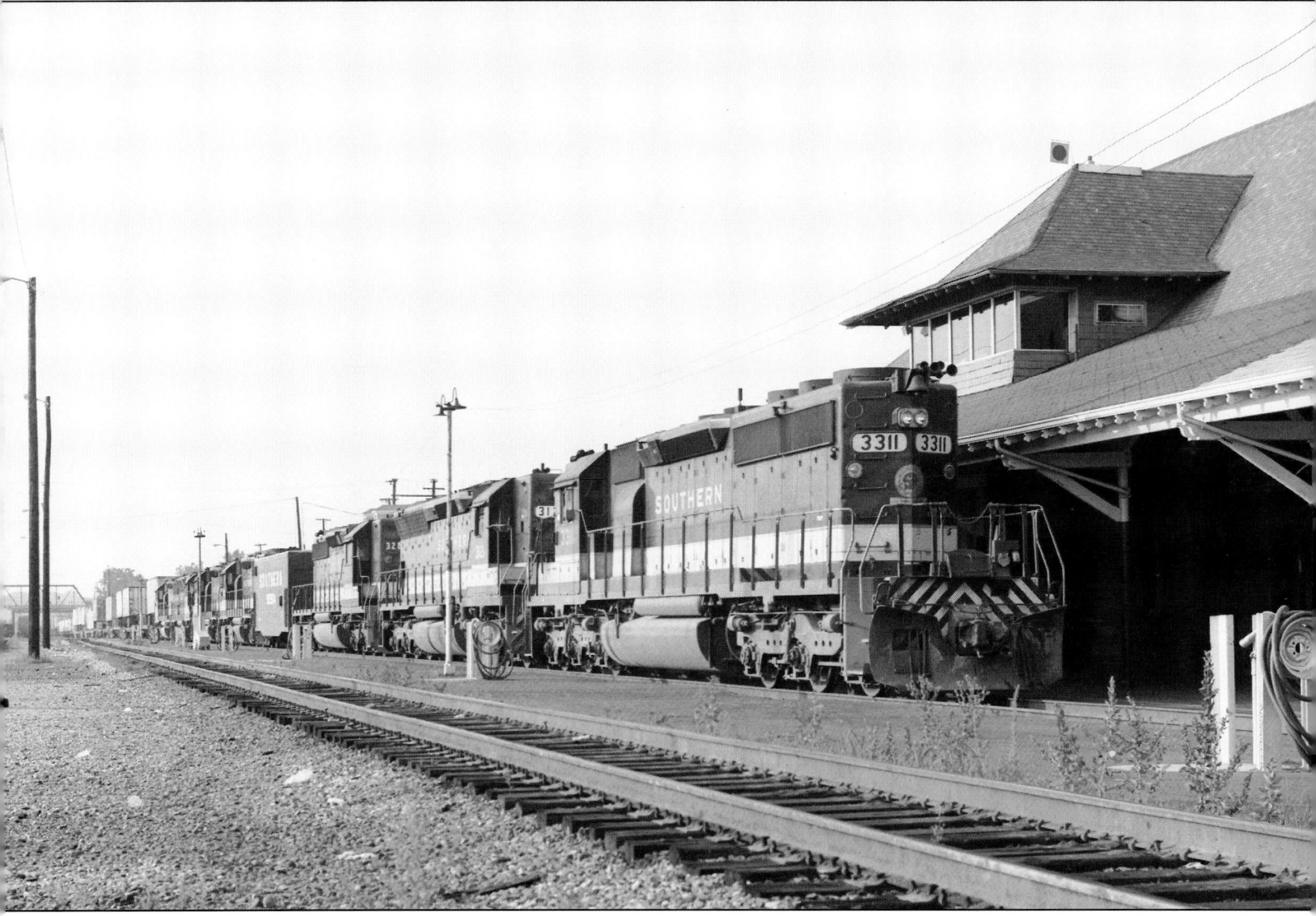

This is truly a most remarkable sight! Standing in front of the Greenville, S. C. station which was also the office for the yardmaster (look at the windows on the depot's roof), the Division Headquarters, the crew change point between Spencer, N. C. and Atlanta, plus the freight station as well, we find SD-40-2 (#3311W), SD-45 (#3121F), SD-40-2 (#3281J), a "radio receiver" car, two GP-50's (#7072H and #7055T), GP-40X (#7001F) and GP-50 (#7037L) – all at the head of this 155-car long freight waiting for the Atlanta crew to take control this July 9, 1984 (7:20 p.m.) with the temperature still at a blistering 92°F.

Believe it or not there was an explanation for this "top heavy" motive power consist. Quite often on Sundays, the Southern –now the NS-combined piggyback No. 219 with high priority, "radio train," No. 173, from Spencer to Atlanta. So, what we have here is two trains combined into one which created this most impressive occasion. The consolidated trains was called No. 219-all on No. 1 track.

The lead engine, SD-40-2 (#3311W), was equipped with 'radio control" equipment since its number boards had a white background with black numbers. Twenty five of the '40-2's had these "locotrol" devices which enabled them to handle "radio trains." No. 3311 came from EMD in March of 1979, had 3,000 h.p., weighed 375,024 lbs., carried 3,900 gal. of fuel and 72 cu. ft. of sand. It was 68' 8 1/2" long and remains in service today, displaying a "thoroughbred" on its front rather than the beautiful Southern symbol.

On any other day in the week, these two trains would have been part of the "parade" which passed through Greenville between 6:30 and 10:30 p.m.: No. 219, No. 173, No. 169, No. 141 – southbound – and No. 152, No. 141 and the "Crescent"-northbound. You could also count on an extra or two or a second section of one of the regular freights as well.

On many of my visits to this beautiful station, I can recall three or four automobiles with families, driving to the station to actually watch this "parade." Seeing this renewed my faith in the fact that other people also liked train watching – maybe even as much as "us" railfans!

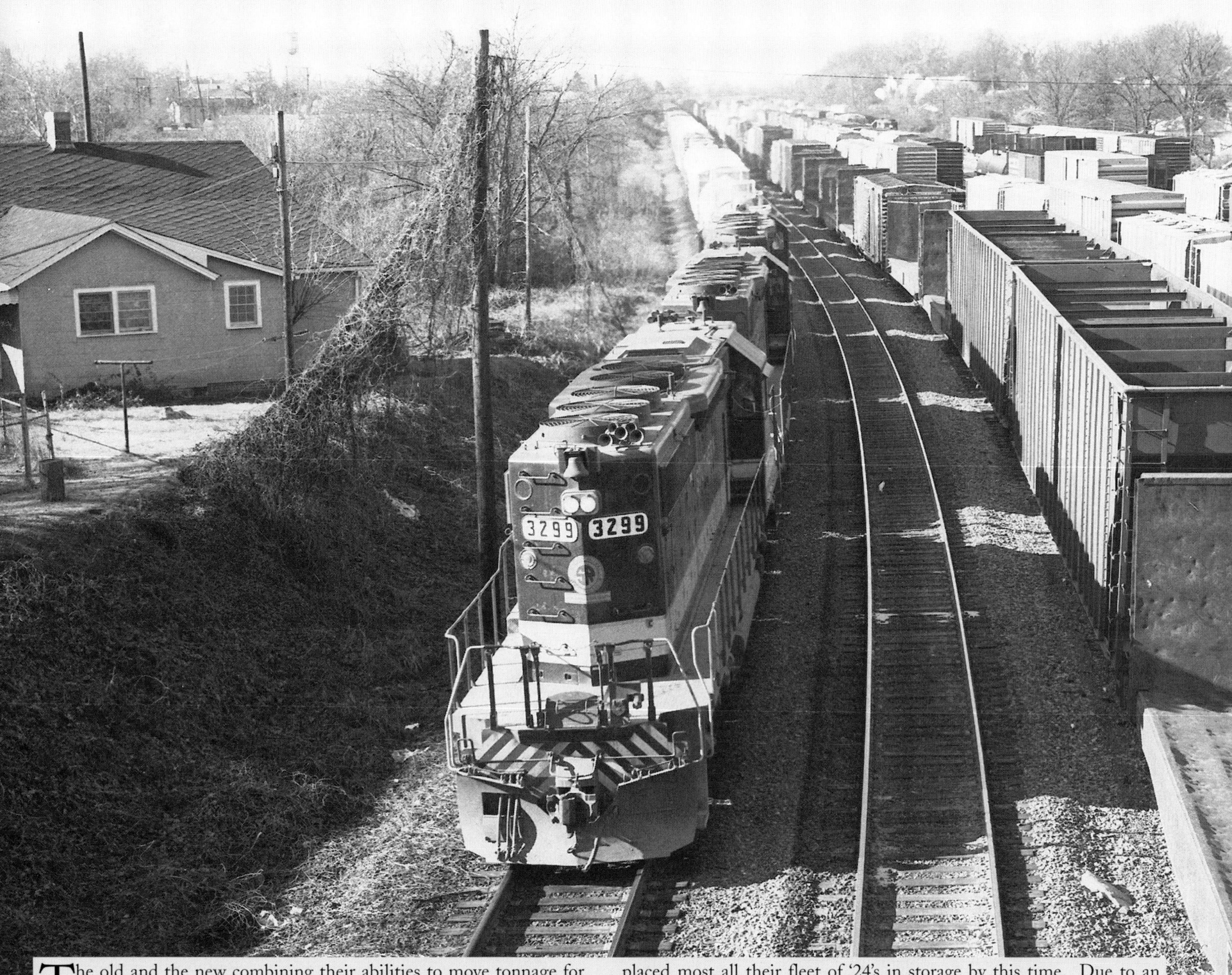

The old and the new combining their abilities to move tonnage for the Southern. That's what we have here in this photo, which was made on June 24, 1975, at 1:19 p.m., in Salisbury, N. C.

At the Jefferson Street crossing in Salisbury, the line from Spencer, N. C. (in the background) to Asheville, N. C. splits from the Washington-Atlanta mainline (the double track on the right) and heads west to the mountains and the "Land of the Sky." No. 165 is shown curving west as its engineer notches-out his throttle (note the exhaust) with SD-40-2 (#3206A), SD-24 (#6307J) and SD-40-2 (#3234H) pulling 75 cars on a journey which offers one of the most scenic trips east of the Mississippi River (especially between Old Fort and Biltmore, N. C.): seven tunnels, curves, grades and sights of majestic mountains. You simply cannot beat mountain railroading for the excitement and beauty made possible by "Mother Nature" and all available for rail photography.

The SD-40-2's were built between 1972 and 1973 while this SD-24 (#6307J) came from EMD in Dec. of 1959. The Southern actually had placed most all their fleet of '24's in storage by this time. Due to an unanticipated upsurge in traffic, the Southern found itself short of the motive power necessary to move this increased tonnage. As a result, the road took several of the old SD-24's off the storage tracks and put them back into service. Finally, in 1978, the old "war horses" were put "out to pasture" for good since, by this time, the Southern had enough, newer power to handle this traffic.

EMD built #3206A in Dec. of 1972, gave it 3,000 h.p., a capacity of 4,000 gal. of fuel, a weight of 370,579 lbs. and the ability to move more tonnage with less fuel than the other SD ("Special Duty") models. It remains in service to this very day (now for the Norfolk Southern).

In the background – on the right – you will see No. 157 leaving Spencer Yard, heading towards Charlotte, N. C. and Columbia, S. C.'s Andrews Yard, with four GP's and 89 cars. Two trains at the same time at this location were a rather common occurrence, "in the good old days!"

SD-45

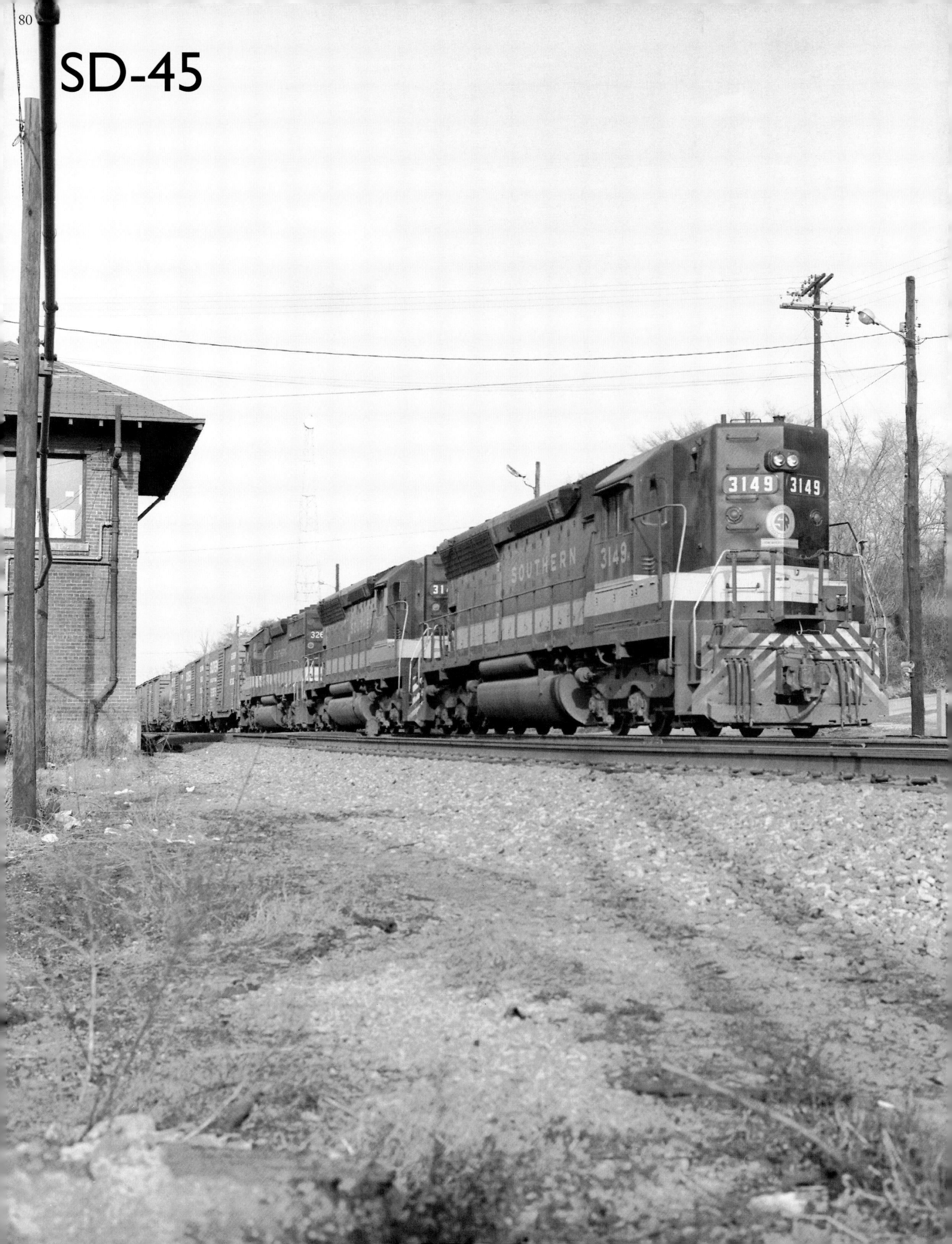

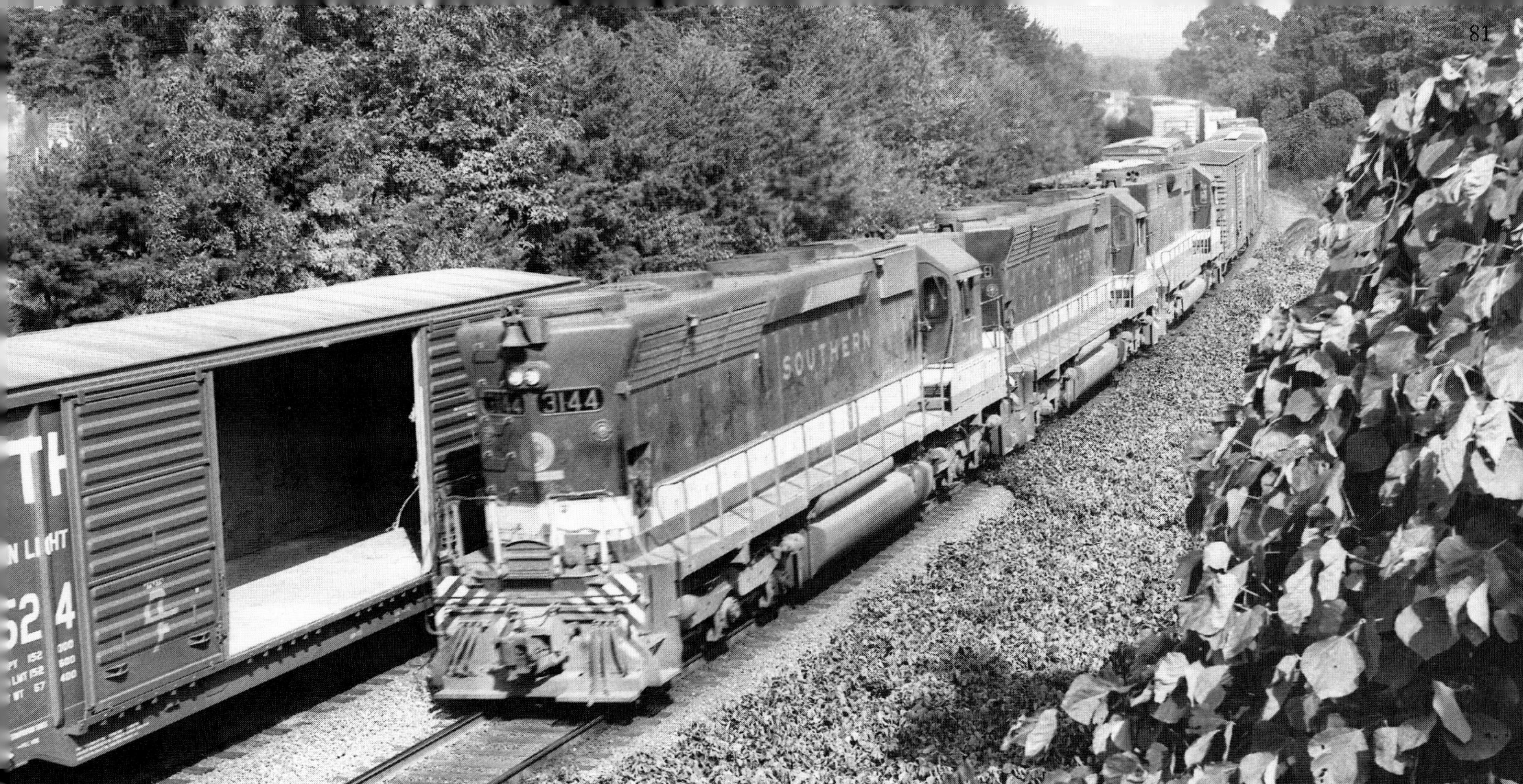

Shown here are the advantages of having double track, centralized traffic control – C.T.C. (called "T.C." by the Southern) and microwave communication: two trains, running in opposite directions, meeting each other, passing, without either being delayed – real efficiency (a form of operation encouraged by the railroads since "efficiency" means more funds for their coffers).

Heading upgrade on No. 1 track (on the right), at approximately 20-25 m.p.h. was No. 159, powered by two massive and powerful SD-45's (#3144 and #3140) along with SD-40-2 (#3227), pulling 138 cars on July 17, 1974 at 1:15 p.m. On No. 2 track was No. 154 – a "radio control" northbounder with three SD's up front and an SD in the middle of the 135-car train – heading to Potomac Yard (from New Orleans) at 45-50+ m.p.h. Both "hot shots," passing through a "sea of kudzu" at Shelton, N. C. were not delayed. This is "my" kind of railroading!

No. 159's lead engine, #3144, came off EMD's assembly line in Nov. of 1967, weighing an impressive 395,109 lbs., carrying 4,000 gal. of fuel and, with 20 cylinders, boasting 3,600 h.p. Since running long end forward was the preferred position by the Southern, its bell was located there; however, its Leslie S-ST-RF model horns were positioned on the short end of this motive power giant.

The SD-45 was the most powerful diesel model owned by the Southern. The road was so impressed with their performance, they put Locotrol apparatus into #3105 through #3121 and put them on "radio-control" train service. And, until the arrival of the GP-50's, the '45's were Southern's premier locomotive even though, due to their excessive weight, they were restricted to "big rail" territory. The 70-unit fleet (#3100-#3169) was retired between 1986 and '87 with many going into the EMD leasing fleet.

Railfans, such as yours truly, live for moments like this: two mainliners meeting at speed on the Washington-Atlanta main. After seeing such action as shown here, you will not be the same ever again. You'll be a more devoted lover of trains, hoping to find many similar experiences.

Massive, extra powerful, long, 20 cylinders, holding an incredible 4,000 gal. of fuel…these and other similar descriptive terms could only refer to one diesel-electric model on the Southern: the SD-45 – the most powerful diesel locomotive on the motive power roster of the road that "Served the South."

When the Southern discovered that the six-axle engines, such as their SD-24's and SD-35's could not only lug tonnage in the mountains effectively, but could do the same thing at a good rate of speed on the mainline (with fewer engines), the road – like several other lines – became interested in obtaining even more powerful locomotives. By reducing the number of units required to move their increasing business, it would not only save money but also enable the road to have more engines to move more trains.

In 1967, GM's Electro-Motive Division (EMD) announced that they had a model with 20 cylinders, producing 3,600 h.p. and had excellent rail adhesion, which would help these new engines use all of their 3,600 h.p. without wheel slippage. The Southern purchased a few of these SD-45's and quickly discovered that EMD's promises were true. As a result, the road eventually had a fleet of 70 of these muscular units (#3100 through #3169). Until the arrival of the SD-40-2's, and especially the GP-50's, the '45's were assigned to move all of the road's priority trains. The one drawback to the 3100's use was that they were restricted to "big rail"territory due to their tremendous weight.

Shown passing the Dundee, Va. Tower (now gone) is No. 159, being powered by two of the SD-45's (#3149 and #3167) plus an SD-40-2 (#3206), pulling 147 cars this Jan. 12, 1974 at 4:31 p.m. No. 3149 went to work on the Southern in Nov. of 1967, weighed 390,759 lbs. It was 65'8" long, 15'5" tall and 11" side. The '45's remained on the road until 1987 (serving the NS for 5 years).

Even though the Southern officials wanted these giants to run long end forward, the crews always tried to run them short end forward, since looking down that long engine was almost as bad as looking down the side of an articulated steamer – you could see very little of the tracks you were on!

The ground truly trembled as these colossal engines went by me; and I was very impressed with the immensity of these locomotives. Even with 20 cylinders operating, the '45's were quiet diesels. Once the Southern added its symbol to these impressive engines – "which really didn't know their own strength" – it made them more attractive and will remain in my memories as one "BIG" and yet effective engine, one that I will never forget – even without such photos as the one shown here.

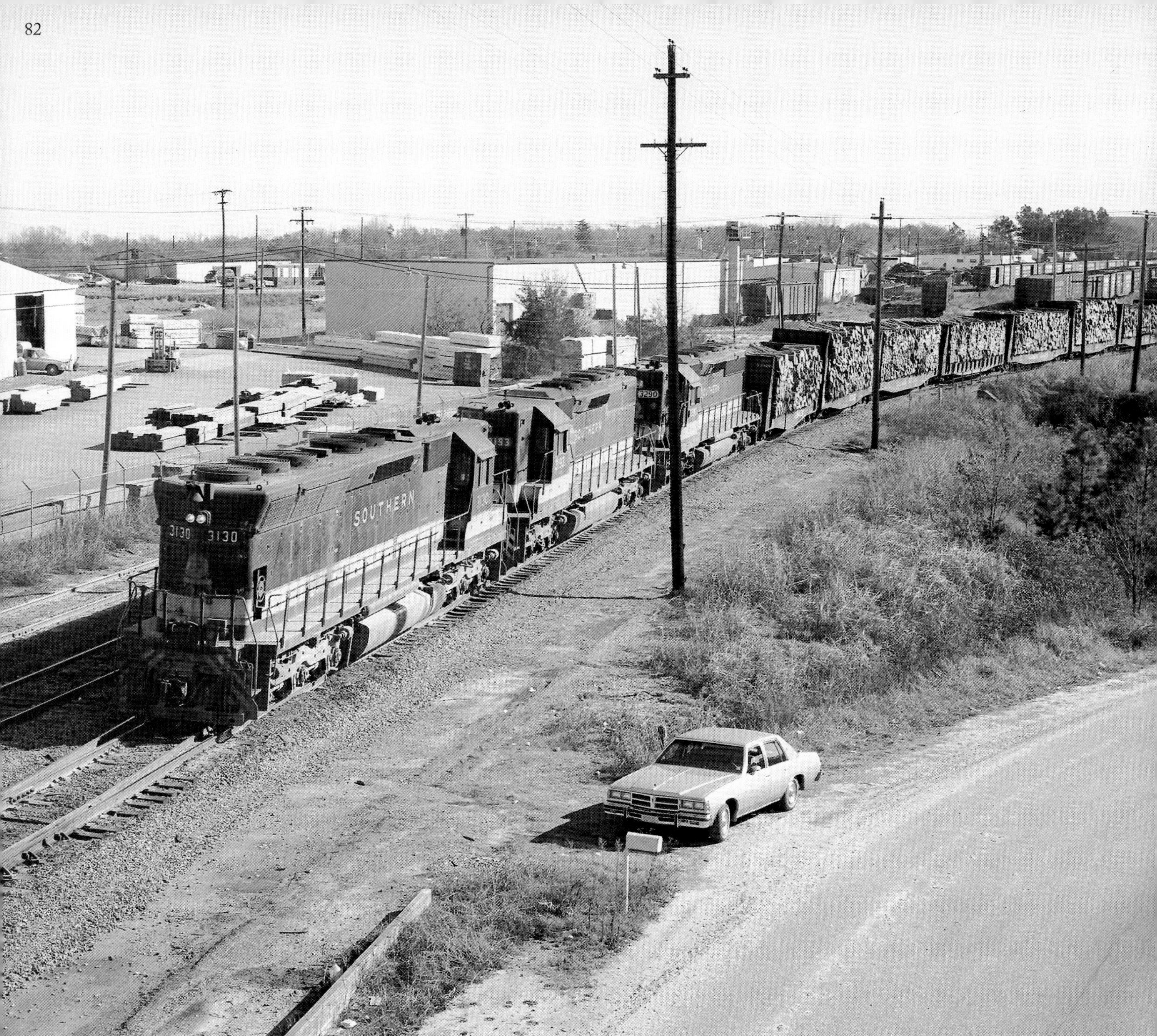

Risking both "life and limbs" since I was standing on an Interstate 85 overpass, I caught Southern Railway's No. 168 departing west Haynes Yard in Spartanburg, S. C., heading for Asheville, N. C. Ahead lies a fight with mighty Saluda Grade; but with an SD-45 (#3130H), an SD-40 (#3193A) plus SD-40-2 (#3290X) providing the power, No.168 should have enough "pull" to conquer this historic obstacle as it carries 83 cars out of town to the "Land of the Sky" this Dec. 8, 1979, at 12:55 p.m. That's my "steed," my "magic carpet on four wheels," parked to the right of this collection of 9,600 horsepower that will be soon taxed to their limits.

The SD-45's could move so much tonnage, and as a result, needed less engines to move its trains. This fact enabled the Southern to have more units available to move more trains. Because of this ability, the road purchased 70 of these massive, 3,600 h.p. locomotives (#3100-#3169) which carried 4,000 gal. of fuel and operated with 20 huge cylinders. No. 3130H, on the head of No. 168, weighed 391,859 lbs.; it was built in Dec. of 1967 and worked until Aug. of 1987 when the 1982-created Norfolk Southern retired it.

On many occasions, I would photograph the big "radio-control" coal train, which came down from Saluda Grade, come into Spartanburg with four SD's on the point and three additional SD's in the middle with the control car. Usually two SD's (up front) would remain in Spartanburg when the heavy train entered the Washington-Atlanta mainline, heading to Beaumont, N. C. (south of Charlotte) and the big Duke Power Company plant, awaiting the arrival of "black gold."

I would not advise other railfans to use such a location as I did to photograph No. 168, with those "18 wheelers" whizzing by my back at 65+ m.p.h. Still, I'm glad I made this exposure so that both you and I can enjoy this scene forever, remembering a time when being a railfan was far more enjoyable – at least for this railfan.

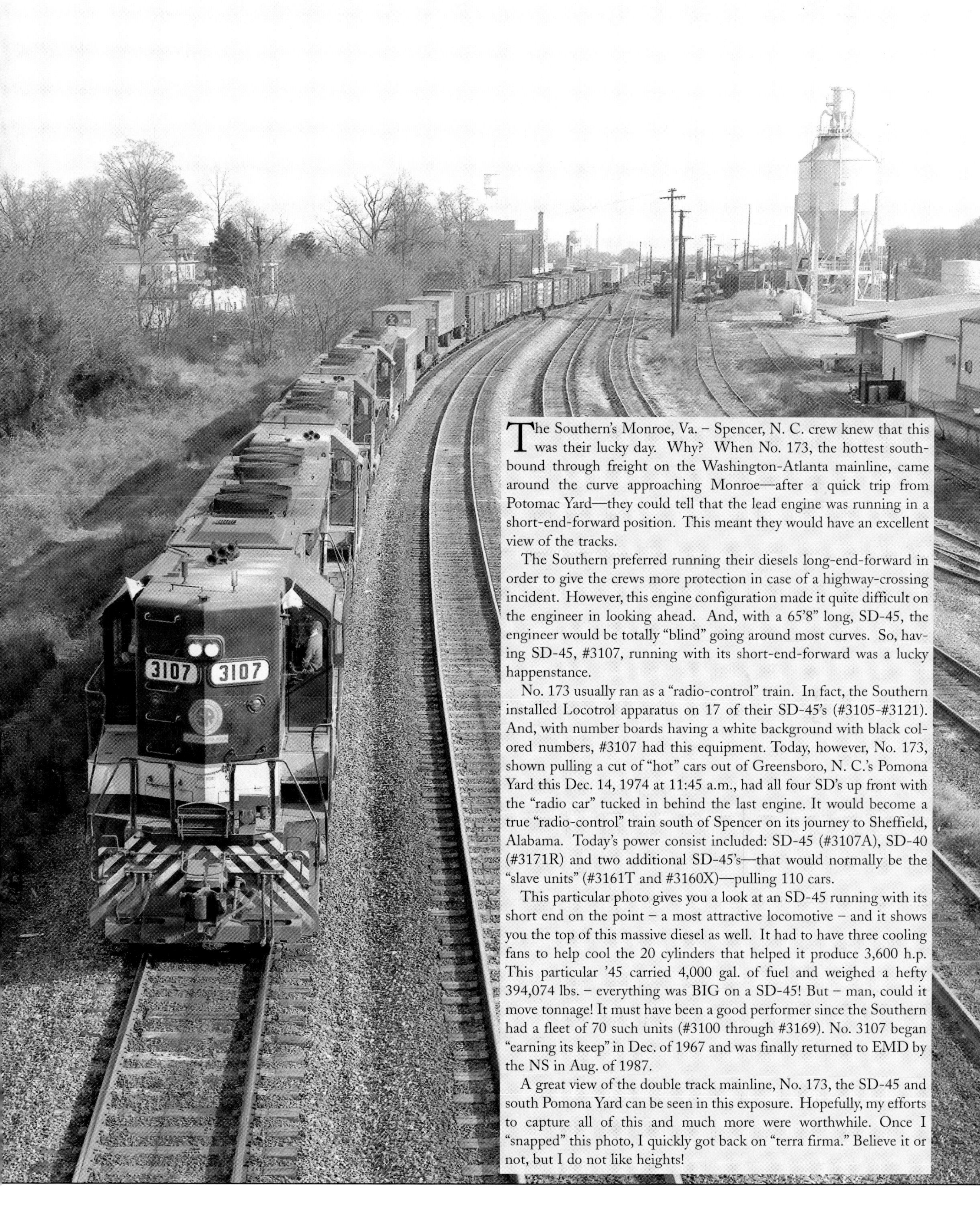

The Southern's Monroe, Va. – Spencer, N. C. crew knew that this was their lucky day. Why? When No. 173, the hottest southbound through freight on the Washington-Atlanta mainline, came around the curve approaching Monroe—after a quick trip from Potomac Yard—they could tell that the lead engine was running in a short-end-forward position. This meant they would have an excellent view of the tracks.

The Southern preferred running their diesels long-end-forward in order to give the crews more protection in case of a highway-crossing incident. However, this engine configuration made it quite difficult on the engineer in looking ahead. And, with a 65'8" long, SD-45, the engineer would be totally "blind" going around most curves. So, having SD-45, #3107, running with its short-end-forward was a lucky happenstance.

No. 173 usually ran as a "radio-control" train. In fact, the Southern installed Locotrol apparatus on 17 of their SD-45's (#3105-#3121). And, with number boards having a white background with black colored numbers, #3107 had this equipment. Today, however, No. 173, shown pulling a cut of "hot" cars out of Greensboro, N. C.'s Pomona Yard this Dec. 14, 1974 at 11:45 a.m., had all four SD's up front with the "radio car" tucked in behind the last engine. It would become a true "radio-control" train south of Spencer on its journey to Sheffield, Alabama. Today's power consist included: SD-45 (#3107A), SD-40 (#3171R) and two additional SD-45's—that would normally be the "slave units" (#3161T and #3160X)—pulling 110 cars.

This particular photo gives you a look at an SD-45 running with its short end on the point – a most attractive locomotive – and it shows you the top of this massive diesel as well. It had to have three cooling fans to help cool the 20 cylinders that helped it produce 3,600 h.p. This particular '45 carried 4,000 gal. of fuel and weighed a hefty 394,074 lbs. – everything was BIG on a SD-45! But – man, could it move tonnage! It must have been a good performer since the Southern had a fleet of 70 such units (#3100 through #3169). No. 3107 began "earning its keep" in Dec. of 1967 and was finally returned to EMD by the NS in Aug. of 1987.

A great view of the double track mainline, No. 173, the SD-45 and south Pomona Yard can be seen in this exposure. Hopefully, my efforts to capture all of this and much more were worthwhile. Once I "snapped" this photo, I quickly got back on "terra firma." Believe it or not, but I do not like heights!

U-23B

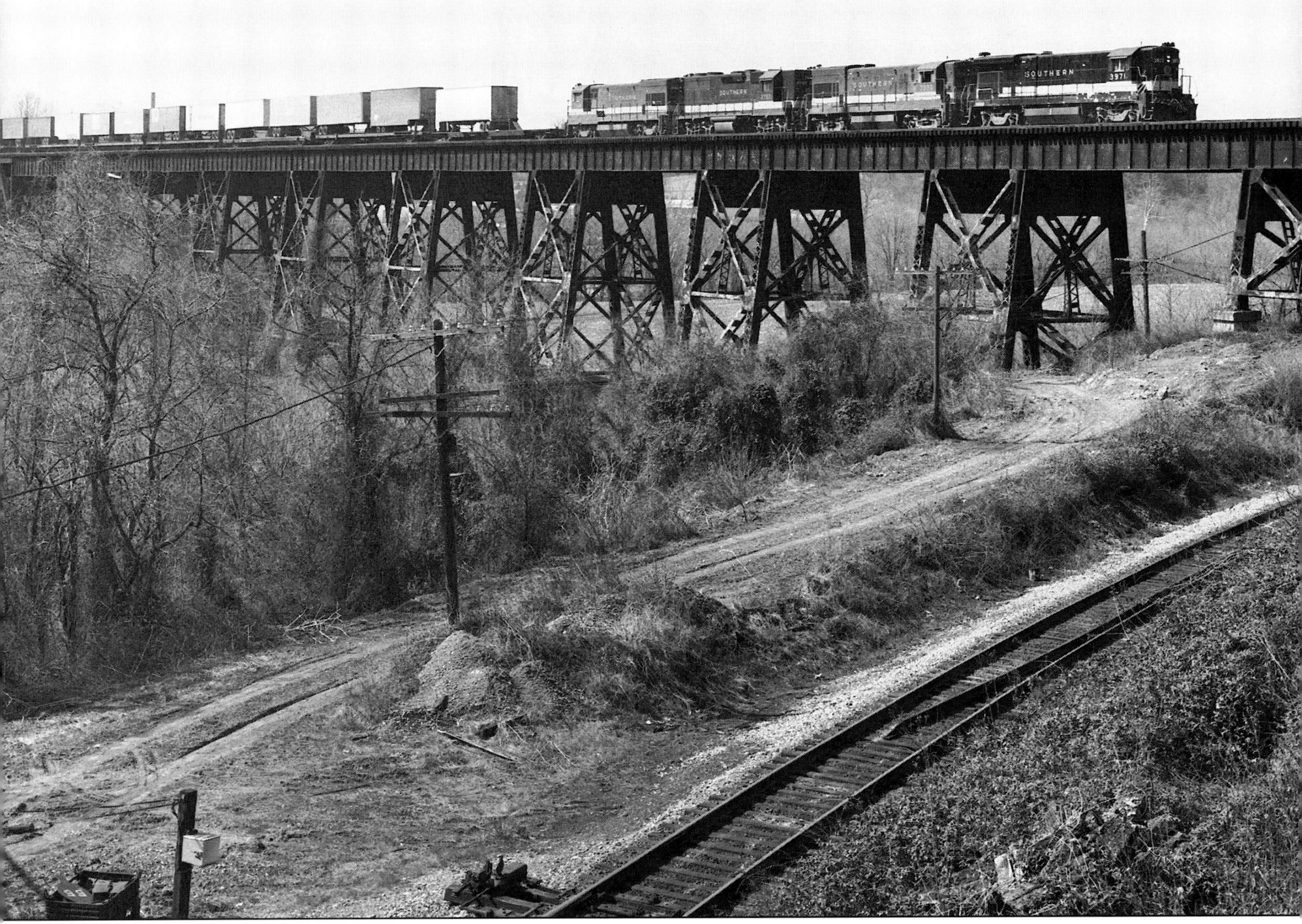

You are looking at one of the "Wonders of the (Southern Railway) World:" the bridge at Altavista, Va. Railfans are familiar with such Southern "wonders" as the James River Bridge, (north of Lynchburg, Va.), Saluda Grade (on the Spartanburg, S. C.-Asheville, N. C. Line) and the bridge at Altavista, which not only crosses over the Staunton River but the ex-Virginian mainline, eventually used by the N&W and now the Norfolk Southern, in order to avoid the stiff Blue Ridge grade east out of Roanoke, Va.

On this day, March 17, 1979 (at 11:08 a.m.), piggyback No. 222 was shown heading north on the Southern's Washington-Atlanta mainline, pulled by B23-7 (#3971K), U-23B (#3937F), GP-38-2 (#5157J) and U-23B (#3946J), with 42 cars – all at approximately 45+ m.p.h.

The two U-23B's and the improved B23-7, represented the two most popular GE built models purchased by the Southern. U-23B (#3937F) – the second engine – was built by May of 1975 and retired as a member of the NS's fleet of diesels in Oct. of 1996. It had 2,250 h.p. (250 more than the EMD GP-38 series) and carried 2,750 gal. of fuel, 350 gal. of cooling water, 300 gal. of lube oil and 48 cu. ft. of sand. The "U-Boat" was 60' 2" long, 15' 4 fl" high and 10' 3" wide; and its weight of 252,653 lbs. gave it good traction, so its pulling power – especially at slower speeds – was very good. Indeed, the GE four axles had to be good or they would not have been assigned to the hot "3-deuces," i.e., No. 222.

This was (and remains) a great spot for observing rail action. If you wait long enough, and get lucky, you could catch a Southern train on the bridge while an N&W coal train passed by below. THAT was great rail action!

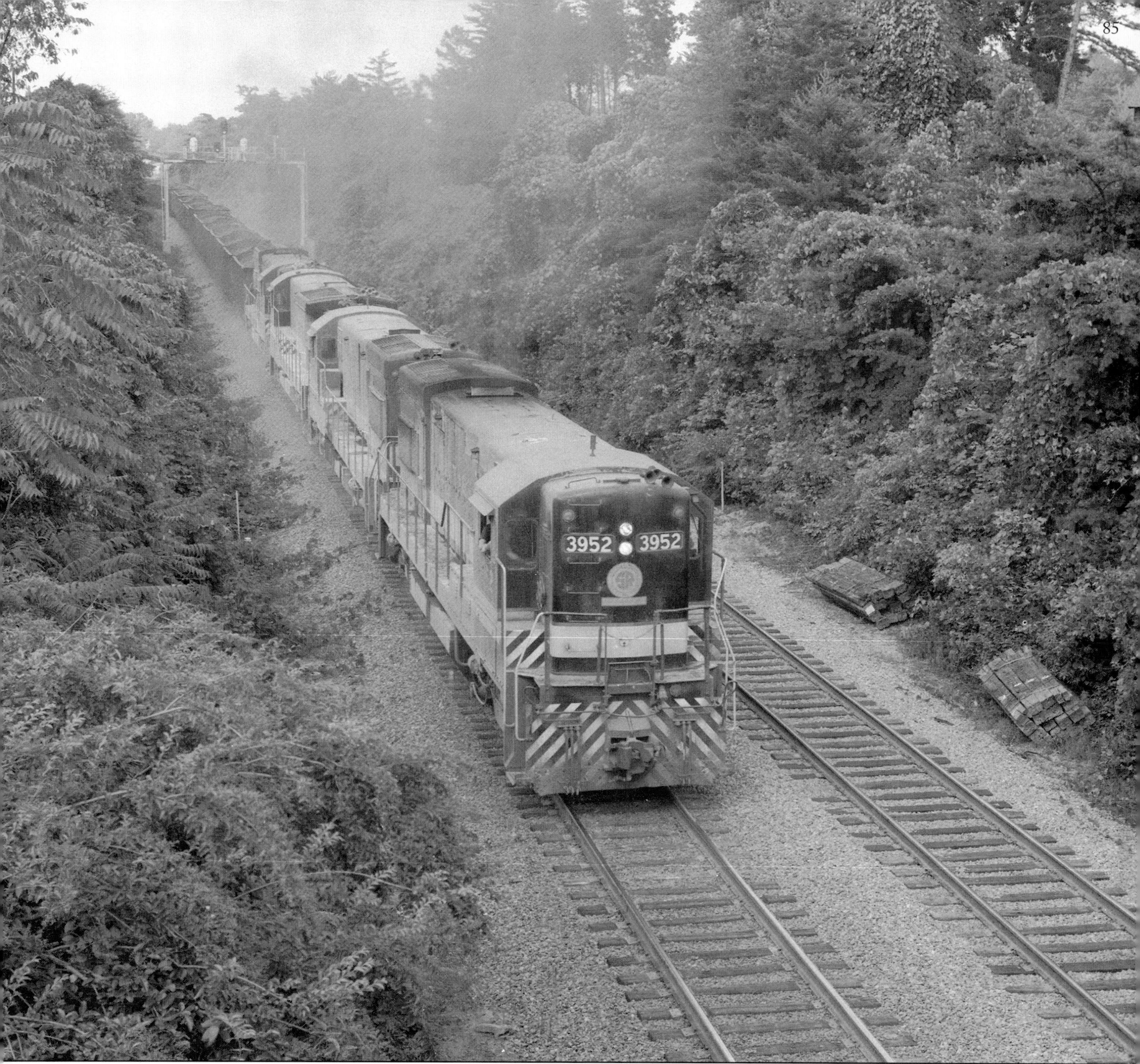

Look at this photo for a few seconds. Now, close your eyes and visualize three U-23B's and one B23-7, with a combined 9,000 h.p., wide-opened, the sand flowing freely under their wheels helping each unit to keep its traction. The sound decibels were at an incredible level and the ground was shaking as they did what the GE's could do the best: lug heavy tonnage (in this case, 68 cars of coal which the four units received from the N&W at Hurt, Va.) at a slow speed (10-15 m.p.h. upgrade on the Southern's Washington-Atlanta mainline. What a spectacle-one you would never forget (I know I won't).

The train in question was Extra 3952 South, passing through Shelton, N. C. on July 28, 1979, at 4:00 p.m., with the temperature at a hot and humid 94°F. As a point of interest, even though this exposure was made in North Carolina, a good portion of the coal train was still in Virginia! The Extra South was powered by two U-23B's (#3952X and #3913F), a B23-7 (#3970F) and a U-23B (#3924W).

Lead engine, #3952X, was built by General Electric in July of 1975 and continued "earning its keep" until it was retired as a Norfolk Southern engine in July of 1996. It had 2,250 h.p., carried 2,750 gal. of fuel and weighed 252,253 lbs. Stretching 60'2", the U-23B's and the improved B23-7's, were built to compete with the popular EMD GP-38 series. The two GE models were popular and many were purchased; however, the Southern ordered hundreds of GP-38's, GP-38AC's and GP-38-2's.

Even though the U-23B's looked more utilitarian than the more aesthetically-designed EMD products, they proved to be good engines although the crews grumbled somewhat about the exhaust fumes which got into the cab with great regularity and the few second's delay of the engines when the engineer opened the throttle before the unit actually began to move.

There was no doubt that big time railroading was going on in Shelton, N. C. this hot afternoon day in July of 1979-no doubts at all!

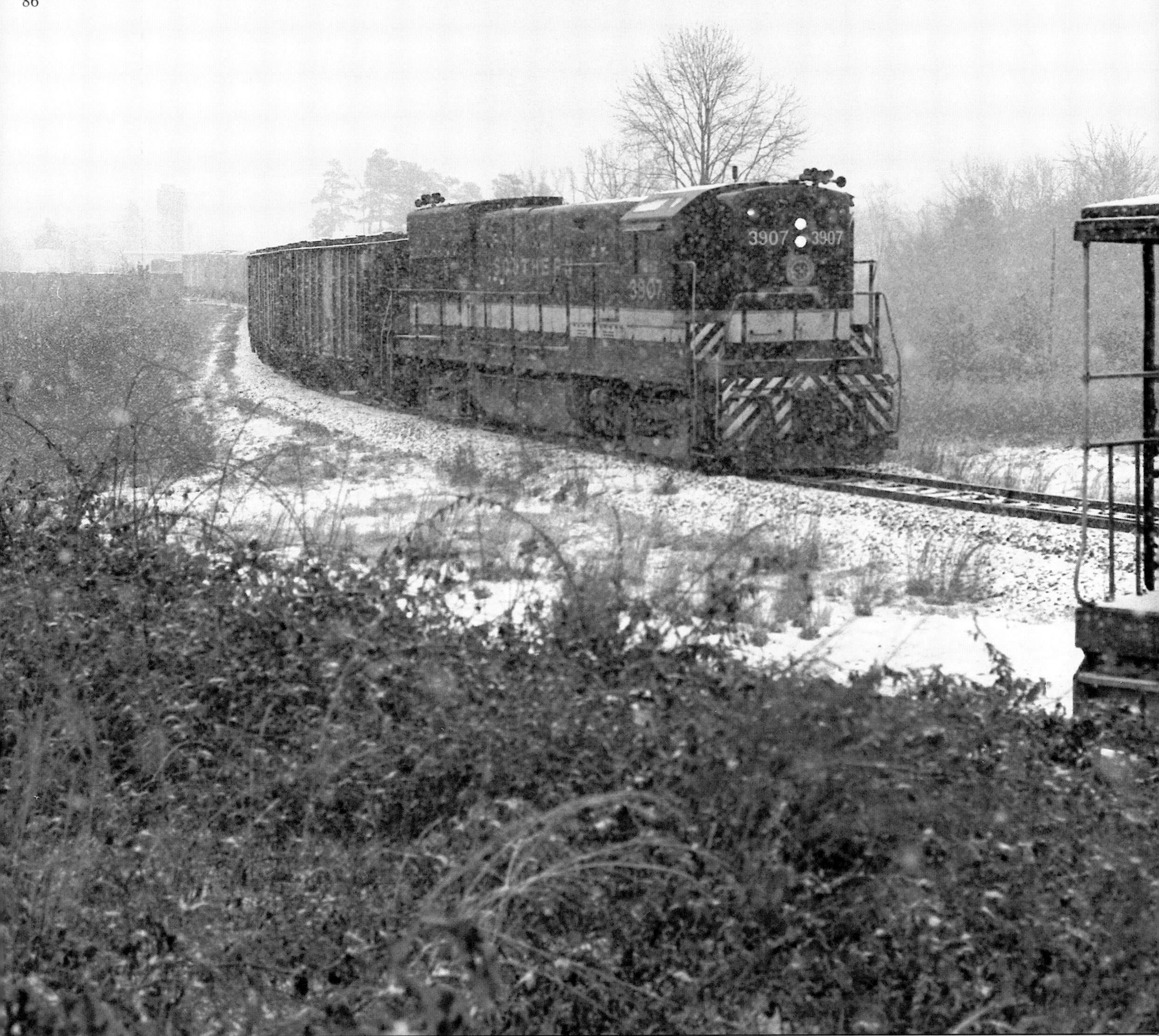

This was an "umbrella" shot. Why an umbrella? I needed it to protect my camera from the falling snow (there was 5-6" on the ground when the "white storm" left the area) and be able to get an exposure of Southern's local freight No. 21-running as an extra south-working the large, five-track yard at the CertainTeed plant in Oxford, N. C. (my hometown) in the snow. The facility makes roofing shingles and remains the No. 1 customer on the East Durham, N. C.-Keysville, Va. line (part of the Southern's old Richmond Division).

No. 21's engine, a GE built U-23B (#3907J), was shown returning to the mainline and its caboose with a long line of empty cars after leaving twenty loads at the plant, which could just barely be seen through the snow in the background.

It's Feb. 27, 1981, at 9:15 a.m. with the temperature at 28°F; and the business at CertainTeed was becoming so great that the two locals, which passed through the area on a daily ex-Sunday basis, could not meet the plant's growing needs. The answer to the dilemma: a rented switch engine to work their yard. Today, the local, now making a Durham-Oxford roundtrip, puts the loads (20-25 cars per day) in the plant's yard, gets the empties and let the "CertainTeed Switcher" do all the other work.

No. 3907J came from General Electric in May of 1973 and was retired by the Norfolk Southern in July of 1996-23 years of using its 2,250 h.p. and 256,245 lbs. of engine with to move tonnage. It held 2,750 gal. of fuel and 48 cu. ft. of sand to keep those wheels from slipping.

The U-23B and B23-7 models served the Southern well; however, the road's "true love" seemed to be with the engines made by the Electro-Motive Division of General Motors.

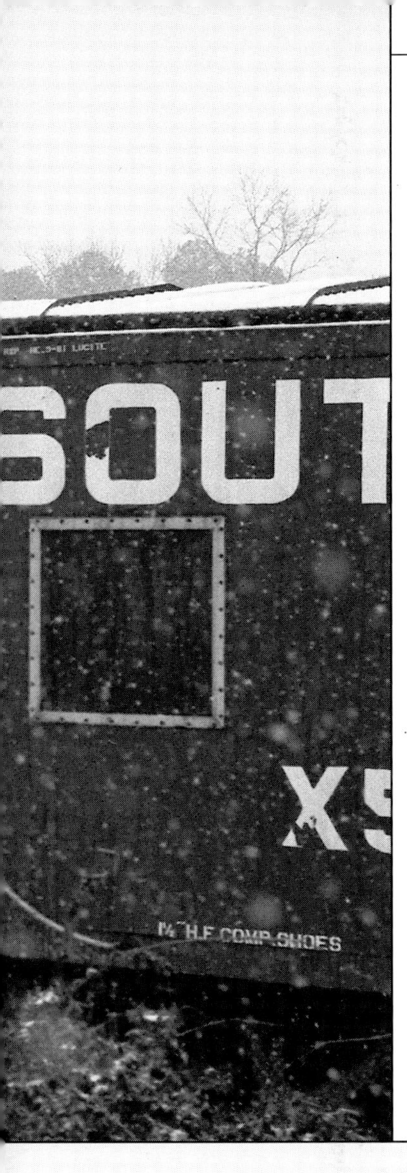

Now this is my idea of railroading in action: a four-unit freight (Southern's No. 141) coming at me with all throttles in the last notch; the ground was shaking; engine sounds were so intense that it would be impossible to find words to adequately describe the magnificent "talking" of four engines, straining to get their 85 cars south. The lead unit (a GE built-May of 1974-U-23B, #3926J) was using all of its 2,250 h.p. muscles and laying a plume of exhaust smoke worthy of old #4501, approaching a super-elevated curve on the Washington-Atlanta mainline-all at 35-40 m.p.h. It was truly a scene that would reinforce the love of trains held in the hearts of all railfans.

No. 141 had worked the Dundee, Va. yard this Dec. 17, 1981, conquered the stiff grade all trains had to face heading south out of Danville ("Cemetery Hill"). Now it was approaching the Va.-N.C. border and facing another grade, so it was building up as much momentum as possible.

Up front of the long, heavy freight, passing through Stokesland, Va. at 8:25 a.m., were: U-23B (#3926J), GP-38 (#2804J), U-23B (#3953T) and GP-38-2 (#5065W) –a combined 8,500 horsepower. I think it would be safe to say that all 4 engines were "on line!"

GE's #9326J was really "showing off" as it lead its companions toward Spencer Yard. It weighed 254,553 lbs. and was 60'2" long, carrying 2,750 gal. of fuel. The "U-Boat" would remain active until the NS retired the four axle "growler" in July of 1996.

I believe this photo is the best way of remembering #3926J doing what it was built to do. Wouldn't you agree?

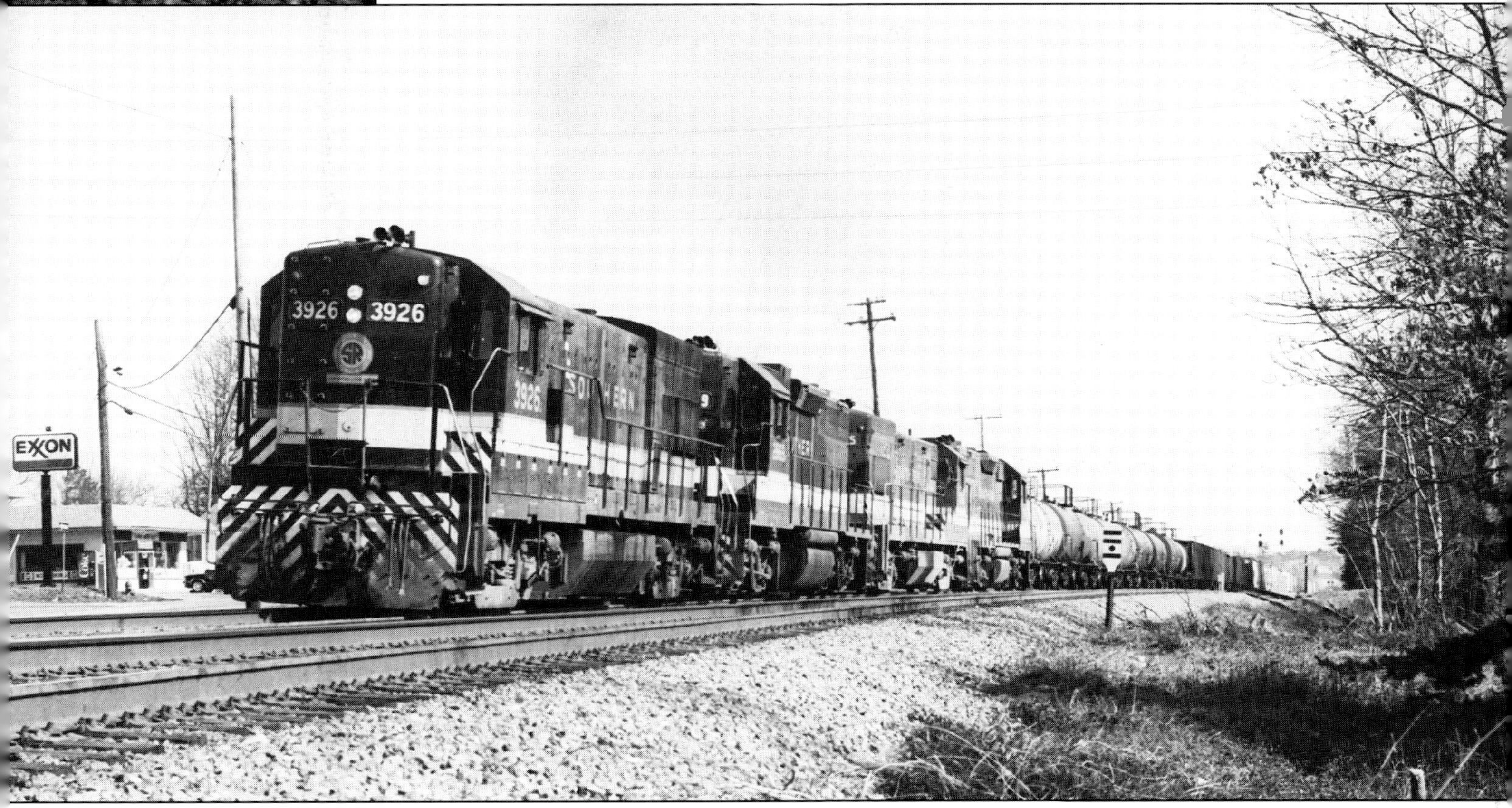

U-30C

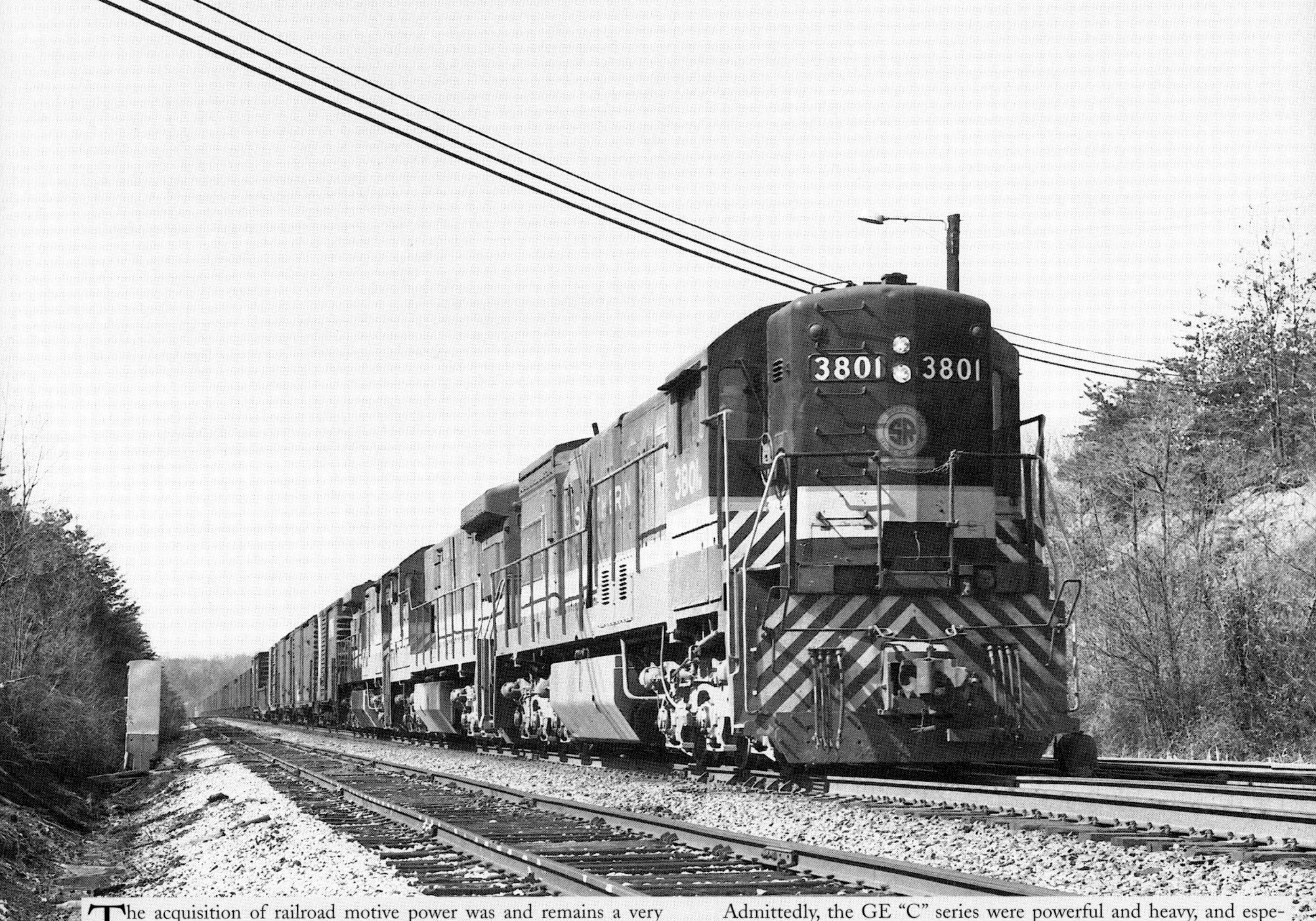

The acquisition of railroad motive power was and remains a very competitive business, with General Motors' Electro-Motive Division (EMD) and General Electric (GE) being the main competitors.

When the Southern Railway began showing a great deal of interest in EMD's GP-30's, '35's and GP-38 series, GE responded with their U-23, B23-7 and other similar models. Even though the road that "Serves the South" purchased a respectable number of the GE built engines, the road tended to favor the EMD products.

During the mid-1960's, the Southern started using six-axle power made by EMD, such as the SD-24's (my favorite), SD-35's, the huge and powerful SD-45's and the old reliable SD-40's and their upgraded brothers, the SD-40-2's. GE's reaction to this move was to produce their massive U-30C's and the improved U-33C models among other similar motive power. Unfortunately, for GE, the Southern only purchased 5 of the U-30C's and just 10 of their U-33C's. And, just like the Southern's satisfaction with four-axle products made by EMD, they found that when it came to the six-axle monsters, EMD was still their favorite company.

Admittedly, the GE "C" series were powerful and heavy, and especially at low speeds, good "pullers;" however, the Southern continued to acquire massive numbers of EMD motive power.

Even though few were purchased by the Southern, the GE heavyweight six-axle units were big and reliable; they also had an aesthetically pleasing appearance about them as well. Look at this U-30C (#3801) approaching the Hurt-Altavista, Va. area with No. 158 on March 17, 1979, at 10:50 a.m. with 110 cars at 40+ m.p.h., along with their 2U-33C companions (#3814 and #3813). Truthfully, they created a most impressive sight: a look of modern railroading at work.

No. 3801 was built in December of 1967, had 3,000 h.p., weighed 392,608 lbs. and carried 4,000 gal. of fuel, 300 gal. of cooling water, 380 gal. of lube oil and 60. cu. ft. of sand. The huge unit was 67'3" long, 10' 2 1 /4" and 16' 1" high. It was retired in 1982. Indeed, #3801 would never receive the paint of the Norfolk Southern. No. 3803 was the only one of the 5 U-30C's to serve the NS. It was retired in January of 1987.

The GE "Big Boys" were good but the Southern found the EMD built six-axles to be better.

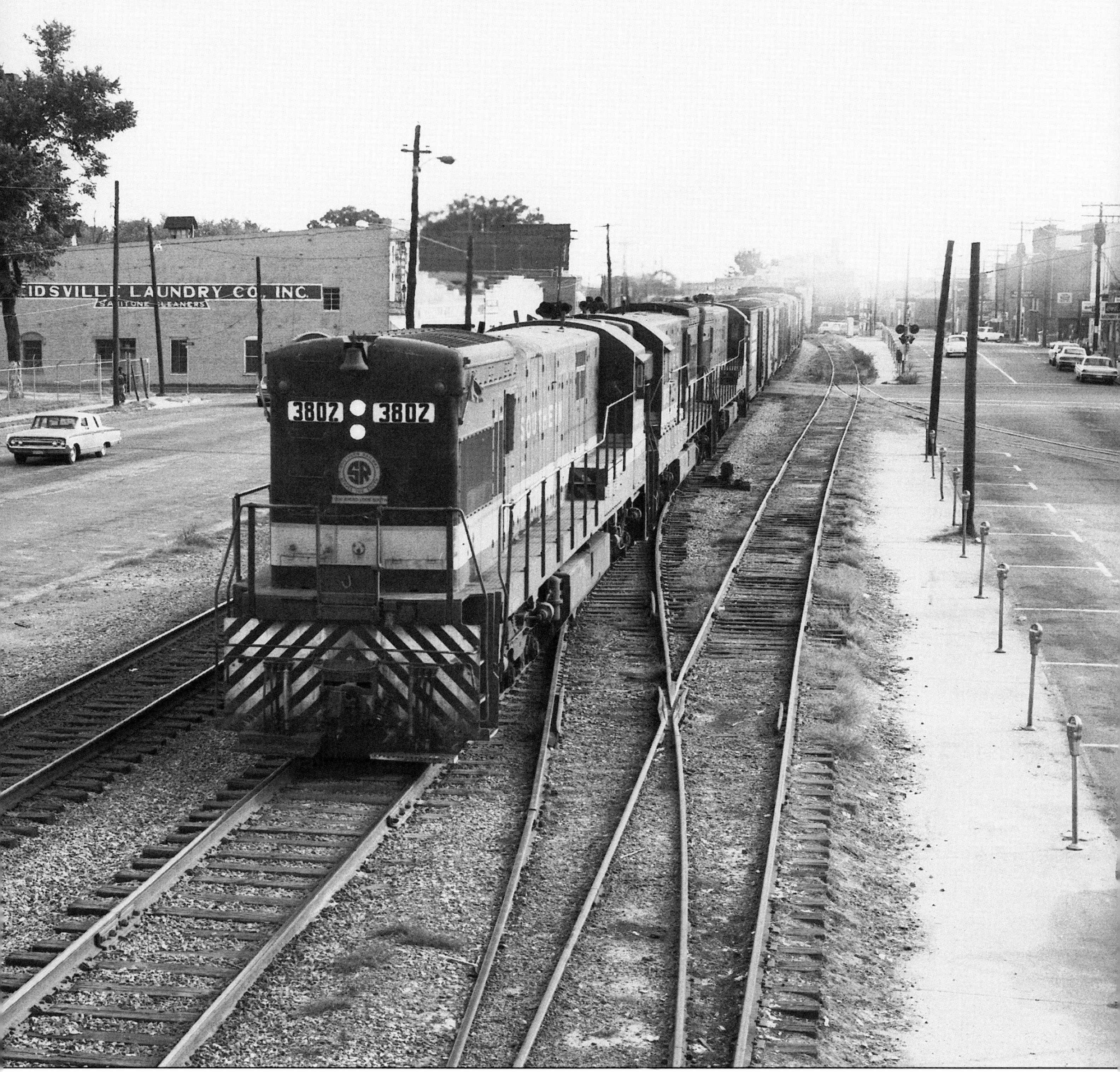

It's a good thing that this is big rail territory since we have 393,608 lbs. of a General Electric built U-30C engine approaching your photographer at a good 35 m.p.h. with 1st No. 220, on October 11, 1970 at 4:11 p.m. with 74 cars.

There are actually three of the five U-30C's purchased by the Southern pulling 1st No. 220 towards Potomac Yard, passing through Reidsville, N. C. (a good train watching location on the hot Washington-Atlanta mainline): #3802, #3800 and #3804.

No. 3802 was born in Dec. of 1967; it had 3,000 h.p., carried 4,000 gal. of fuel and was slightly over 67 ft. in length.

At the time this photo was made, the Southern preferred their engines to run long end forward. Believe me, #3802 looked far better with the short end up front; the crews also preferred this arrangement so the exhaust fumes did not enter the cab.

GE lost out to EMD (Electro-Motive Division-GM) when it came to six-axle power. While the road only acquired 5 of GE's U-30C's and 10 U-33C's, the Southern purchased hundreds of EMD's SD-24's, '35's, '45's and possibly the most successful six-axle engine ever built, the SD-40 and SD-40-2 series.

Fortunately, we have such photos as this one to help us remember the big GE's in action, moving the tonnage that helped make the Southern one of the most successful, innovative and financially blessed railroads in history.

U-33-C

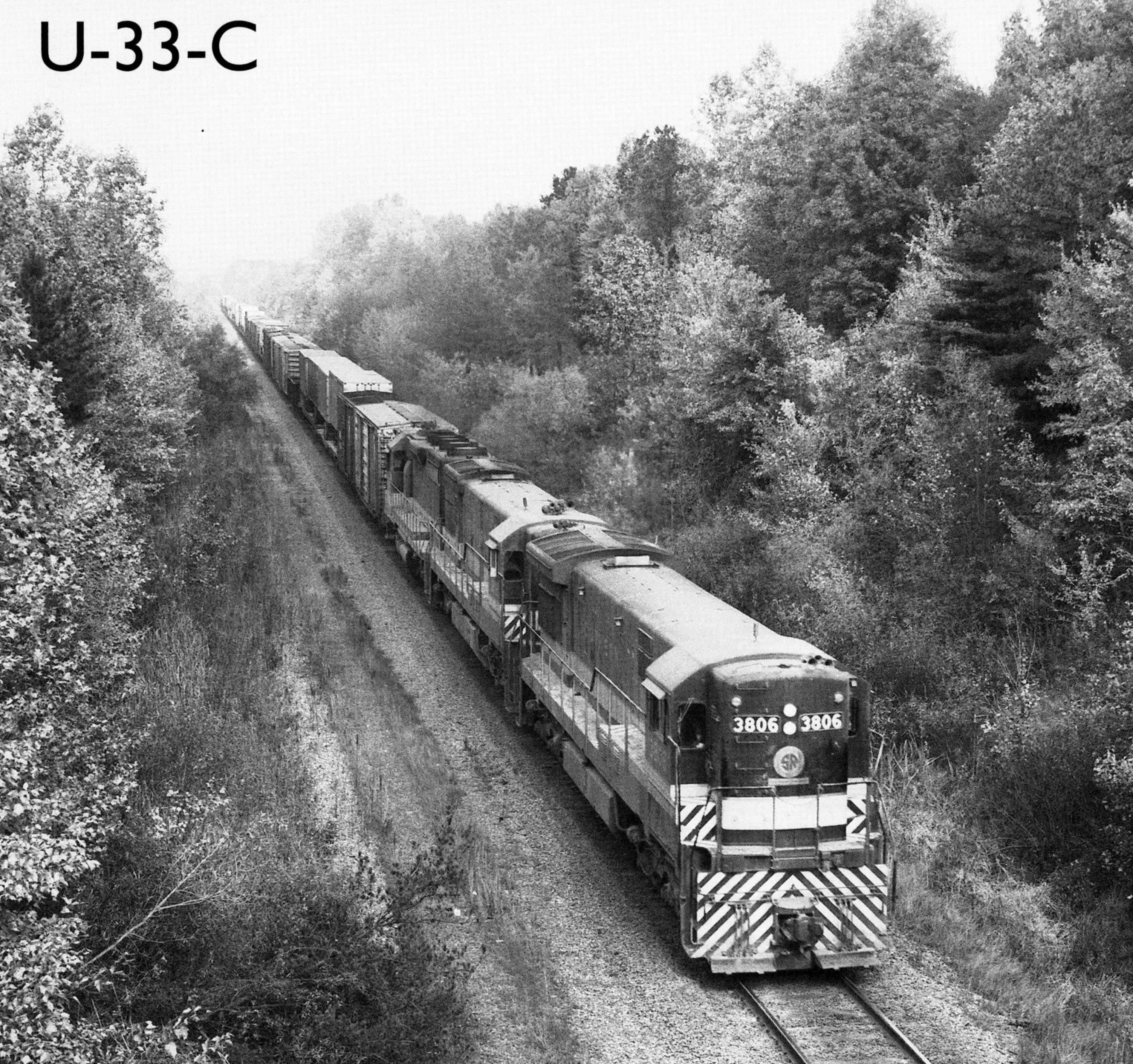

Coming down White Oak Mountain (famed by the "Wreck of Old 97" incident), not at 90 m.p.h., but more in the 45-50 range, No. 219 is shown passing through Blairs, Va. on one of the many short, single-track sections of the Southern's Washington-Atlanta mainline, with a trio of six-axle motive power hustling 65 cars towards Atlanta and points south.

Today's power consist of this "hot shot" freight included a big General Electric built U-33C (#3806) and U-30C (#3801) along with an EMD SD-35 (#3015) on Oct. 24, 1970 at 12:40 p.m. It will be in Atlanta's Inman Yard by midnight.

Due to the poor sales of their U-30C model, GE introduced the even more powerful and improved U-33C series. The Southern had purchased five of the U-30C's; however, they obtained ten of the U-33C engines: #3805 through #3814. Even with the improvements of the GE six-axles, the Southern still preferred, both four and six axle diesels built by GM's Electro-Motive Division (EMD).

No. 3806 was built in April of 1970, weighed 393,135 lbs. and produced 3,300 h.p. (300 more than the U-30C series); it carried 4,000 gal. of fuel and, stretching 67'3" long, both the U-30C's and U-33C's proved to be the longest engines purchased by the Southern.

Unlike the U-30C's, where only one unit was placed on the roster of the 1982 created Norfolk Southern, all ten U-33C's served the NS for several years. No. 3806 was finally retired in March of 1986.

When running short end forward, the massive U-33C's were very impressive looking engines. And since the GE's were "smokers," the crews appreciated this position of travel since the fumes from the exhaust outlet did not enter their cabs; they also had a better view of the tracks as well.

The big six-axle GE's were good. The Southern, however, was an EMD believer and they simply felt that GM made excellent motive power.

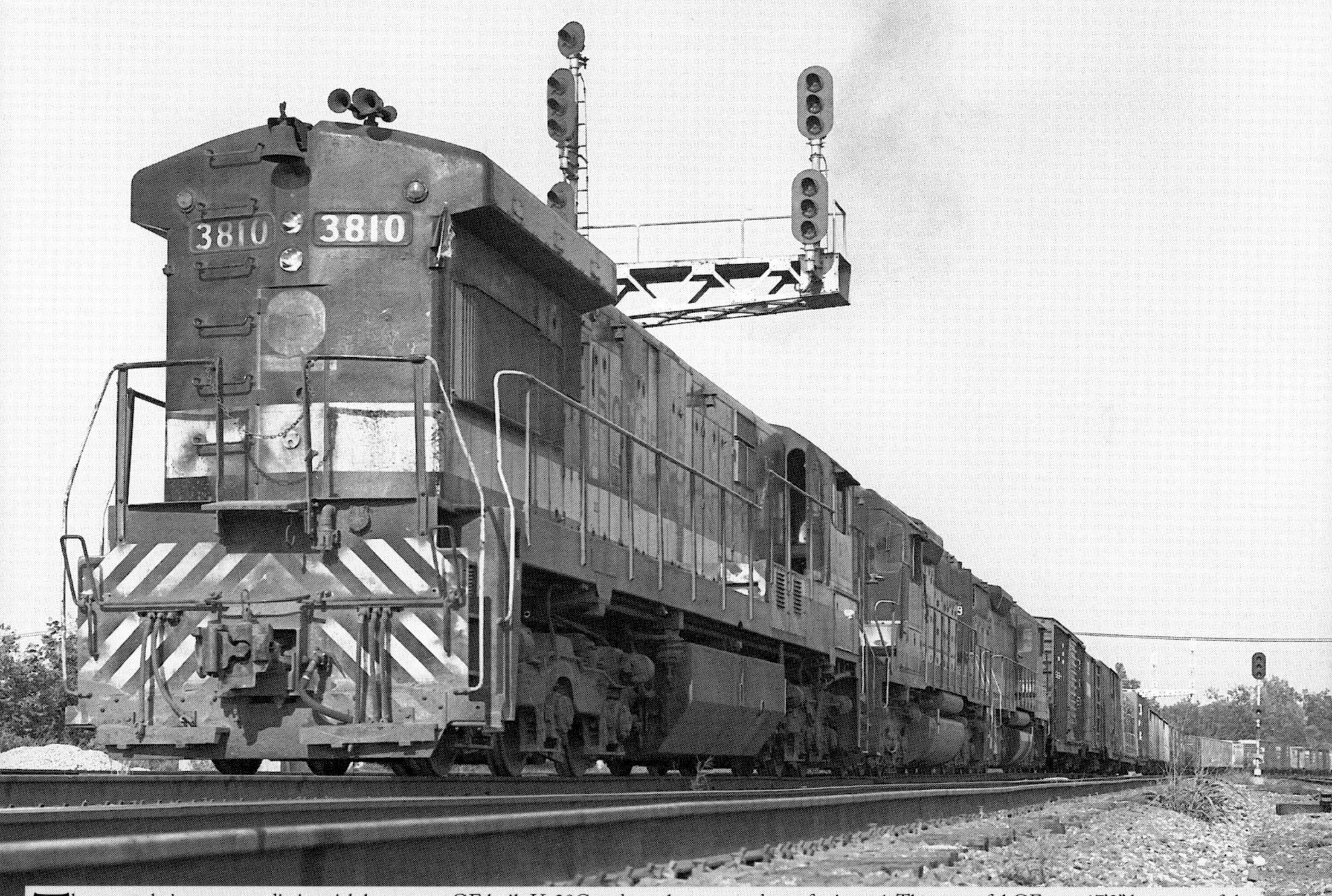

The most obvious way to distinguish between a GE built U-30C and a U-33C is shown here with great prominence: the "wings!" The U-30C's had a straight, long end while the U-33C's had a flared top (sometimes called "bat wings"). Indeed, the "wings" shown in this photo-taken at Greensboro, N. C. on Sept. 16, 1978 at 5:10 p.m. with the temperature at 88° F-was a harbinger of things to come since most all future GE engines would have "wings," even until this very day.

The big six axle was the lead engine on 1st No. 159, which had finished working Greensboro's Pomona Yard and was running a brake test, will soon proceed to its final destination: Spencer Yard, with 103 cars in tow. Behind the huge U-33C was an EMD SD-40 (#3197F) and SD-35 (#3089H).

No. 3810X came off GE's assembly line in Jan. of 1972, worked for both the Southern, until June 1, 1982 and the Norfolk Southern, where it was retired in Feb. of 1987. It had 3,300 h.p., weighed 396,090 lbs. and carried 4,000 gal. of fuel; if it looked longer than most engines, you have a good eye, for it was! The powerful GE was 67'3" long one of the longest diesels owned by the Southern.

Since the Southern only had ten of the U-33C's, it was rare to find one in action on the 8,000+ mile long railroad, and to find one as the lead unit in this power consist: WOW! The "wings" actually gave the U-33C's an improved appearance when running long end forward (the Southern's preferred position for its locomotives at this time) than the "plain Jane" looks of the U-30C's.

As a point of interest, No. 3801X and its two companions are shown at the exact location where the line from Winston-Salem, N. C. enters the Washington-Atlanta mainline (off to the left of No. 3810X).

They were big and powerful; however, the Southern preferred the locomotives built by the Electro-Motive Division of General Motors, so the U-33C's and U-30C's were few in numbers. Even so, they could really pull the tonnage and, when working at full throttle, sounded great.

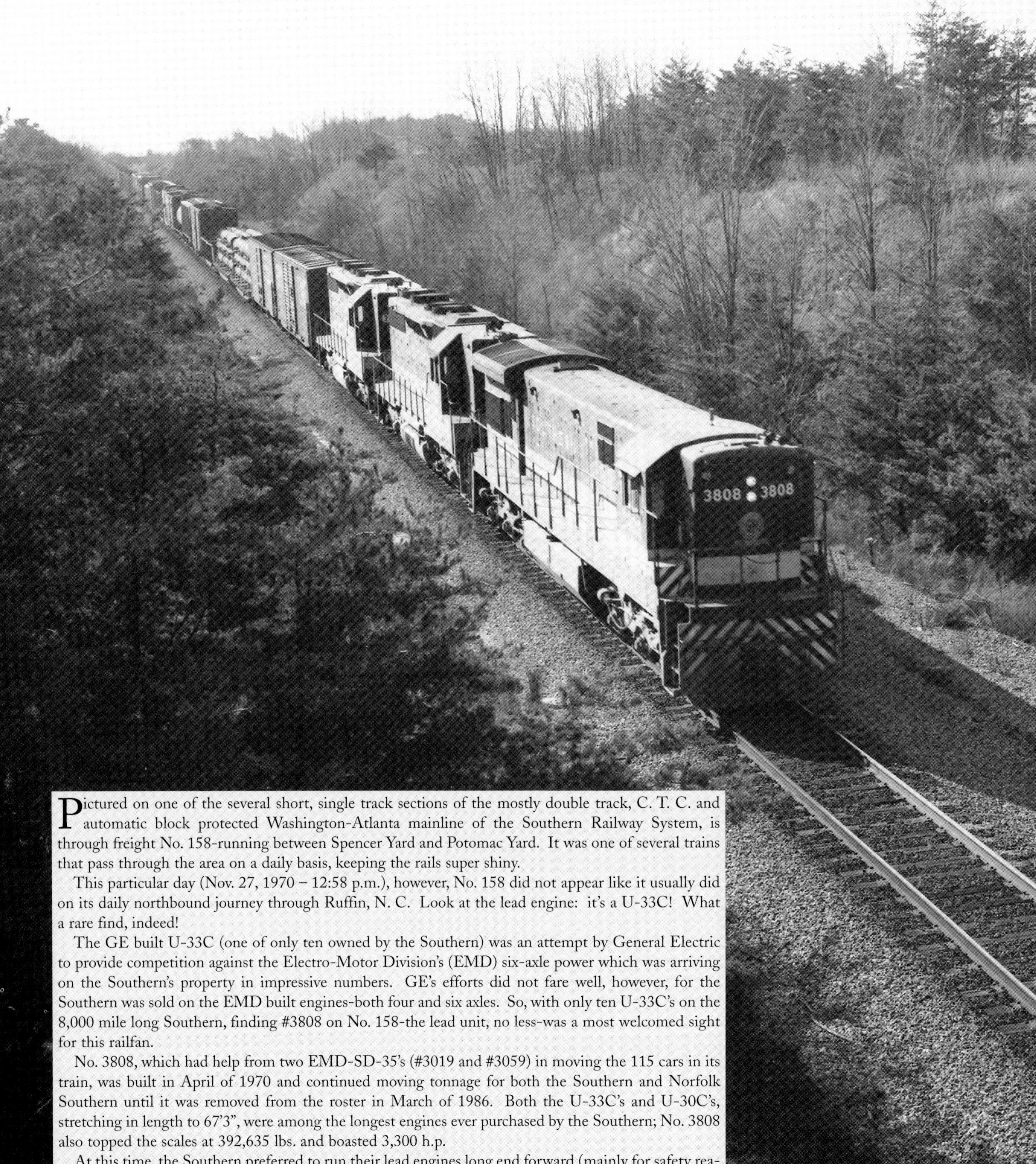

Pictured on one of the several short, single track sections of the mostly double track, C. T. C. and automatic block protected Washington-Atlanta mainline of the Southern Railway System, is through freight No. 158-running between Spencer Yard and Potomac Yard. It was one of several trains that pass through the area on a daily basis, keeping the rails super shiny.

This particular day (Nov. 27, 1970 – 12:58 p.m.), however, No. 158 did not appear like it usually did on its daily northbound journey through Ruffin, N. C. Look at the lead engine: it's a U-33C! What a rare find, indeed!

The GE built U-33C (one of only ten owned by the Southern) was an attempt by General Electric to provide competition against the Electro-Motor Division's (EMD) six-axle power which was arriving on the Southern's property in impressive numbers. GE's efforts did not fare well, however, for the Southern was sold on the EMD built engines-both four and six axles. So, with only ten U-33C's on the 8,000 mile long Southern, finding #3808 on No. 158-the lead unit, no less-was a most welcomed sight for this railfan.

No. 3808, which had help from two EMD-SD-35's (#3019 and #3059) in moving the 115 cars in its train, was built in April of 1970 and continued moving tonnage for both the Southern and Norfolk Southern until it was removed from the roster in March of 1986. Both the U-33C's and U-30C's, stretching in length to 67'3", were among the longest engines ever purchased by the Southern; No. 3808 also topped the scales at 392,635 lbs. and boasted 3,300 h.p.

At this time, the Southern preferred to run their lead engines long end forward (mainly for safety reasons). In my opinion, the big GE-and all the other engines (GE's and EMD's)-looked far more attractive and efficient running short end forward. Wouldn't you agree?

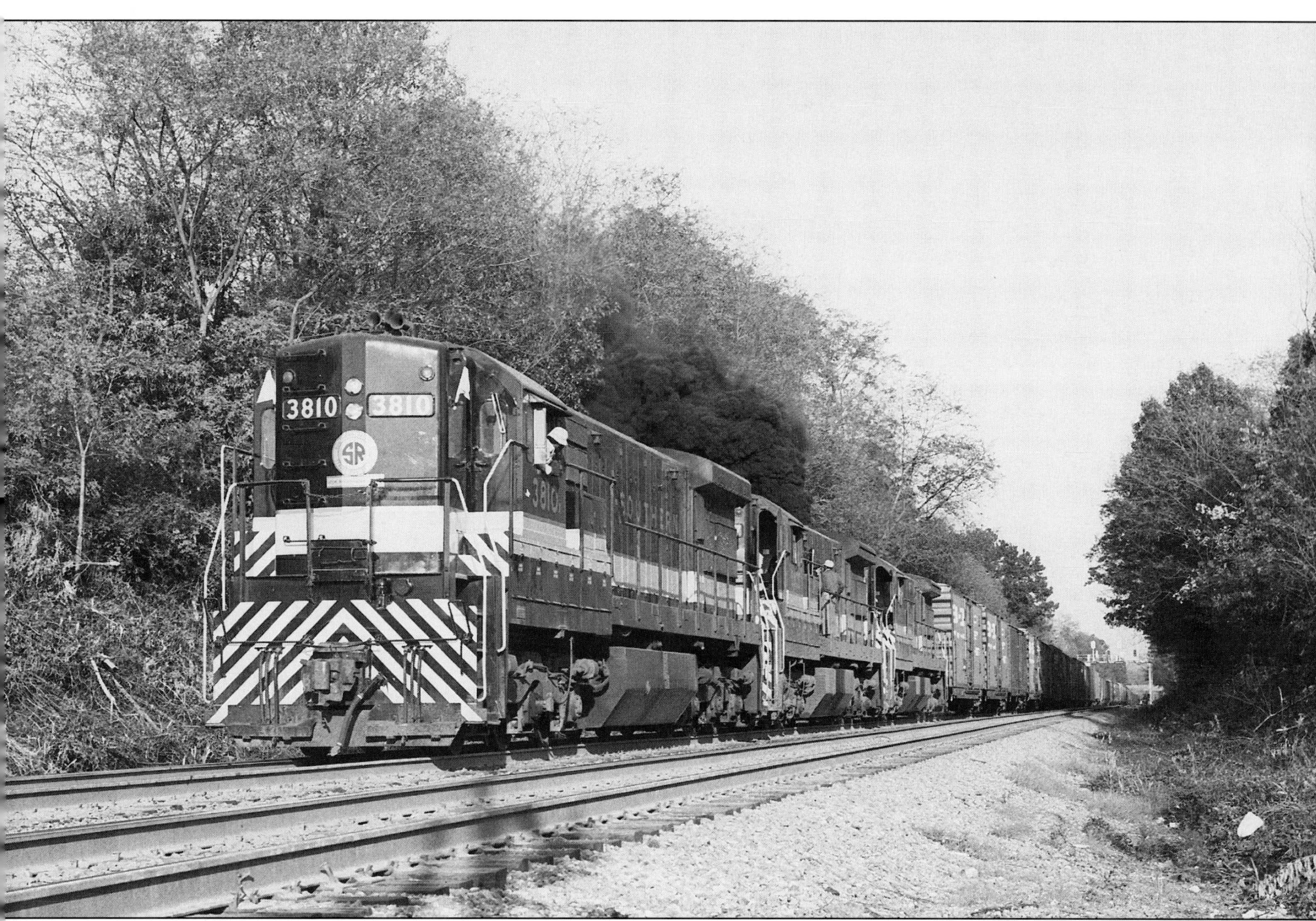

October 27, 1979 was not a good day for the Southern Railway crew on this extra south freight, shown struggling up the sharp grade that all southbound trains out of Danville, Va. must face (it was called "Cemetery Hill").

The southbound extra had worked the yard at Dundee, Va., roared by the Danville, Va. passenger, trying to build up as much momentum as possible in order to help it top the hill. Then it happened: the second engine began spewing huge volumes of black smoke and then went "off line." Almost immediately, the extra, now with only two engines to pull its 92 cars, stalled only halfway up the grade at 4:55 p.m. Fortunately, a mechanic at the Dundee diesel shop got the second unit back on line within an hour and the southbounder finally topped the grade and continued its journey to Spencer Yard.

Look at the motive power of this Extra South: three GE built U-33C's-all together (three of the ten owned by the Southern)!!! What a lucky find for me. There they were: #3810X, #3807L and #3805X, with #3807L looking like Mt. Vesuvius in an eruption.

With a crossing signal shadow in the foreground, the engineer on #3810X looks back in disgust at his middle engine, seconds before it stopped. One can only imagine what he was saying about this predicament!

No. 3810X was built in January of 1972 (retired as an NS engine in Feb. of 1987), #3807L was created in April of 1970 (retired by the NS in March of 1986) and #3805X-first of the Southern owned U-33C's-was born in April of 1970 (removed from the NS roster in March of 1986).

All three U-33C's had 3,300 h.p., weighed between 393,395 and 396,090 lbs. and carried 4,000 gal. of fuel.

I consider this photo to be one of the luckiest pictures I ever made of "my" Southern: three U-33C's-all in the same power consist-on this warm afternoon, pulling tonnage on the Washington-Atlanta mainline. Enjoy viewing this atypical but beautiful action. Boy, the three big GE's were roaring loud enough to even make the rail gods take notice!

B-23-7

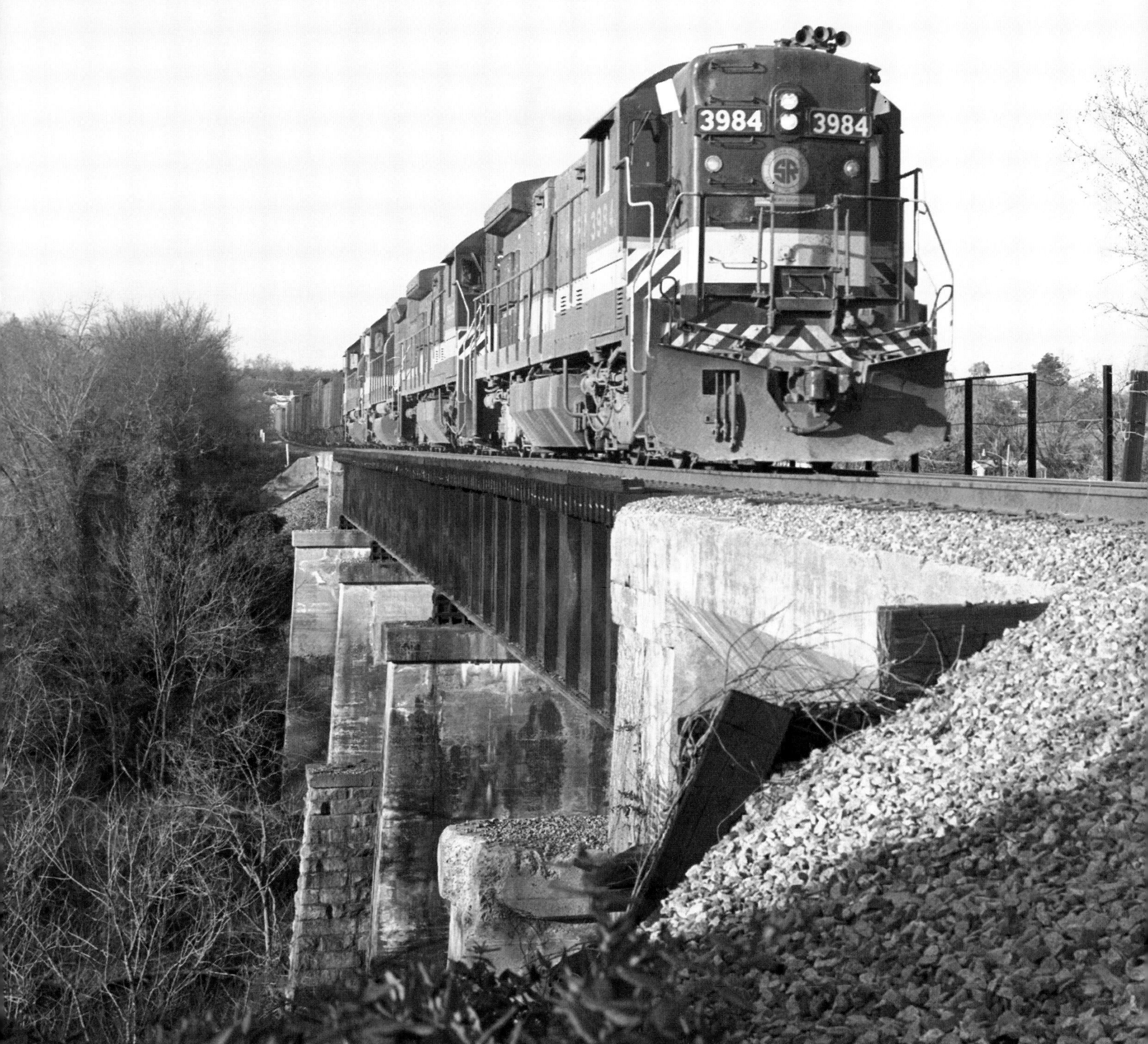

Two competing diesel manufacturers (General Electric and General Motor's Electro Motive Division – "EMD") have their engines operating together in moving this solid coal train over the Haw River Bridge in Haw River, N. C. on the busy Greensboro-Raleigh, N. C. line, thereby adding more finances to the Southern's coffers.

What a wonderful way to start a railfan's day: two GE built B23-7's (#3984 & #3992) and two EMD's GP-38-2's (#5088 & #5050) have 90 cars of coal moving east to Raleigh at a good 35-40 m.p.h. pace on this beautiful Nov. 21, 1981. It's 8:35 a.m. and the temperature stands at 49° F as the "ground shaking" tonnage passes by.

The B23-7's were an improvement over GE's older U-23B models and designed to out-perform EMD's GP-38 series (GP-38, GP-38AC & GP-38-2's). Unfortunately for GE, the Southern – and a vast majority of their crews – favored the GP's over the U-23B's and B23-7's. The "Geeps" were more responsive to the engineer's touch and were very reliable. Still, when it got down to lugging heavy tonnage at a low speed, the GE's prove to be good pullers and what a tremendous sound they could make!

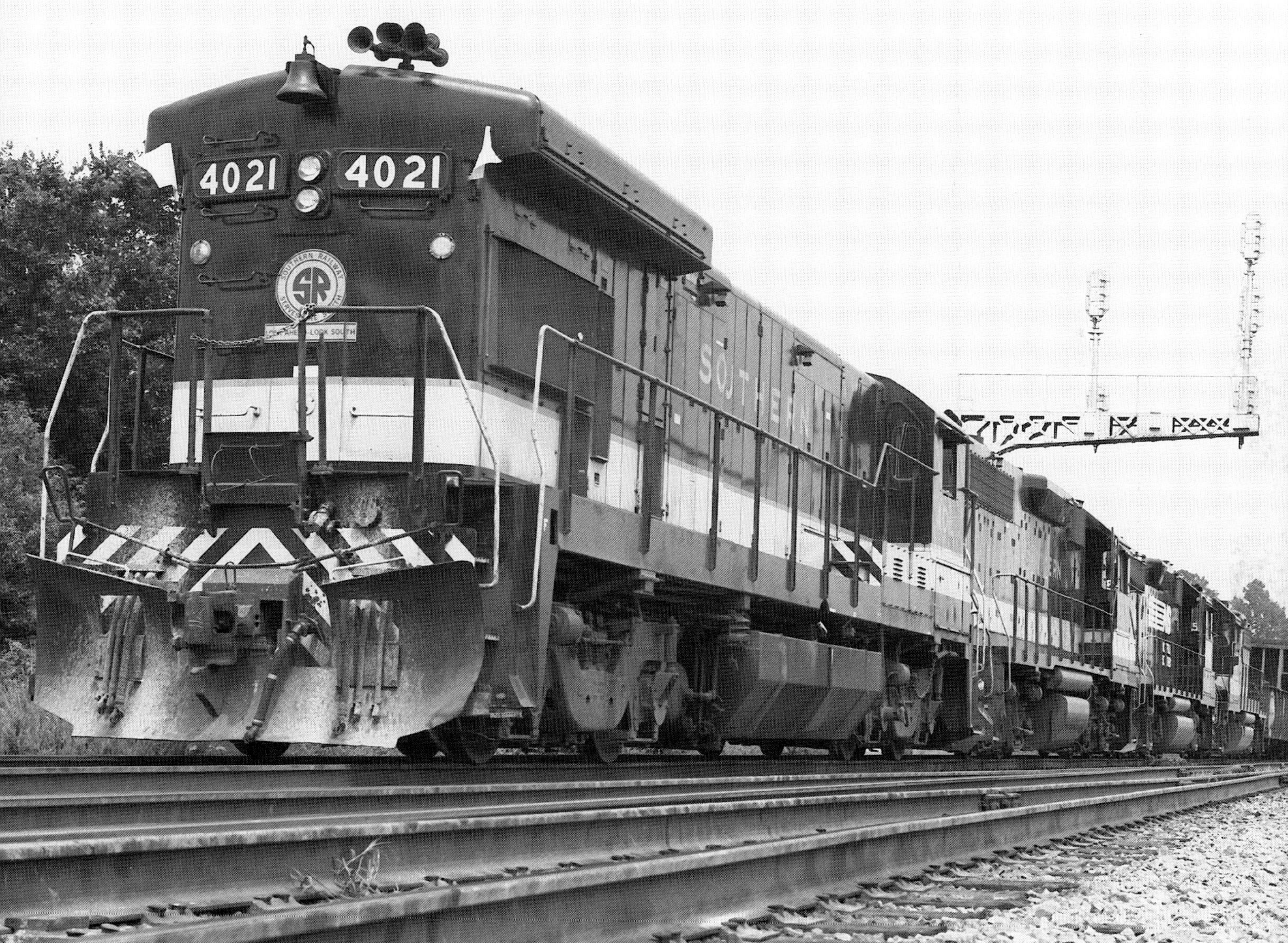

On occasion, when the freight yards accumulated too many cars and the yardmasters wanted to make room for incoming tonnage, the Southern would run an extra freight to relieve the congestion.

Here, in Greensboro, N. C. on Aug. 11, 1982 at 2:37 p.m. – running a brake test – is such a train. The extra, pulled by GE's B23-7 (#4021H – built in April of 1981 and weighing 256, 600 lbs.) plus three EMD's, GP-38 (#2784T), and 2 GP-38-2's (#5163F and #5155T), helped the yardmasters at Raleigh's Glenwood Yard, East Durham and here at Pomona Yard. As a result of this help, its length has grown to 137 cars – all bound for the huge and modern Spencer Yard in Linwood, N. C.

This is the place to be if you are a railfan, i.e., South Pomona Yard. Why? Because not only do you have the tremendous number of train on the Washington-Atlanta mainline passing by, you also have the frequent movements to and from Raleigh. The line from Winston-Salem, N. C. enters the mainline from the left in this photo – almost exactly where the #4021H stands. And, on many occasions, an extra train will come to Pomona Yard from Spencer Yard with a long cut of piggyback cars and return to Spencer with piggybacks from the huge "pig" yard at Pomona (located just behind your photographer). This movement would help the hot, mainline piggyback trains avoid making a stop at Pomona Yard, thereby saving time and saving time saves money!

Yes, here's the place to be, if you are just a "looker" or a photographer, for a great deal of rail action.

B-30-7

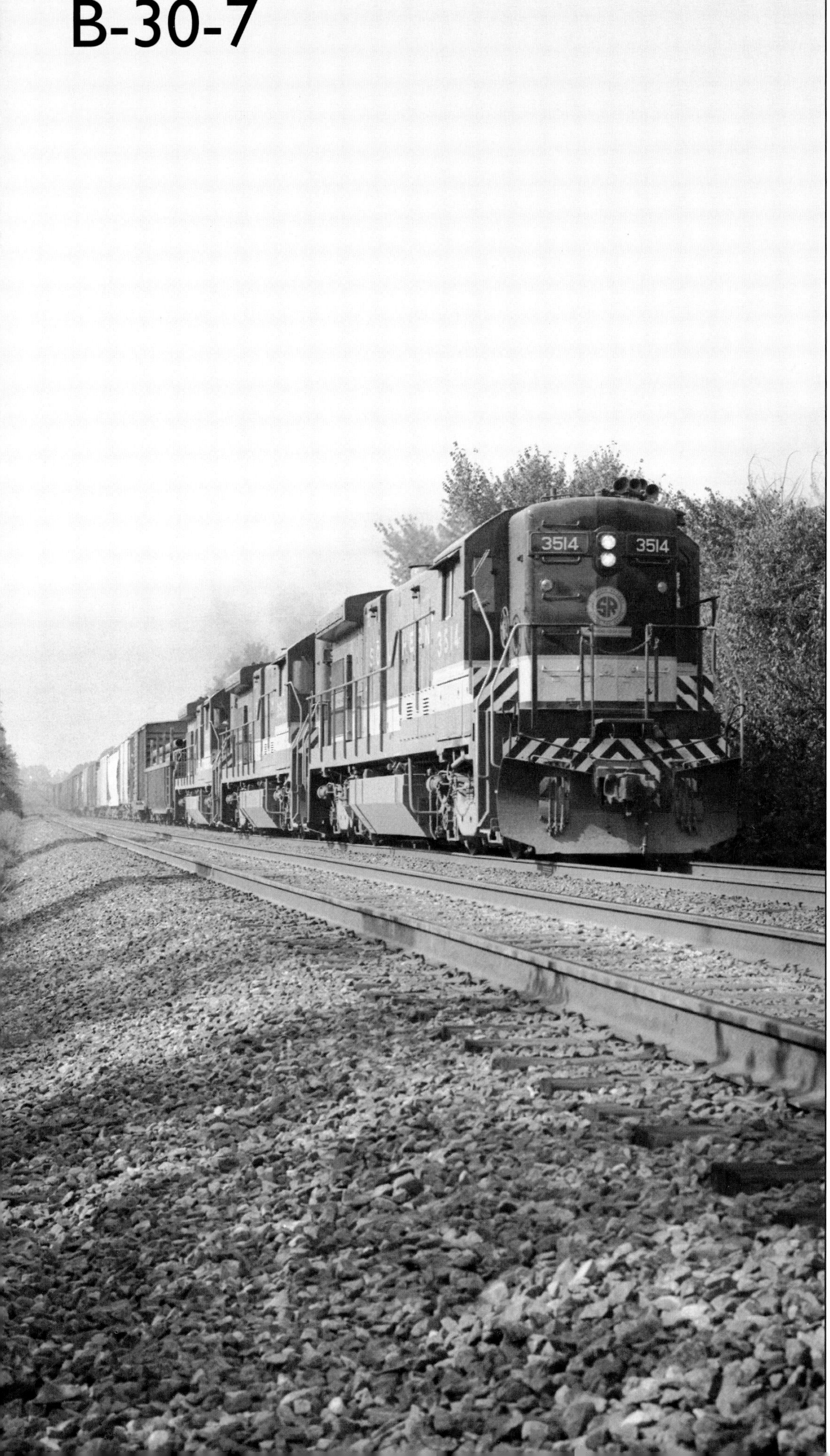

After leaving Spencer Yard (by the time of this photo, the yard was located in Linwood, N. C. – approximately seven miles north of Spencer, N. C. – and was an ultra-modern, huge facility), "former" Southern's through freight, No. 158, is shown nearing High Point, N. C. on the Washington-Atlanta main-line, making its daily trip to Potomac Yard – all at a good 50+ m.p.h.

There are two things that make this picture unique: 1) this exposure was made on Oct. 2, 1982 (10:24 a.m.), four months after the Southern and N&W merger, so we are actually viewing a Norfolk Southern freight, not Southern; 2) the Southern ordered the GE-built B30-7A1's so close to the June 1, 1982 merger date, that most exposures made of these high horsepower (3,000), fuel-efficient (3,350 gal.) and increased dynamic braking capacity engines, were made when they were serving the NS. Fortunately, the big four axles retained their Southern colors and lettering plus that magnificent Southern symbol for a few years after the merger.

As an example of the two factors mentioned above, No. 158's three B30-7A1's (#3514T, #3513X and #3500R) – pulling 144 cars – were built in April of 1982 (two months before the merger). The B30-7A1's were 63'2" long, carried 48 cu. ft. of sand and weighed over 278,000 lbs. They were the engines built by GE, designed to match and, hopefully, exceed the performance of Southern's successfully and beloved EMD's GP-50's.

The area between Greensboro and Linwood, N. C. was and remains the busiest section of the Washington-Atlanta main, for it hosted not only the normal mainliners but the considerable traffic to and from the Greensboro-Raleigh route as well. Today you can also find six Amtrak's among all the freights: the "Crescent," "Carolinian" and "Piedmont" – the latter two used the line to Raleigh. Indeed, Jamestown, High Point, Thomasville and Lexington would be ideal locations for railfans to stay for awhile to see the action roll by. I know this to be true, from personal experience!

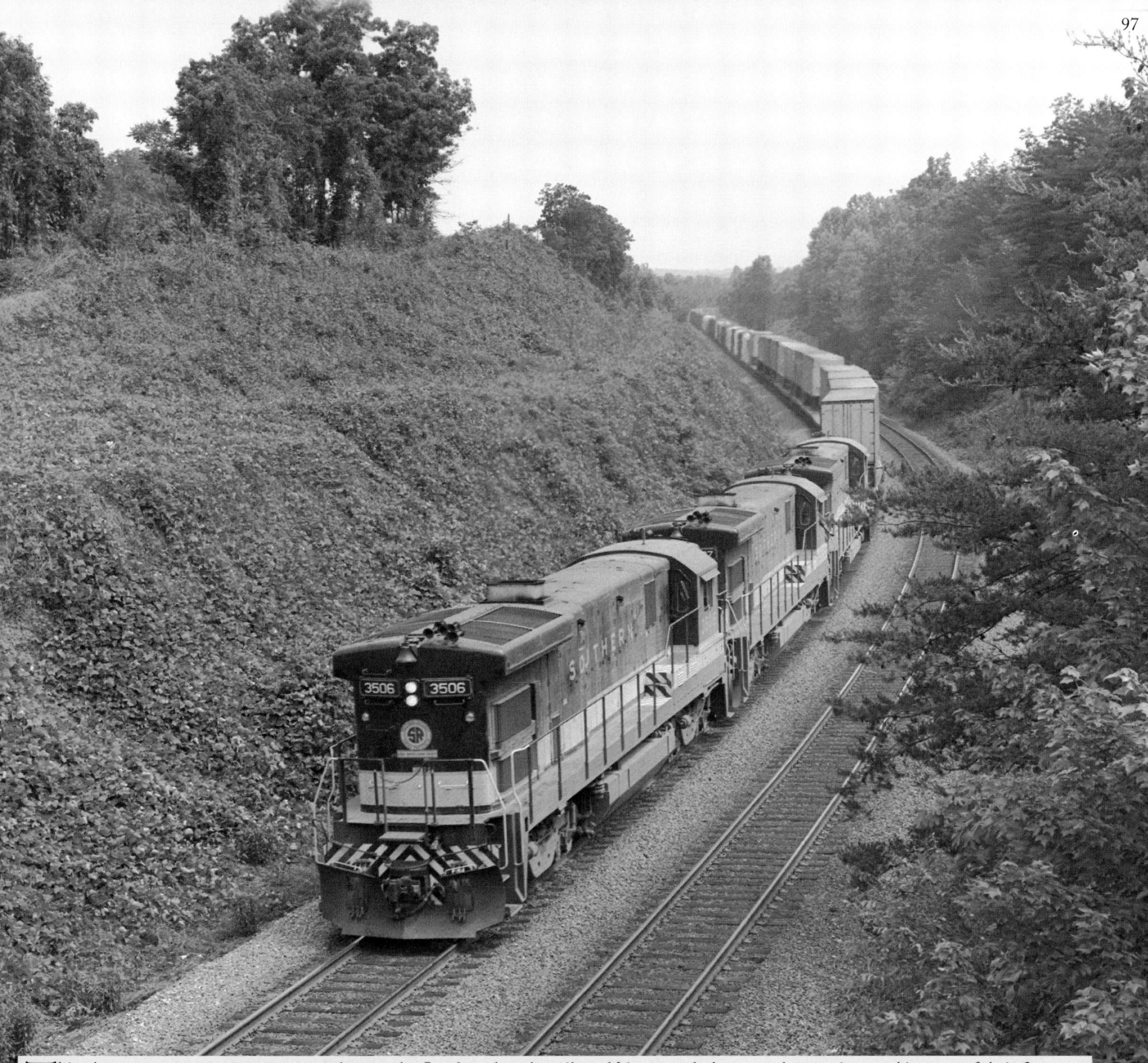

This photo captures a rare moment, not just on the Southern but the rail world in general: three new locomotives, making one of their first runs in revenue service.

Three brand new GE-built B30-7A1's (constructed in April of 1982) are shown working upgrade through Motley, Va. pulling No. 173's 92 cars, including a long line of piggybacks, this May 29, 1982 at 11:46 a.m. Only a month old, their paint was still shiny, the lettering and numbers were unblemished. Even their exhaust stacks still had the silver paint applied by GE. I could almost swear that I could actually smell fresh paint as the big four axles rolled by.

The Southern had a policy of placing their most modern power on their high-priority trains. No. 173 left Potomac Yard near Sunrise and would arrive in Atlanta's Inman Yard by midnight – 633 miles before the end of the day: the Southern really moved their freights!

The three B30-7A1's (#3506J, #3507F, and #3502H) were high horsepowered (3,000 h.p. each), four-axle diesels which had increased dynamic braking capacity. The road that "Served the South" also felt that it should run their engines in match sets to optimize their performance because of their high speed gearing and other specifications.

No. 173 is shown passing through a "sea of kudzu" on the busy, well-maintained Washington-Atlanta mainline. Because the new GE's arrived just before the June 1, 1982 merger of the Southern with the N&W, most of their service was for the newly created Norfolk Southern, for which they continue to toil to this very day, all 22 units purchased by the Southern (#3500-#3521).

To me, this super-elevated curve in Motley was one of the most photogenic locations in the area. I not only photographed several other freights at this spot over the years but I also made numerous exposures of most all steam locomotives used during the wonderful steam excursion era, for this grade made all the steam power operate at full throttle; the smoke and sounds were terrific! By the way, the sounds coming from these three, wide-opened, new B30-7A1's were not all that bad either!

B-36-7

What a pleasant surprise I found at the north end of Greensboro, N.C.'s Pomona Yard this cloudy July 21, 1982, at 1:30 p.m. There, at the head of Southern's No. 156, were three of the elusive B36-7's. I called the B36-7's elusive because the Southern only purchased six of these powerful road switchers from General Electric. Indeed, No. 156 actually had half of all these engines on the road's motive power roster – WOW!

GE delivered the six B36-7's (#3815-#3820) to the Southern in March of 1981, giving their latest diesels glowing reports. The B36-7's were GE's answer to EMD's highly successful GP-50's.

No. 3815W, #3817K and #3816R were waiting to back into the yard to leave its "Greensboro's cut" and retrieve several "hot" piggyback cars before continuing its journey from Florida to Potomac Yard. No.156 was known as the "Bean Train" – a nickname from the days of steam operations when the Southern gave the SAL competition for the Florida – New York business.

The northbounder's lead unit had 3,600 h.p., carried 2,650 gal. of fuel, 380 gal. of lube oil, 365 gal. of cooling water and 48 cu. ft. of sand. Stretching 61'2" in length, the B36-7's lived up to their reputation as 1st class locomotives.

One problem kept the Southern from purchasing more of these remarkable engines. During the negotiations between the Southern and the N&W, which would eventually result in the June 1, 1982 creation of the current Norfolk Southern, both roads agreed that they would not purchase additional high horsepower four-axle locomotives. Instead, they would use the six-axle "monsters" for muscle power. As a result, the six B36-7's were the last of their kind on the Southern.

No. 3815W still works for the NS. Unfortunately, I only caught the B36-7's on film twice – both times in Greensboro. So, even though it was a cloudy and hot day, who cared?

I got photos of the B36-7's! To me, the day was sunny and mild and I had a "BIG" smile on my face and a happy memory.

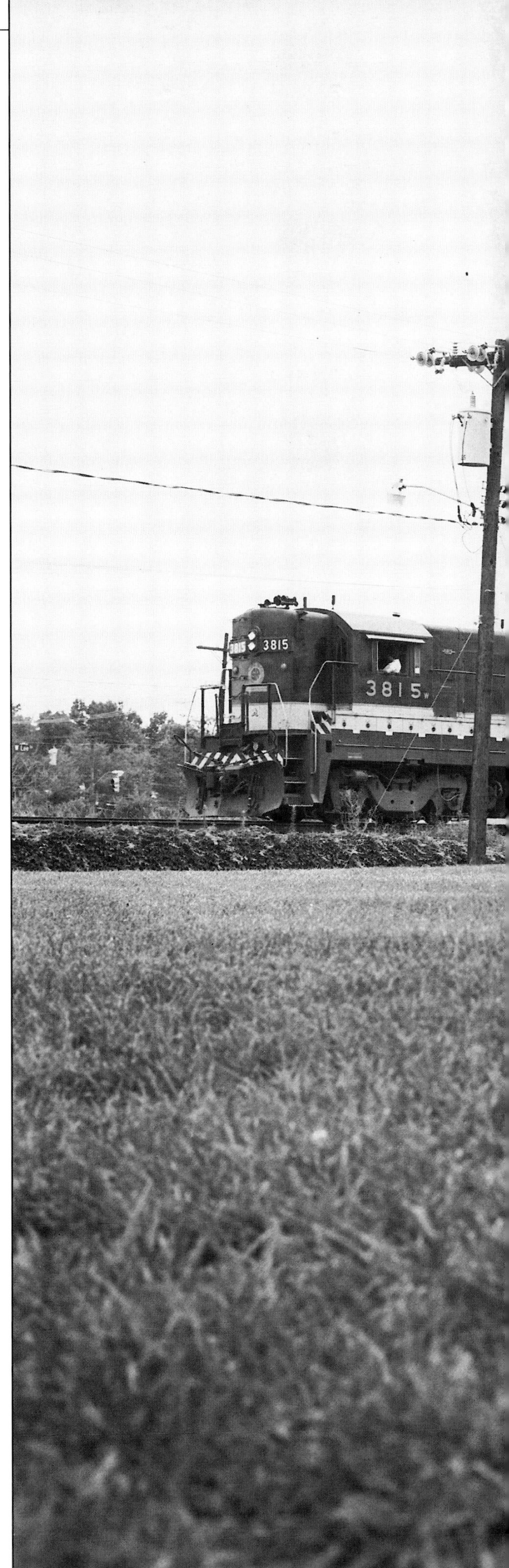

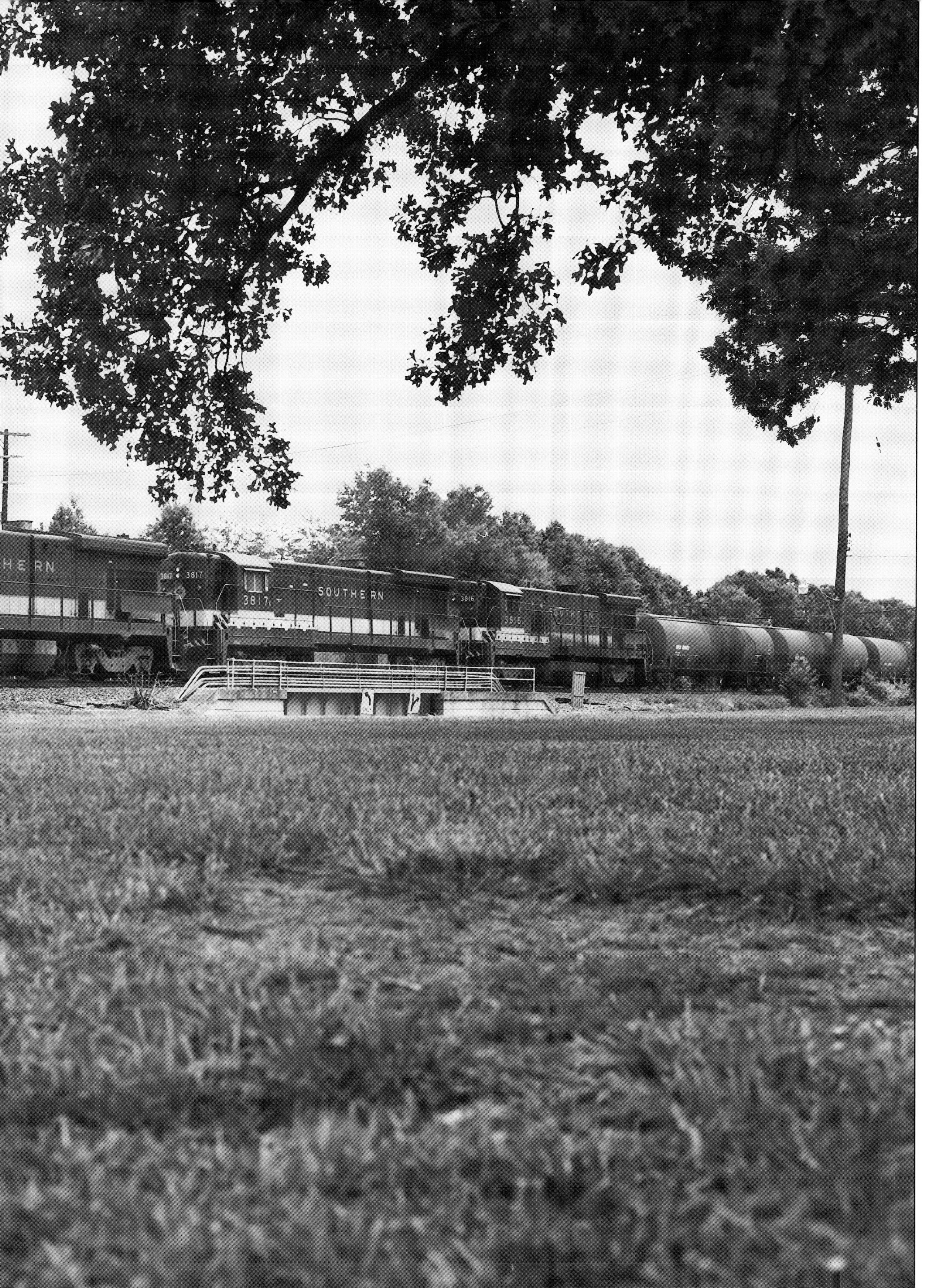
3817
SOUTHERN
3817
3816
SOUTHERN
3816

SWITCHERS

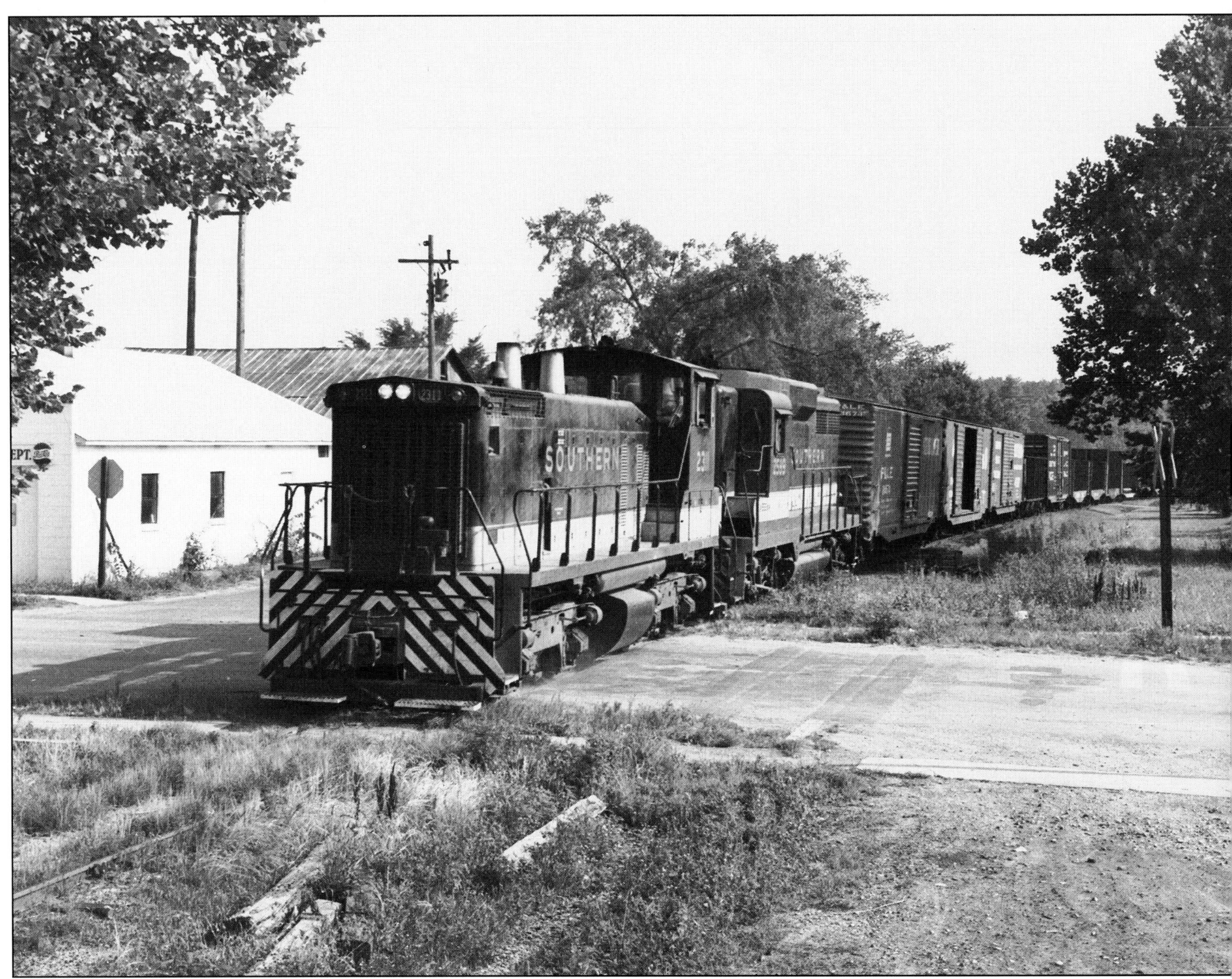

The EMD built SW-1500 was one of the most successful and popular switchers owned by the Southern. Indeed, their performance was so impressive the road purchased 65 units. They had great power (1,500 h.p.), excellent visibility for the crews and their fast response to the engineer's demands was greatly appreciated.

They were so effective in yard work that for a year or so the Southern assigned several of the SW-1500's to local freight work – this was a mistake. True, when working local yards and industrial tracks, they were very good. However, when traveling between towns, they were rough riders, slow and their weight on such a short frame was bad on the tracks. As an example of this problem, No. 2311 (shown here) weighed 257,153 lbs. on a frame that was just 44'8" long. The crews and track people finally convinced the officials to keep the SW-1500's (usually called simply "SW-15's") in the yards and let the "GP" series handle the freights.

The quietness of Stovall, N. C. (my mom's hometown) was interrupted twice a day (except Sundays) with the passage of local freight's No. 78 (from East Durham, N. C. to Keysville, Va.) and No. 77 (Keysville to East Durham). In fact, each day several people would come out of their buildings and/or homes to watch the freights go by. On occasion, No. 78 (shown here) would stop, pull out loaded cars of pulpwood (a pile of which I was standing on to make this exposure) and place empty wood "racks" into the siding for more loads.

Today's train was different: there were two engines on the point of the normal one engine powered train. With 32 cars in tow, the northbound local was assigned SW-15 (#231) and GP-30 (#2646) to pull the heavy train this June 28, 1969 at 2:10 p.m. No. 78 is shown crossing the Main Street in Stoval at 25 m.p.h.

The crew did not like the rough riding SW-15 (#2311). Built in Nov. of 1968-not quite a year old when this portrait was made – it carried 1,100 gal. of fuel and 30. cu. ft. of sand and remains in service today, working for the Norfolk Southern.

What a difference in sights and sounds: an SW-15 plus GP-30 working together. The SW-1500's were not very photogenic, but they were powerful although short engines. In fact, their rough riding qualities and heavy-short configuration finally confined them to mostly yard work. However, it made for an interesting photo this afternoon and the people who came out to see No. 78 got quite a sight to remember!

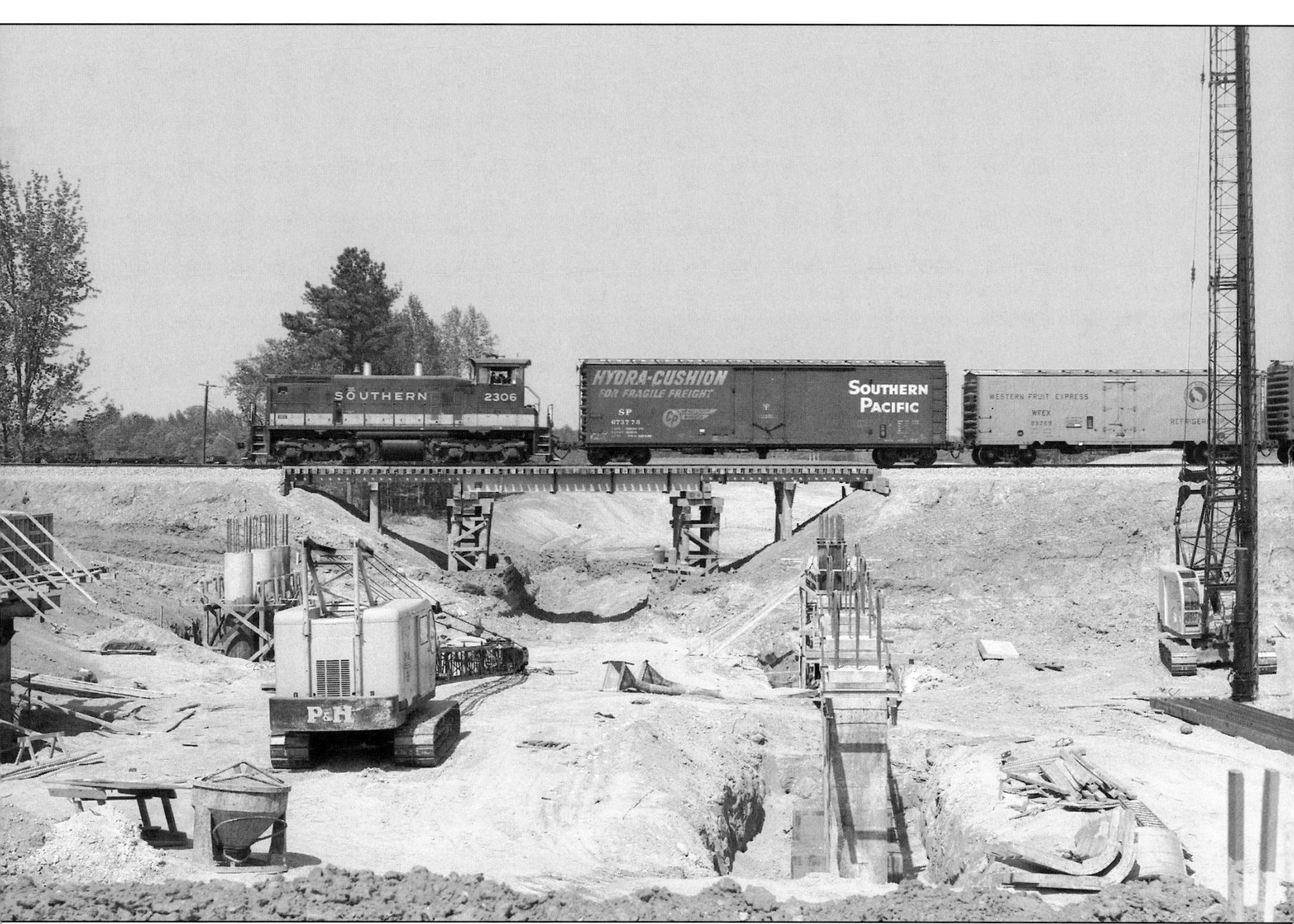

You have a view of the creation of Interstate 85 through the Henderson, N. C. area on May 3, 1969, at 3:29 p.m. To complete the four-lane "speedway," a new bridge had to be built to go under Dabney Drive (the highway I'm standing on while taking this photo). The D.O.T. (Department of Transportation) also had to build a new bridge which would carry train traffic over the Southern's Oxford-Henderson, N. C. branch.

In order to keep rail traffic moving while the new overpass was being built, they had to construct a "shoo-fly" – a temporary structure – that would enable No. 168 (Oxford-Henderson) and No. 167 (shown here) to complete their trips.

Today's No. 167 is shown crossing over the "shoo-fly" at 10 m.p.h. with a powerful and short SW-1500 (#2306) pulling 15 cars on its way back to Oxford. Once back in my hometown, No. 167 would become No. 78 and complete its East Durham, N. C. to Keysville, Va. run (No. 78 was required to make a round trip between Oxford and Henderson and its southbound counterpart, No. 77, would pass through Oxford – on its Keysville to East Durham run – while No. 78 was on the Henderson branch (running as No. 168 and No. 167).

The SW-15's were among the finest switch engines ever owned by the Southern (the road eventually had 64 units on its roster); however, they did not prove to be good local freight motive power: they were rough riders, slow and did damage to the tracks since they were so short – 44'8" long – and heavy – No. 2306 weighed 256,537 lbs. As a result, the Southern kept most of them doing what they were designed to do: yard work. No. 2306 was built in Nov. of 1968 and remains in service today (for the Norfolk Southern).

Unfortunately, the NS abandoned the Oxford-Henderson branch. The bridge remains in place to this very day; and whenever I pass this area, I think back to that May 3, 1969 when I made this historic portrait and thank the Lord that I took this exposure (I almost decided not to record this moment in rail history).

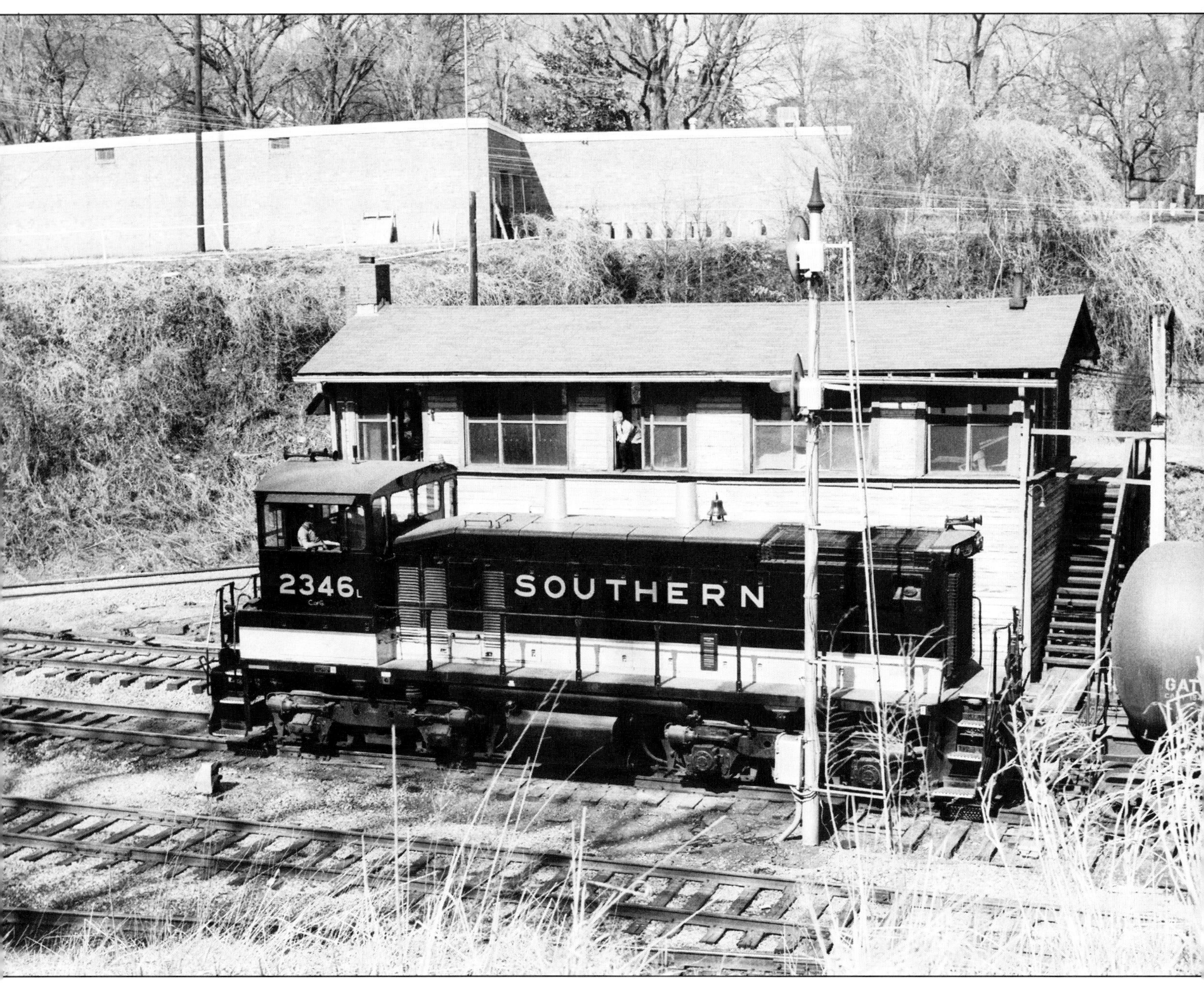

It was a "lazy" Saturday afternoon, this Feb. 28, 1976 (at 1:50 p.m.). Since no trains were due around Boylen Tower, here in Raleigh, N. C., for nearly an hour, Southern's SW-1500, #2346L, was able to work a long cut of cars in their "old yard." After the Southern purchased the Norfolk Southern in Jan. of 1974, it was decided to use the much larger ex-NS Glenwood Yard as the main switching facility in Raleigh. Once this decision was made, the Southern's original yard became known as the "old yard." Even the tower operator had time to watch #2346L do what it was designed to do: work the yards.

For many years, the old Norfolk Southern operated the tower to protect this busy location. The track on the left of the engine (running behind the tower) was the former NS, Norfolk, Va. – Charlotte, N. C. mainline. It crossed over the jointly operated double-track territory. The Southern's Greensboro-Goldsboro, N. C. line and the SCL's Richmond-Miami mainline kept the rails of the double track very shiny. This was also a connection point for all three roads although the SCL's major connection with the ex-NS was located at the east end of Glenwood. This was also the place to be in Raleigh if you wanted to watch and/or photograph the majority of rail action.

No. 2346L entered the Southern's roster in March of 1970 and remains in service today) for the current NS) – over 30 years of service. The "little giant" had 1,500 h.p., weighed 254,477 lbs., carried 1,100 gal. of fuel and 30 cu. ft. of sand. Two sets of air-chime horns were on top, along with its bell. It was 44'8" long, 10'1" wide and 15'11" high (counting the height of the horns).

This area was visited by railfans from in and outside the Raleigh area. I always tried to select a new position to get my photos. It remains the hottest rail action area in Raleigh to this very day; however, the tower is long gone, unfortunately. Six Amtraks, 16+ freights and numerous switching movements continue to function like a magnet in drawing railfans back to this location time and time again, including yours truly!

Color Gallery

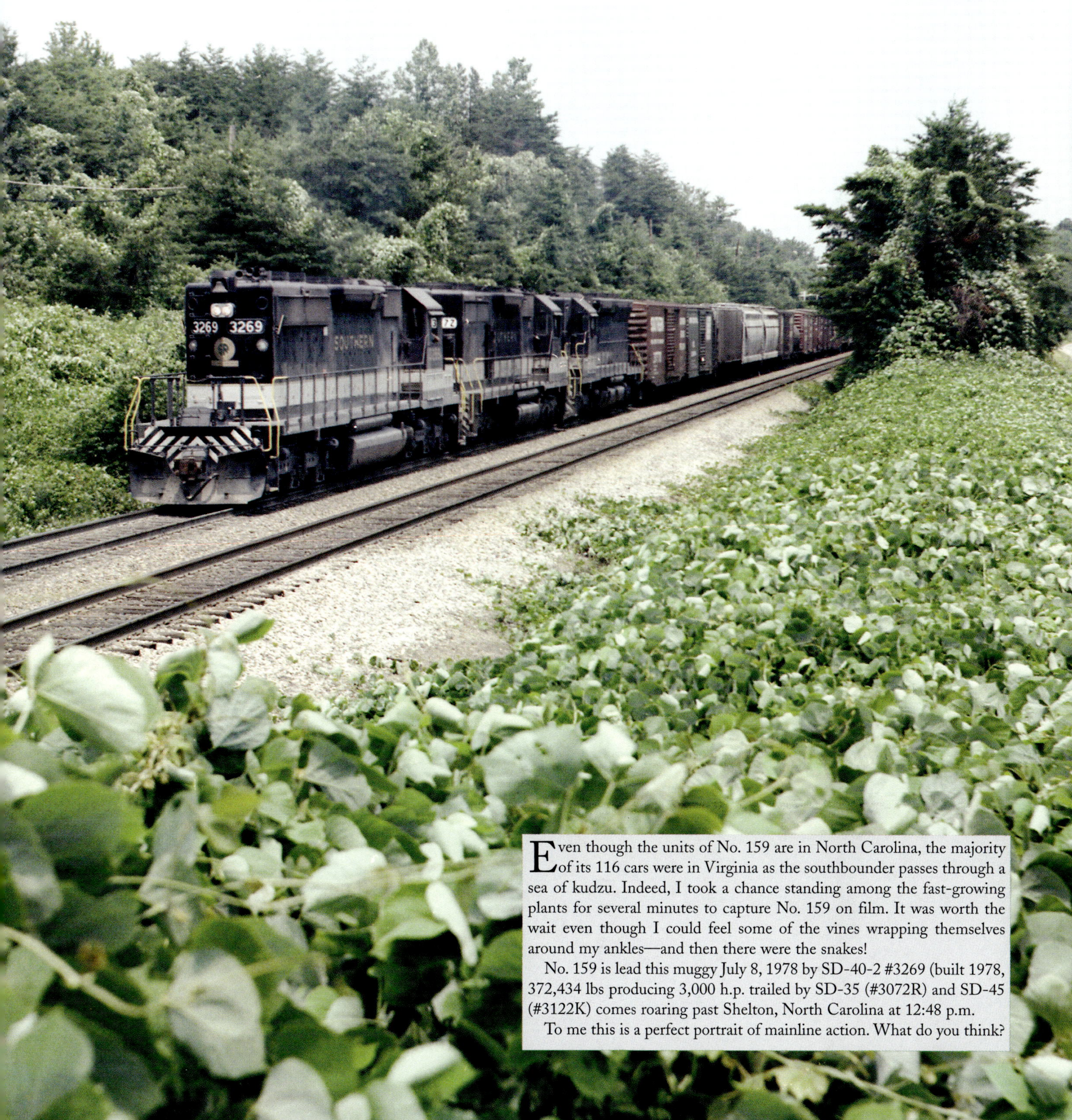

Even though the units of No. 159 are in North Carolina, the majority of its 116 cars were in Virginia as the southbounder passes through a sea of kudzu. Indeed, I took a chance standing among the fast-growing plants for several minutes to capture No. 159 on film. It was worth the wait even though I could feel some of the vines wrapping themselves around my ankles—and then there were the snakes!

No. 159 is lead this muggy July 8, 1978 by SD-40-2 #3269 (built 1978, 372,434 lbs producing 3,000 h.p. trailed by SD-35 (#3072R) and SD-45 (#3122K) comes roaring past Shelton, North Carolina at 12:48 p.m.

To me this is a perfect portrait of mainline action. What do you think?

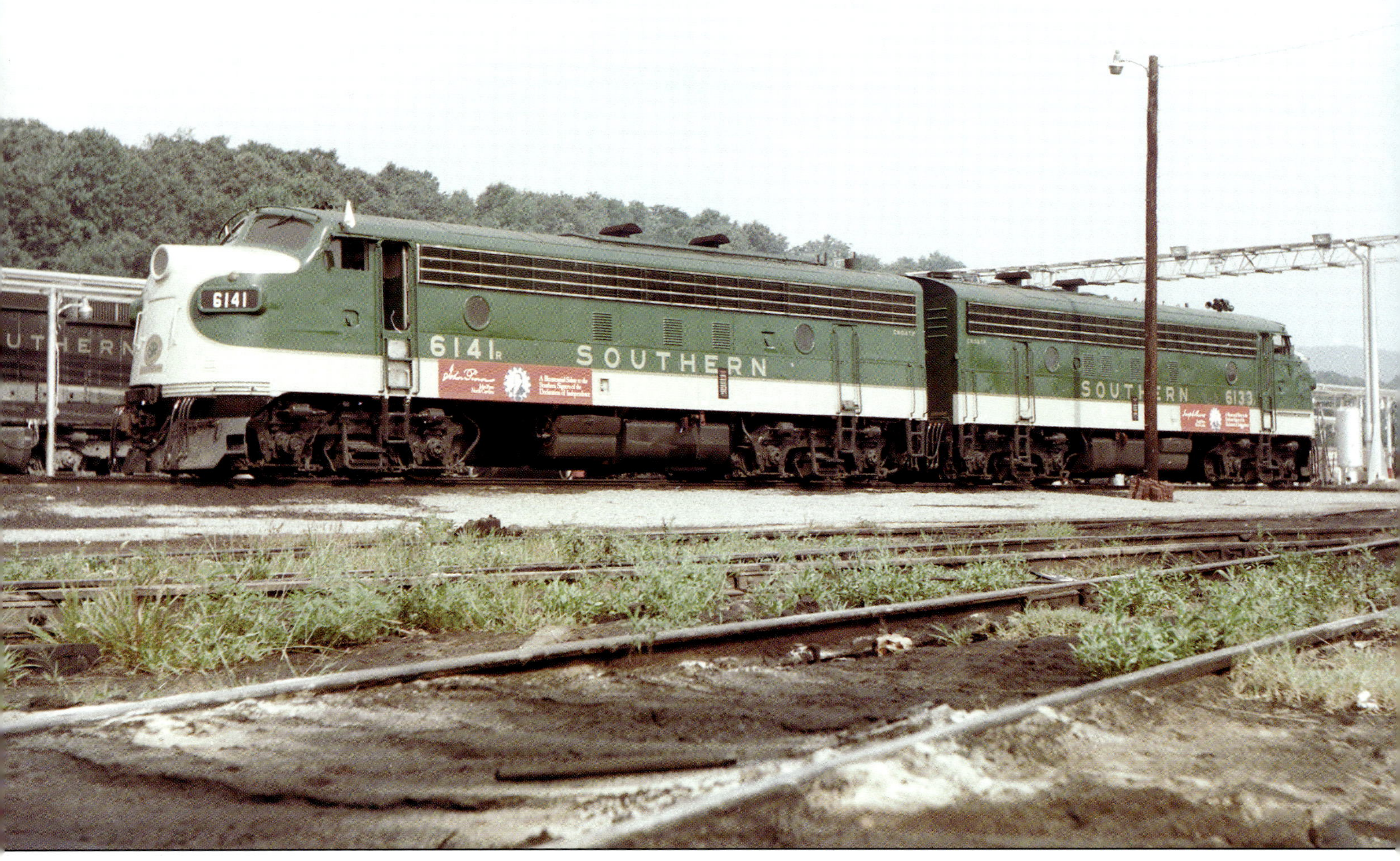

During the Bicentennial of our Nation's Birth, the southern decided to celebrate this historic occasion by placing red-colored decals on the sides of all of their E-8 and FP-7s. Each decal contained, among other information, the signature and portrait of a southerner who signed the Declaration of Independence.

Examples of the decals were found on two, super clean, beautiful, green, white and gold colored Southern FP-7As on this quiet, lazy afternoon near the old Asheville, North Carolina roundhouse. No. 6141R's decal had the signature and portrait of John Penn, while the 6133J recognized Joseph Hewes.

It was a wonderful afternoon for yours truly. The FP-7As would pull the "Skyland Special" the next morning from Asheville (actually Biltmore), to Old Fort, North Carolina and return—one of the most scenic rides this side of the Mississippi River. Mom, Dad, three Aunts and myself would take the trip.

When I arrived in this area, there was no one there—no railfans or employees. It was just me, the two beauties and that wonderful afternoon sun. I had a most outstanding time photographing two of the most impressive FP-7As to roll off of EMD's assembly line (with the help of the Southern).

Here we see the Southern's excursion train the "Skyline Special," taking on over 100 passengers at Biltmore, North Carolina before heading east on its round-trip to Old Fort.

During the Nation's bicentennial celebration of our nation's birth, the Southern ran this scenic trip behind two freshly painted FP-7As, with a consist of three open cars, a dome car (once used on the Central of Georgia's streamliner "Nancy Hanks") plus three regular coaches.

Mom, Dad, three of my Aunts and yours truly rode the "Sky" this day. The family rode in the dome car; I chose to ride in the first car which was coupled just behind 6141R—I almost froze. I never considered just how cold the morning mountain air could even be in October (I would do it again without any hesitation).

This ride was on the busy Asheville-Salisbury, North Carolina line; and between Ridgecrest and Old Fort your were surrounded by the spectacular grandure of the Blue Ridge Mountains. Their were unbelievable curves, deep cuts, numerous grades and seven tunnels. By the way, the engineer of the "Sky" was an old friend: rail historian, photographer and author: Frank Clodfelter.

The "Skyland Special" left Biltmore at 9:00 a.m., arriving in Old Fort at 10:20 a.m. on Saturdays and holidays. On Sundays the eastbounder departed Biltmore at 11:00 a.m., arriving in Old Fort at 2:20 p.m.

As a point of interest the "Sky" was located at the best "train watching" location in the area: it was where the line from Spartanburg, S.C.—over Saluda grade—and Salisbury joined and headed toward the big yard at Ashville.

This was a ride I will never forget!

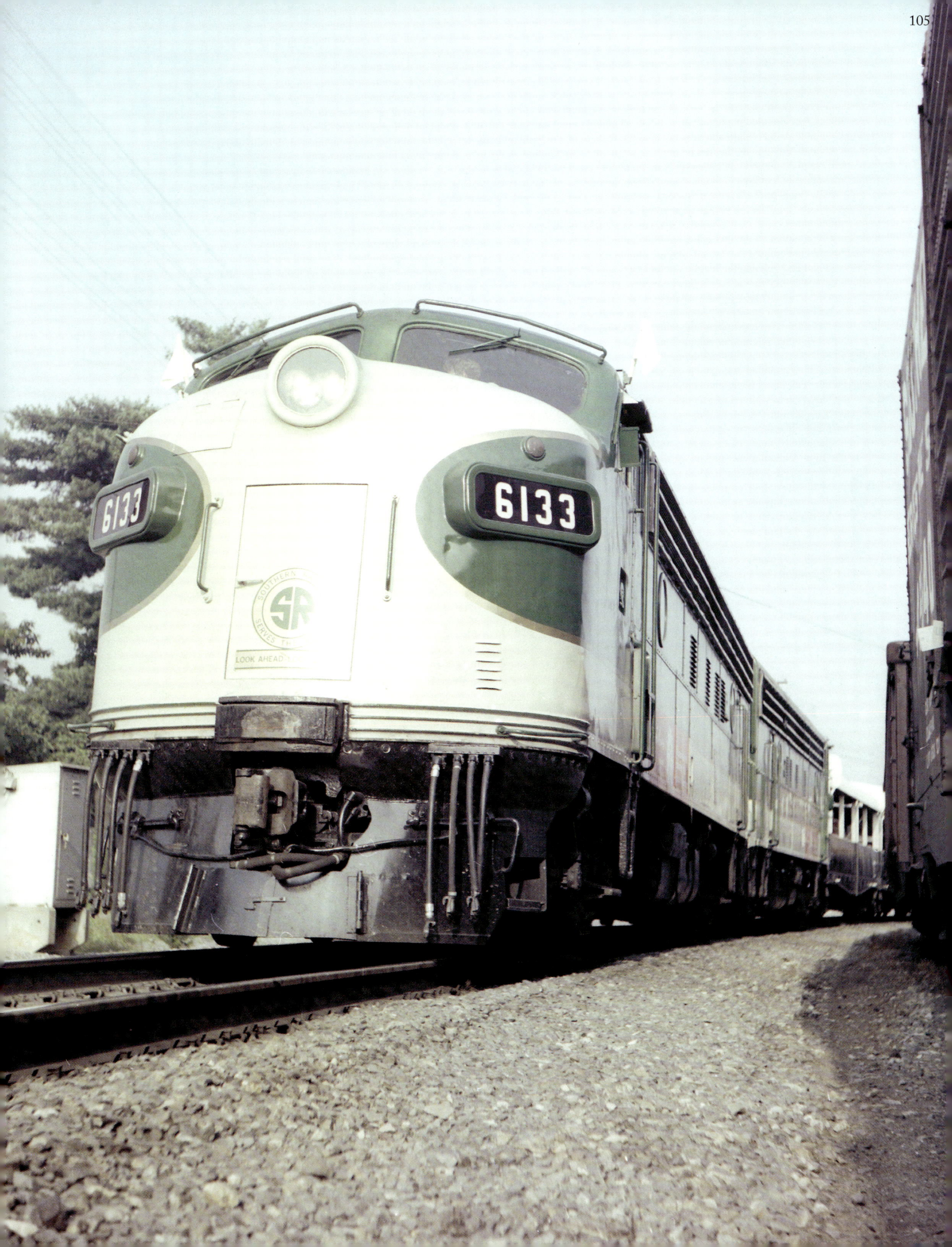
6133
6133
SOUTHERN
SR
LOOK AHEAD

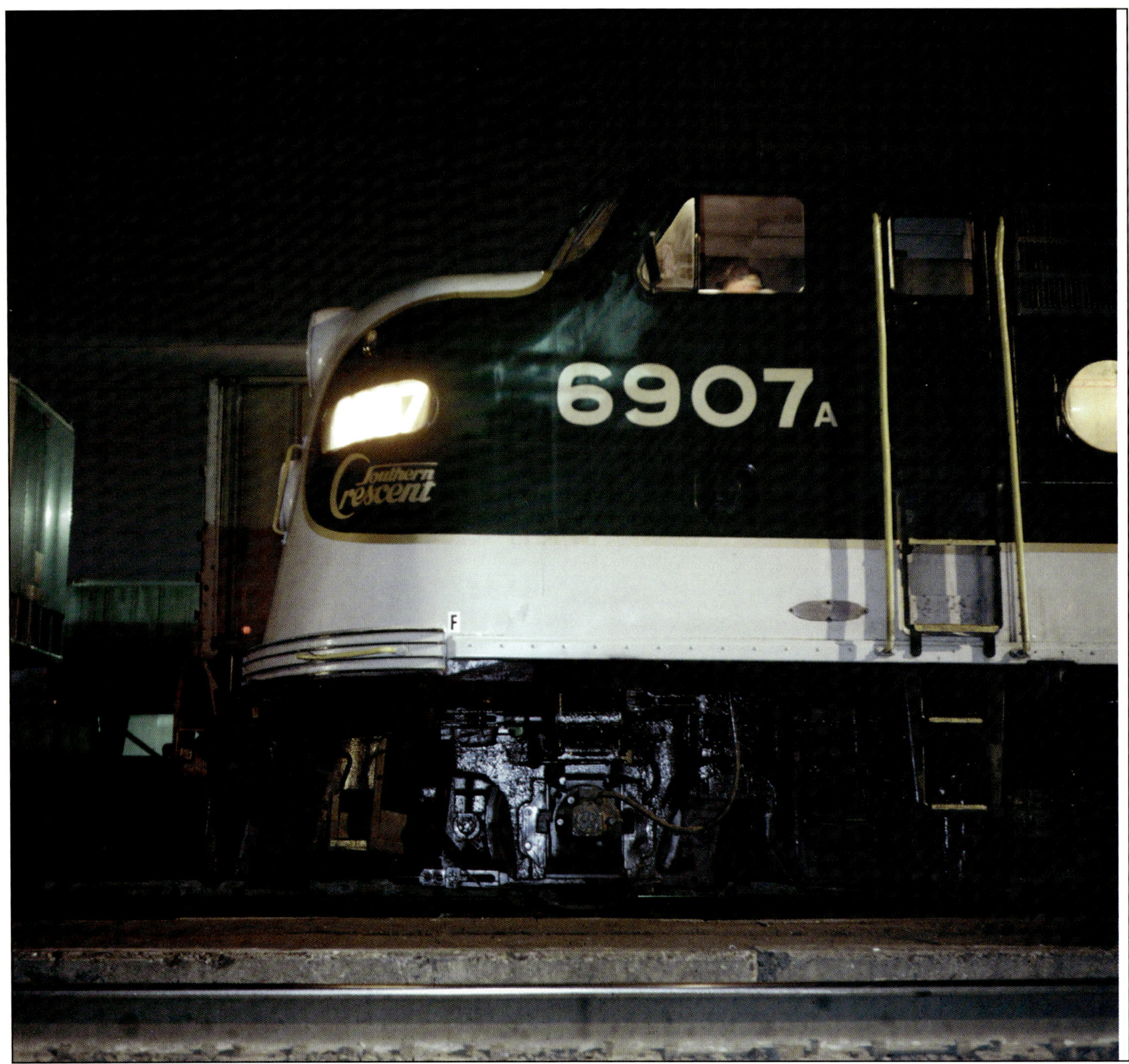

Mix a mainline with the darkness of night and you have two ingredients that will make a railfan's heart beat somewhat faster than normal. The mainline provides the traffic, while the night—ah that's the mystery, that's the fun!

During the night, practically every sound you heard makes you think that a train was approaching. When one actually heads your way, the fascination sets in: that headlight grows larger and larger while the ground begins to shake. When the mainliner plunges back into the darkness on the nocturnal journey to its destination—now that's a moment that one would find very difficult to forget!

A case in point is shown here: one of those sounds in the night turned out to be the Southern's pride and joy, the "Southern Crescent," now taking on passengers and fuel plus a new crew in Greenville, South Carolina. Because it took 15 minutes to fill the fuel tanks on the three E-8As., I was able to make this time exposure of No. 2's lead unit. At this time, November 4, 1972, No. 1 and No. 2 were the only two long-distance luxury passenger trains not running under Amtrak. By 1979, however, the Southern finally joined the organization designed to "save the American passenger train." Now Amtrak's No. 19 & 20—called the "Crescent"—now makes the same run between New York and New Orleans, but it will never be the same. At least this photo helps us to remember how wonderful it used to be.

The three E-8As 6907A, 6914R, 6913W, were leading fourteen cars in this 9:50 p.m. photo of the northbound "Southern Crescent" as it awaits its plunge into the blackness once again.

Leaving Greensboro, N.C.'s Pomona Yard on No. 2 track of the Washington-Atlanta mainline, we find one of the last new types of motive power purchased by the Southern, before the June 1, 1982 merger with N&W, heading south to the huge and modern Spencer Yard, located at Linwood, N.C. Indeed, this photo of Train No. 183 was made just fifteen days before the creation of the current Norfolk Southern.

The B30-7A1's proved to be good engines even with the usual crew complaints of exhaust fumes coming back into the cab and delay of movement when the engineer opened the throttle plus a few others.

Although it did not have the sleek look of and EMD locomotive, those chime horns, the "wings" plus that beautiful Southern symbol on the flat front of #3503A actually (at least to me) enhanced its appearance.

In the background is No. 75. As soon as No. 183 (from Raleigh) clears the area, the three GP-30s and 52 cars will move over to the No. 2 track and just behind the photographer—will leave the double track and head west to Winston-Salem, North Carolina. This location was, and remains, the "hot-spot" for train watching in the "Gate City" of Greensboro.

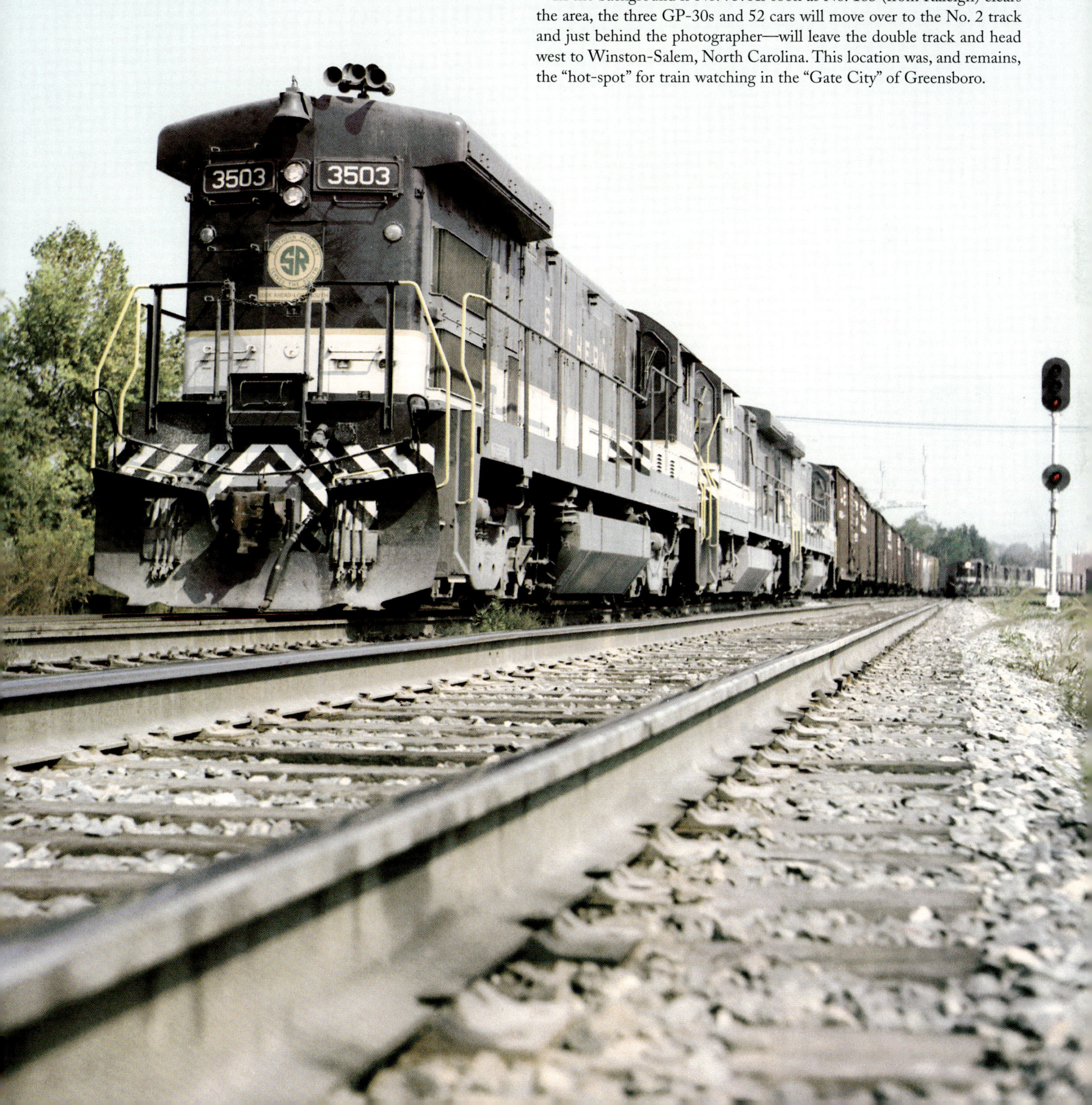

Most through freights entering Greenville, S.C. did so on No. 1 track (next to station). No. 2 track would be used if No. 1 was occupied or if the train was going to leave and/or receive cars from North Greenville yard (on the left). Some freights used No. 2 track to work the South Greenville yard—approximately 1/2 mile south of this historic and magnificent, multi-purpose station.

One of the Southern's "hottest" freights—No. 173— is shown here in front of the station. Here it will be supplied with a crew that will take the priority freight on to Atlanta. Providing crews is just one of the many procedures performed at this important facility: the yardmaster's office can be seen on top of the station, it was both the passenger and freight location, the Piedmont Division's superintendent (and all his "helpers") called the station "home;" the track people and railroad police had their offices there as did the dispatchers and C.T.C. boards—Wow!

My favorite part of the station was the long shed which stood between the tracks and the building. The shed gave me relief from that hot, South Carolina summer sun (there was always a welcome breeze there) and if it rained, the cover would still allow me to get my photos of mainline action.

Alas, the station and shed are now gone, replaced by several "modern" structures. Today's passengers getting on or off Amtrak's "Crescent" will get wet when the two streamliners arrive when it is raining! Who said progress is great? I tend to disagree with this statement on many things, especially the changes made in Greenville. Man, I sure miss that old protective shed!

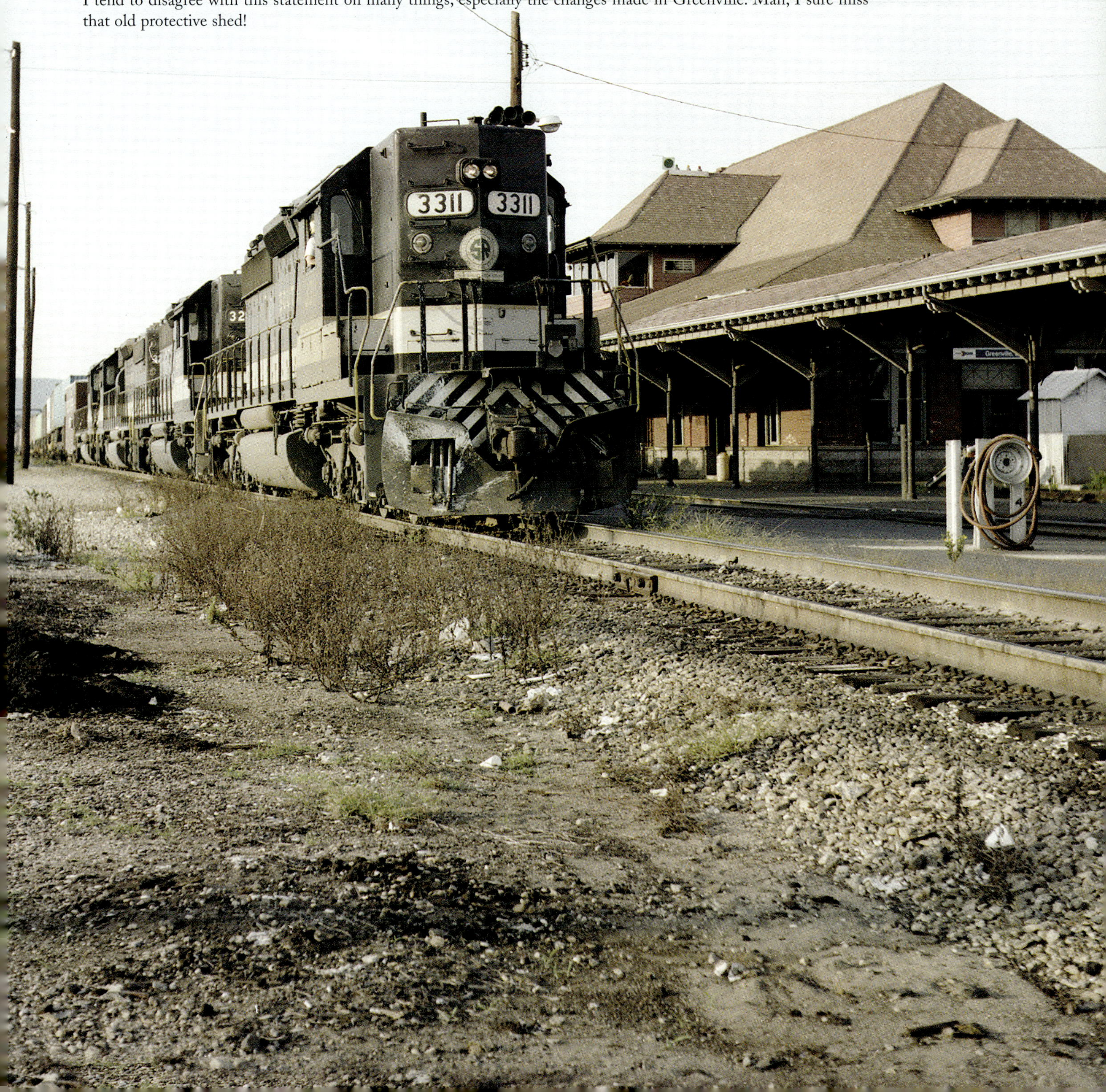

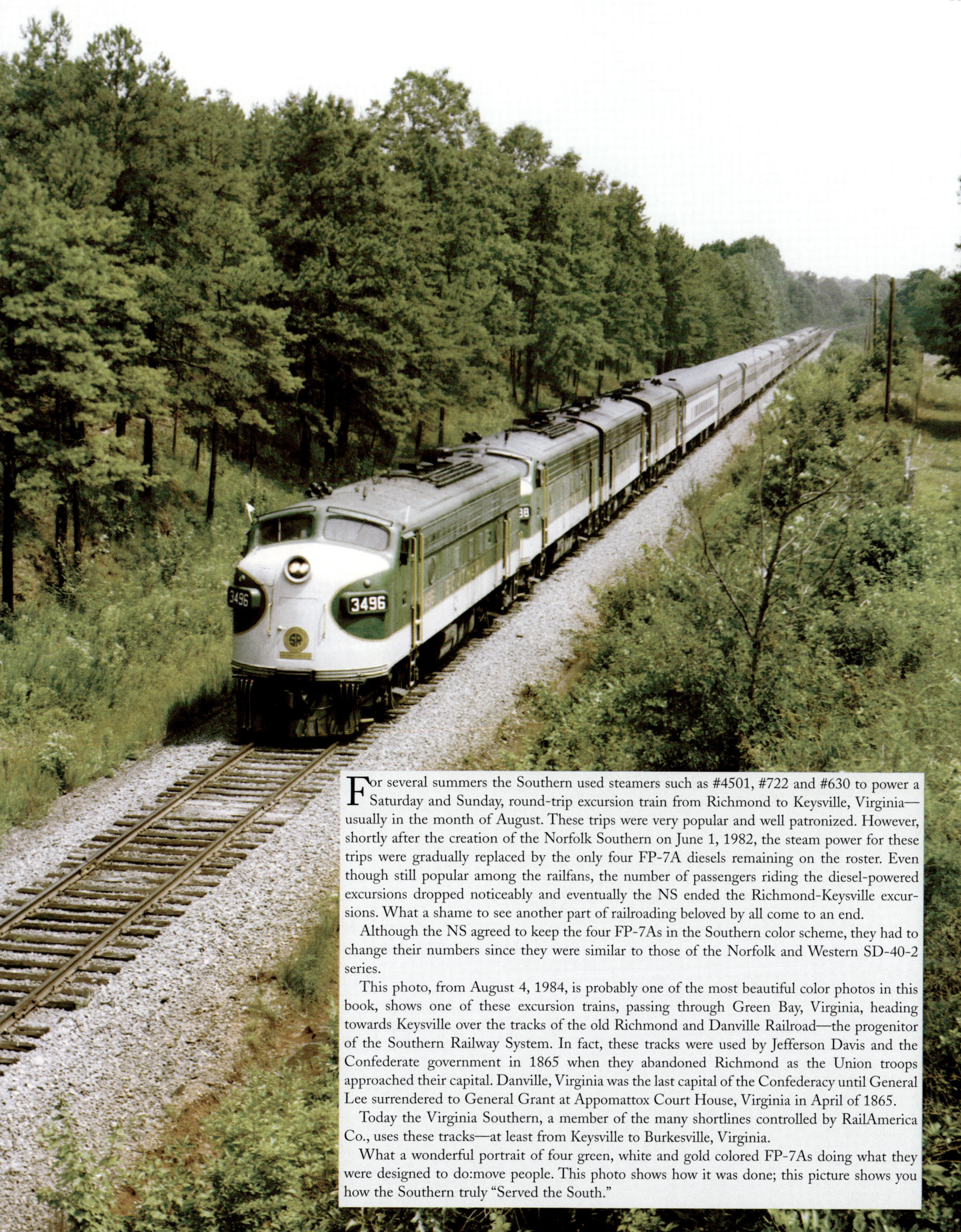

For several summers the Southern used steamers such as #4501, #722 and #630 to power a Saturday and Sunday, round-trip excursion train from Richmond to Keysville, Virginia—usually in the month of August. These trips were very popular and well patronized. However, shortly after the creation of the Norfolk Southern on June 1, 1982, the steam power for these trips were gradually replaced by the only four FP-7A diesels remaining on the roster. Even though still popular among the railfans, the number of passengers riding the diesel-powered excursions dropped noticeably and eventually the NS ended the Richmond-Keysville excursions. What a shame to see another part of railroading beloved by all come to an end.

Although the NS agreed to keep the four FP-7As in the Southern color scheme, they had to change their numbers since they were similar to those of the Norfolk and Western SD-40-2 series.

This photo, from August 4, 1984, is probably one of the most beautiful color photos in this book, shows one of these excursion trains, passing through Green Bay, Virginia, heading towards Keysville over the tracks of the old Richmond and Danville Railroad—the progenitor of the Southern Railway System. In fact, these tracks were used by Jefferson Davis and the Confederate government in 1865 when they abandoned Richmond as the Union troops approached their capital. Danville, Virginia was the last capital of the Confederacy until General Lee surrendered to General Grant at Appomattox Court House, Virginia in April of 1865.

Today the Virginia Southern, a member of the many shortlines controlled by RailAmerica Co., uses these tracks—at least from Keysville to Burkesville, Virginia.

What a wonderful portrait of four green, white and gold colored FP-7As doing what they were designed to do:move people. This photo shows how it was done; this picture shows you how the Southern truly "Served the South."

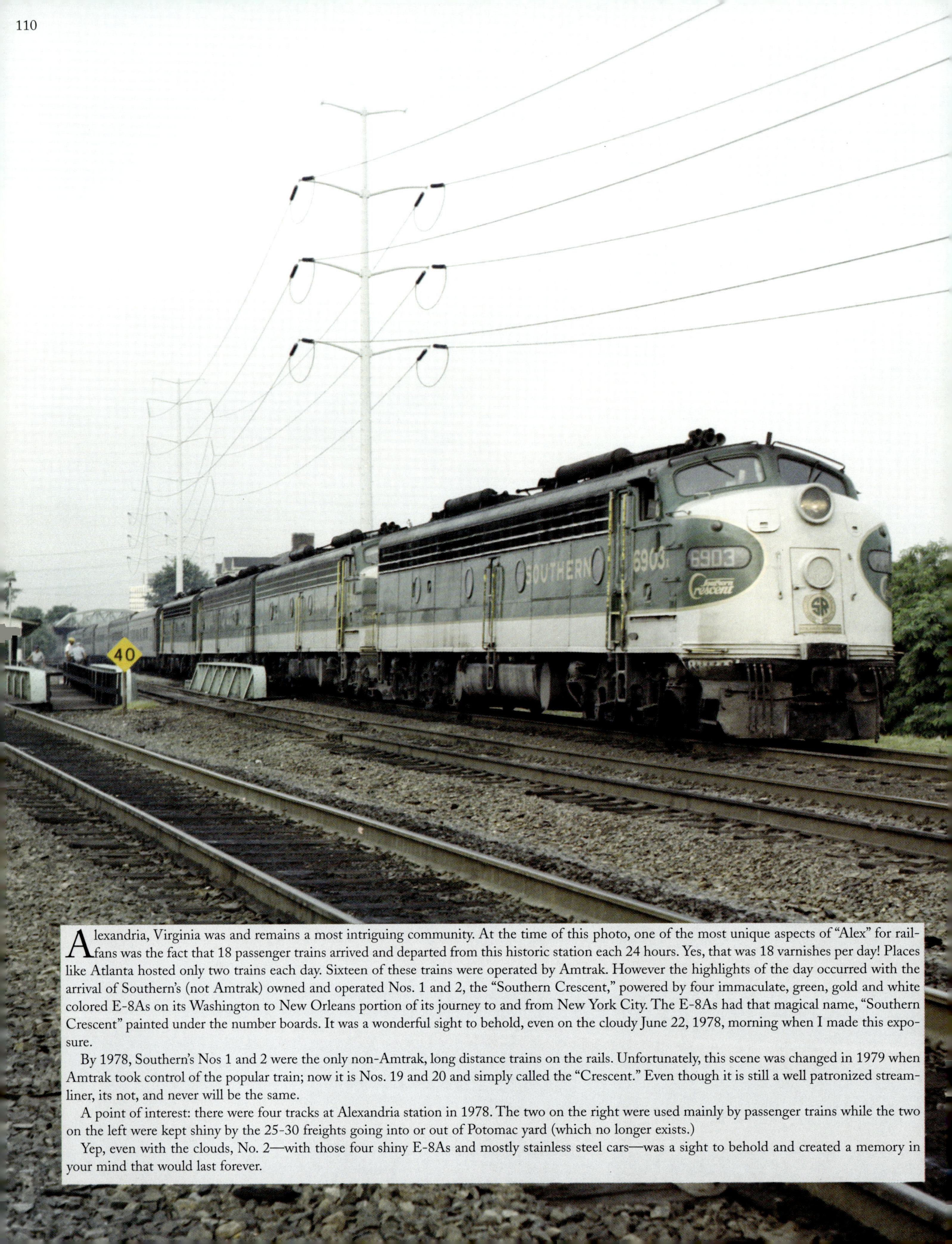

Alexandria, Virginia was and remains a most intriguing community. At the time of this photo, one of the most unique aspects of "Alex" for railfans was the fact that 18 passenger trains arrived and departed from this historic station each 24 hours. Yes, that was 18 varnishes per day! Places like Atlanta hosted only two trains each day. Sixteen of these trains were operated by Amtrak. However the highlights of the day occurred with the arrival of Southern's (not Amtrak) owned and operated Nos. 1 and 2, the "Southern Crescent," powered by four immaculate, green, gold and white colored E-8As on its Washington to New Orleans portion of its journey to and from New York City. The E-8As had that magical name, "Southern Crescent" painted under the number boards. It was a wonderful sight to behold, even on the cloudy June 22, 1978, morning when I made this exposure.

By 1978, Southern's Nos 1 and 2 were the only non-Amtrak, long distance trains on the rails. Unfortunately, this scene was changed in 1979 when Amtrak took control of the popular train; now it is Nos. 19 and 20 and simply called the "Crescent." Even though it is still a well patronized streamliner, its not, and never will be the same.

A point of interest: there were four tracks at Alexandria station in 1978. The two on the right were used mainly by passenger trains while the two on the left were kept shiny by the 25-30 freights going into or out of Potomac yard (which no longer exists.)

Yep, even with the clouds, No. 2—with those four shiny E-8As and mostly stainless steel cars—was a sight to behold and created a memory in your mind that would last forever.

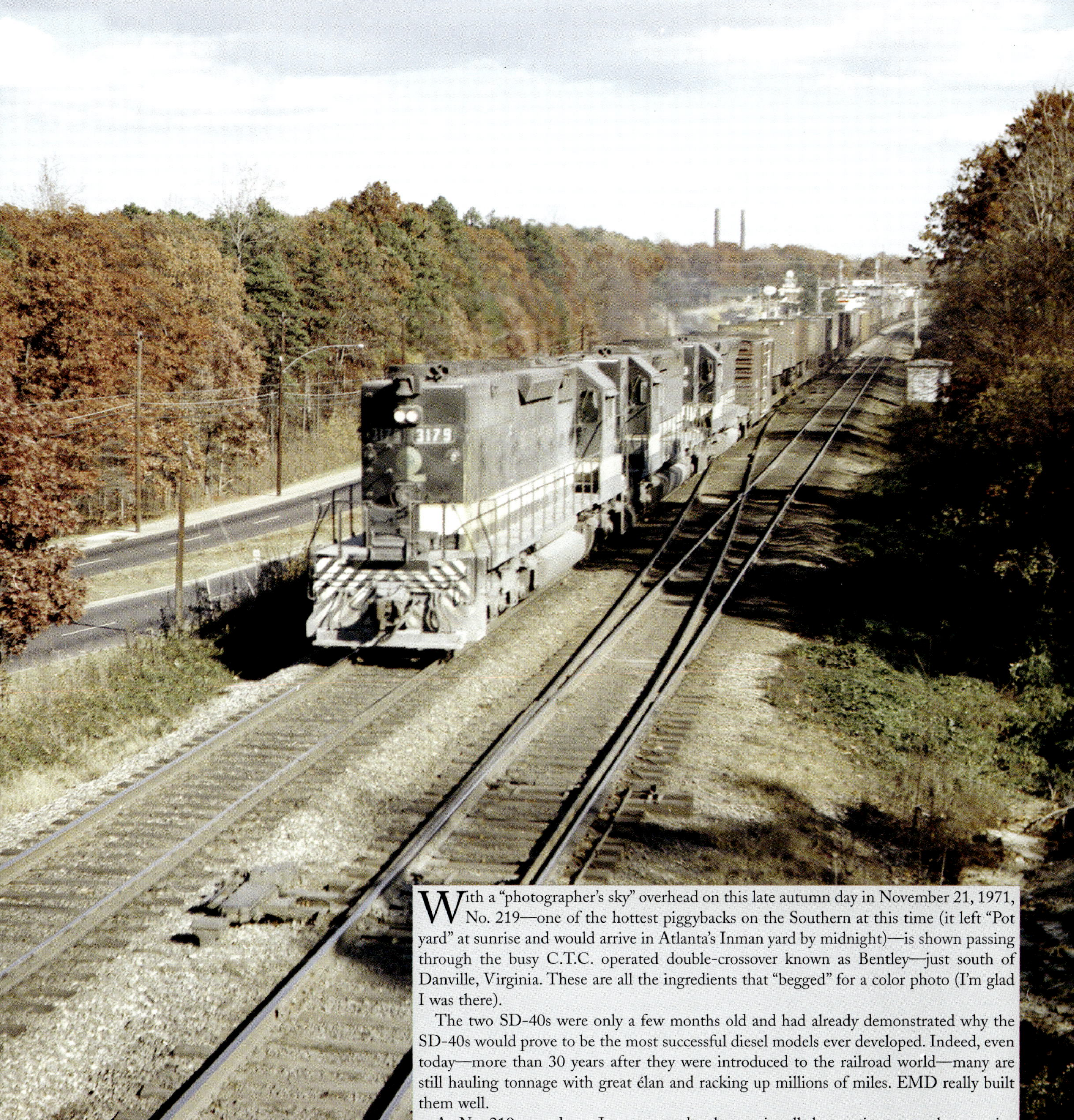

With a "photographer's sky" overhead on this late autumn day in November 21, 1971, No. 219—one of the hottest piggybacks on the Southern at this time (it left "Pot yard" at sunrise and would arrive in Atlanta's Inman yard by midnight)—is shown passing through the busy C.T.C. operated double-crossover known as Bentley—just south of Danville, Virginia. These are all the ingredients that "begged" for a color photo (I'm glad I was there).

The two SD-40s were only a few months old and had already demonstrated why the SD-40s would prove to be the most successful diesel models ever developed. Indeed, even today—more than 30 years after they were introduced to the railroad world—many are still hauling tonnage with great élan and racking up millions of miles. EMD really built them well.

As No. 219 passed me, I was amazed at how quiet all three units—even that massive SD-45—sounded, even though working at full-throttle.

I've seen dozens of times when the dispatcher used this double-crossover to direct a faster train around a slower one: modern railroading at its best!

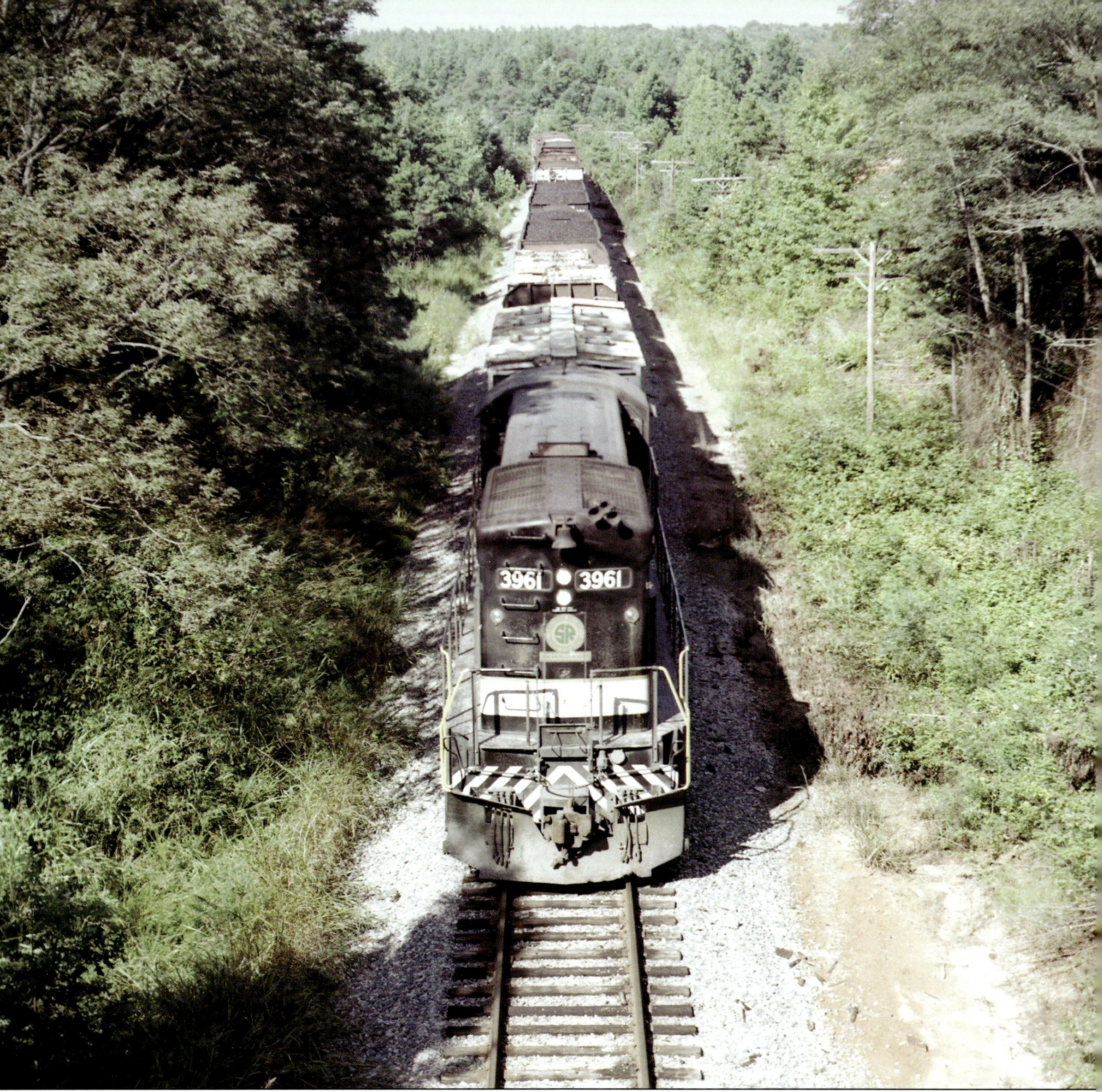

Coming straight towards you is Southern's daily except Sunday local freight No. 21, preparing to pass under the highway overpass (U.S. 15) just north of Clarksville, Virginia. No. 21 had a GE built U-23B (#3961A) on the point, pulling 18 cars and running long-end forward—rats! Most diesels looked far more impressive running in the short-end configuration (at least in my opinion).

No. 21 ran from Keysville, Virginia to East Durham, North Carolina. This was "my line." In fact No. 21 will pass my house (in Oxford, North Carolina) in approximately one hour. It usually met its northbound counterpart, No. 22, in Oxford as well.

GE's U-23B series (and its improved version, the B-23-7) was its first true competition for EMD's highly successful GP-38, GP-38-2 models. Indeed the Southern was so impressed with the performance of the GE "U-Boats"—as railfans called them—that they purchased a large number of them and never regretted their investment in this form of motive power. As a matter of fact, the GE's had 2,250 h.p. while the EMD GP-38 series only had 2,000 h.p. Even the road crews grudgingly admitted that the GE's rode well and were good pullers, especially at low speeds, even though they did not like the fumes from it's big exhaust stack coming back into the cab plus the slow response of the series as the engineer manipulated its throttle.

They were truly good engines and with that most impressive Southern symbol on its nose, not bad in appearance as well. However, EMD still remained Southern's favorite builder when it came to motive power.

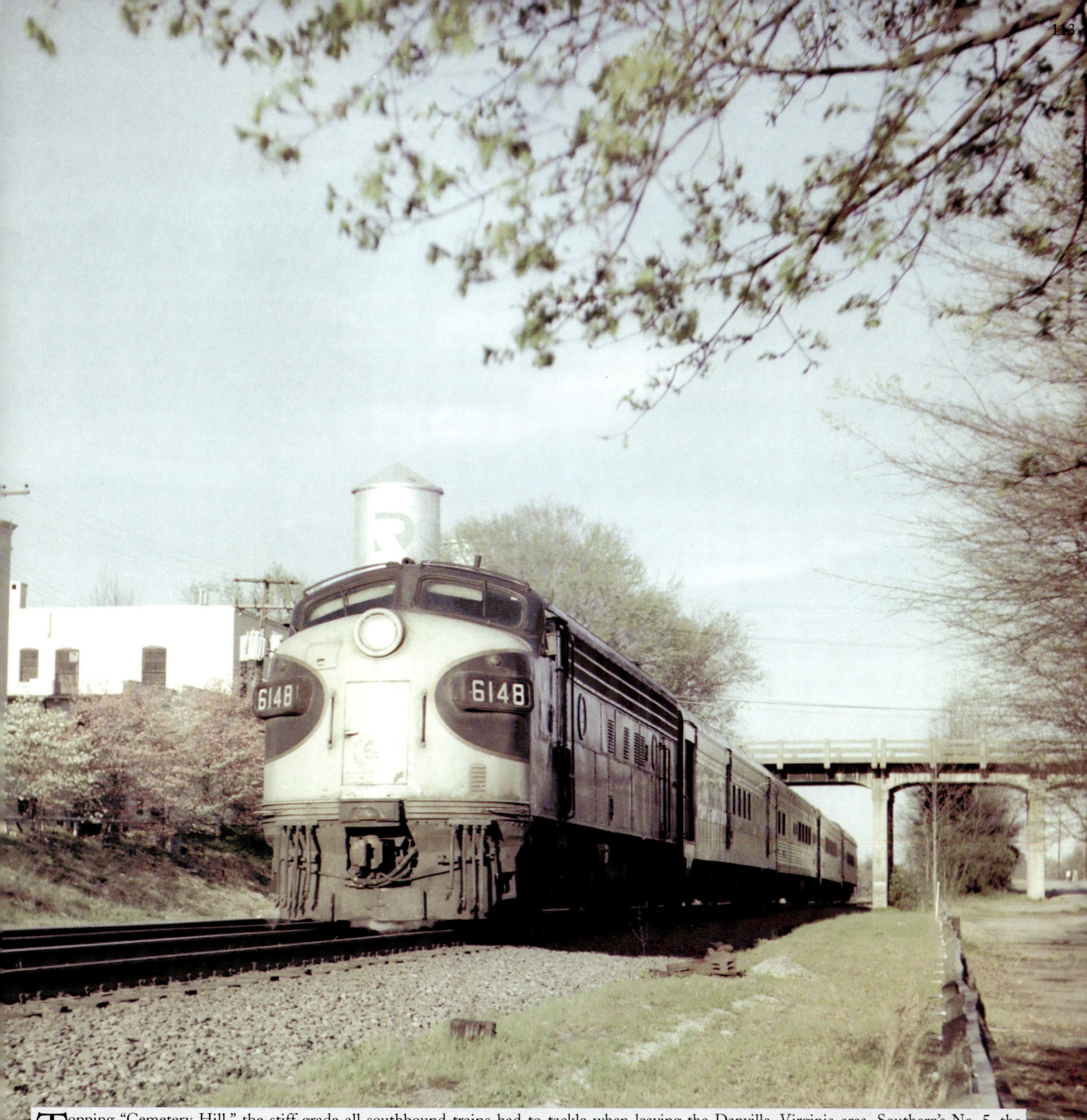

Topping "Cemetery Hill," the stiff grade all southbound trains had to tackle when leaving the Danville, Virginia area, Southern's No. 5, the "Piedmont," is shown making good time. In fact, the FP-7A (#6148F) has its 4 cars up to 45 m.p.h. climbing as it headed south on its Washington-Atlanta "adventure." On several occasions the Southern would add more piggyback cars to the rear of No. 5 than it had passenger equipment, in order to made some revenue.

Since it is late March; spring is busting out all over. The dogwood (seen on left) were beautiful as No. 5 passes through the Dan River Mill's headquarters—notice the "DR" painted on the water tank, shown just above the FP-7A.

Nos. 5 and 6 plus the luxury streamliner, the "Southern Crescent" (Nos. 1 and 2) were all that remained of the grand fleet that the railroad that "Served the South" could be proud of.

In 1979, when the Southern joined the Amtrak system—one of the last major railroads to do so—the "Southern Crescent" and "Piedmont" became part of the history of this historic road. Today, Amtrak runs the still popular Nos. 19 and 20, the "Crescent" between New York and New Orleans.

It is truly amazing that the United States remains the only major nation in the world that does not take advantage of the railroad's capacity of moving not only freight but people as well, in the safest and most efficient mode of transportation ever conceived by man.

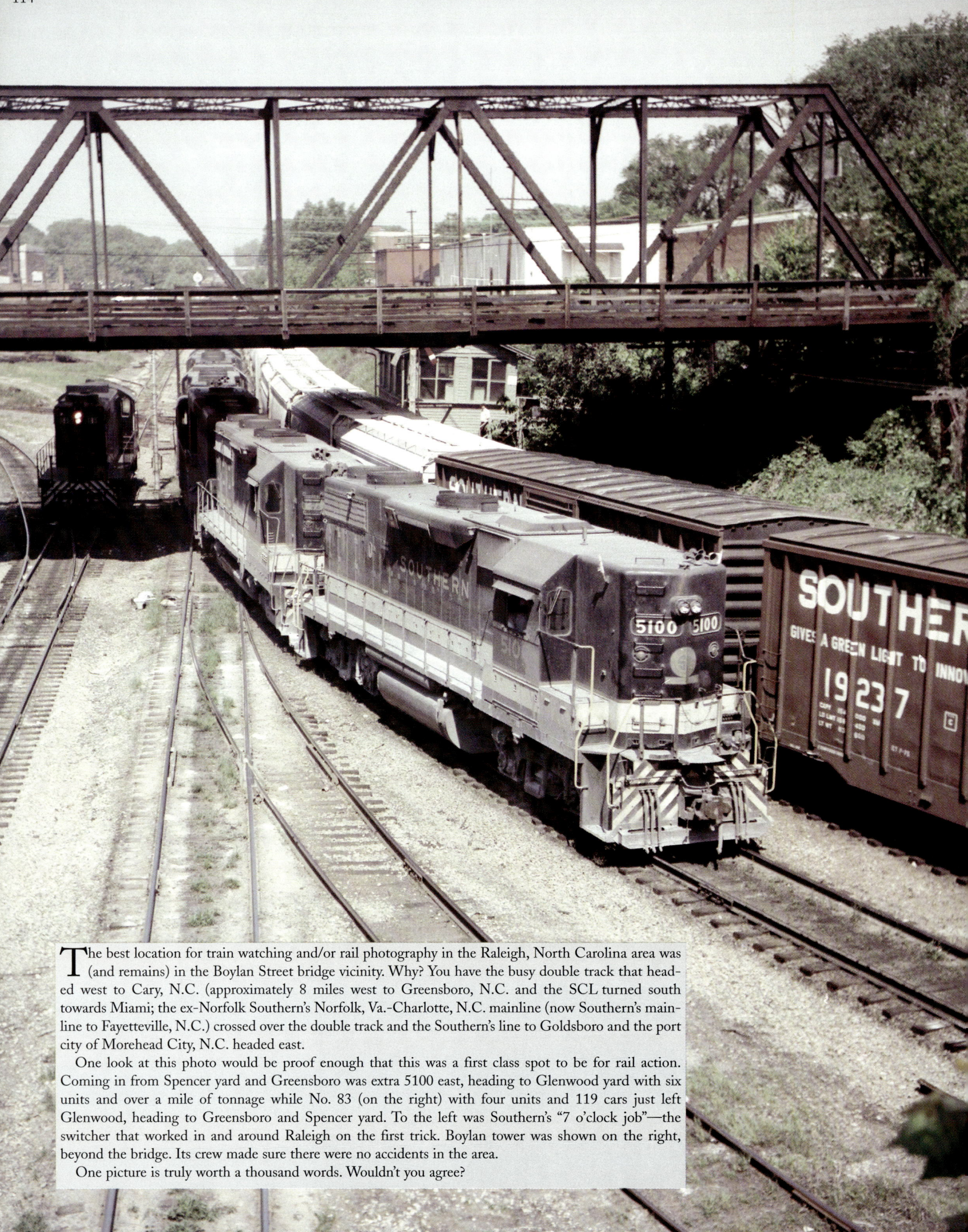

The best location for train watching and/or rail photography in the Raleigh, North Carolina area was (and remains) in the Boylan Street bridge vicinity. Why? You have the busy double track that headed west to Cary, N.C. (approximately 8 miles west to Greensboro, N.C. and the SCL turned south towards Miami; the ex-Norfolk Southern's Norfolk, Va.-Charlotte, N.C. mainline (now Southern's mainline to Fayetteville, N.C.) crossed over the double track and the Southern's line to Goldsboro and the port city of Morehead City, N.C. headed east.

One look at this photo would be proof enough that this was a first class spot to be for rail action. Coming in from Spencer yard and Greensboro was extra 5100 east, heading to Glenwood yard with six units and over a mile of tonnage while No. 83 (on the right) with four units and 119 cars just left Glenwood, heading to Greensboro and Spencer yard. To the left was Southern's "7 o'clock job"—the switcher that worked in and around Raleigh on the first trick. Boylan tower was shown on the right, beyond the bridge. Its crew made sure there were no accidents in the area.

One picture is truly worth a thousand words. Wouldn't you agree?

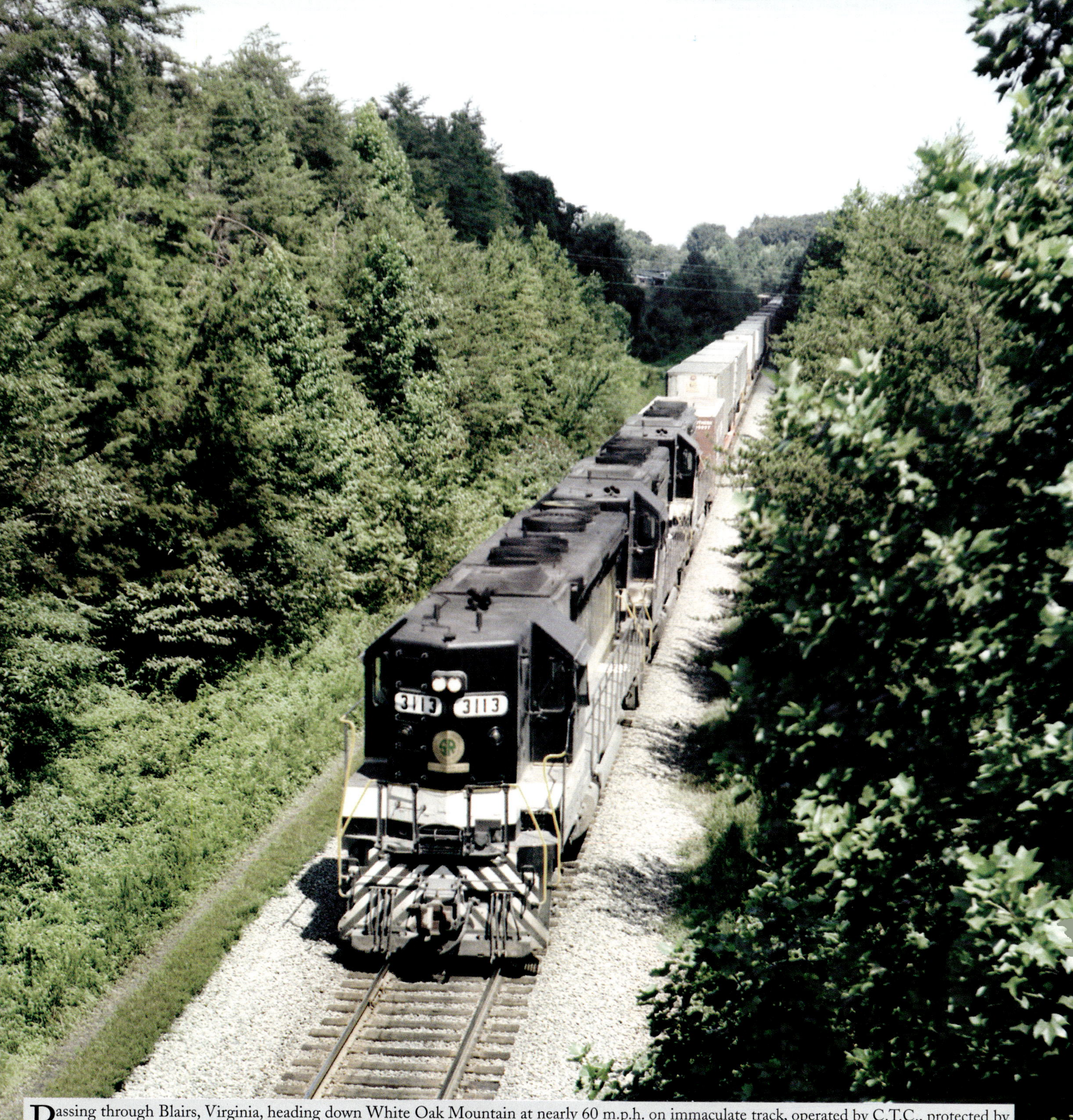

Passing through Blairs, Virginia, heading down White Oak Mountain at nearly 60 m.p.h. on immaculate track, operated by C.T.C., protected by Automatic Block Signals, using microwave communication., Southern's No. 173 epitomized modern railroading at its best—not to mention creating a beautiful scene at the same time.

Indeed, imagine old train No. 97 with engineer Joseph A. "Steve" Broady at the throttle in September of 1903, passing the area at "90 miles an hour," according to the song, "The Wreck of Old 97." Now look at White Oak Mountain's descending grade in August of 1979 with a huge, powerful SD-45 on the point, plus two SD-40s doing a mile-a-minute speed. What a contrast between the old and new. Yet, they had a few things in common: both movements were dramatic and created the excitement that filled a railfan's heart (not the actual wreck itself, of course). I'm glad I remembered to release the shutter on my Rollei; so that you could share my adventure with No. 173.

This location was one of the several short sections of the mostly double-tracked Washington-Atlanta mainline; No. 173 will be in Atlanta's Inman yard by midnight of this same day—that's good railroading!

Just look at this scene; let it soak in. Then decide if this photo captures the true essence of railroading as it should be!

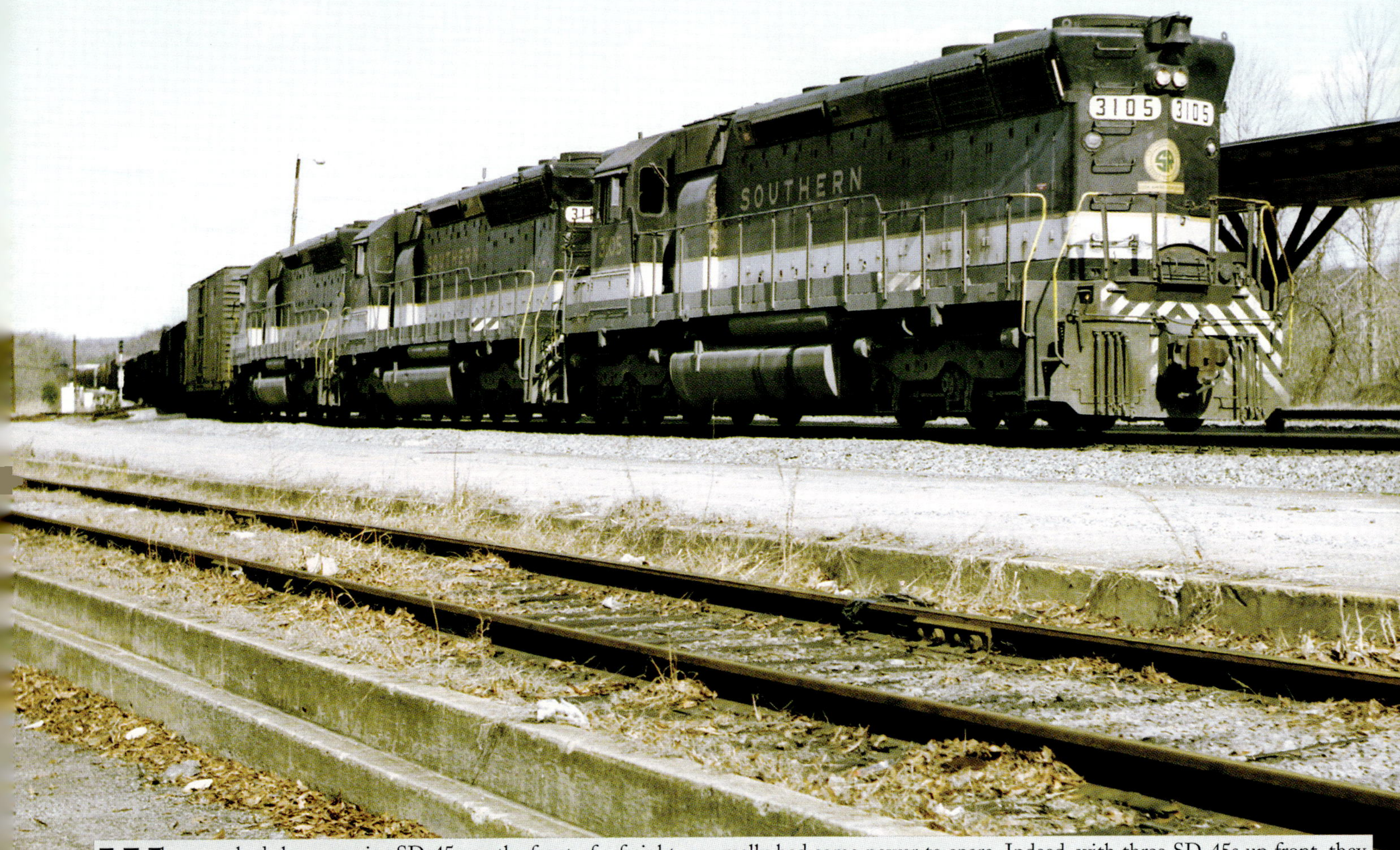

When you had three massive SD-45s on the front of a freight, you really had some power to spare. Indeed, with three SD-45s up front, they could move anything a yardmaster could tie one it, easily; most grades were "no problem" for these monsters.

If running long end forward; it reminded one of an engineer looking down the long barrel of an articulated steam locomotive. Neither engineer— the one on the SD-45 or the steamer— could really see much of the track ahead. The SD-45 was truly the diesel equivalent of a "Big Boy" during its day.

Extra 3105 south (shown here) had completed its work at Dundee (Va.) yard—just north of the Dan River bridge—and was just passing through the Danville, Va. passenger station—where the infamous "Cemetery Hill" started (the stiff grade all southbound trains had to encounter). With a combined 10,800 h.p., the extra, even with 147 cars, topped the grade at a good 15-20 m.p.h.—boy, could they pull!

Even this far away from the long freight, I could feel the ground shaking as the three SD-45s, pulling nearly 1.5 miles of tonnage—wide opened going by yours truly towards Greensboro, N.C. and points south.

To say this scene was "thrilling" would be inadequate when trying to describe the event. Yet, with its throttles in "notch 8" and making the ground tremble, the three "big boys" were very quiet. Still I am glad that I was able to capture this moment on fill, so that you could share my "adventure."

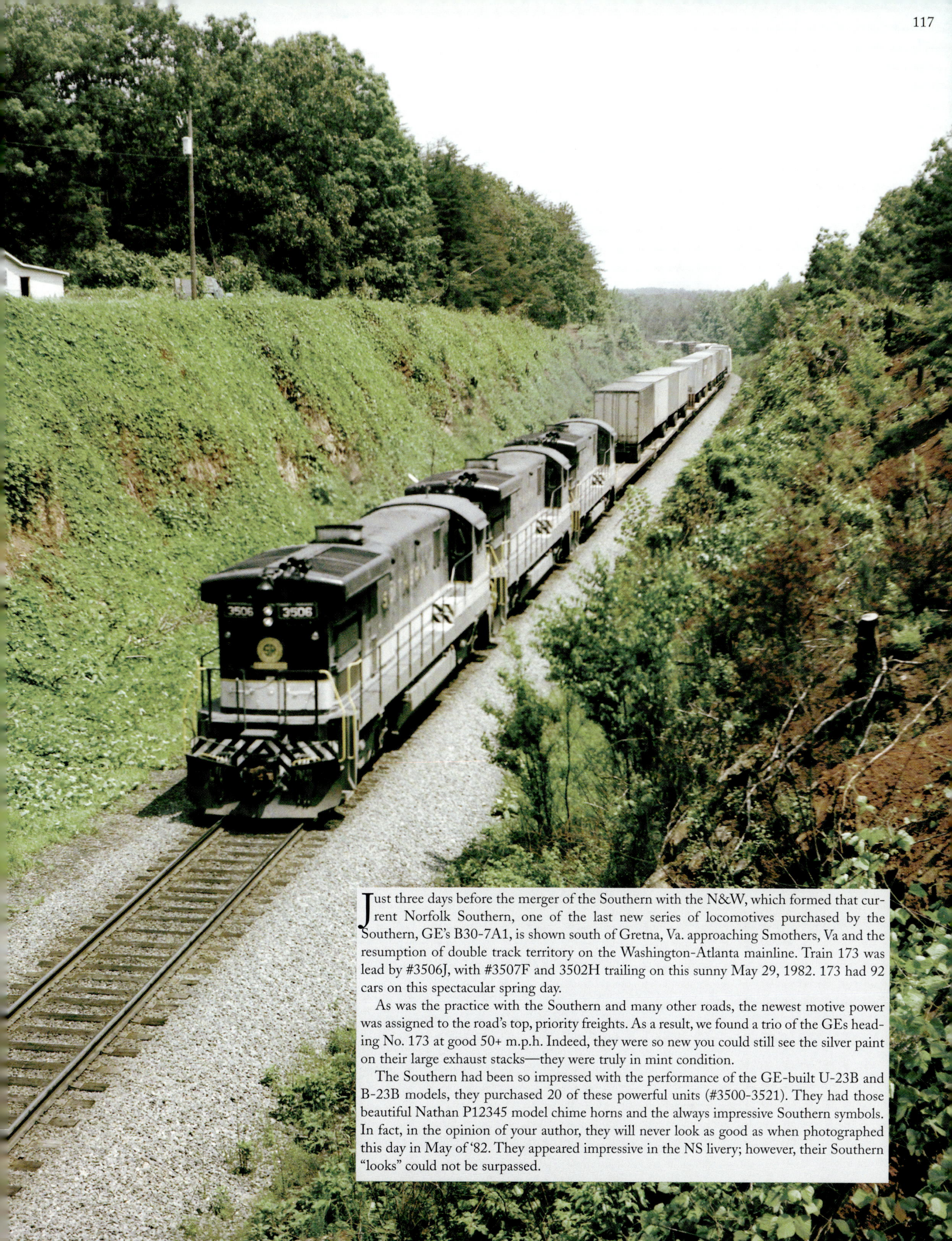

Just three days before the merger of the Southern with the N&W, which formed that current Norfolk Southern, one of the last new series of locomotives purchased by the Southern, GE's B30-7A1, is shown south of Gretna, Va. approaching Smothers, Va and the resumption of double track territory on the Washington-Atlanta mainline. Train 173 was lead by #3506J, with #3507F and 3502H trailing on this sunny May 29, 1982. 173 had 92 cars on this spectacular spring day.

As was the practice with the Southern and many other roads, the newest motive power was assigned to the road's top, priority freights. As a result, we found a trio of the GEs heading No. 173 at good 50+ m.p.h. Indeed, they were so new you could still see the silver paint on their large exhaust stacks—they were truly in mint condition.

The Southern had been so impressed with the performance of the GE-built U-23B and B-23B models, they purchased 20 of these powerful units (#3500-3521). They had those beautiful Nathan P12345 model chime horns and the always impressive Southern symbols. In fact, in the opinion of your author, they will never look as good as when photographed this day in May of '82. They appeared impressive in the NS livery; however, their Southern "looks" could not be surpassed.

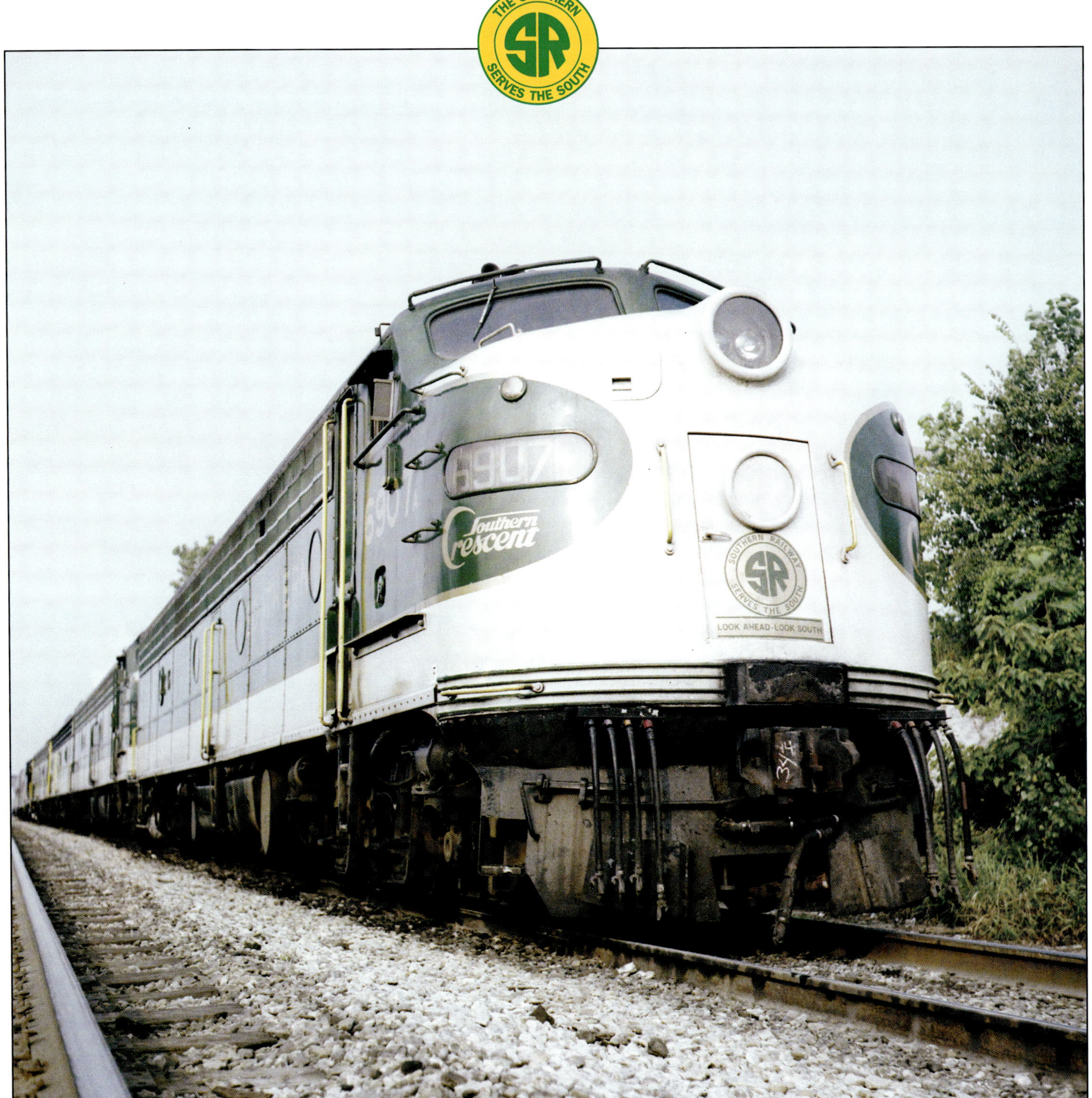

On this particular July morning in 1978, I found a deep blue sky—not a cloud in sight— and a beautiful, albeit very hot sun: the perfect ingredients to enhance the attractiveness of the most beautiful E-8As to ever ride the rails—shown here in Atlanta, Georgia.

By 1978, the Southern's "Southern Crescent" (Nos. 1 and 2) ran from New York City to New Orleans. From Washington south, the streamliner was powered by four green, white and gold painted Southern E-8As with every unit having "Southern Crescent" painted under each number board.

The four E-8As that pulled No. 1out of Washington were replaced by four fresh E-8As in Atlanta while stopped in Peachtree Station (this change also occurred for No. 2 on its northbound journey).

Here we find the super clean E-8As waiting for the arrival of No. 1 from Washington. They would take the popular train from Atlanta to New Orleans. Nos. 1 and 2 were the only long distance passenger runs not controlled by Amtrak by 1978. Unfortunately, in 1979, the Southern had to allow its pride and joy to be operated by Amtrak, which numbered them to No. 19 and 20 and called the streamliner the "Crescent."

Just look at those clean, green, white and gold colored units with the train name painted under those modern looking number boards. Now do you agree with my previous statement that they were among the most attractive E-8A's ever to keep the rails shiny?

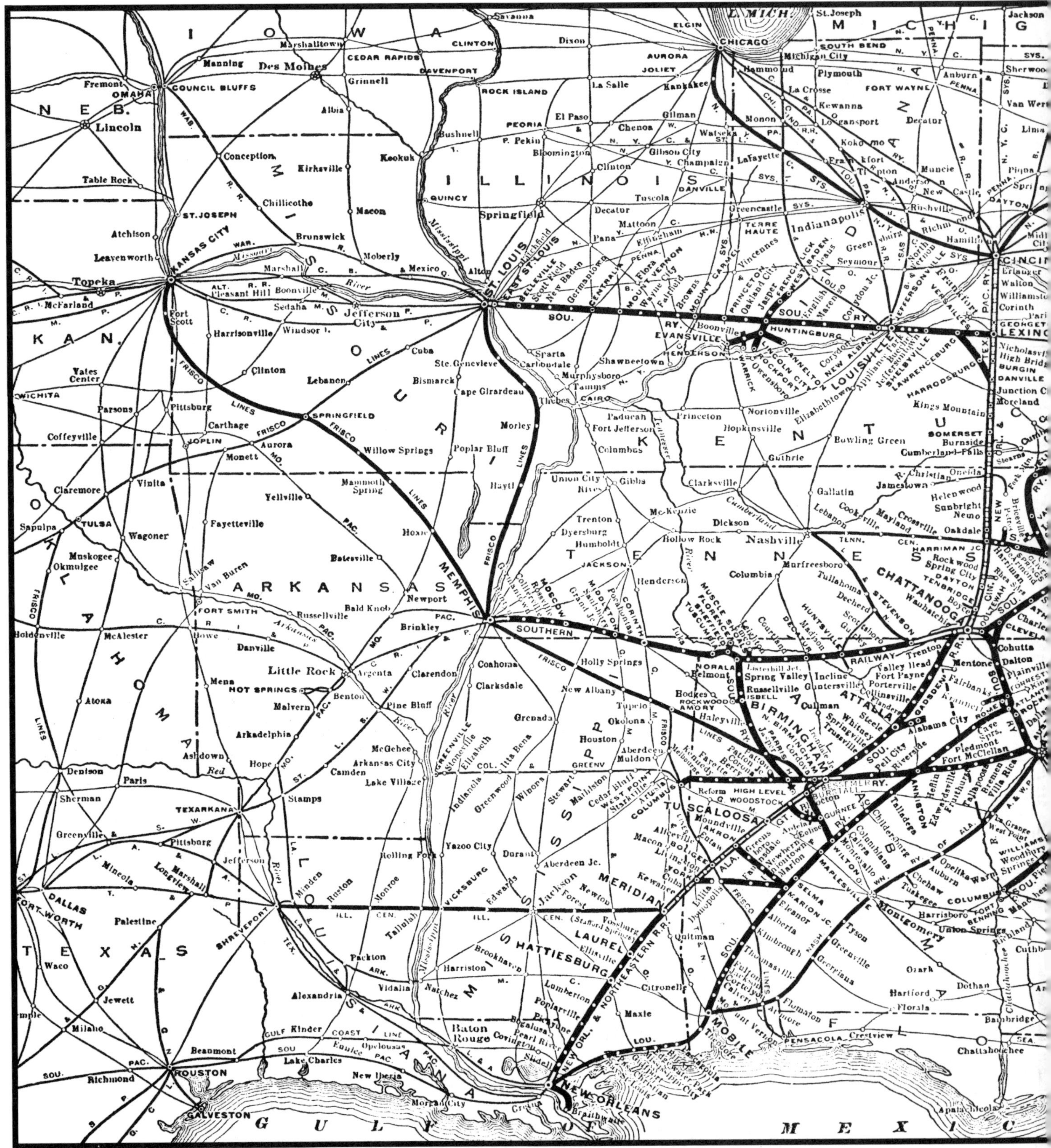
I O W A
N E B.
Lincoln
Fremont
OMAHA
COUNCIL BLUFFS
Manning
Des Moines
Marshalltown
CEDAR RAPIDS
CLINTON
DAVENPORT
Grinnell
Albia
Keokuk
Savanna
Dixon
ELGIN
CHICAGO
L. MICH
AURORA
JOLIET
La Salle
ROCK ISLAND
Kankakee
PEORIA
El Paso
P. Pekin
Bushnell
Chenoa
Gilman
Bloomington
Gibson City
Champaign
Clinton
I L L I N O I S
QUINCY
Springfield
Tuscola
DANVILLE
Decatur
Mattoon
Pana
Effingham
TERRE HAUTE
Greencastle
Indianapolis
Lafayette
Monon
Watseka
Michigan City
Hammond
SOUTH BEND
Plymouth
La Crosse
Kewanna
Logansport
FORT WAYNE
Kokomo
Frankfort
Tipton
Anderson
Muncie
New Castle
Rushville
Richmond
Hamilton
Decatur
Auburn
St. Joseph
M I C H I G
Jackson
Sherwood
Van Wert
Lima
Piqua
DAYTON
CINCIN
Greensburg
North Vernon
Seymour
Vincennes
Conception
Kirksville
Table Rock
ST. JOSEPH
Atchison
Chillicothe
Macon
Brunswick
Moberly
Leavenworth
KANSAS CITY
Topeka
McFarland
Marshall
Mexico
Alton
ST. LOUIS
EAST ST. LOUIS
BELLEVILLE
Boonville
Pleasant Hill
Sedalia
Jefferson City
Fort Scott
Harrisonville
Windsor
Clinton
Cuba
Lebanon
Ste. Genevieve
Bismarck
Cape Girardeau
Sparta
Carbondale
Murphysboro
Tamms
Thebes
CAIRO
Shawneetown
EVANSVILLE
HENDERSON
Boonville
HUNTINGBURG
LOUISVILLE
Owensboro
Elizabethtown
Princeton
Nortonville
Hopkinsville
Paducah
Fort Jefferson
Columbus
K E N T U
Bowling Green
Guthrie
SOMERSET
Burnside
Cumberland Falls
Kings Mountain
Moreland
Junction City
DANVILLE
HARRODSBURG
LAWRENCEBURG
Frankfort
Erlanger
Walton
Williamstown
Corinth
GEORGETOWN
LEXINGTON
Nicholasville
High Bridge
BURGIN
K A N.
M I S S O U R I
Yates Center
WICHITA
Parsons
Pittsburg
Carthage
JOPLIN
Coffeyville
Aurora
Monett
SPRINGFIELD
Willow Springs
Morley
Poplar Bluff
Mammoth Spring
Yellville
Claremore
Vinita
Sapulpa
TULSA
Wagoner
Fayetteville
Muskogee
Okmulgee
O K L A H O M A
Hoxie
Batesville
Hayti
Union City
Gibbs
Trenton
Dyersburg
McKenzie
Clarksville
Dickson
Nashville
Hollow Rock
Humboldt
JACKSON
Henderson
Gallatin
Lebanon
Cookeville
Jamestown
Crossville
Mayland
Oakdale
Helenwood
Sunbright
Nemo
Oneida
T E N N E S S
HARRIMAN JC.
Rockwood
Spring City
DAYTON
Columbia
Murfreesboro
Tullahoma
Decherd
CHATTANOOGA
STEVENSON
Wauhatchie
A R K A N S A S
Van Buren
FORT SMITH
Russellville
Bald Knob
Newport
MEMPHIS
Brinkley
Holdenville
McAlester
Howe
Danville
Little Rock
Argenta
Clarendon
Atoka
Mena
HOT SPRINGS
Benton
Malvern
Pine Bluff
Arkadelphia
Coahoma
Clarksdale
Holly Springs
New Albany
Tupelo
Okolona
Houston
Aberdeen
Muldoon
Grenada
McGehee
Arkansas City
Lake Village
Camden
Ashdown
Hope
Stamps
Denison
Paris
Sherman
TEXARKANA
Greenville
Pittsburg
Mineola
Marshall
Longview
Jefferson
Shreveport
DALLAS
FORT WORTH
Palestine
T E X A S
Waco
Jewett
Milano
HOUSTON
Richmond
Beaumont
GALVESTON
Minden
Ruston
Monroe
Rolling Fork
Yazoo City
VICKSBURG
Tallulah
Jackson
Edwards
Durant
Aberdeen Jc.
MERIDIAN
Newton
Forest
Fossburg
LAUREL
Ellisville
HATTIESBURG
Brookhaven
Harriston
Natchez
Vidalia
Packton
Alexandria
Kinder
Opelousas
Eunice
Lake Charles
New Iberia
Morgan City
Baton Rouge
Covington
Bogalusa
Pearl River
Slidell
NEW ORLEANS
Braithwaite
Lumberton
Poplarville
Citronelle
Maxie
MOBILE
PENSACOLA
Crestview
Flomaton
Atmore
Florala
Hartford
Dothan
Ozark
Bainbridge
Chattahoochee
Apalachicola
TUSCALOOSA
Moundville
AKRON
Eutaw
Livingston
York
Cuba
Demopolis
Thomasville
SELMA
MARION JC.
Alberta
Kimbrough
Tyson
Greenville
Georgiana
Montgomery
Union Springs
Harrisburg
Tuskegee
Chehaw
Auburn
Opelika
COLUMBUS
BIRMINGHAM
BESSEMER
Woodstock
Haleyville
Cullman
ATTALLA
GADSDEN
Steele
Alabama City
Anniston
Talladega
Childersburg
Columbiana
Calera
Montevallo
Pell City
Riverside
Piedmont
Fort McClellan
Heflin
Fruithurst
Tallapoosa
Bremen
Villa Rica
Mentone
Fort Payne
Valley Head
Trenton
Collinsville
Spring Valley
Russellville
Guntersville
Belmont
NORALA
Tuscumbia
Sheffield
Florence
Muscle Shoals
Decatur
Huntsville
Courtland
Scottsboro
Corinth
Iuka
Cohutta
Dalton
Plainville
ROME
Cuthbert
Fort Benning
G U L F   O F   M E X I C O